FOREIGN CURRENCY CLAIMS IN THE CONFLICT OF LAWS

Problems in assessment of damages remain among the most contentious aspects of private law disputes. The assessment exercise becomes particularly difficult when one of the parties asks that damages be assessed in a foreign currency or claims that, even though damages should be assessed in the currency of the forum, foreign exchange losses should form a head of loss.

The 1975 decision of the House of Lords in *Miliangos v George Frank (Textiles) Ltd* was revolutionary in that it permitted English courts to award damages in a foreign currency. *Miliangos* has been influential throughout the common law world and courts in the commonwealth and the United States now contemplate awarding damages in currencies other than their own. However, that modernisation has hardly eliminated the problems in this area. When may a judge assess damages in a currency other than that of the forum? If a court elects to assess damages in its own currency, what date should it select in converting from a foreign currency that was relevant to the obligations between the parties? In an age of fluctuating currencies questions of this nature present judges with choices involving significant financial implications.

This book takes a comparative look at how common law courts have addressed damages claims when foreign currencies are involved, and at statutory responses to that issue. It describes the practices of UK, Commonwealth and American courts in this field and draws both on principles of private international law and of damages assessment to analyse current practice.

Volume 2 in the series Studies in Private International Law

Studies in Private International Law

Volume 1: Electronic Consumer Contracts in the Conflict of Laws
Zheng Sophia Tang

Volume 2: Foreign Currency Claims in the Conflict of Laws
Vaughan Black

Foreign Currency Claims in the Conflict of Laws

Vaughan Black

·HART·
PUBLISHING
OXFORD AND PORTLAND, OREGON
2010

Published in North America (US and Canada) by
Hart Publishing
c/o International Specialized Book Services
920 NE 58th Avenue, Suite 300
Portland, OR 97213-3786
USA
Tel: +1 503 287 3093 or toll-free: (1) 800 944 6190
Fax: +1 503 280 8832
E-mail: orders@isbs.com
Website: http://www.isbs.com

Hart Publishing Ltd, 16C Worcester Place, Oxford, OX1 2JW
Telephone: +44 (0)1865 517530 Fax: +44 (0)1865 510710
E-mail: mail@hartpub.co.uk
Website: http://www.hartpub.co.uk

British Library Cataloguing in Publication Data
Data Available

ISBN: 978-1-84113-892-3

Typeset by Compuscript Ltd, Shannon
Printed and bound in Great Britain by
Lightning Source UK Ltd

To my parents, Alan and Maisie Black

ACKNOWLEDGEMENTS

Three institutions deserve particular thanks. The Hague Academy of International Law asked me to give a series of lectures on foreign currency obligations in the summer of 2003 and subsequently published them in the *Recueil des cours*. I give special thanks to Peter Trooboff for his part in initiating that invitation and to the Academy for permission to build on those 2003 lectures in writing this book. The Foundation for Legal Research awarded me a grant to hire a research assistant. The staff of the Sir James Dunn Law Library at Dalhousie University were unfailingly competent and pleasant in responding to my many requests for assistance. I especially thank research librarians David Michels, Mark Lewis and Jennifer Adams.

Several people provided help along the way, in particular Barry Glaspell, Archie Kaiser, Mohammed Khimji, Scott Millar, Richard Frimpong Oppong, Angela Swan and Jacob Ziegel. Finally, thanks to everyone at Hart, especially Mel Hamill and Rachel Turner, for their co-operation, competence and patience.

CONTENTS

TABLE OF CASES

Australia

Barbados

Canada

Cyprus

East Caribbean

France

Germany

Ghana

Greece

Guyana

Hong Kong

India

Ireland

Kenya

Malaysia

Netherlands

New Zealand

Nigeria

Papua New Guinea

Singapore

South Africa

Tanzania

United Kingdom

United States

Zimbabwe

European Court of Justice

TABLE OF LEGISLATION

National Legislation

Australia

Botswana

Canada

International Legislation

Introduction

So much of barbarism ... remains in the transactions of most civilized nations, that almost all independent countries choose to assert their nationality by having, to their own inconvenience and that of their neighbours, a peculiar currency of their own.

John Stuart Mill
Principles of Political Economy

The subject of this book may be helpfully introduced by a brief account of what was at stake in the 1994 decision of the House of Lords in *The Texaco Melbourne*.[1] There the plaintiff demanded compensation for breach of an agreement under which it had shipped fuel oil on the defendant's vessel. The defendant was held liable but then a question arose as to what currency should be used to denominate damages for non-delivery of the cargo. No one contended for sterling, the money of the forum. Rather, the choice was between US dollars and Ghanaian cedis. Due to fluctuations between those currencies in the considerable period between the of breach of the contract and the date when judgment was to be rendered—specifically, the precipitate fall of the notoriously unstable cedi[2] vis-a-vis the dollar—the choice of which unit of account should be selected for the calculation of damages meant the difference between an award then valued at $US 2,886,187 and one worth only $US 21,165. Put another way, the court's selection of the medium in which its award should be assessed made the difference between two awards, one of which was worth 136 times the other.

Few disputes raising the question of which country's money should provide the reference point for the assessment of damages present such a dramatic instance of the discrepancy that can result depending which money is selected. However, *The Texaco Melbourne* is not the only case where the answer to the currency-of-judgment question makes a large difference. It is not infrequently the case that the resolution of that matter involves a non-trivial sum. More to the point, and crucial to the ensuing chapters, the difference is often big enough to be worth litigating. It is that litigation—its arguments, presuppositions, discourse and consequences—that is examined in this book.

When the parties to a case like *The Texaco Melbourne* go to court over what currency should be selected for the calculation of damages their core disagreement is

[1] *AG of the Republic of Ghana v Texaco Overseas Tankships Ltd (The 'Texaco Melbourne')* [1994] 1 Lloyd's Rep 473 (HL) (*The Texaco Melbourne*).

[2] A Ghanaian judge once lamented that the cedi was 'a falling star ever plunging downward into the abyss': *Hungarotex Foreign Trading Co v Boateng* [1984–86] 1 GLR 611 (CA) 619.

not over which coin the losing defendant should employ to reward the victorious plaintiff. In the great majority of instances the moneys in question are freely convertible hard currencies. So if the successful party does not wish to retain the currency in which it is paid then it can readily exchange it for its equivalent in some other money, and of course that party could also easily convert its award into some other commodity in which it preferred to retain its wealth—gold, shares in some corporation, soy bean futures, fine art, real estate and so on. Equally, if the unsuccessful party does not possess the money in which it is ordered to pay then it can readily obtain it, at least provided it has the wherewithal in some exchangeable form (and if it does not then it does not much matter what the currency of judgment is). We will see that some court rulings implicitly recognise this and take the following form: 'the defendant will pay the plaintiff 1 million euros or the equivalent in US dollars of 1 million euros on the date that payment is made'. A losing party can be given the option of satisfying the judgment in either of two currencies, since by definition the alternative media of exchange are of equal value; the choice between a judgment in that form and one which simply takes the form 'the defendant shall pay the plaintiff 1 million euros' is not one that concerns me or anyone I know. That is not the currency-of-judgment question.

Rather, the currency-of-judgment question comes down to which monetary yardstick is employed to measure the value of the plaintiff's compensable loss. What disputes about foreign currency obligations (and the remedies for their breach) are about is the exchange value of the award that the successful claimant is to receive in substitution for the remediable harms it has suffered. That value may vary according to which currency is used to assess damages because, at least in the majority of civil cases, an award of damages is arrived at by determining the amount of money which will, so far as money ever permits, fairly compensate the claimant for the loss of some right *at the time the right was abrogated.* While it is known to all that there are scores of currencies in the world, in the great majority of legal disputes the question '*which* money?' never crosses the parties' minds. Nor does it occur to the court. Most cases have no significant international aspect and it goes without saying and without complaint that the money in which the value of the plaintiff's compensable injuries will be calibrated will be that of the forum. That is the medium of exchange both parties are used to employing and the metric they use to assess their worth, and although in some cases a plaintiff might grumble that it has to make do with the substitutionary remedy of damages instead of specific performance, or that some injuries are deemed too remote to warrant compensation, it never gives a moment's thought to *which* currency it is being forced to accept as so-called compensation. Sometimes, however, the question 'which money?' does arise, and since over time currencies fluctuate in value with respect to one another, the choice of a currency in which to quantify damages will have an effect on the ultimate value of the award.

I began with an account of what was at issue in *The Texaco Melbourne* in the hope of demonstrating to the reader that, even if the subject of this book might seem like an esoteric niche, it is at least a niche where substantial sums might be at stake.[3] There is a second respect in which *The Texaco Melbourne* nicely illustrates a key aspect of the pages to come: it reveals the considerable doubts that continue to afflict the practical resolution of the currency-of-judgment question. The trial judge in that case, expressly adverting to the unfairness that would result to the plaintiff if it had to take judgment in now nearly valueless cedis, held that in light of that unstable currency's steep fall a just resolution of the remedial aspect of the case required judgment in US dollars. That is, a court should evaluate the lost cargo in the amount of US dollars that the oil would have been worth at the time of non-delivery and use that as the basis for the award. That, as noted, would produce an award worth $US 2,888,187 at the time of judgment.[4] Soon after that, the trial judge's decision was considered by the United States Court of Appeals for the Seventh Circuit in another dispute where the judges of that court were wrestling with a similar question. In that case, *The Amoco Cadiz*,[5] the Seventh Circuit overruled the decision of the Federal Court trial judge. It approved the reasoning of the English trial judge in *The Texaco Melbourne* and reached an analogous conclusion. Meanwhile, back in London *The Texaco Melbourne* was working its way up the courts. The English Court of Appeal allowed the defendant's appeal and held that the plaintiff would be most fairly compensated by a judgment in now-greatly-devalued cedis, an award worth just a tiny fraction of that granted at first instance.[6] However, a dissenting judge in the Court of Appeal held that the trial judge was correct. Unlike the trial judge, however, that dissenting appeal judge did not buttress his conclusion

[3] Often, of course, the sums at stake *are* trivial. This raises problems of its own. As we will see in later chapters, sometimes judges deal with the currency-of-judgment question in a cavalier and sloppy fashion, probably because the lawyers involved have failed to address it in argument or have done so only as an afterthought. It is easy to see how this might happen in a case where, although the currency-of-judgment question technically arises, the moneys involved have not fluctuated significantly relative to one another during the course of litigation. In such instances the values at stake in choosing one currency or another are slight and consequently judges are not inclined to put much thought into the matter or to offer much explanation for their choice. However, since the rendering of a judgment necessarily involves the selection of some currency they willy-nilly end up making a choice. That choice may not make much difference to the parties in the situation I have just described. However, to the extent that such practices may operate to establish precedents which have some effect in later cases where there *has* been significant currency fluctuation, the resultant problem is obvious.

[4] [1992] 1 Lloyd's Law Rep 303 (QB).

[5] *Matter of Oil Spill by The Amoco Cadiz* 954 F 2d 1279 (7th Cir 1992) 1328 (*The Amoco Cadiz*). Although the Seventh Circuit, in dealing with this aspect of the appeal, overruled the trial judge's decision to award damages in sterling and substituted a judgment in US dollars, on another claim in that same case it did sustain a judgment in French francs. This made *The Amoco Cadiz* the first American appellate judgment to sanction an award in a foreign currency. Another Federal Circuit Court of Appeals followed suit: *Sea-Roy Corp v Parts R Parts Inc* 173 F3d 851 (4th Cir 1999).

[6] [1993] 1 Lloyd's Law Rep 471 (CA). The Court of Appeal then awarded interest at the Ghanaian rate. As we will see, once interest is figured in, the difference between the value of the judgments in the two possible currencies narrows significantly. Briefly, this is because courts have (rightly) decided that the applicable interest rate should be that in effect in the country whose currency is selected for judgment. Since countries whose currencies are falling typically have high domestic interest rates, and those whose currency is rising commonly have lower ones, once the interest component of the award is added the difference in value between the initial judgments (that is, the judgments without the interest component) tends to get smaller. It might even disappear, though it will not necessarily do so.

by pointing to the cedi's post-breach collapse. Rather, he simply thought that, according to other criteria, the cedi was the proper money of judgment and would be so regardless of which way the relevant currencies had fluctuated during the course of litigation. The plaintiff appealed the Court of Appeal's decision but the House of Lords dismissed that appeal, 'notwithstanding the rampant inflation that had reduced the cedi to only a small fraction of its former worth'.[7] Commentators, however, have had the occasion to be sharply critical of that holding. For instance, JA Knott wrote:

> Surely it is not a satisfactory outcome of a dispute under English law that a party who is entitled to compensation for the loss of valuable goods which he was about to sell should, over 10 years after that loss, be awarded a sum which (even including interest) then had a purchasing power of about 2% of the purchasing power he would have obtained 10 years earlier if he had not been deprived of his goods.[8]

It is not my ambition in this introduction to engage the question of whether *The Texaco Melbourne* or its American analogue *The Amoco Cadiz* were correctly decided. At this stage I only point out that in addition to involving a large dollar amount the currency-of-judgment issue is one which has the capacity to divide judges and to provoke adverse comment from those who write about what judges do. Even in areas where the law regarding the currency of judgment appears settled, its application in a given case can be a matter of doubt. And even where the law seems settled and certain in one country that solution may not be the same as that adopted in another country. As we shall see, the judicial uncertainty and attendant scholarly debate on this point are not limited to the United Kingdom and the United States. Other legal systems continue to grapple with the same question. Moreover, this is not an area where the uncertainty can invariably be eliminated by a little foresight and an appropriately drafted clause in a contract. While most of the cases arise out of contractual dealings, the problem also arises in torts cases, such as *The Amoco Cadiz*, where the parties will have had no interaction prior to the cause of action arising. Even in contract cases many courts consider the currency-of-judgment question to be a procedural matter that is, at least in some respects, insulated from the dictates of private party autonomy. Nor, as we shall see, can resort to arbitration eliminate all the uncertainties.

Discord in this area is not confined to straightforward arguments about what money should be employed to denominate an award of damages, or the differently formulated but functionally equivalent inquiry into which date should

[7] M Cohen, 'Foreign Currency Judgments—A Coda' [1996] *Lloyd's Maritime and Commercial Law Quarterly* 323.

[8] J Knott, 'The Currency of Damages in Contract: *The Texaco Melbourne*' [1994] *Lloyd's Maritime and Commercial Law Quarterly* 314. Knott expressed similar views in 'Currency Erosion in Contract Damages' [1994] *International Maritime Law* 88. See also C Proctor, 'Changes in Monetary Value and the Assessment of Damages', in D Saidov & R Cunnington (eds), *Contract Damages: Domestic and International Perspectives* (Oxford, Hart Publishing, 2008) 482.

be selected for the conversion from a foreign currency to that of the forum.[9] Certainly there are debates that take that form, with participants contending for a variety of conversion dates: the date of breach, the day the plaintiff's action is launched, the time the trial started (or finished), the date of payment, or some other time, combination of times or average of times. As we shall see, such discussions are vigorously pursued. The difference of opinion here runs deeper, however, and takes place at the level of a clash over the nature and form of the ideal rule. Some courts and scholars take the view that it really does not much matter what currency of judgment or conversion date is selected so long as the answer is a certain one. That is, they contend what is needed is a dependable yardstick, one ascertainable in advance by objective criteria, known to (or at least knowable by) both parties and under the unilateral control of neither of them. For those analysts, the fundamental goal is certainty and, as a consequence, rules regarding the currency of judgment should not, as the trial judge in *The Texaco Melbourne* did, attend to the direction in which the relevant currencies may *in fact* have fluctuated during the pendency of the litigation. That is, since the tendency and extent of that change cannot be ascertained until trial, making the direction of that fluctuation a factor in selecting the currency of judgment is antithetical to having the currency of judgment be something that is predictable from the outset (the outset in this context being the time of breach at the latest, if not the time of contract formation). The argument here is that a fixed, predictable conversion date promotes settlement and affords litigants the ability to hedge if they wish to avoid the effects of the assessment of damages in a given national currency, and that a fair law of damages requires no more.

Other judges and scholars, however, believe that what is needed is quite the opposite—that is, that no single rule will ensure a just outcome in all instances and that fairness necessitates an adaptable methodology where courts are given the authority to choose from among a variety of dates according to particular circumstances of the case. This power might be constrained by guidelines (such as, 'choose the currency of judgment that benefits the plaintiff') or, in the views of others, would be better expressed as a discretion to select the currency of judgment that best does justice under all the circumstances. At times this is even labelled an 'equitable' approach— connoting both a high degree of judicial discretion in the selection of the applicable currency (or the conversion date), and also

[9] At this stage I refer to the currency-of-judgment question and the conversion-date question almost interchangeably, since courts do the same. A court that is prepared, in certain circumstances, to give judgment in a currency other than its own may have to decide in a given case whether to give judgment in the local money or some foreign currency. That decision may be called the currency-of-judgment question. Some courts, however, only give judgment in their own currency. When they do so in a case where the underlying obligation is regarded as being in some foreign currency such courts will face the question of when to 'convert' that obligation into the money of the forum. That is the conversion-date question. Obviously a conversion from a foreign currency to the local one at the date the obligation is in fact paid is the practical equivalent of rendering judgment in that foreign currency. The currency-of-judgment question and the conversion-date question may be different ways of framing the issue, but they can come down to the same thing.

the related notion that a wide variety of circumstances is relevant to the exercise of that judgment. In the view of some, the circumstances to which a judge should have regard in selecting a conversion date even—or especially—include the ways the pertinent currencies have oscillated in relation to one another during the course of litigation. That is, the relevant currency of judgment (or conversion date) should not be determined until the date of trial, since only then will it be clear how the contending currencies have fared vis-a-vis each other. In short, rather than promoting a certain rule—a solution they commonly characterised by such pejoratives as 'inflexible', 'wooden', 'rigid', 'mechanical' and the like—such courts and scholars advocate a generous, unstructured measure of judicial freedom of choice. For them, some amount of lack of certainty with respect to the conversion-date for foreign currency obligations is a desirable thing and the only guarantor of fair results. (One point I hope to make convincingly in this work is that those who champion certainty have the better argument, but pursuit of that will have to wait for later chapters.)[10]

There is yet a further level of disagreement and uncertainty. Even where there is consensus within a given national legal system as to the formulation of the rules respecting the currency of judgment and the result those rules will lead to in any given case, that does not mean that for any given legal *dispute* there is certainty on the currency-of-judgment question. This is owing to the availability of more than one national forum. National legal systems have adopted different solutions to the question of whether and when damages should be assessed with regard to foreign currency obligations. Of course, the fact that the internal law of states differs from that of other states is not unusual; it is the norm. However, the potential injustice arising from that fact is often tempered by two things: first, with many disputes there may be only one country whose law respecting adjudicative jurisdiction (including *forum non conveniens*) renders its court available for hearing that dispute, and secondly, where there is more than one available forum the application of choice of law rules sometimes conduces to uniformity of result.

In many clashes involving the currency of judgment, however, those factors may be of limited effect. Such cases are often ones where there is more than one available forum; the same factors which raise the possibility that more than one forum is available for resolution of a given dispute are the factors which make more than one national currency a contender to be the denominator of damages. Indeed, an important sub-class of such cases is one involving the enforcement of foreign country judgments. There by definition there are two fora (and two

[10] If it appears that things are starting to get complex, that is because they are. While I hope to defer entering the thicket of the argument at this early point, in essence it is this. With some legal rules—for example, whether one should drive on the right-hand side of the road or the left—there may be no strong a priori argument for either position but there is good reason for saying that whatever choice is made be clearly established and not vary according to, say, the day of the week or the gender of the driver. Moreover, if the neighbouring state has already made a choice and there is likely to be a lot of cross-border traffic there may be reasons for making the same choice as one's neighbour. The currency-of-judgment question is just such a rule.

fora's currency-of-judgment rules) involved. Secondly, many courts regard the currency-of-judgment issue as a procedural issue, and thus beyond the reach of choice of law rules. That is, some courts will always apply their own solution to the currency-of-judgment question, regardless of the governing substantive law. Consequently, even in those disputes where a given country's currency-of-judgment rules seem to provide predictable results, the results in any dispute may be hard to foresee, simply because it is hard to foretell which forum and which law will eventually govern. Furthermore, this problem is not confined to the international arena; it occurs within federal states—mostly notably the United States and Canada—where the sub-federal components of such countries can have resolutions of the conversion-date question which differ from that of other coordinate jurisdictions in that federal system.[11] To offer a simple illustration, the currency of judgment that will apply in enforcing a UK judgment (in sterling) in Canada will differ depending on the province in which enforcement is sought.

This raises the prospect of addressing the matter through international agreements on the currency-of-judgment question—agreements that might promote certainty through the promulgation of a uniform multilateral solution to the currency-of-judgment question. If implemented, such a response would not only provide for predictability within those national systems which adopted it, but would, if widely accepted, produce certainty with respect to any given dispute, regardless of where it was litigated. Such international agreements hold out the promise of reducing the supposed evil—if evil it is—of forum shopping, at least with respect to the currency-of-judgment issue, by bringing about a state of affairs where the currency of judgment must be the same regardless of where a matter is litigated. As we will see, there have been some efforts in that direction, though they have been incomplete and their efficacy is open to question.

One explanation for the variety of views about the question of foreign currency obligations is that the subject may be approached from disparate legal perspectives. It sits at an intersection of disciplines. This may be seen by brief reference to the different sort of texts that give some treatment to the matter. Obviously the subject is one that is dealt with in specialised books dedicated to the study of the legal nature of money, such as FA Mann's classic *The Legal Aspect of Money*,[12] Arthur Nussbaum's seminal *Money in the Law*[13] and Rémy

[11] As we shall see, within federations it is common for the sub-national components to possess the power to impose distinct resolutions of the conversion-date rule, since that matter has, at least in the past, been viewed as a procedural one (and thus of purely local interest) rather than as raising a matter worthy of a uniform national response.

[12] The current edition is C Proctor, *Mann on the Legal Aspect of Money*, 6th edn (Oxford, Oxford University Press, 2005).

[13] A Nussbaum, *Money in the Law* (Chicago, Foundation Press, 1939). This was an updating and expansion of a book published in German in 1925. It was further expanded and considerably revised in 1950 under the title *Money in the Law: National and International* (Brooklyn, Foundation Press, 1950). A useful shorter version of Nussbaum's insights is A Nussbaum, 'Basic Monetary Conceptions in Law' (1937) 35 *Michigan Law Review* 865.

Libchaber's *Recherches sur la Monnaie en Droit Privé*.[14] It is also dealt with by scholars on conflicts of law.[15] They commonly wrestle with the relevance of choice of law rules to resolving the conversion date, and with the related issue of whether the appropriate rule on the matter should be part of the *lex causae* or is instead a procedural matter to be disposed of by the law of the forum. In addition, the currency-of-judgment issue is touched on in books and articles focussing on the law of damages[16] and in other texts dealing with substantive law, for example, of contract or tort. At other times the issue is categorised as procedural and dealt with in treatises on civil procedure.

Sometimes the currency-of-judgment issue is even seen as not being confined to any of the foregoing private-law fields, but rather, or in addition, as engaging public law concerns—in particular those of sovereignty. In modern times most countries have elected to have their own national money, though of course the euro is a bold departure from that and there is also the example of El Salvador which since 2001 has used only the US dollar and does not even have a central bank. Thus we will see that soon after their respective foundings as independent countries both the United States and Canada, in efforts to signal their escape from colonial status and support their newly established mints, enacted legislation confirming the primacy, within their respective legal systems, of their newly created national currencies. At the times these statutes were passed it seems unlikely that they were intended to have any effect on the currency-of-judgment question. Rightly or wrongly, however, both statutes eventually came to have such an effect. Specifically, at least at times, they have both been interpreted as barring courts in those two countries from rendering damages awards in any currencies other than their respective state moneys. National currencies remain important indicators of independent national status, and thus even today the currency-of-judgment question may retain features that go beyond merely selecting the appropriate yardstick of compensation with which to bring about justice between the two parties to a private law dispute.

Of course judges faced with resolving the currency-of-judgment question may consciously adopt or be unconsciously influenced by analytical frameworks derived from one or more of the foregoing approaches, and such frameworks may change over time. It will surprise no one, then, that the selection of a given discursive approach, and the concomitant rejection or downplaying of others, can have an impact on the eventual resolution of a dispute and on the formulation of any more general rule which may emerge from a given case.

Such problems with analytical framework are not uncommon. The borders between legal categories are often uncertain and porous, especially in common law

[14] R Libchaber, *Recherches sur la Monnaie en Droit Privé* (Paris, Librairie générale de droit et de jurisprudence, 1992).

[15] L Collins, *Dicey, Morris & Collins: The Conflict of Laws*, 14th edn (London, Sweet & Maxwell, 2006) 2015–23; JJ Fawcett & JM Carruthers, *Cheshire, North & Fawcett: Private International Law*, 14th edn (Oxford, Oxford University Press, 2008) 101–09; C Kleiner, *La Monnaie dans les Relations Privées Internationales* (Paris, LGDJ, 2010).

[16] H McGregor, *McGregor on Damages*, 18th edn (London, Sweet & Maxwell, 2009) ch 16.

adjudication, which is the focus of this study. However, the currency-of-judgment question is one where such problems seem especially acute, in part because money itself is a slippery and sometimes mysterious concept in the law. Even if we decline to engage with post-modern musings on the nature of money,[17] it remains a protean and chimeric thing, sometimes corporeal, but increasingly a de-physicalised[18] matter of trust and belief, untethered from any grounding in other materials such as gold. It may be viewed as a mere device for measuring the value of other commodities, as a commodity and store of value in its own right,[19] or as a *sui generis*[20] form of property with a unique relationship to the nation state which creates it. At times the currency-of-judgment question is seen to turn on whether judges of one country view the currency of others as a commodity or as having a genuine monetary character, though these labels themselves appear to have shifting and uncertain meanings and may function more as masks for conclusions than as aids to analysis.[21] Like other legal concepts its nature has changed over time and continues to evolve.

One of the themes of this book will be that analysis of the currency-of-judgment has too often suffered from approaches that fail to take into account more than one or two perspectives on the problem. For instance, those who have approached it from a conflicts of laws stance, concerned to see that the currency issue is resolved in a way that is consistent with other features of their preferred choice-of-law theory, have failed to attend to the importance of some aspects of the law of damages—the role of remoteness and mitigation for instance. And those whose starting point lies in private law remedies have not always taken proper account of the conflict of laws features of the problem—for instance the part played by the substance/procedure distinction or the problems created by the existence of multiple fora. I will try to demonstrate that a good resolution of the issues involves some integration of perspectives but this is not the place to expand on that point.

A word about two other subjects, one of which is not addressed in the pages that follow, though some readers might expect it to be, while the other *is* the subject of description and commentary in this work, despite the fact that some might question whether it rightly belongs here. First, the subject not taken

[17] For those interested in what Baudrillard and Goux have to say on the matter the place to start is JJ Chung, 'Money as Simulacrum: The Legal Nature and Reality of Money' (2009) 5 *Hastings Business Law Journal* 109, 145–52.

[18] I borrow the phrase from D Fox, *Property Rights in Money* (Oxford, Oxford University Press, 2008) 42.

[19] That is, not so much as something which is used to measure the value of other things, but as a type of merchandise which may be bought and sold but whose value is thought of in terms of something else (that 'something else' typically being some other currency); in short, not as an evaluator but as a something to be evaluated.

[20] Particularly in the ways in which it is exempted from the full force of the *nemo dat* rule.

[21] The English Court of Appeal has commented on the lack of utility of the commodity/currency distinction in this context: 'This [distinction] I confess to having found at first blush persuasive if somewhat elusive. The closer it was examined, however, the more elusive I came to find it to the point where I now regard it as wholly illusory'. *Camdex International Ltd v Bank of Zambia* [1997] EWCA 798, [1997] 1 All ER 728, para 12 (CA) (Simon Brown LJ).

up: the substantive canons regarding foreign currency obligations. Legal systems typically have rules for interpreting contractual provisions that call for payment in a certain currency. For instance, an agreement for the sale of goods might call for the price to be paid in a currency that is not the national money of the place at which payment is to be made. Contract law may then have to address the question of whether payment under such an agreement *must* be made in the currency denominated in the contract, or whether, in the alternative, the payor has the option of tendering instead the national money of the place of payment (at the rate of exchange in effect at the time and place of payment). Answering this question may be done by way of gap-filling interpretative rules—rules which leave the matter up to the contracting parties but which in the absence of evidence of their intention provide a default rule on the matter. Alternatively, there may be statutes that limit freedom of contract and provide that, regardless of what the parties have stipulated, payment may always be made in a certain currency, typically the money of the place of payment. There may even be laws stipulating that payments made in certain places must be made in certain currencies.

Such laws, which vary from country to country, obviously deal with one aspect of foreign currency obligations. Accordingly they might be thought to lie within the scope of this book. However, my focus here is on remedies. More specifically, it deals with the assessment of damages and other monetary awards, and I say little about contractual interpretation or the delineation of substantive obligations. Admittedly the line between substance and remedy is not always easy to draw. Be that as it may, the question of defining the content of contractual obligations concerning money is dealt with in the current edition of *Mann on the Legal Aspect of Money*[22] in an exemplary fashion. I do not seek to explore that question here but rather to focus on what judges do when deciding which money should be used to denominate an award of damages.

There is, however, one other subject that cries for inclusion here: compensation for foreign exchange losses resulting from breach of contract.[23] Sometimes a claimant who had a contractual right to be paid in, for example, sterling wants to argue that, for instance, its damages should be calculated in US dollars. However, that argument on the currency-of-judgment question may be rejected and the claimant may be told by the court that it must be content with judgment in sterling. A litigant in that position might then turn around and say that, had it been paid in sterling on the day that it was contractually entitled to be paid, it would promptly have converted those pounds into US dollars. It might then further assert that when it failed to receive timely payment of the contracted-for sterling it was deprived of the chance to convert those pounds into dollars and that, since dollars have appreciated vis-a-vis sterling in the meantime, it has suffered a loss—one for which it is entitled to be compensated (in sterling).

[22] Above, n 12, ch 7.

[23] In theory such losses could result from the breach of other private law obligations, such as tort, but in practice it is contract cases that give rise to such claims.

It might well be the case that such an award of damages for being deprived of the chance to convert pounds into dollars would, when added to damages for the original non-payment in sterling, bring the value of the claimant's award up to that of an award calculated entirely in dollars (ie, to the value of the award that was initially rejected by the court).

Awarding damages for being deprived of the opportunity to change one currency into another can be used to evade the effect of the rules regarding currency-of damages and achieve the same result by different means. If there are two rules, rule A which affords a claimant a greater recovery and rule B which gives it a lesser one, and the claimant is told that the law requires it to accept the result dictated by rule B but that it can tack on a claim for consequential damages in the amount of the difference between rule A and rule B, then such a claimant has been given the result that would follow under rule A. While I do not here claim that the issues associated by so-called damages for foreign-exchange losses[24] are no more and no different than the issues raised by the currency-of-judgment question, the foregoing illustration, and the fact that the two approaches often generate extensionally equivalent results, should at least show why an inquiry into one cannot easily proceed in the absence of some discussion of the other.

In examining claims for so-called foreign-exchange losses here I am not being heterodox. As we will see, courts and other commentators[25] have noted the close practical connection between the currency-of-judgment question and the question of consequential damages for exchange losses. They have argued for the law's approach to each of those issues to take cognisance of its approach to the other. Troubling questions of classification arise here, however. For while the question of awarding damages for foreign exchange losses must, on the one hand, attend to the neighbouring question of the currency of judgment, it has a neighbour on the other side as well: consequential losses generally. There seems no significant difference between (1) a creditor's argument that had it been paid on time it would have converted that money into some other currency and—that other currency having since appreciated—the creditor should be compensated for that loss (something explored in this work) and (2) a creditor's argument that had it been paid on time it would have taken that money and invested it in shares in some company and, shares in that company having since risen dramatically, the creditor should be compensated for that loss (which is something I do not explore here). Both of those arguments are claims that a plaintiff has a right to be compensated for losses flowing from the fact that, had it been paid on time, it

[24] The phrases 'foreign-exchange losses' or 'exchange-loss damages' are less than ideal since they might seem to refer to losses resulting from unsuccessful speculation on currency fluctuation, which is not which is under consideration here. However, no short unambiguous phrase seems available.

[25] *Di Ferdinando v Simon, Smits & Co* [1920] 3 KB 409 (CA) 416 (Scrutton LJ); *Barclays Bank International Ltd v Levin Brothers (Bradford) Ltd* [1977] 1 QB 270 (QB) 283; O Kahn-Freund, 'Foreign Money Debts—Conversion into Sterling' (1940) 3 *MLR* 228, 231; R Brand, Exchange Loss Damages and the Uniform Foreign–Money Claims Act: The Emperor Hasn't All His Clothes' (1991) 23 *Law and Policy in International Business* 1.

would have employed that payment to acquire some other commodity which has, it turns out, risen in value.[26] Both arguments are species of the same genus: claims to be compensated for consequential losses. So examining foreign-exchange losses involves considering the issues pertinent to consequential losses generally, issues such as foreseeability and mitigation.

The problem, of course, is that the question of liability for consequential losses in private law is too vast a subject to address here. We have here yet another instance of trying to focus on just a couple of threads in the common law's seamless web. For the purposes of this introductory note I must be content with making just two points. First, as the foregoing discussion should bear out, the problem of foreign exchange losses is closely related to both the currency-of-judgment question, on the one hand, and to the question of recovery for consequential losses on the other hand. An abrupt discontinuity between the currency-of-judgment question and the exchange-loss question, or between the exchange-loss question and consequential losses generally, would signal that something was amiss. Analysis of the exchange-loss question must be attentive to the way those other two matters are approached and resolved. My second point is, at this stage, simply an assertion: some of the problems in judicial resolution of foreign exchange loss claims may be traced to the fact that courts have not always been attentive to the first point. In particular, some courts have treated claims for exchange losses much differently than they have approached other claims for consequential losses. In particular, they have been inclined to be more sympathetic to the first—the situation where the plaintiff claims that it would have converted the contract-for money into some foreign money—than they would be to the second. They thus open the door for awards of damages that, at least from one angle, appear to address the currency-of-judgment issue through other means.

I have written about all this before. In the summer of 2003 I had the pleasure of delivering a week-long course in foreign currency obligations at The Hague Academy of International Law. The Academy later published my lecture papers.[27] The pages that follow are indebted to that earlier work. However, while some sentences in this book remain unchanged from the version published five years ago, most parts have been substantially reworked. I have tried throughout not only to update my lectures at The Hague but also to correct errors, reduce infelicities, reformulate arguments and restructure their presentation.

The following chapters explore questions described above. Since most of them deal with how these matters have been dealt with within a given national system, readers interested primarily in one such country may be tempted to read the

[26] At least this is true if we can regard money as a commodity.

[27] V Black, 'Foreign Currency Obligations in Private International Law' (2003) 302 Recueil des Cours de l'Académie de Droit International 9. I had earlier made preliminary forays into the area: V Black, 'Damages for Foreign Exchange Losses in Contract Actions' [1991] *New Zealand Recent Law Review* 190; V Black, 'Loose Change: Problems with Foreign Currency Conversions' (2001) 35 *Canadian Business Law Journal* 123. Any readers familiar with the arguments in those two articles will have to endure some repetition of them here.

chapter on that country and ignore the rest. I hope that some benefits could be gained from such a use of this book. However, the chapters are designed to be read in the order in which they are placed. Although in places they are predominantly descriptive, the chapters attempt to chart the effects which developments in some systems have had on others. In addition, the book does attempt to offer an identification of problems which have arisen in this branch of the law. There is also a normative thread. Although the common law's handling of the currency-of-judgment question has improved, it remains less effective and less fair than it could be. The book has an argument to make about what the preferred approach should be and offers some suggestions as to how that might be implemented, both at the national level and through international co-operation.

1

Foreign Money in English Courts: The Impact of *Miliangos*

Why have we in England insisted on a judgment in sterling and nothing else? It is, I think, because of our faith in sterling. It was a stable currency which had no equal. Things are different now. Sterling floats in the wind. It changes like a weathercock with every gust that blows.

Lord Denning MR[1]

I. Introduction

I start with English law, with particular focus on developments in the last quarter of the last century. While I make some reference to older decisions, this is not principally an historical inquiry and I mention the pre-1975 cases mainly insofar as they set the stage for modern ones or inform the present debate.

The reasons for starting in England are several. It is a significant site for international commercial dispute resolution. Many matters involving parties who have little connection with England are nevertheless resolved before its courts or by arbitrators sitting there and applying English law. This is especially the case with marine cargo claims, maritime collision cases, marine insurance disputes and charter parties. All of these are frequently brought before arbitrators and courts in London and all have been a fruitful source of jurisprudence on the currency-of-judgment question. The problem of foreign currency obligations has been before all levels of English courts numerous times in a variety of contexts. Many experienced commercial judges have had the occasion to consider the matter, some of them on several occasions, and the resulting case law is thoughtful and nuanced.

In addition, as we shall see in the following chapters, English developments in this field have had an effect in other countries, both in courts and legislatures. That this should be so throughout the Commonwealth is not surprising, since English judgments on many matters—and especially on the common law, within which the currency-of-judgment question falls in Commonwealth legal systems—are often

[1] *Schorsch Meier GmbH v Hennin* [1975] 1 QB 416 (CA) 424 (*Schorsch Meier*).

influential there. Indeed, for a dwindling number of Commonwealth countries—most of them islands in the English Channel, the Caribbean or the mid-Atlantic—the Privy Council in London remains the court of last resort. However, on the currency-of-judgment question the effect of the English cases is not confined to the Commonwealth. The matter of foreign currency obligations is one of those rare areas where English judgments continue to have some effect in the United States. As we will see in chapter four, English judicial innovations have swayed American judges and also American scholars, law reform bodies and legislatures. Indeed it is hard to think of another area of the law where, in recent decades at least, American courts and academics have been so influenced by innovations in England. English judicial decisions on the currency question have even received favourable notice in France, though admittedly that is more because they have at length brought English practice into line with that which has for many years prevailed across the channel.[2]

At the heart of all this is a single case. Any account of the problem of awarding damages in foreign currency must give a prime place to the revolutionary 1975 decision of the House of Lords in *Miliangos v George Frank (Textiles) Ltd*,[3] where, contrary to the view that had prevailed up to that time, it was held that in certain circumstances English courts might—in fact, must—award judgment in a foreign currency. Although carefully confined to one narrow point, in the years since its appearance *Miliangos* has been applied expansively, so much so that the leading English text on damages refers to it as effecting 'a sea change',[4] and a judge two years after it was handed down was able to write that 'no case decided prior to *Miliangos* ... on the general question of rates of exchange can now be considered good law if inconsistent with *Miliangos*'.[5]

Although scrutiny and criticism of the currency-of-judgment question will be deferred until later chapters, it is worth noting here that the reasoning and result in *Miliangos* is by and large taken by courts, scholars and the English business community alike to constitute an enlightened, progressive and commercially astute resolution of the remedial problems raised by foreign currency obligations. The case has come in for minimal negative commentary. It is widely viewed as a modernising decision—a veritable *fiat lux*, which liberated legal doctrine on the foreign currency question from the grip of medieval attitudes and the benighted

[2] D Tallon, 'Les Dettes Libellées en Monnaie Étrangère devant Le Chambre des Lords' (1977) 66 *Revue Critique de Droit Internationale Privé* 485.

[3] *Miliangos v George Frank (Textiles) Ltd* [1976] AC 443 (HL) (*Miliangos*). The adjective is an overstatement of course. The House of Lords is not the site of revolutionary activity. However, the term has been applied to *Miliangos* on several occasions. Lord Simon used it in *Miliangos* itself (at 482), and in *George Veflings Rederi A/S v President of India* [1979] 1 WLR 59 (CA) Lord Denning claimed that *Miliangos* 'revolutionised' the law in this area (at 62). To similar effect see also *Barclays Bank International Ltd v Levin Brothers (Bradford) Ltd* [1977] 1 QB 270 (QB) 282; *Ozalid Group (Export) Ltd v African Continental Bank Ltd* [1979] Lloyd's Rep 231 (QB) 233 and *Camdex International Ltd v Bank of Zambia* [1997] EWCA 798 [21].

[4] H McGregor, *McGregor on Damages*, 18th edn (London, Sweet & Maxwell, 2009) 684.

[5] *Monrovia Tramp Shipping Co v President of India (The Pearl Merchant)* [1978] 2 Lloyd's Law Rep 193 (QB) 197 (Donaldson J), aff'd [1979] 1 WLR 59 (CA).

hold of monetary nominalism[6] and laid the groundwork for an approach to this matter which was more in accord with general principles of remedial law, more responsive to the realities of fluctuating currencies, and more conducive to the fair and orderly globalisation of economic activity.[7] *Miliangos* is seen as a House of Lords ruling in the field of English private international law which, along with certain other House of Lords and Privy Council judgments of the 1970s and 1980s,[8] departed from the parochialism which had previously characterised English private international law. It is regarded as taking a welcome and overdue step away from an Anglocentric world-view in which England was regarded as the fount and measure of all things, and substituting a more appropriate cosmopolitan world outlook where the English legal system was simply one among many equals and needed to give consideration to co-ordinating its justice system with those of other countries.

It is not my goal here to protest or malign the enthronement of *Miliangos* or advance dissident claims that it and the judicial developments it spawned were ill-conceived. Although I will later suggest that there are aspects of its reasoning that have been under interrogated and which start to crumble when pressed, when the time comes for critical evaluation I will line up with those who rate *Miliangos* as a welcome advance. Certainly it is the master key for understanding subsequent happenings in this area. Arguably, however, the degree to which that touchstone case has been praised and celebrated by courts and academics, especially in some countries other than England, has not always been matched by the degree to which it has been understood. As we shall see, the fact that *Miliangos* is almost universally lauded has not preserved it from being interpreted and applied in diverse and not easily reconcilable ways. Indeed, the new religion of *Miliangos* has split into competing sects, and as a consequence of this schism that case has been cited in support of more than one resolution of the currency-of-judgment issue. However, the reception, amplification and possible misunderstanding of *Miliangos* outside England are subjects for later chapters. The goal here is the unambitious one of describing that case and related subsequent developments in the land of its origin.

Readers might fairly wonder whether the world really needs yet another retelling of the *Miliangos* story. Descriptions and discussions of the cases leading up to that decision, of *Miliangos* itself, and of the litigation which immediately followed

[6] More about nominalism in the next chapter, but for the moment it can be characterised as the stand that, unlike other commodities, money—or at least the money of one's home country—is an unshakeable constant that can only be measured in terms of itself (and hence not really measured at all). As Scutton LJ put it, 'A pound in England is a pound whatever its international purchasing power': *The Baarn* [1933] P 251 (CA) 265. The following statement from Denning LJ in *Treseder-Griffin v Co-operative Insurance Society* [1956] 2 QB 127 (CA) 144 has become a classic illustration of nominalism: 'Sterling is the constant unit of value by which in the eye of the law everything else is measured. Prices of commodities may go up or down, other currencies may go up and down, but sterling remains the same'.

[7] *McGregor on Damages* says that the effect of *Miliangos* 'is most salutory': above n 4, 709.

[8] See, eg: *Chaplin v Boys* [1971] AC 356 (HL); *The Atlantic Star v Bona Spes* [1974] AC 436 (HL); *MacShannon v Rockware Glass Ltd* [1978] AC 795 (HL); *Spiliada Maritime Corp v Cansulex Ltd* [1987] AC 460(HL); *SNI Aérospatiale v Lee Kui Jak* [1987] 3 WLR 59 (PC).

and interpreted it are not hard to come by. Accounts can be found in the leading English text dealing with the legal treatment of money,[9] the leading English text on damages,[10] the leading English texts on conflict of laws[11] and elsewhere.[12] The tale lends itself to narrative for a variety of reasons. It features a particularly abrupt reversal of a common law rule—an about-face assisted by some dubious judicial interpretations of previous case law,[13] a strange and arguably bad faith interpretation of an international treaty, and a dubious attitude to the rules of precedent. In fact there continues to be legal scholarship which, although it has no special interest in the foreign currency puzzle, grapples with the *Miliangos* case simply because of what that case can tell us about stare decisis.[14] Indeed, 'the transformation of judicial attitudes'[15] evident in the *Miliangos* story is as much the focus of some accounts as is the change in legal doctrine. On top of that, the *Miliangos* tale offers the bonus of some characteristically colourful and quotable language from Lord Denning. All of that has prompted several scholars to recount the story and it is with some hesitation that anyone ventures on yet another telling.

Nevertheless, repetition of that account here is unavoidable. A reiteration of the *Miliangos* story permits a necessary elucidation of the foreign currency question in general and of many of the principal ways in which that question has been conceived and resolved. The reasoning in *Miliangos* encapsulates much that appears elsewhere in discussions of this matter, so an exposition of the case, starting with the situation which prevailed before it was decided, has some analytical value.

II. Before *Miliangos*

Prior to *Miliangos*, it was settled law that foreign currency claims could not be brought in English courts. It is necessary to expand on what this meant. Obviously it did not imply that a claim based, for example, on an unfulfilled

[9] C Proctor, *Mann on the Legal Aspect of Money*, 6th edn (Oxford, Oxford University Press, 2005) 209–14.

[10] *McGregor on Damages*, above n 4, 684–710.

[11] L Collins, *Dicey, Morris and Collins: The Conflict of Laws*, 14th edn (London, Sweet & Maxwell, 2000) 2015–27; JJ Fawcett & JM Carruthers, *Cheshire, North & Fawcett: Private International Law*, 14th edn (Oxford, Oxford University Press, 2008) 101–09.

[12] JHC Morris, 'English Judgments in Foreign Currency: A Procedural Revolution' (1977) 41 *Law and Contemporary Problems* 44; M Howard, 'Foreign Currency Judgments in Contractual Claims' in FD Rose (ed), *Consensus Ad Idem: Essays in Honour of Guenter Treitel* (London, Sweet & Maxwell, 1996).

[13] Interpretations described by Lord Wilberforce as 'some distortion of the judicial process': *Miliangos*, above n 3, 459.

[14] See, for instance, the discussions of *Miliangos* in R Cross & JW Harris, *Precedent in English Law*, 4th edn (Oxford, Clarendon, 1991) 135–39 and N Duxbury, *The Nature and Authority of Precedent* (Cambridge, Cambridge University Press, 2008) 127, 158.

[15] Howard, above n 12.

promise to pay French francs could not be pursued in the English judicial system. Rather, it simply indicated that legal claims that had a foreign currency aspect had to be, in a sense, domesticated. If the underlying obligation had a foreign money component—for instance, a promise to pay an amount that was stated in a currency other than English pounds—a civil action in England based on that claim had to be both expressed (in the parties' pleadings) and assessed (by the court) in pounds sterling. The cases supposed that judgment could only be awarded in sterling were venerable ones,[16] and the principle was perceived as 'fundamental'.[17]

The foremost modern authority for this was the 1960 judgment of the House of Lords in *Re United Railways of Havana and Regla Warehouses*,[18] which affirmed the rule that had existed throughout most of the first part of the twentieth century. It is unnecessary here to go into the details of *Havana Railways*, which involved complex issues in a grievance relating to the financing of Cuba's national railway, expropriated by the Cuban government with inadequate compensation. This was against the background of the 1947and 1949 devaluations of the pound which drastically reduced its exchange value vis-a-vis US dollars. The important thing is the decision's affirmation of the rule that judgments issuing from English courts must be in sterling. The words of Lord Denning in that case afford a sense of how this principle was regarded as beyond doubt, in fact nearly inevitable:

> if there is one thing that is clear in our law, it is that the claim must be made in sterling and the judgment given in sterling. We do not give judgment in dollars any more than the United States courts give judgments in sterling.[19]

The idea in the closing words—namely, that the rule which prevailed in England was one which was neither idiosyncratic nor parochial but which in fact operated elsewhere—is one we will see repeated. The passage operates to convey the impression that the local rule was an almost unavoidable consequence of a world in which there were national judicial systems with accompanying national currencies, and that any other approach would be unworkable.

Since judgments were required to be rendered in pounds, and since pounds obviously might fluctuate in value vis-a-vis the currency in the underlying claim, another question necessarily arose: what date should be selected for conversion from the foreign currency into sterling? Pre-*Miliangos* law answered this by saying that the mandatory date for exchange from the foreign currency into sterling was the time at which the obligation was breached. In a contract claim, this was the

[16] *Bagshaw v Playn* (1594) Cro Eliz 536, 78 ER 783 (KB); *Rastell v Draper* (1605) 1 Cro Jac 88, 80 ER 55 (KB); *Ward v Kidswin* (1625) Latch 77, 82 ER 283 (KB). The last-mentioned is in Norman French, but an English translation is provided by Viscount Simonds in *Re United Railways of Havana and Regla Warehouses Ltd* [1961] AC 1007 (HL) 1044 (*Havana Railways*).

[17] See, eg: O Kahn-Freund 'Foreign Money Debts—Conversion into Sterling' (1940) 3 *MLR* 228, 229.

[18] Above n 16.

[19] Ibid, 1068-69. Lord Reid expressed a similar view at 1052.

date at which the contractual obligation should have been performed,[20] though of course complications might arise in the cases of anticipatory breach, ongoing breaches and breaches of multiple obligations. This rule was thought to be just an instance of the more general rule of accurate compensation. As Denning LJ put it in 1952,

> I take it to be clear law that when a creditor comes to the courts to enforce a debt payable in a foreign currency the creditor is entitled to be put into as good a position as if the debtor had done his duty under the contract and had paid the debt in the foreign currency without the intervention of the courts. To do this, judgment must be given for the creditor for the debt turned into sterling at the rate of exchange ruling at the date when it should have been paid.[21]

What is more, this standard—which accorded with the more general private-law rule that damages are presumptively calculated by assessing the value of the abridged right in sterling as of the date the right was violated—should be applied regardless of whether English currency had appreciated[22] or depreciated[23] as against the foreign money, irrespective of the parties' residence or nationality,[24] and regardless of whether the plaintiff or defendant appeared to benefit therefrom. Furthermore the rule should operate both in actions for debt and in damages claims, and regardless of what state's substantive law was held to govern the cause of action.[25]

The operation of the rule merits some closer examination. Arguably, it is best understood as three rules operating in conjunction. The first is simply the easily complied with procedural requirement that claims must be pleaded in sterling. So regardless of the fact that the parties might have employed foreign currencies in denominating their underlying obligations—for instance, in a contract for sale of goods by stating that the price was payable in some currency other than sterling—when it came time to go to court to have such obligations enforced, the plaintiff had to articulate its prayer for relief in English pounds. The rule did not go so far as to say that evidence which a party might lead must not make mention of foreign currencies, or even that foreign money might not be mentioned in a party's pleadings—for instance, by making reference to a contract which

[20] See, eg: *Havana Railways*, ibid; *Di Ferdinando v Simon, Smits & Co* [1920] 3 KB 409 (CA) (*Di Ferdinando*); *Celia (Owners) v SS Volturno (Owners)* [1921] 2 AC 544 (HL) (*The Volturno*); *Re Chesterman's Trusts* [1923] Ch 466 (CA); *Peynal v Wilkinson* [1924] 2 KB 166 (KB); *Anderson v Equitable Assurance Society of the United States* (1926) 134 Law Times 557 (CA); *The 'Canadian Transport'* [1932] Lloyd's List L Rep 409 (CA); *Madeleine Vionnet et Cie v Wills* [1940] 1 KB 72 (CA). The breach-date rule was adopted by the Privy Council in an appeal from the Supreme Court of Palestine: *Syndic in Bankruptcy of Salim Nasrallah Khoury v Khayat* [1943] AC 507 (PC).

[21] *Cummings v London Bullion Co* [1952] 1 KB 327 (CA) 335–36.

[22] See, eg: *Di Ferdinando*, above n 20, where due to the collapse of the Italian lire and the operation of the forum-currency/breach-date rule the Italian plaintiff was awarded the sterling equivalent of twice his loss in the original currency (as valued at judgment day); and *Madeleine Vionnet et Cie v Wills*, above n 20.

[23] See, eg: *Barry v Van der Hurk* [1920] 2 KB 709 (KB).

[24] *Re British American Continental Bank Ltd* [1922] 2 Ch 589.

[25] *Re American Continental Bank* [1922] 2 Ch 589 (Ch); *Havana Railways*, above n 16.

stipulated for payment in pesetas. However, a prayer for relief which requested an English court to order payment in anything other than sterling was regarded as defective.

The second aspect of the pre-*Miliangos* sterling-only rule was closely allied with the first. It dealt with the way a judge should go about communicating any monetary remedy she might grant. It mandated that judicial awards for debt or damages in an English court must be expressed in English pounds.[26] Again, it did not forbid judges from making any reference to foreign currencies in their reasons; but when it came to the bottom line—the amount that the loser would be told to pay the winner—it required that such amounts be articulated in pounds and in pounds only. As noted, at times English courts appear to have taken the view that it was practically inconceivable that any court, English or otherwise, could award damages in other than the local currency. The rule seemed almost to possess the status of natural law, and accordingly some judicial pronouncements gave the impression that the rule was but the local English instance of some universal state of affairs. For instance, in 1898 a judge of the Court of Appeal wrote that

> if the defendants were within the jurisdiction of any other civilised State and were sued there, as they might be, the courts of that State would have to deal with precisely the same problem, and to express in the currency of that State, the amount payable by the defendants instead of expressing it in [the money of the contract].[27]

The third key element of the pre-*Miliangos* response to remedying breached foreign currency obligations concerned the conversion date to be employed in order for a court to come up with an award in pounds. This was the aspect of the pre-*Miliangos* regime which, when combined with the fact that over time currencies vary in value with respect to one another, generated the situation in which the ultimate value of the judicial remedies could differ according to the date selected. If the underlying obligation was a foreign currency, but the ultimate award had to be claimed, calculated and granted in sterling, then an exchange rate is required. But since such rates change over time a date must be chosen for establishing that rate. The third aspect of the sterling-only rule stipulates that the exchange rate at which that foreign currency had to be converted[28] into sterling was the rate prevailing at the date the relevant obligation was breached. It was the breach-date rule.[29]

[26] The modern origin of this rule is *Manners v Pearson & Son* [1898] 1 Ch 581 (CA) 587 (Lord Lindley). The case has been said to stand for the proposition that English courts lack *jurisdiction* to order recovery in anything other than pounds: BFM, Case Note (1923) 1 *Cambridge Law Journal* 325. The use of the term 'jurisdiction' serves to mark the fundamental status accorded to the rule.

[27] Ibid, 587.

[28] Of course at this stage we are dealing with incorporeal money and 'converted' in this context does not, of course, mean that there is any actual exchange of currency. It simply indicates that, where the underlying obligation is one valued in a foreign currency (as, for example, a promise to pay a given amount of such money), the value of the breached obligation is assessed by ascertaining the number of English pounds it would take to buy that amount of foreign currency, and then reckoning further damages calculations with reference to that number of pounds.

[29] For instance, in the case of a suit based on an obligation to pay money, the rate would be the one prevailing on the date at which the payment should have been made. The two-rule explanation is

This third rule is sometimes perceived as simply an instance of a more general common law rule of damages, namely that—as part of the principle of compensation or *restitutio in integrum*—damages are generally calculated by assessing the value of the obligation breached as of the date of breach.[30] That statement is incomplete unless there is agreement on what measures that 'value'. The answer is the currency of the forum. So if the plaintiff seeks damages for non-delivery of some contracted-for commodity—goods, land, corporate shares—then a court inquires into the market value in the currency of the forum that commodity would have had at the time and place of the contracted-for delivery. Similarly, if the plaintiff's right to bodily integrity or non-interference with its property is violated, then that is the right that is evaluated at the time of breach in the currency of the forum. Pre- and post-judgment interest are usually added to take account of the fact that the plaintiff is kept out of the use of that money between the time of that breach and the ultimate receipt of the money, but apart from that (and of course any consequential and punitive awards) plaintiffs have to be content with an award of money in supposed replacement of the right which the defendant has infringed.

When assessing damages, breach-date evaluation is no longer an absolute rule. Case law has acknowledged that a variety of factors may justify the selection of some later date, up to and including the time of trial, for measuring the value of the claimant's loss.[31] Nevertheless, though breach-date assessment is not an absolute, it is the starting point. Generally some convincing explanation is required for departing from it—typically an explanation as to why the obligation on a claimant to mitigate its losses may justifiably be relaxed, or at least postponed.

The forum-currency/breach-date rule, then, may simply be viewed as applying that general breach-date rule to the right to receive a certain amount of a foreign currency. That is, the foreign currency, even if owed as a debt, could be treated as a commodity, and any claim for non-payment could be treated as a damages claim in which the remedy had to be evaluated by reference to the currency of the forum at the date the cause of action arose. Arguably, this operated to restore the injured plaintiff to the position it would have occupied had the breach not occurred, insofar as money can do so. Additionally, the rule was not out of step with one core principle of damages in contract and tort cases—namely that damages are normally calculated as of the time of the loss by assessing in the currency of the forum the loss to the plaintiff, at that time, brought about by the defendant's wrong.

found in RA Bowles & CJ Whelan, 'Judicial Responses to Exchange Rate Instability', in P Burrows and CG Veljanovski (eds), *The Economic Approach to Law* (London, Butterworths, 1981) 253, 254.

[30] *Johnson v Agnew* [1980] AC 367 (HL). This case did not establish a breach-date damages assessment as a new principle. Rather, it recognised it as a venerable one. It was re-affirmed in *Golden State Corp v Nippon Yusen Kubisha Kaisha* [2007] UKHL 12. Also, the remedies of specific performance and injunction are generally inconsistent with a breach-date assessment of the claimant's loss.

[31] *Dodd Properties (Kent) v Canterbury City Council* [1980] 1 WLR 433 (CA); *Johnson v Agnew*, ibid; and in Canada, *Asamera Oil Corp v Sea Oil & General Corp* [1979] 1 SCR 633.

In combination, these three rules might be labelled the sterling/breach-date rule. However, since, as we shall see, a similar regime prevailed elsewhere (though by no means everywhere), I shall more generally drop the reference to sterling and refer to it as the forum-currency/breach-date rule.

It has been credibly argued that in England the forum-currency/breach date rule—at least insofar as it took the shape of a mandatory requirement—arose partly out of a series of misunderstandings and was not nearly so deeply rooted in English law as some, such as Lord Denning in the quotation above, have suggested.[32] Before the twentieth century, English case law on the foreign currency question (like its American counterpart, as we shall see in chapter four[33]) was rather messier and less consistent than is sometimes acknowledged. In the days before textbooks and modern law reports, many aspects of the common law were less regularly applied than is the case today, so claims that the forum-currency/breach-date rule had been applied since time out of mind may be regarded with some suspicion. Indeed, even on the eve of the Privy Council's 1921 decision in *The Volturno* it is possible to find English decisions that employed different conversion dates.[34] However, my focus here is principally on the modern era and there is no need to probe the question of where the rule's ancient pedigree is valid or a mere fabrication of modern courts. Certainly by the mid-twentieth century the forum-currency/breach-date rule was comfortably established in English law, and the claims that it was fundamental, possessed of a long lineage and practically a matter of necessity were by then regarded as entirely orthodox.

However, even though by he mid-twentieth century English support for the forum-currency/breach-date rule was solid among the judges, among academics there were scattered signs of dissent. Foremost among these was FA Mann, whose text *The Legal Aspect of Money* was the pre-eminent English authority on that subject. In each of that book's first three editions—1938, 1953 and 1971—Mann had attacked the forum-currency/breach-date rule as being founded on dubious authority. He also pointed out that the rule was hardly an inevitable one. He noted that, contrary to some English judicial pronouncements, there was nothing inconceivable in granting judgment in a currency other than that of the forum. He further reported that judges in some countries were in the habit of doing exactly that. Most importantly, Mann asserted that the forum-currency/breach-date rule was out of touch with modern commerce and potentially productive of

[32] FA Mann, *The Legal Aspect of Money*, 3rd edn (Oxford, Oxford University Press, 1971) 336. This was the last pre-*Miliangos* edition and accordingly had a fuller discussion of the breach-date rule than the post-*Miliangos* editions.

[33] See ch 4, nn 11 and 12. And see the observations on Canadian law at pp 98–99.

[34] In *Kirsch v Allen, Harding & Co* (1919) 122 LTR 159 (KB) Roche J converted at the time of his judgment; in (1920) 123 LTR 105 the Court of Appeal allowed the appeal on grounds of liability and did not address the conversion date. In *Cohn v Boulken* (1920) 36 TLR 767 (KB) a date-of-trial conversion was applied. For discussion of these and other cases arising after World War I and mostly concerned with currency devaluations associated with the aftermath of that conflict see R Gottschalk, 'The Law Relating to Devaluation of Currency' (1935) 17 *Journal of Comparative Legislation* 47.

injustice. For instance, in his third edition he asserted that 'the Anglo-American countries have failed to produce persuasive arguments in favour of a rule which, on cogent grounds, the rest of the Western world has rejected'.[35]

Mann's core claim about the unfairness of the existing English situation was that, in situations where during the litigation the pound had declined against the relevant foreign money, application of the forum-currency/breach date rule produced an award which did not fully compensate the successful claimant. He thought that, depending on how the relevant currencies behaved in the post-breach period the breach-date rule might operate to under-compensate the claimant. Mann's view was not common, but he was not quite alone in this. Otto Kahn-Freund espoused similar reservations.[36]

Then there began to be rumblings on the judicial front. We have noted that the forum-currency/breach-date rule had been affirmed by the House of Lords as fundamental as recently as 1960. However, even that case contains some passing reference to the fact that the rule might not invariably be productive of fair results.[37] A decade later in his judgment in *The Teh Hu* Lord Denning MR observed that the rule could result in injustice in the form of under-compensation of a foreign plaintiff whose currency had recently appreciated versus the pound pending trial.[38] Lord Denning had altered his views since *Havana Railways* and in *The Teh Hu* he would have abandoned the traditional rule. But his judgment there was a dissenting one; the other two judges stuck with the old law.[39]

Just a few years later, however, that same judge took the opportunity to make two notable breaches in the old rule. First, in his 1974 judgment in *Jugoslavenska Oceanska Plovidba v Castle Investment Co*[40] Lord Denning joined the other two

[35] Above n 32, 376. Even back in the 1920s one voice had been raised in criticism of the rule: R Negus, 'Rate of Exchange in Reference to Foreign Debts Expressed in Foreign Currency' (1924) 40 *LQR* 149.

[36] O Kahn-Freund, 'Foreign Currency Obligations and the Devaluation of Sterling' (1952) 68 *LQR* 163 esp 167; Mann, above n 21, 371. And note that there were statutory exceptions which allowed for escaping the old rule: *Carriage of Goods by Air Act 1961*, sch 1, art 22(5); *Carriage of Goods by Road Act 1965*, sch 1, art 27(2), *International Convention and Additional Protocol Concerning the Carriage of Goods by Rail 1961*, Art 31(2), Brit TS 67 (1965).

[37] *Havana Railways*, above n 16, 1053 (Lord Reid).

[38] [1970] P 106 (CA).

[39] And the view of the majority later met with the approval of Megarry J in *Hawkins v Hawkins* [1972] 1 Ch 714 (Ch D).

[40] *Jugoslavenska Oceanska Plovidba v Castle Investment Co* [1974] QB 292, [1973] 3 WLR 847 (CA) (*Jugoslavenska*). The rule adopted in this case was that the amount of the foreign currency award should be converted into pounds sterling as of the date of the arbitral award. Foreigners might well have become hesitant to arbitrate in England if the courts had not adopted such a view, since at this time the pound was falling against many other currencies. Certainly Lord Denning in his dissent in *The Teh Hu* had argued that clinging to the old rule would diminish the attractiveness of England as a site for commercial arbitrations (ibid, 127). The power of arbitrators to express their awards in foreign currency has now been confirmed by statute: Arbitration Act 1996, s 48(4), which will be discussed in ch 5. In 2005 this provision received consideration by the House of Lords in *Lesotho Highland Development Authority v Impreglio SpA* [2005] UKHL 43. There it was argued that the arbitrators had exceeded their powers in the way they had chosen the currency of their award, which was partly in Italian lire, partly in sterling, partly in French francs and partly in Deutschmarks. In a decision which

members of the Court of Appeal in holding that English courts might give effect to arbitrators' decisions expressed in a foreign currency. In this undefended appeal from an interlocutory order of Kerr J, who said that he would have preferred to have ordered judgment in the foreign currency but felt bound by authority to refrain from doing so,[41] the Master of the Rolls reasoned that there was no reason to extend the forum-currency/breach-date rule to arbitral decisions, since the principal justification for that rule was that there were procedural problems associated with collecting judgments in currencies other than that of the country where such collection must take place. He claimed that, with arbitral awards, 'there is rarely any need to call in the sheriff or his officer to enforce the award'.[42]

In another case the following year, *Schorsch Meier*,[43] Lord Denning led the Court of Appeal in holding that the rationale for the forum-currency/breach-date rule had ceased to exist and that where the plaintiff was a resident in one of the member states of the European Economic Community, s 106 of the Treaty of Rome (which by statute was part of English law) permitted that plaintiff to claim for a debt expressed in a foreign currency. More could be said about the reasoning in these two cases. *Jugoslavenska*'s claims that the rationale for the forum-currency/breach date rule was simply the existence of procedural difficulties in executing foreign currency judgments and that arbitral awards never posed problems of collection are both open to question. The same can be said for *Schorsch Meier*'s assertion that legislation implementing the Treaty of Rome should be construed as abrogating the old rule (even if only for EEC residents), since it appears s 106 of the Treaty of Rome has little to do with the issue of currency of judgment.[44] Arguably, those arguments were no more than pretexts for Lord Denning's declining to follow a rule he no longer favoured, at least as it would have applied in those cases.

Schorsch Meier was not unanimous. While Foster J offered only a brief concurrence with the result and reasons given by Lord Denning, Lawton LJ would have allowed the appeal. However, this was only because he felt bound by the authorities mandating the breach-date/forum-currency rule. As for the merits of that

accorded wide deference to arbitrations, or at least to those conducted according to the International Chamber of Commerce Rules, which go further than most in seeking to insulate awards from judicial scrutiny, the House of Lords held that even if the arbitrators' handling of the currency point was an error of law, it was it was not in excess of their powers. Accordingly the arbitral award should be enforced.

41 *Jugoslavenska*, ibid, 294 QB.

42 Ibid, 299 QB.

43 Above, n 1. As FA Mann, *The Legal Aspect of Money*, 5th edn (Oxford, Clarendon Press, 1992) 356, noted, the reasons offered in this case 'in strict law were far from convincing'. However, he thought the result was right. Mann described Lord Denning MR's work in the Court of Appeal on the foreign damages question as a 'most beneficial initiative': FA Mann, 'Case Note on *Miliangos*' (1976) 92 *LQR* 165, 167.

44 On this point see G White, 'Judgments in Foreign Currency and the EEC Treaty' [1976] *Journal of Business Law* 7.

rule, which went back to the seventeenth-century decision in *Ward v Kidswin*,[45] he sided with the other two members of the court: 'It is disturbing to find that a rule which does injustice to a foreign trader is founded on archaic legal nonsense of this kind. It is, however, my duty to apply the law, not to reform it'.[46]

Lord Denning's trilogy in *The Teh Hu*, *Jugoslavenska* and *Schorsch Meier* has been dissected with skill elsewhere.[47] There is room for debate about whether the reasoning he offered for refusing to follow the traditional rule in *Schorsch Meier* and *The Jugoslavenska* stand up to scrutiny. I will not pursue that because soon after those two cases appeared they were overtaken by the House of Lords decision in *Miliangos*. With that case, English law's rejection of the forum-currency/breach-date rule does not rest on considerations peculiar to arbitral awards or the Treaty of Rome, but rather on a more fundamental rethinking of the currency-of-judgment question.

III. *Miliangos*: A Landmark Judgment

Miliangos was a suit brought in England by an unpaid seller of goods. It was an action for price, which had been expressed in the contract as an amount in Swiss francs. In its original claim the seller had asked for judgment in English pounds, calculated by reference to the sterling equivalent of the price in Swiss francs at the date that payment should have been made. That is, initially the plaintiff advanced a claim in complete accordance with what was then understood to be the mandatory approach in English courts, the forum-currency/breach-date rule. However, because of doubts cast upon the wisdom and scope of this rule after the drafting of its claim but before the matter came on for hearing—in particular, the decision of the Court of Appeal in *Schorsch Meier*, which was handed down just a week before the trial in *Miliangos* started—the plaintiff amended its claim and requested judgment expressed in Swiss francs in the amount of the stated price of the goods. The plaintiff's incentive to alter its pleadings in this fashion is easily understood: in the period between the breach of contract and the start of the trial the Swiss franc had appreciated considerably in relation to the pound. Due to this fluctuation, an award expressed in pounds, as calculated by the sterling equivalent of the price at the time of breach, would be worth far less than an award in Swiss francs, at their then-current value.

45 Above n 16.

46 *Schorsch Meier*, above n 1, 430.

47 See JHC Morris, 'English Judgments in Foreign Currency: A Procedural Revolution', above n 12, 48–53. Lord Denning was not the only judge to play a role in weakening the reign of the breach-date rule. In *The Halcyon The Great* [1975] 1 WLR 515, [1975] 1 All ER 883 (QB) Brandon J ruled that an order to cause a vessel to be sold for the highest obtainable price enabled court officials to sell it for a price expressed in a foreign currency. This decision was mentioned in *Miliangos*.

It should not escape notice that, had the fluctuation gone the other way—that is, had the pound risen vis-a-vis the Swiss franc between the breach date and the trial date—the unpaid seller would have had no such incentive to request the court to abandon the forum-currency/breach-date rule. It would not have done so. Indeed, in that instance the effect of such a rule would have worked to the Swiss plaintiff's great advantage. The plaintiff seller would have reaped the benefit of sterling's rise as against the franc. Whether such a benefit should be viewed as a windfall or as an appropriate implementation of the objective of fair compensation is a question to which we will return.

In any event, the pound had not risen. It had gone the other way, and the plaintiff seller did have an incentive to seek the application of a rule that would give it the benefit of the franc's corresponding appreciation. While the trial judge allowed the plaintiff to amend its pleading, he went on to hold that he was bound by the authority of the longstanding forum-currency/breach-date rule. So judgment was awarded in pounds, to the detriment of the plaintiff seller.[48] The Court of Appeal, however, emboldened by its previous departures from that rule, allowed an appeal on the basis that it was bound by its own recent decision in *Schorsch Meier*, not by the old rule.[49] Not surprisingly the defendant appealed. On Guy Fawkes Day of 1975 the House of Lords dropped a bombshell and rejected the position it had adopted just fifteen years before in *Havana Railways*.[50] By a four-to-one majority it decided that the forum-currency/breach-date rule should not be applied in the case before it. It held that instead the plaintiff could and should be granted judgment in Swiss francs or in the equivalent in English pounds at the date of payment, or when the court authorised enforcement of the judgment.[51] That is, the defendant buyer might pay either in Swiss francs or in pounds, but if the latter were chosen then the conversion would not be the date of breach, as it would have been under the old rule, but rather the date of payment (which of course is the same as paying in francs).

This amounted to an abrogation of all three rules stated above. The sterling rule was abandoned in that claimants in debt actions were now free to request

[48] *Miliangos v George Frank (Textiles) Ltd* [1975] 2 WLR 555 (QB).

[49] *Miliangos v George Frank (Textiles) Ltd* [1975] QB 487 (CA).

[50] Above n 16.

[51] One minor matter on which there has been subsequent litigation concerns precisely when this point is. The holding in *Miliangos* sought to push the conversion date to the latest possible time, but depending on the method of enforcement there could be a measure of doubt about what that date was. In *Carnegie v Giessen* [2005] EWCA Civ 191 the Court of Appeal dealt with a case where, judgment having been obtained against the defendant, a master had made a charging order for the sale of the defendant's properties and expressed the amount in US dollars. It was contended that enforcement took place when the charging order was made and that, accordingly, conversion from US dollars to sterling should have taken place on that day. The Court of Appeal upheld the master's decision and its reasons offer a discussion of what the precise conversion date should be depending on the form of enforcement. Comparable problems have also arisen with respect to maintenance orders. Although post-*Miliangos* decisions have been prepared to grant such orders in foreign currencies, for practical purposes the conversion into sterling must be made when the enforcement procedure is commenced: *R v Cambridge Country Court, ex p Ireland* [1985] 15 Fam Law 23 (Fam Div).

judgment in a currency other than pounds and courts were then permitted—at least in certain circumstances—to express any ultimate damages award in a foreign currency. Finally, the third element of the breach-date rule was jettisoned: conversion from the foreign currency now took place either (1) never (in the case where the judgment debtor exercised its option to pay in the foreign currency), or (2) at the date of payment (in cases where it elected to pay in pounds).

The reasoning in *Miliangos* provides the groundwork for many subsequent developments both in England and elsewhere. As noted above, the justifications which the House of Lords offered for abandoning the forum-currency/breach-date rule and adopting one based on the date of payment have been generally applauded and seen to represent an enlightened, commercially astute updating of the law—a freeing of it from outdated and unrealistic rules.[52] Evaluation of that will be postponed until the next chapter, but some skeletal description of that reasoning is needed here. The focus is on the speech of Lord Wilberforce, which was the majority judgment in the case[53] and has been the one most quoted and embraced by subsequent courts, both in England and elsewhere.

Lord Wilberforce's reasoning in *Miliangos* is based on pursuit of the principle of compensation—putting a successful plaintiff into the position it would have occupied had the defendant not breached the plaintiff's rights, at least insofar as money permits. In that respect it does not differ from the reasoning that had been used to support the old breach-date rule. It differed only in its thinking as to how compensation was best achieved in circumstances of fluctuating currencies. In the opinion of Lord Wilberforce, the old pre-*Miliangos* rule—the forum-currency/breach-date rule encapsulated in cases such as *Havana Railways*—was perceived to deviate from the compensation principle, notably by operating to under-compensate a victorious plaintiff in cases, like *Miliangos*, where the forum's currency had weakened during the course of litigation. Such under-compensation was thought to flow from the fact that, if the right in question was the plaintiff's right to receive a certain amount of some foreign currency, compensating a plaintiff for a breach of that right by calculating damages based on the sterling value of such currency as of the date of breach would shortchange a claimant in those instances where sterling had fallen as against that currency in the post-breach period.

However, Lord Wilberforce did not go so far as to argue that cases such as *Havana Railways* had erred in failing to accord with the compensation principle. Rather, he took the view that things had changed in the fifteen years since *Havana Railways* so that matters could now be considered afresh. In his view things had

[52] See, eg: B Riordan, 'The Currency of Suit in Actions for Foreign Debts' (1978) 24 *McGill Law Journal* 422.

[53] Fifteen years before *Miliangos*, as Wilberforce QC, he had been lead counsel for the losing respondent in *Havana Railways*, above n 16. In *Miliangos* Lord Fraser and Lord Edmund-Davies both expressed agreement with the reasoning of Lord Wilberforce, though each went on to offer additional reasons of his own. Lord Cross wrote a separate speech agreeing with the result. Lord Simon dissented.

changed in two ways. One was that arbitrators and, in cases such as *Schorsch Meier*, courts had developed and become comfortable with a procedure under which orders for payment in foreign money might be made.[54] More significantly, however, Lord Wilberforce observed that, recently, frequent currency fluctuations had become the norm. He noted that in this regard things had altered even in the interval since *Havana Railways*[55] and that it was now the case that currencies floated as against one another and had no fixed and relatively stable value. In his view, changes of relative value between the breach date and the time of judgment or payment used to be exceptional occurrences, occurrences the law could legitimately ignore in formulating and applying its general rules. However, due to changes in the world monetary system, currency fluctuation during the course of litigation was now likely in almost every case.[56]

In this connection Lord Wilberforce did not expressly advert to the announcement of the United States in the summer of 1971 that henceforth the dollar would be fiat money and that the United States would no longer convert dollars to gold or other reserve assets.[57] Nor did he mention the disintegration of the Bretton Woods system of fixed exchange rates that followed hard on this decoupling. However, he appeared to take judicial notice of that state of affairs which had prevailed since early 1973 in which the countries which issued the world's major trading currencies no longer undertook to maintain any agreed-upon monetary exchange rates, either with other currencies or with commodities such as gold, and no longer promised to enter into the currency exchange market in order to maintain some pre-arranged par of exchange—in short, the state of affairs known as floating currencies. In claiming that the volatility of world currency markets was a new thing Lord Wilberforce was echoing a statement Lord Denning had made in *Schorsch Meier*, the one that serves as the epigraph for this chapter:

> [Sterling] was a stable currency which had no equal. Things are different now. Sterling floats in the wind. It changes like a weathercock with every gust that blows.[58]

[54] *Miliangos*, above n 3, 462–63.

[55] It is noteworthy that in *Havana Railways* (above n 16) the English pound had fallen as against the relevant foreign currency (US dollars). So *Miliangos* was hardly the first case to raise the foreign currency issue in the context of declining sterling. However it was certainly true that sterling was not a generally declining currency in 1960, as it was by 1975.

[56] *Miliangos*, above n 3, 463. Lord Wilberforce makes no reference to any particular event that had taken place between 1960 and 1975 that would have brought about this fundamental change.

[57] See Announcement of President Richard Nixon, The Challenge of Peace, 7 Weekly Comp Pres Doc 1170 (15 August 1971). As we will see in the discussion of American law, *The Restatement (Third) Foreign Relations* expressly relies on these events as justifying a comparable rethinking of the American position: Vol 2, 313–15.

[58] *Schorsch Meier*, above n 1, 424. To similar effect are the words of Steven Stern that foreign exchange rates are fluctuating 'ever more rapidly': S Stern, 'Judgments in Foreign Currencies: A Comparative Analysis' [1997] *Journal of Business Law* 266, 267. Everyone seems to think that the time in which they are writing is a time of especially rapid currency fluctuation, but empirical evidence is rarely offered to support such claims. It is true that, looking at things as at the time *Miliangos* was being decided, in recent memory English currency would only have been floating for three years, so the phenomenon of daily fluctuations might have appeared new. However, even before 1972, when par

In his dissenting speech in *Miliangos* Lord Simon took issue with this. He made the point that currency fluctuations were by no means unprecedented and that fifteen years earlier, in the course of affirming the forum-currency/breach-date rule in *Havana Railways*, the House of Lords had shown express awareness of currency fluctuation and of the possibility of the depreciation of sterling.[59] He did acknowledge that things were *slightly* different in an age of periodic revaluations as compared with one of daily fluctuations, but went on to observe that he could not 'see that it makes any difference that currencies float instead of staggering up and down'.[60]

It is unnecessary here to decide whether the better argument on this point is that of Lord Wilberforce and Lord Denning or that of Lord Simon. It is worth pointing out, however, that claims to the effect that 'the present is a time of unprecedented flux' are not confined to the mid 1970s. Observations about fluctuations in currency and their effect on the foreign damages question hardly originated then. Discussing the conversion date problem in 1956 Charles Evan has remarked on the 'unprecedented scale and rapidity range'[61] of post-war currency fluctuations. A generation before that, William McNair had occasion to note that the

> chaotic condition of the world's exchanges since the Armistice has brought into prominence in the English Courts an important question on contracts and torts involving sums expressed in foreign currency, namely, at what date the debt or damages stated in foreign currency must be converted into English money for the purpose of judgment.[62]

Indeed the entire period from about 1914, when the gold standard was abandoned, until the founding of the Bretton Woods regime in 1945 was one characterised by considerable currency fluctuation. And when it instituted the firm breach-date rule in 1921 in *The Volturno* the House of Lords had expressly adverted to currency instability. Lord Sumner there noted that '[f]luctuations in

rates prevailed, that there had been devaluations of sterling (1931, 1942, 1949 and 1967). And of course many other currencies had likewise undergone devaluations or revaluations—the hyperinflation in Germany in the years 1920 to 1924 being the premier example in the twentieth century. Nevertheless, even today the House of Lords takes the view that the about-face which occurred in Miliangos was justified because of a change of circumstances which had taken place in the world: *Persimmon Homes Ltd v Chartbrook Ltd* [2009] UKHL 38 [70] (Lord Rodger).

There is some objective basis to the claim that exchange-rate volatility in the four years immediately preceding *Miliangos* was greater than it had been for the decade before that: Bowles & Whelan, 'Judicial Responses', above n 29, 253, 256. More generally, the mid 1970s was a time of economic crisis in the UK, with a variety of *dirigiste* intercessions by the Labour government and eventually a deal with the International Monetary Fund to stabilise the pound. Influence is notoriously hard to prove, but there is no doubt that *Miliangos*'s new openness to foreign currency coincided with a time of national retrenchment.

[59] *Miliangos*, above n 3, 485.

[60] Ibid.

[61] C Evan, 'Rationale of Valuation of Foreign Money Obligations' (1956) 54 *Michigan Law Review* 307. As we will see, it is common to find judges taking a little trip down nummary lane and claiming that currency fluctuations are a recent phenomenon.

[62] WL McNair, 'Rate of Exchange in English Law' (1921) 37 *LQR* 38.

foreign exchanges inevitably introduce a speculative element into all transactions and affairs'.[63] Yet this did not keep him from insisting on a rigid breach-date conversion. Finally it was hardly a secret that many of these devaluations and periods of hyperinflation had produced or at least contributed to legal changes.[64]

There was no response to these points (or to Lord Simon) by Lord Wilberforce or any of the assentient speeches in *Miliangos*. Rather, the position of the majority in *Miliangos* was simply to declare that currency fluctuations were now the norm, as they had not been when the breach-date rule was crafted and promulgated, so that circumstances were different than when *Havana Railways* had been decided and the House of Lords might accordingly approach the problem unfettered by authority. It is an open question whether this assertion is a genuine misunderstanding of history or a disingenuous ploy to get rid of authorities now viewed as wrongly decided.

There is a related consideration that may have given an additional incentive for the House of Lords to overrule *Havana Railways*. It has been argued that the breach-date rule generally benefitted foreign claimants when sterling was strong and appreciating, but would systematically harm them when it was depreciating. It has been claimed, therefore, that, quite apart from fairness considerations between the parties, continuing to cling to the breach-date rule at a time when the pound was falling and likely to continue to fall would have the effect of making London an unattractive litigation forum for foreigners.[65] This in turn would harm the English economy (especially that of lawyers), which benefitted from London's being an attractive location for settling international disputes. Although it has been said that this consideration was well-known to the House of Lords in *Miliangos* and may have played a role in the result in the case, it did not form part of Lord Wilberforce's reasoning. In orthodox fashion he confined himself to considerations which bore on fairness to the parties (including future parties which might be affected by the rule which emerged from the case) and adverted neither to the interests of the London litigation industry nor to the broader public good. However, later House of Lords judgments on this point have taken some cognisance of this consideration.[66] Moreover in his dissenting speech

[63] *The Volturno*, above n 16. There was a similar observation by Scrutton LJ just a couple of years earlier in *Di Ferdinando*, above n 20, 414.

[64] E Hirschberg, *The Impact of Inflation and Devaluation on Private Legal Obligations*, (Ramat-Gran, Israel, Daf-Chen Press, 1976).

[65] For expression of this point see J Knott, 'A Matter of Some Interest' [1994] *Lloyd's Maritime and Commercial Law Quarterly* 4, 5; J Knott, 'Currency of Damages for Breach of Contract: Further Adventures in the Wealth-Time Continuum' [1996] *London Maritime Arbitrators Association Law Review* 41, 42. Francis Mann made the point very strongly in his canonical book. In the first post-*Miliangos* edition he claimed that the shift to awarding damages in foreign currency in arbitrations 'was necessary to prevent the death of London as a centre of international arbitration'. (FA Mann, *The Legal Aspect of Money*, 4th edn (Oxford, Clarendon Press, 1982) 352.) And he went on to note that once the shift was made at the arbitral level it would have been paradoxical for the House of Lords in *Miliangos* to arrive at any other result. See also the statements by Lord Denning, above n 38.

[66] *AG of the Republic of Ghana v Texaco Overseas Tankships Ltd (The 'Texaco Melbourne')* [1994] 1 Lloyd's Rep 473 (HL) 477 (*The Texaco Melbourne*).

in *Miliangos* Lord Simon made brief reference to it, declining to take it into account on the grounds that, as a judge, he was not in a good position to evaluate the general welfare or the country's balance of payments.[67] In chapter four we will see this same argument successfully advanced as a reason why New York State should abandon its forum-currency-breach date rule—that is, to remain an attractive and competitive location for international litigation—and it will be necessary in due course to evaluate whether considerations of this sort truly and properly bear on the currency-of-judgment issue. The argument relies on a number of far-from-obvious assumptions, including that persons making claims to have damages assessed in some currency will be foreigners while defendants in those cases will be locals.[68]

In any event, although Lord Wilberforce did not rely on the public-welfare argument as a ground for overthrowing the breach-date rule, he did rely on the other arguments sketched out above to free himself from the bonds of authority and consider afresh how the currency-of-judgment question should be addressed. He began his analysis with the basic principle of *restitutio in integrum*, which he defined as complete, but not excessive, compensation. This was a goal which legal rules should help to attain with certainty: 'The relevant certainty which the rule ought to achieve is that which gives the creditor neither more nor less than he bargained for'.[69] In light of this criterion the forum-currency/breach-date rule was regarded as defective since, in a case like *Miliangos*, that rule appeared to produce under-compensation: 'in a case such as the present, justice demands that the creditor should not suffer from fluctuations in the value of sterling'.[70]

However—and this is a point sometimes overlooked by some judges and scholars who have expressed admiration for *Miliangos*—Lord Wilberforce's worry

[67] *Miliangos*, above n 3, 481.

[68] It is helpful to think through the logic of this argument, which is rarely spelled out in detail by those relying on it. It would seem to be roughly as follows: (1) most cases raising the issue of foreign currency obligations involve a claimant from one country and a defendant from another; (2) in the majority of those cases the claimant will be the foreigner and the defendant a national, or at least resident, of the forum state (presumably due to the claimant's having to bring its action in the defendant's home state to maximise the chances of any judgment being enforceable in the place where the defendant's property is located); (3) a legal rule which systematically has the effect of favouring a local party over a foreigner will harm the international reputation of the forum as a fair place to litigate disputes; (4) such reputational harms are to be avoided; so (5) while a breach-date conversion rule is good when the local money is generally appreciating it is bad in periods when that currency is depreciating. Clearly there are a number of empirical claims here—untested, to the best of my knowledge. There are also countervailing considerations: while a country may have an interest in maintaining a reputation as being a fair place to litigate or arbitrate, it may also have an interest in encouraging persons to hold its currency rather than some alternative money. (On this point see S Fischer, 'Seigniorage and the Case for a National Money' (1982) 90 *Journal of Political Economy* 295.) Arguably an early conversion-date rule such as breach-date rule encourages traders to maintain more of their wealth in the money that their claim must be assessed in. Thus, if macroeconomic factors are to be taken into consideration in the currency-of-judgment question then arguably they pull both ways. It seems doubtful that judges are well placed to decide which is the stronger pull, or even which is the more legitimate one.

[69] Ibid, 466.

[70] Ibid, 465.

with the way in which the forum-currency/breach-date rule undermined the compensation principle of *restitutio in integrum* was not confined to a concern with *under*-compensation. While he acknowledged and deprecated the under-compensation that appeared to result from application of the forum-currency/breach-date rule in a case like *Miliangos* where the forum's currency had fallen, he was also concerned to avoid over-compensation of claimants. His concern was with *exact* compensation. He noted that the compensation principle should give the plaintiff 'neither more nor less than he bargained for'.[71] In the specific context of *Miliangos* he noted that what mattered for the plaintiff seller was that 'a Swiss franc for good *or ill* should remain a Swiss franc'.[72] It was the perceived failure to accord with the general principle of compensation—and in particular the prospect of under-compensation in the specific case before it—that motivated the House of Lords in *Miliangos* to reject the forum-currency/breach-date rule. Having disposed of concerns over difficulties of implementation of an alternative rule, Lord Wilberforce concluded that it would be appropriate for an English court to enter judgment in a foreign currency in an appropriate case. As to what would amount to such an appropriate case, that was defined narrowly as

> obligations of a money character to pay foreign currency arising under a contract whose proper law is that of a foreign country and where the money of account and payment is that of that country, or possibly of some other country but not of the United Kingdom.[73]

To summarise, in order better to fulfill the fundamental remedial principle of accurate and certain compensation, the majority in *Miliangos* held that in claims for debts originally expressed in a foreign currency and governed by that foreign law, English courts should give judgment in that currency. That judgment might then be satisfied either by payment in that foreign currency or in the sterling equivalent at the time when the payment was made. In the words of Lord Hoffmann, summing up the effect of *Miliangos* in a 2003 Privy Council appeal from the courts of Trinidad and Tobago:

> The writ … asked simply for payment in United States currency. Judgments in this form have been possible since *Miliangos v George Frank (Textiles) Ltd*, a decision of the House of Lords which has been followed in Trinidad and Tobago. The fact that the judgment may express the obligation in US dollars does not necessarily mean that a defendant has to pay in that currency. It means that US dollars are the unit of account for measuring the sum which has to be paid. If the defendant pays in a different currency (eg dollars of Trinidad and Tobago) they must be the equivalent of the US dollar debt at the time of payment.[74]

[71] Ibid, 466.
[72] Ibid, 466 (emphasis added).
[73] *Miliangos*, above note 3, 467.
[74] *Trinidad Homes Developers Ltd v IMH Investments Ltd* [2003] UKPC 85 [3].

IV. Post-*Miliangos* Developments

Several important questions were left unresolved by the House of Lords in *Miliangos*, deliberately so. The change which that case had effected involved the abrogation of a longstanding rule. In such circumstances a typically restrained view of the judicial function required that the House of Lords confine itself to the claim before it and decide no more than was necessary to resolve that case. This was so even though it was obvious that a consequence of *Miliangos* would be that lower courts would soon be faced with arguments to extend it to other situations—that is, to render judgment in foreign currency in actions other than those to recover a monetary obligation originally expressed in a foreign currency. Those sorts of claims did arise and the five years following *Miliangos* saw a flurry of litigation working out the ramifications of that decision and transforming the English law regarding foreign currency obligations. Those developments will be chronicled in this section.

None of these post-*Miliangos* changes was revolutionary; at least they were not perceived to be so by the judges who brought them about. Rather, they were regarded as no more than the uncontroversial extension of the *Miliangos* payment-date rule to new sorts of claims—uncontroversial in the sense that the extensions seemed to follow almost as a matter of logic from *Miliangos* itself. *Miliangos* had been a suit in debt and the House of Lords was clear that whether it should be extended to cases involving damages claims in contract or tort was a matter rightly left for another day. But that day was not long in coming and when it did there was virtually no resistance to the extension of *Miliangos* to other causes of action—apart, of course, from resistance arising from a couple of statutes that required a different result in certain defined areas.[75] The general sense was that, while the House of Lords in *Miliangos* had shown proper restraint in declining to express views on matters other than claims in debt, there could be no good argument for drawing the line there. To do so would have been to let the forms of action have too much sway and thus constitute a betrayal of the modernising force of *Miliangos*. Extending *Miliangos* to other forms of action would involve developing some additional rules, but that was just busywork.

There is a second aspect to the immediate post-*Miliangos* judicial developments. The expansion of *Miliangos* to other types of claims involved refinements to the rule that entailed choices that did not have to be made in *Miliangos* itself. In particular, they seemed to involve choices between certainty, on the one hand,

[75] The Carriage by Air Act 1961, c 27, sch 1, art 22(6) gives effect to the 1929 Warsaw Convention as amended at The Hague in 1955. In determining the limits on damages, set in Special Drawing Rights, it requires a judgment-date conversion into the currency of the forum. The Merchant Shipping Act 1995, c 21, sch 6, Part I, art 9, dealing with the limitation of damages, likewise requires a judgment date conversion for determining the amount of that limitation in the currency of the forum. The Maintenance Orders (Reciprocal Enforcement) Act 1972, s 16 requires conversion into pounds at the date the order is registered.

and protection of plaintiffs on the other. Whether matters were that simple is a question to which we will return.

In addition to the question of whether the *Miliangos* payment-date rule operated beyond actions in debt there was a further question: whether the new rule should be confined to cases where the proper law of the contract was that of some foreign country, as it was in *Miliangos*, or extended to those governed by English law. A related concern was, now that a court had the authority to assess damages in some foreign currency, what was the triggering factor—that is, what facts or features of a dispute indicate when a court might (or perhaps must) take this step? In *Miliangos* the House of Lords thought that Swiss francs were the proper currency of judgment, but in arriving at that conclusion it had regard to a number of factors that appeared to point to Switzerland—(1) the plaintiff resided there, (2) the contract was governed by Swiss law, (3) the money of payment under the agreement was Swiss francs, and (4) so was the money of account. With those four factors all pointing toward the same country it was not surprising that that country's money should be selected to be the currency of judgment. However, a moment's reflection reveals that there will be no shortage of cases where perhaps only one of those four factors points to a foreign country, while the others point to England, or perhaps to one or more other foreign countries. While it might have been possible to interpret *Miliangos* narrowly and conclude that it should apply only where all four of those factors pointed to the same country, such a confined reading of the case would have been at odds with those passages in its reasons which were phrased as a much more general condemnation of the effects of the old forum-currency/breach-date rule. But which of the four factors should be determinative?

A final unknown after *Miliangos* was whether its new approach was one that either party might invoke or instead one that a plaintiff might appeal to at its option but which, if the plaintiff did not raise it, could not be argued by the defendant (in which case the old rule would continue to apply). That is, in a given case could a plaintiff who preferred the results that flowed from the old forum-currency/breach-date rule elect that rule instead of the new one? In his dissenting speech in *Miliangos*, Lord Simon took the view that the new rule which emerged from that case was one only available to plaintiffs, who might call upon it when it was to their advantage (that is, where sterling had depreciated, as it had in *Miliangos*) but ignore it when sterling had risen. This one-way street did not, in his view, accord with principles of remedial law: it was 'highly unjust to the English debtor, as well as importing an undesirable element of monetary speculation into English litigation'.[76]

Yet in offering this criticism Lord Simon may have been mistaken in thinking that the majority was putting forth a non-compulsory rule. As noted above, while one concern of the majority in *Miliangos* was undoubtedly with guarding against

[76] Ibid, 482.

under-compensation of the plaintiff in that case, there are passages in Lord Wilberforce's speech which suggest that the *Miliangos* rule is one which defendants might also bring into play in the event of sterling's appreciation vis-a-vis the foreign currency in question. As noted, he observed that the 'creditor has no concern with pounds sterling: for him what matters is that a Swiss franc for good *or ill* should remain a Swiss franc'.[77] The italicised words lend some force to an interpretation of *Miliangos* different from that of Lord Simon—one which would allow a court to grant judgment in foreign currency even when neither party requested it (only when the appropriate triggering circumstances were established, of course), or at least for a defendant to request such judgment even where a plaintiff did not. However, it was not clear that *Miliangos* led to this, so the question of whether its new rule was mandatory or plaintiff-optional remained to be definitely settled.

The following sections explore the answers which English courts supplied to these questions that *Miliangos* had declined to answer, and also to some questions that *Miliangos* seems not to have anticipated.

A. Contract[78]

As noted, the House of Lords in *Miliangos* was careful not to pre-judge the question of whether its reasoning should apply to claims of damages for breach of contract. Given the considerable doctrinal change wrought in *Miliangos* it is unsurprising that no one criticised that judgment for failing to deal with the more general issue of the currency of judgment in cases where damages are to be awarded for contractual breach, even though that was issue was bound to arise soon thereafter. It was obvious that the consequences of *Miliangos* were going to require considerable working out, but that chore was properly left to later cases.

Certainly in the pre-*Miliangos* period the old breach-date rule had applied to claims for damages for breach of contract,[79] so the question was whether the new payment-date rule would also apply to such claims. Soon after *Miliangos*, in *Jean Kraut AG v Albany Fabrics Ltd*[80] the Swiss seller under a sale of goods

[77] Ibid, 466 (emphasis added).

[78] Availability of damages in a foreign currency is a matter of procedure, and so governed by the law of the forum. Thus courts in contract cases are able to award damages in a foreign currency, regardless of whether the contract is governed by English or foreign law. But the conversion date appears to be a different matter. The currency in which contractual damages are to be awarded must be selected in accordance with the proper law of the contract: *Rome Convention on the Law Applicable to Contractual Obligations (Contracts (Applicable Law) Act 1990*, sch, art 10(1)(c). This does not mean that the currency must be that of the governing law, only that governing law will determine the currency.

[79] See, eg: *Di Ferdinando* above n 20 (unliquidated damages for breach of contract); *Madeleine Vionnet et Cie v Wills*, above n 10 (contractual debt); *Graumann v Treitel* [1940] 2 All ER 188 (KB) (contractual debt).

[80] *Jean Kraut AG v Albany Fabrics Ltd* [1977] QB 182 (QB) [*Jean Kraut*]. The notion that judgments in foreign currency were not limited to claims in debt had been prefigured by a practice direction issued just six weeks after *Miliangos*. It gave the profession detailed guidance on how a claim for

contract attempted to claim damages expressed in a foreign currency which had appreciated in relation to sterling between the date of the alleged breach and the date of trial. The original pleadings asked for damages in pounds. However, after *Miliangos* appeared, the plaintiff seller, in order to reap the benefits of the new rule, amended its pleadings to claim damages in that foreign currency. The defendant, of course, maintained that the *Miliangos* rule applied only to actions to recover a monetary obligation originally expressed in non-forum currency, not to claims for damages for breach of contract.[81] Eveleigh J had little difficulty in concluding that since the proper law of the contract, the money of account and the money of payment were all that of a foreign country, the *Miliangos* reasoning should be extended to permit the plaintiff to claim in that foreign country's currency.[82] The decision was not initially regarded as holding that *any* claim for contract damages might be made in a foreign currency, since it rested in part on the holding that the claim was governed by Swiss contract law which regarded the claim as being one for debt. However, in another case three months later, a second judge of the same court concurred with the holding in *Jean Kraut*.[83] And the month after that, in the third post-*Miliangos* case to be decided, another judge of the same court extended this reasoning to apply to a case where, although the proper law of the contract was that of England, the currency was that of a foreign country. In that case, *Barclays Bank International Ltd v Levin Brothers (Bradford) Ltd*,[84] Mocatta J was of the view that the *Miliangos* reasoning applied with equal force to the case before him and that 'it cannot be a sine qua non to a judgment being entered in a foreign currency that the proper law of the contract giving rise to the obligation must be other than the law of England'.[85] It was sufficient that the currency of account in the contract, which was the same as the currency of the dishonoured bills of exchange in respect of which damages were sought, was a foreign one.

Four months later, just about a year after *Miliangos*, that view was accepted by the Court of Appeal in another case, *The Maratha Envoy*.[86] The lead judgment, at

liquidated damages in foreign currency should be pleaded: *Practice Direction (Judgment: Foreign Currency)* [1976] 1 WLR 83, as modified a year later by *Practice Direction (Judgment: Foreign Currency) (No 2)* [1977] 1 WLR 197.

[81] *Jean Kraut*, ibid, 186.

[82] Ibid, 189.

[83] *The Folias*, [1977] 3 WLR 176, [1977] Lloyd's Law Rep 39 (QBD) 44 (Goff J). Other parts of this judgment were later varied by the House of Lords. See n 94 below and accompanying text.

[84] Above n 3.

[85] Ibid, 279.

[86] *Federal Commerce and Navigation Co Ltd v Tradax Export SA (The Maratha Envoy)* [1977] 1 Lloyd's Rep 217 (CA) (*The Maratha Envoy*). It should be noted that Lord Denning characterised the claim in this case, which was for demurrage, as one for debt rather than for breach of contract, thus minimising the departure from the strict ruling in *Miliangos*. But he is heterodox on this point: generally demurrage is seen as damages, not debt (as in the House of Lords decision in *The Lips*, n 182 below). In any event, Lord Denning did say that if he were wrong on the demurrage point that the judgment should apply to damages (225). *The Maratha Envoy* was reversed by the House of Lords on other grounds, [1978] AC 1, [1977] 2 Lloyd's Rep 201, but nothing was said on the damages issue.

least on the currency point, was written by Lord Denning. He confirmed that the payment-date rule should apply to damages for breach and contract and that it should do so even if English law governed the contract

> in contracts where the currency of the contract is a foreign currency, but the proper law of the contract is English law, the Court can and should give judgment in the foreign currency: and this is both when it is for a debt due under the contract… or damages for breach of contract (as of the implied term).[87]

In addition to providing appellate authority for the extension of *Miliangos* to other sorts of claims, *The Maratha Envoy* addressed and resolved yet another matter that had not been decided in *Miliangos*. If, in a given contract, the money of account and money of payment are different, in which of those two currencies should damages be awarded? *The Maratha Envoy* stated that the relevant foreign currency was the money of account under the contract.[88] That is, where the money of account and the money of payment are different it is the former that should designate the currency in which damages should be awarded.[89]

As well as confirming that the *Miliangos* rule applied to all contract claims and that the triggering feature was the money of account, *The Maratha Envoy* had something to say about a further subject that arose from *Miliangos* but had not been definitively resolved by it: was the new payment-date rule a mandatory or an elective one? *Miliangos* had not unambiguously decided that point. Moreover, in a decision rendered just a few months after *Miliangos* one trial judge had expressed the view, in obiter, that the new rule was one that a plaintiff might invoke at its option.[90] However, in a pre-*Miliangos* case Lord Denning had taken the position that the payment-date rule was a compulsory one.[91] In *The Maratha Envoy* he had a chance to repeat that view:

> Once it is recognised that a judgment *can* be given in a foreign currency, justice requires that it *should* be given in every case where the currency of the contract is a foreign currency: otherwise one side or the other will suffer unfairly by the fluctuations of the exchange.[92]

[87] Ibid, 225. The other two members of the Court of Appeal gave judgments which addressed other matters, but on the topic of currency they did no more than to express brief concurrence with the reasoning of Lord Denning MR.

[88] This had been defined by the Court of Appeal in *Woodhouse AC Israel Cocoa Ltd v Nigerian Produce Marketing Co* [1971] 2 QB 23 (CA) 54 as the money which 'tells the debtor how much he has to pay'.

[89] This same approach was taken then following year by Donaldson J in *George Veflings Rederi SA v President of India* [1978] 1 WLR 982 (QB). This decision was upheld on appeal, above n 3, though the appeal judgment did not deal with this point.

[90] *Barclays Bank International Ltd v Levin Brothers (Bradford) Ltd*, above n 3, 280. To comparable effect are the words of Donaldson J in *Ozalid Group (Export) Ltd v African Continental Bank Ltd*, above n 3, 233–34.

[91] *Jugoslavenska*, above n 40, 298.

[92] *The Maratha Envoy*, above n 86, 225. The other two members of the Court of Appeal agreed, as did England's pre-eminent academic commercial lawyer, Roy Goode: RM Goode, *Payment Obligations in Commercial and Financial Transactions* (London, Sweet & Maxwell, 1983) 138–40.

The rule that emerges from *The Maratha Envoy* is thus one that seems nearly as rigid as the old forum-currency/breach-date rule: in contracts cases, regardless of whether the claim is for debt or unliquidated damages, there is one and only one currency in which judgment should be given: the money of account in the contract. Either party could ask for judgment in this currency, and where one of them did then courts were required to award it, at least providing the appropriate preconditions were established. Thus the currency of judgment was not a matter of judicial discretion but was to be judicially established in light of objective factors.[93] In particular, there was no suggestion that any currency other than sterling or the contractual money of account could ever become the currency of judgment in a contract case (though perhaps that was because in *The Maratha Envoy* no other currency—for instance, the plaintiff's home currency—was advocated by either party). The same was true of two other early post-*Miliangos* cases to award contract damages in a foreign currency.[94]

As we will see in subsequent chapters, although *Miliangos* has been favourably regarded in virtually every jurisdiction that has taken notice of it, the question of whether its payment-date rule was mandatory or optional (at the plaintiff's choice) is one that has been answered in different ways in different countries. In the United States, Canada and some other jurisdictions *Miliangos*, though viewed with undiluted admiration, is commonly interpreted as permitting a plaintiff to opt for a payment-date conversion if it prefers that to the old breach-date rule, but not as providing that same option to a defendant. More accurately, it is interpreted as providing courts with a discretion to select among conversion dates, and as providing for a general rule that urges courts to exercise that discretion so as to favour plaintiffs. There are passages in *Miliangos* that lend support to such an interpretation; it is possible to read that case as shuffling off an old, rigid rule with under-compensatory implications and ushering in an era of flexibility. We will return to the details and ramifications of that treatment of *Miliangos* in due course. For the moment, however, the focus is England, and while some commentators on *Miliangos* favoured an interpretation of it that favoured flexibility and adaptability,[95] that country's courts regarded the payment-date rule as a mandatory one.

[93] Doubts might have remained about whether, under this new approach, courts should award judgment in the foreign currency even if neither party asked for it, and doubts might arise about what the currency of judgment should be in cases where damages were sought for breach of a contract which did not provide a currency of account (for instance, a contract for a straight barter of goods). However, neither of those instances would frequently arise, so in most cases the new payment-date rule seemed every bit as conducive to predictability of outcome as the breach-date rule it replaced.

[94] In both *Jean Kraut* (above n 80) and *Barclays Bank International Ltd v Levin Brothers (Bradford) Ltd* (above n 3) the dispute was simply about whether judgment should be awarded in sterling or in the contractual money of account; no other currency was on the horizon.

[95] For instance J Knott 'A Quarter of a Century of Foreign Currency Judgments: The Wealth-Time Continuum in Perspective' [2004] *Lloyd's Maritime and Commercial Law Quarterly* 325. Knott views *Miliangos* as releasing English courts from 'the straight-jacket procedure of awarding all judgments in sterling' (325) but regards later judicial developments as an unwelcome trend 'towards too rigid a

Thus, within a couple of years of *Miliangos* its extension to claims for damages for breach of contract was assured by the lower courts.[96] In addition, this process answered a number of the other questions left unaddressed by *Miliangos*—in particular, the payment-date rule might apply regardless of whether the proper law of the contract was English or foreign, the relevant determining factor was the currency of account under the contract, and both defendants and plaintiffs were free to invoke the rule.

The next step was a return to the House of Lords. Just three years almost to the day after *Miliangos* the application of the *Miliangos* approach to claims for damages for breach of contract was confirmed by a unanimous House of Lords in *The Folias*.[97] Lord Wilberforce, who, as in *Miliangos*, gave the principal judgment in *The Folias*, found it relatively easy and uncontroversial to approve the lower-court consensus to extend the *Miliangos*[98] thinking to damages for breach of contract.

However, while *The Folias* added a measure of certainty to the law in confirming the lower courts' views that the *Miliangos* rule should be extended to claims for damages for breach of contract, it at the same time revealed—or perhaps created—new and perhaps previously unanticipated problems which arose in consequence of the *Miliangos* transformation. Indeed, *The Folias* introduced a significant innovation relating to how the relevant foreign currency should be determined. In *Miliangos*, once the decision had been made that judgment should be awarded in a foreign currency, there was no difficulty in selecting which one. It had to be Swiss francs. No other foreign currency was even in the picture. The lower court cases that extended *Miliangos* to damages claims for contractual breach—*Jean Kraut* and *The Maratha Envoy*—likewise had little difficulty in selecting which currency to award damages in; it was the currency of account in the contract.

The Folias, however, while providing the endorsement of final appellate authority that damages in a breach of contract claim might be awarded in money other than sterling, removed the certainty that the foreign currency should necessarily be the currency of account in the contract in question. The claim in *The Folias* was brought by charterers against the owners of the ship they chartered. The ship's refrigeration system had failed, resulting in harm to perishable cargo, and the charterers had consequently made compensatory payments to the cargo's

system of compensation' (345). He expressed a similar liking for flexibility on the currency issue in 'Loss of Profit Caused by the Total Loss of a Ship: Its Relationship to Value and Interest' [1993] *Lloyd's Maritime and Commercial Law Quarterly* 502, 526. In this Knott appears opposed to the views of Roy Goode, above n 92, who supported the mandatory interpretation of the payment-date rule.

96 For two other Court of Appeal cases in which contract damages were awarded in a foreign currency see *Monrovia Tramp Shipping Co v The President of India (The Pearl Merchant)* and *Marperfecta Compania Naviera SA v The President of India (The Doric Chariot)*, both reported at [1979] 1 WLR 59.

97 *Services Europe Atlantique Sud (SEAS) v Stockholms Rederiaktiebolag Svea of Stockholm* [1979] AC 685 (HL) (*The Folias*).

98 He had already written in *Miliangos* that it would be wrong 'to allow procedure to affect, detrimentally, the substance of the creditor's right'. (Above n 3, 465.)

owners. They sought reimbursement from the ship owners for having to make those payments. But what currency should measure that compensation? Everyone agreed it was not sterling, which seemed to bear no relevance to the action apart from the fact that England was the forum. The currency of account under the charterparty was US dollars, and on the basis of post-*Miliangos* developments in *The Maratha Envoy* and *Jean Kraut* that currency would have a strong claim. However, the plaintiffs had made expenditures to repair the loss caused by the defendant's breach of contract and had done so in Brazilian cruzeiros. That raised the prospect that perhaps the currency of expenditure was the appropriate one in which to calculate a damages award. There was even a third currency in play. The plaintiffs were a French company with their main place of business in Paris. They claimed that their loss was really felt in French francs, and that in order for the compensation principle to be implemented, damages should be assessed in that currency.

The London arbitrators who decided the case at first instance had selected francs, the exchange medium in which the plaintiff conducted most of its operations. The trial judge had rejected that conclusion and opted for cruzeiros, the money of the plaintiff's initial curative expenditure. As for the currency of account of the contract, US dollars, he reasoned that simply because the parties had agreed upon a currency of payment and other monetary obligations under the contract that indicated no contractual intention with respect to the assessment of damages. If the contract gave rise to a claim in debt, then the *Miliangos* reasoning would require that such a claim be expressed and governed by the currency of account under the contract, but when it gave rise to a claim for unliquidated damages things were different. In that situation, the trial judge thought, there was 'no connection between the loss and the U.S. dollar at all'.[99] He held that the currency of expenditure was the metric that justly measured the plaintiff's true loss. The Court of Appeal restored the arbitrators' selection of francs, with Lord Denning MR, in what would be his final judicial encounter with the currency-of-judgment issue, expressing the view that in selecting the correct currency for the assessment of damages 'the plaintiff should be compensated for the expense which most truly expresses his loss'.[100]

In unanimously dismissing the appeal the House of Lords embraced Lord Denning's notion of finding the currency which best measures the plaintiff's loss. It agreed with the trial court that the currency of account need not govern—a point on which all four levels of judgment in *The Folias* were in agreement. In reaching this conclusion the House of Lords did not indicate that cases such as *Jean Kraut* and *The Maratha Envoy* had been wrongly decided. Those decisions had selected the currency of account as the proper money in which to assess a damages claim for breach of contract and in the view of Lord Wilberforce both

[99] Above n 83 at 506 QB.
[100] [1979] QB 491 (CA) 514.

had correctly identified the contractual money of account as the currency which best expressed the claimant's loss.[101] However, they should not be read as deciding the currency of account must *necessarily* be the correct resolution of such an inquiry. Rather, '[i]n some cases the "immediate loss" currency may be appropriate, in others the currency in which it was borne by the plaintiff. There will be others in which the appropriate currency is the currency of the contract'.[102]

In this case the Law Lords were of the view that the arbitrators had not erred in selecting the plaintiff's general operating currency as the one in which it felt its loss, so they agreed with the Court of Appeal that the arbitral decision should be restored. In reaching this result Lord Wilberforce adopted 'a *flexible* rule in which account must be taken of the circumstances in which the loss arose, in which the loss was converted into a money sum, and in which it was felt by the plaintiff'.[103]

Although critical analysis of this point will be postponed to the next chapter, a couple of observations must be made at this point. As a consequence of the holding in *The Folias* there will sometimes be doubt as to which currency damages will be assessed in, a doubt which may not be resolved until the conclusion of a trial. This gives rise to a situation which differs fundamentally from that which prevailed before *Miliangos*, where the forum-currency/breach-date rule, whatever its deficiencies, at least provided the parties with certainty on this point. It also differs from the post-*Miliangos* situation in actions for debt, where the money of account will continue to be the currency of judgment, thus ensuring a setting in which, at least in the vast majority of cases, the parties will have little difficulty in ascertaining in advance the money of judgment. What is more, it also creates more uncertainty than a rule which might have emerged from *Jean Kraut* and *The Maratha Envoy*—a rule that said in any action for breach of contract damages must be assessed in the currency of account of the contract. In pondering this it is worth recalling that the lone dissenting judge in *Miliangos*, Lord Simon, had declined to join the other Law Lords largely because he thought that the unforeseeable consequences of the proposed revolutionary change in the law were beyond the capacity of the judiciary to deal with. He thought that to abrogate the breach-date rule was to open a can of worms and that any change in that rule should be left to Parliament, not the judiciary.

Secondly, it is worth taking note of the context in which Lord Wilberforce in *The Folias* endorsed the need for a flexible rule. As we shall see when we examine the reception of *Miliangos* and its progeny in some other countries, judges in some places have regarded those English decisions as authorising an approach which allows courts the *discretion* to select a conversion date which best does justice in the individual case—a choice which may be exercised, at least in part, in light of which way the relevant currencies may have fluctuated over the course of the litigation. Usually, though not invariably, this is a preference which is

[101] *The Folias*, above n 97, 701.
[102] Ibid, 703.
[103] Ibid, 703 (italics added).

exercised in the plaintiff's favour, and sometimes Lord Wilberforce's approval of flexibility in *The Folias* is called on in support of such an approach. However, it seems doubtful whether anything in *The Folias* can be faithfully read as calling for any change to the position that Lord Wilberforce took in *Miliangos* that held that the Swiss franc was the proper currency of judgment in that case and that the plaintiff must be taken to claim in that currency 'for good or ill'.[104] The flexibility embraced by the House of Lords in *The Folias* is flexibility in the inquiry into which currency—contractual currency of account, currency of immediate expenditure to cure the loss, general operating currency, or conceivably some other currency—most accurately and fairly measures the plaintiff's loss. Once that currency is identified then—for good or ill—it becomes the currency of judgment and the question of which way the currencies may have fluctuated following the breach plays no part in that investigation.

The remainder of the cases in this section are ones which grapple with applying the rules which come out of *The Folias*. They provide good illustrations both of the lack of predictability which emerges from that case and the fact that the flexibility in the relevant inquiry is not one which considered whether the currencies in question have risen or fallen and does not always operate to the benefit of the claimant. After *The Folias* then, the position in England with respect to claims for damages for breach of contract may be briefly summarised as follows: (1) Damages may be claimed and expressed in a foreign currency, and if so expressed then the judgment debtor has the option of paying either in that currency or in the sterling equivalent at date of payment. (2) If the terms of the contract reveal the parties' intention that damages should be awarded in any particular currency then that is the currency in which courts should calculate and award damages; the money of account may reveal such an intention.[105] (3) However, in some cases it will be apparent from the contract and the circumstances that the parties had formed no intention as to what the currency of damages should be. That is, despite the fact that their contract had a clear money of account there may have been no shared expectation that damages for breach of contract—or at least damages for the particular breach that occurred in the case before the court—should be awarded in that currency. (4) In such circumstances damages should be assessed in the currency which most truly expresses the plaintiff's loss, which is most likely the currency in which the plaintiff normally conducts its business, but may be the currency in which the loss immediately arose, typically as ascertained by the currency first expended to cure it.

Not surprisingly, the new wrinkle introduced by *The Folias* gave rise to a measure of uncertainty in subsequent cases. A plaintiff might argue that the default rule—currency of account under the contract—should be displaced by one of the

[104] *Miliangos*, above n 3, 466.

[105] But in a case where the contract provides an agreed-upon exchange rate between the money of payment and the money of account, then damages should normally be assessed in the currency of payment: *President of India v Tayhetos Shipping Co (The Agenor)* [1985] 1 Lloyd's Rep 155 (QB).

currencies in rule (4) above. This was the result in *Ozalid Group (Export) Ltd v African Continental Bank*,[106] a case decided four months after *The Folias*, where the court held that the plaintiff's normal operating currency should be the currency of judgment. However, such an argument will not be successful where the court concludes that the proper construction of the contract is that the parties intended that any damages claim be brought in the currency of account.[107] Of course discerning contractual intent is an enterprise fraught with doubt. Assuming that inquiry leads to a conclusion that the currency of account under a contract reveals no intent as to the currency of judgment, a court must then embark upon an inquiry into the money in which the plaintiff truly felt its loss. Indeed, the entire concept of 'feeling the loss' is a novel and elusive one. In the case of a claimant which is a multinational enterprise, with offices in many countries and bank accounts in many currencies, the notion that such an entity might be said to 'feel' any given loss in one currency but not another seems one of questionable coherence.

In theory this will be tempered by the requirement that the currency in which the plaintiff feels its loss is a foreseeable one, but in practice this has not proven to be a difficult hurdle for claimants to cross. For instance, in *Virani Ltd v Manuel Revert y Cia SA* the claimant sued for damages for breach of a sales contract.[108] The defendant was a Spanish company and the money of account in the contract was pesetas. The claimant, although it was an English company, gave evidence that it operated in US dollars and that when it entered a contract for some other currency it hedged its currency risk in dollars, as it had done in this case. It requested damages in dollars, which meant that its award would be worth about £57,000 more than if the claim was in pesetas, due to the Spanish currency's decline. The court granted it. It held that since the dollar was the currency in which the English company operated that must be the money in which it felt its loss. The court then turned to foreseeability, and despite the fact that there was no evidence that the claimant had told the defendant that it operated in dollars, the Court of Appeal found that it 'must be within the reasonable contemplation of anyone engaged in foreign transactions to expect that steps will be taken to protect the value of the particular transaction by covering it in the way the claimant did'.[109]

[106] Above n 3. This case will be discussed in more detail below at pp 62–64, where the question will be raised whether it is rightly regarded as a currency-of-judgment case or an exchange loss case. However it is regarded, the court in *Ozalid* certainly made a *finding* as to what the currency of judgment should be, and that finding is the basis for the comment in the text.

[107] As was held in *Metallhandel JA Magnus BV v Ardfields Transport Ltd* [1988] Lloyd's Rep 197 (QB), where the court assessed damages in the currency of account and payment, despite the plaintiff's argument that damages should be assessed in its normal operating currency.

[108] *Virani Ltd v Manuel Revert y Cia SA* [2003] EWCA Civ 1651, [2004] 2 Lloyd's Rep 14.

[109] Ibid [20] (Ward LJ, with whom Tuckey and Lightman LLJ agreed). The same approach has been taken to assessing the effect of contractual limitation of liability when that limitation is expressed in some non-national-currency commodity such as gold or special drawing rights: *Kinetic Technology Ltd v Cross Seas Shipping Corp (The 'Mosconici')* [2001] 2 Lloyd's Rep 313 (Com). In that contractual damages case the claim the parties had agreed to settle the claim for SDRs141,000; however, the value of that settlement depended on whether it was converted into lire or US dollars. Although the claimant was an Italian company which had lost goods that it had acquired in Italy for lire, it prevailed in its

Another case which arguably illustrates the plaintiff-favouring nature of the new rule is *The Dione*,[110] a claim by shipowners against charterers. There neither party contended for the currency of the contract. The defendant charterers argued for the currency in which the plaintiff had made the initial expenditure to cover the loss—Argentine pesos (which would work to the defendant's advantage since they had fallen disastrously in the period subsequent to the loss). The claimant owners relied on *The Folias* to support a claim in US dollars. They did not show that US dollars were their normal operating currency, only that that had used dollars to buy the pesos to cover the initial loss. The court held for the plaintiff, deferring to the arbitrator's decision that the currency to which the plaintiff had turned to buy the currency that was used to mend the loss was the currency which best expressed the loss.

The Federal Huron[111] was yet another case in which the plaintiff prevailed in having the court assess damages in the currency it proposed. There the plaintiff was a French company that had expended French francs to cover a loss arising from damage to a cargo of soy beans that the defendant had carried from the United States to France. However, it claimed in US dollars, which had recently appreciated vis-a-vis the franc. Despite the defendant's claim that damages should be assessed in francs, the court chose dollars on the basis that dollars were the currency in which the French plaintiff normally conducted its soy bean operations.

On the basis of the cases just discussed the new rule which emerged from *The Folias* might appear to operate as a plaintiff-favouring one. The plaintiff's information about which currencies it employed for a given transaction is likely to be far superior to the knowledge of the defendant on that point. Plaintiffs may then rely on the presumptive rule (currency of account, and failing that, the currency of the state in which they conduct most of their business) when it benefits them. When it does not they will cast around for some other currency—say, the currency which they used to acquire the money to pay for repair of their loss (as in *The Dione*) or the money in which they normally conduct the sort of operation in question (as in *The Federal Huron*) and claim that that is the metric in which they should be held to have felt their loss.[112] So long as the currency has some plausible connection with the transaction the requirement of foreseeability will be met. Under such circumstances, plaintiffs appear to have a choice of several currencies-of-judgment and seem likely to select the one that has appreciated in the period

claim that the currency that truly expressed its loss was US dollars. This was not because, as in *Virani v Manuel Rivert*, it generally conducted its business in US dollars, but simply because the larger venture to which this particular contractual loss related was one that it was conducted in US dollars.

[110] *The Food Corporation of India v Carras (Hellas) Ltd* (*The Dione*) [1980] 2 Lloyd's Rep 577 (QB).

[111] *Société Francaise Bunge SA v Belcan NV* (*The Federal Huron*) [1985] 3 All ER 378, [1985] 2 Lloyd's Rep 189 (QB).

[112] Of course defendants may be able to use the pre-trial discovery process to get access to this information and thus equalise their capacity to argue about the currency in which the claimant should be deemed to have felt its loss. But it seems open to question whether, in practice, this will really level the playing field with respect to this issue.

between the loss and the time at which they must make their selection—which could be the time of launching their claim, or later if they are permitted to amend their pleadings.

However, as the government of Ghana found out in *The Texaco Melbourne*,[113] it goes too far to claim that *The Folias* rule will invariably operate in a claimant-friendly fashion. The reader will recall that this was the case used in the introduction to illustrate the subject matter of this book, show that the financial stakes could be high and demonstrate the complexity and unsettled state of the governing rules, or at least of predicting the results of their application. Aside from passing reference to the currency point in 2005 in *Lesotho Highland Development Authority v Impreglio SpA*,[114] *The Texaco Melbourne* is the last of the House of Lords cases to deal with the currency-of-judgment issue, and the only one where the leading speech was not written by Lord Wilberforce, who by this time had retired. The key speech was delivered by Lord Goff, who as trial judge in *The Folias* had reversed the arbitrators' decision on the currency issue only then to see his decision on that point overturned on appeal. Unlike the earlier House of Lords judgments on this issue—*Miliangos*, *The Folias* and *The Despina R*—*The Texaco Melbourne* did not purport to lay down any new rule. It was simply an application of the law laid down in those earlier cases, mainly *The Folias*.

The case illustrates the problem that can arise in determining the currency in which a claimant is said to feel its loss, and in particular the difficulties in choosing between a plaintiff's 'home currency' and that of the immediate expenditure it may have made to cure the defendant's breach. Because the claimant's home currency, the Ghanaian cedi, had collapsed during the lengthy period between breach and trial, it had an incentive to seek damages calculated in some other money. Since the contractual right which had been violated—delivery of a cargo of oil—was one which throughout the world was bought and sold in US dollars, the plaintiff contended for judgment in that currency. That was the money it used to buy a replacement cargo of oil; that was the money everyone used to buy large quantities of oil. Although the trial judge accepted this argument, as did Hirst LJ in the Court of Appeal,[115] the other judges who heard the case, including the five Law Lords, agreed that here the plaintiff felt its loss in its home currency, the now almost worthless cedi.

[113] *The Texaco Melbourne*, above n 66. In the 15 years between 1979, when it decided *The Despina R* and *The Folias*, and 1995, when it decided *The Texaco Melbourne*, the House of Lords had handed down judgments in foreign currency: *Universe Tankships Inc of Monrovia v International Transport Workers* [1983] 1 AC 366 (HL); *National Bank of Greece SA v Pinos Shipping Co* [1990] 1 AC 637 (HL). However, it had not dealt with a case in which the currency of judgment was an issue under appeal.

[114] Above n 30. The Judicial Committee of the Privy Council had a skirmish with the currency-of-judgment question in an appeal from New Zealand, *Gilrose Finance Ltd v Gould* [2000] 2 NZLR 129, but its discussion was short and did not purport to advance the analysis, and see *Candlewood Navigation Corp v Mitsui OSK Lines Ltd* [1986] AC 1 (JCPC).

[115] [1993] 1 Lloyd's Rep 471 (CA).

Lord Goff's speech for the House of Lords confirmed that the flexible approach to selecting the currency of judgment did not permit considering appreciation or depreciation of the currencies in question. He reiterated throughout his speech that in determining the money in which the claimant felt its loss no consideration should be given to currency fluctuations, even dramatic ones, in the post-breach period. Doing so was the error that had led the trial judge to award damages in dollars. The search for the currency of judgment was essentially a factual inquiry, a search for an objective fact which requires a judge 'to look at the reality of the situation in order to discover in what currency the plaintiff has in fact felt his loss'.[116] *The Texaco Melbourne* thus confirms that defendants faced with claims for damages in one foreign currency are able to contend that a damages award should instead be granted in some other foreign currency. Moreover defendants have some chance of prevailing in such arguments, even when that results in damages awards that operate to the plaintiff's considerable disadvantage.

Although *The Texaco Melbourne* might appear to demonstrate a strong preference for selecting the claimant's general operating currency as the money of judgment, thus bringing a measure of certainty and predictability to the nebulous concept of 'feeling the loss', later cases have shown that the matter can still be hard to predict. It remains possible for things to work the other way—that is, for a plaintiff to assert that damages should be assessed in its normal operating currency but for the courts to decline to adopt that solution and instead to evaluate the claim in the currency of the original loss. That was the result in *Barings plc v Coopers & Lybrand*,[117] one of the cases spawned by the unauthorised futures trading by the rogue Nick Leeson which occasioned the collapse of the venerable merchant bank Barings. Numerous claims among numerous parties arose from that debacle, but the one that gave rise to a dispute of the currency of judgment was a suit by Barings Futures (Singapore) Ltd (BFS) against one of its accountants, Deloitte & Touche (Singapore) (D&T) for negligent performance of an auditing contract. BFS claimed that D&T's competent performance of those auditing services would have resulted in early detection of Leeson's unauthorised trading and allowed BFS to take action to prevent further losses. Most of Leeson's trades had been in Japanese yen and when those trades proved unwise the effect was to require BFS to meet margin calls and make other payments in yen. Initially the yen was the currency in which BFS denominated its claim against its auditors. During the course of the litigation, however, the yen plunged and BFS sought

[116] *The Texaco Melbourne*, above n 66, 480.

[117] *Barings plc v Coopers & Lybrand* [2003] EWHC 2371 (Ch) (*Barings*). Another case with a similar structure and result is *Empresa Cubana Importadora de Alimentos v Octavia Shipping Co SA (The 'Kefalonia Wind')* [1986] 1 Lloyd's Rep 273 (QB). A case decided the same year as *Barings* gives yet another illustration of the vagaries of the feeling-the-loss rule in that the court held that different losses were felt in different currencies: in *Nomura International plc v Credit Suisse First Boston International* [2003] EWHC 160 (Comm) the court allowed the claimant to succeed in dollars, since that was the currency of the contract, yet to claim certain losses in pounds, which was the currency expended to cure those losses.

permission to amend its pleadings and bring its claim in Singapore dollars. It pointed out that it was incorporated in Singapore, conducted its internal affairs in Singapore dollars, paid its employees in that currency, was statutorily required to render its accounts in Singapore dollars and was being wound up in Singapore 'where all liquidations must, by statute, be conducted in Singapore dollars'.[118]

In a decision which is not easy to reconcile with *The Texaco Melbourne* the court rejected the plaintiff's arguments and held that the currency of the initial loss—the yen which Leeson's unauthorised trading caused BFS to lose—was the proper currency of judgment. Quite possibly the court was influenced by the fact that the yen was the currency in which the claimant had originally brought its claim and that the request to revise the pleadings when the yen declined smacked of illegitimate opportunism. However, the holding of the case was not based on the fact that the claimant had started off in yen but rather on the conclusion that the currency of expenditure was the starting point for claims of this sort and that the claimant had not discharged the burden of showing that its general operating currency was more appropriate 'in accordance with the principle of restitution'.[119]

The cases described in the last couple of pages reveal that the feeling-the-loss test associated with *The Folias* may sometimes render it difficult to decide in advance what the currency of judgment will be. Most commentators who have considered the matter of foreign currency obligations for breach of contract have arrived at the view that the English law on this point has benefitted from *Miliangos* and its progeny.[120] Any uncertainty in the task of selecting the currency of damages, such as might be illustrated by the results of *The Folias* and the subsequent cases that wrestled with applying the rule which emerged from it, is either not seen as problematic, or is viewed as well worth the cost of a regime charged with identifying the one currency that most truly expresses the loss the plaintiff has felt. There have been a few reservations. Roger Bowles and Christopher Whelan have pointed out that the former certainty provided by the breach-date rule has been replaced by a situation where there are three possible currencies in which damages might be awarded—the expenditure currency, the plaintiff's currency and the currency of the contract.[121] They raise the issue of whether this truly constitutes an improvement. I take up that question in the final chapter.

[118] Ibid [37].

[119] Ibid [30]. The court never got to the question of whether BFS should be allowed to amend its statement of claim by changing the currency of its claim. It decided that, since the yen was the proper money of the claim it did not matter whether a change of pleadings should be allowed, since in any event judgment should be given in yen.

[120] For instance, DG Powles, 'Foreign Currency Judgments' [1979] *Lloyd's Maritime and Commercial Law Quarterly* 485.

[121] RA Bowles and CJ Whelan, 'Law Commission Working Paper No. 80: Private International Law: Foreign Money Liabilities' (1982) 45 *MLR* 434, 436 ff.

B. Tort

Before *Miliangos*, it was clear the forum-currency/breach-date rule prevailed in tort cases. That was the ruling of the House of Lords in *The Volturno*.[122] Curiously, although *The Volturno* is generally cited as supporting the forum-currency/breach-date rule, close reading of the case reveals that the date selected for conversion into sterling was not in fact the date the ships collided, but the date (a couple of weeks later) when the subsequent detention came to an end. The House of Lords, however, did not advert to the distinction, and given the relatively short period in question it may have made no difference. *The Volturno* was a case where sterling had appreciated vis-a-vis the foreign money in question, so the effect of the sterling/breach-date rule was arguably to overcompensate the claimant. There was an interesting dissent by Lord Carson. He noted that the authority of the sterling/breach-date rule was dubious and would have imposed a judgment-date conversion from the foreign currency (Italian lire) into pounds. His reasons for doing so were in many respects similar to the reasons offered by Lord Wilberforce in *Miliangos* 54 years later, namely that faithful elaboration of the compensation principle dictated a late conversion date.

In some other instances it was agreed that damages must be reckoned in sterling at the date when the loss was incurred, but this was found to be the time when the plaintiff made expenditures to fix the damages the defendant had caused.[123] These two times of assessment—the time of the tort and the time of the expenditure to cure it—could obviously be different. But both seemed to fall under the general heading of 'the date at which the loss was suffered'—and there does not appear to have been much litigation about the possible difference.

The contract cases discussed at the end of the previous section should alert us to the fact that if *Miliangos* is extended to tort claims then the certainty afforded by the old breach-date rule will be forgone. The same sort of dispute that we saw in cases like *The Folias*, *The Dione*, *The Federal Huron*, *The Texaco Melbourne* and *Barings plc v Coopers & Lybrand* will arise in tort cases. This will be so because any rule which says that damages may be assessed in foreign currency will immediately produce the follow-on question, *which* foreign currency? Nevertheless, as with contractual claims, the *Miliangos* approach was extended to tort with little hesitation. Again it is noteworthy that, as with *Miliangos* and the other modern decisions mentioned in this chapter, this change took place in a case where the relevant foreign currencies had appreciated against the pound in the interval between breach and trial, thus raising the spectre of under-compensation if the old, breach-date rule were to be maintained.

[122] Above n 16. For a positive appraisal of *The Volturno* and an account of its implementation in contract cases in the 1920s see Anon, 'Fluctuations in Rates of Exchange and English Contract Law' (1930) 172 *Law Times* 317.

[123] *The Baarn*, above n 6.

In fact in tort the problem of uncertainty in selection of the currency of judgment is even more acute. In contract there is almost always a contractual money of account. That may be used to indicate a presumptive currency in which damages for breach of contract should be awarded. Only when the contractual currency of account is held not to be indicative of the parties' intentions with respect to the currency of judgment must a court contend with the troublesome inquiry of identifying a currency in which the plaintiff may be said to really experience its loss. In tort, on the other hand, there will not—or at least not often—be a contract to turn to for even a default currency of judgment. So if the thinking in *Miliangos*, as modified in *The Folias*, is to be extended to causes of action in tort then the feeling-the-loss inquiry would seem to present itself in almost every case.

That, as it turns out is pretty much what has happened. The change came in *The Despina R*,[124] a case arising from a collision between two Greek vessels in the vicinity of Shanghai giving rise to a damages claim in respect of repair expenses incurred in a number of foreign currencies. The trial court held that *Miliangos* freed it from the constraints of the old forum-currency/breach-date rule and ruled that the plaintiff might claim damages in the currencies of the various expenditures (or, as in *Miliangos*, the equivalent in pounds at the time the defendant/judgment debtor eventually paid). The Court of Appeal was also of the view that, in the wake of *Miliangos*, the old breach-date rule need not be followed in tort claims. However, it took the view that general principles of compensatory damages dictated that damages should generally be assessed in the plaintiff's currency—that is, the currency in which the injured party usually operated and would therefore have felt the loss, provided that damages assessed in such currency did not offend the principles of foreseeability and remoteness.[125]

The further appeal to the House of Lords was heard and decided in conjunction with that in *The Folias*, and gave rise to a judgment which laid down the principle in tort that prevails in England today.[126] The two judgments are much of a piece, and since the reasoning in *The Folias* was described above in some detail there is little need to spend much space on its tort counterpart *The Despina R*. Freed from the old rule in *The Volturno*, Lord Wilberforce considered that the result should follow from the normal principles which govern damages assessment in tort. These he considered to be compensation as tempered by foreseeability.[127] (Interestingly, mitigation was not mentioned.) Full compensation was achieved by awarding damages in the money in which the plaintiff felt its loss, which would normally but not necessarily be the currency in which the plaintiff conducted its

[124] *Owners of MV Eleftherotria v Owners of MV Despina R* [1977] 3 WLR 597, [1977] 1 Lloyd's Rep 618 (QB).

[125] *Owners of MV Eleftherotria v Owners of MV Despina R* [1977] 3 WLR 617 (CA).

[126] *Owners of MV Eleftherotria v Owners of MV Despina R* [1979] AC 685, [1979] 1 Lloyd's Law Rep 1(HL) (*The Despina R*).

[127] *The Despina R*, ibid, 697.

trading operations. The key difference between the reasoning in *The Folias* and that in *The Despina R* is that in the latter case Lord Wilberforce took the time to counter the argument the new feeling-the-loss rule produced justice at too high a price in terms of uncertainty:

> I do not see any reason why legal advisors, or insurers, should not be able, from their knowledge of the circumstances, to assess the extent of probable liability. The most difficult step is to assess the quantum of each head of damage. Once this is done, it should not be difficult, on the basis of information which the plaintiff must provide, to agree or disagree with his claim for the relevant currency. … To say that this produces a measure of uncertainty is true, but this is an uncertainty which arises in the nature of things from the variety of human experience. To resolve it is part of the normal process of adjudication.[128]

In other words, under the new rule a defendant might not know what currency damages were being claimed in until it received a statement of claim, might not be able to assess the legitimacy of that claim until the discovery process allowed it to find out more about the claimant's internal operations, and would not know for sure which measure the court would settle on until the time of judgment, but the negative consequences of that uncertainty, which did not exist before *Miliangos*, did not outweigh the advantages of a rule which permitted courts to assess damages in a currency in which the plaintiff truly felt its loss.[129]

As with contractual damages in such cases as *The Federal Huron*[130] and *The Texaco Melbourne*,[131] disputes may arise in tort cases as to whether the currency of the plaintiff's normal trading operations should be displaced by some other currency, or even as to how the former is to be selected. In such cases the defendant has the option of contending for some currency other than the one in which the plaintiff has claimed damages. For example, in *The Lash Atlantico*,[132] the plaintiff argued that it felt its loss in US dollars, since that was the normal operating currency of the company that managed the ship the defendant had damaged. The defendant, however, argued that damages should be assessed in drachmas, since the plaintiff managed its ship through an agent and kept the accounts of that management contract in drachmas. By a majority, that argument was rejected and it was held that damages should be assessed in dollars, since that was 'the currency in which the plaintiff's investment in its ship had its closest

128 Ibid, 698–99.

129 One matter open to some doubt after the *The Despina R* is whether this rule was confined to cases where the tort law applicable to the substantive issues in the case is that of England. In *The Despina R* the tort had occurred in China, but the House of Lords made no reference to Chinese law on assessment of damages in foreign currency. However, it appears that the applicability of Chinese tort law was not argued for by either of the parties; nor was the content of that law pleaded. So arguably the approach of *The Despina R* on this point can be explained on the basis that English tort law was applicable.

130 Above n 83.

131 Above n 85.

132 *The Lash Atlantico* [1987] 2 Lloyd's Rep 115 (CA).

commercial connection',[133] even though that currency was 'at one remove'[134] from the business which suffered the harm.

However, in *The Transoceanica Francesca and Nicos V*[135] the plaintiff requested damages in dollars and led evidence to show that it kept operating accounts for the damaged ship in that currency. However, the defendant succeeded in convincing the court that the plaintiff really felt its loss in Italian lire, since it was an Italian company carrying on business in Italy. Also relevant to that conclusion was the fact that when the relevant operating accounts accrued dollars in excess of a certain amount, the plaintiff converted the excess to lire.

There is yet a further complication. The rule emerging from *The Despina R* can result in different parts of a plaintiff's tort claim being assessed in different currencies. For instance, in a personal injury claim brought by an American injured while visiting England, the plaintiff's damages for pain, suffering and loss of amenity were assessed in sterling, since the court thought it was impossible for it to view such losses otherwise than in pounds.[136] However, losses for such matters as medical expenses, alterations to the plaintiff's motor vehicle and lost salary were calculated in dollars, since they were held to be closed linked with the currency of the plaintiff's residence.

To summarise this brief account, the extension of the *Miliangos* rule to tort was relatively uncontroversial. Damages must now be awarded in the currency in which the plaintiff felt its loss, which in an individual case might be the currency the plaintiff expended to cure the harm in question, the currency it employed with respect to the individual enterprise involved in the tort, or the currency in which it conducts its general operations. Obviously one effect of that has been to introduce a measure of uncertainty that was not present when the forum-currency/breach-date rule operated.[137]

[133] Ibid, 118.

[134] Ibid, 121.

[135] *The Transoceanica Francesca and Nicos V* [1987] 2 Lloyd's Law Rep 155 (QB). That decision also dealt with the question of collision suits where there are two claims which must be set off against one another and where the money in which damages is to be assessed is different for each claim. It held that there was no difficulty in originally assessing the two claims in different currencies. Then, in order to arrive at a single net judgment in one currency, the currency of the smaller claim should be converted into that of the larger, and subtracted. To similar effect see *The Lu Shan* [1993] 2 Lloyd's Rep 259 (QB (Admlty)).

[136] *Hoffman v Sofaer* [1982] 1 WLR 1350 (QB). Courts in other countries have taken the same approach, granting damages for loss of income in the currency in which that income would have been earned, but falling back on the forum currency when it came to assessing non-pecuniary losses. See ch 3, nn 45 and 118.

[137] I do not intend that as a criticism of the development in question. While it is probably beyond contention that, other things being equal, certainty in legal matters is a good thing, it is obviously not the only value. In many areas we may prefer to tolerate a legal standard that, while it seems to offer less certainty than some alternative approach, has other virtues—for example, ease and economy of administration, a greater ability to respond to the unique circumstances of individual cases or, for some other reason, simply more fairness. Whether the rule that emerges from *The Despina R* has this characteristic is a matter that I defer to the final chapter. Other observers have remarked on the

C. Restitution

Claims for restitution are less common than those for debt, breach of contract or tort, but it did not take long after *Miliangos* for the question to arise as to whether its reasoning extended to that sort of claim as well. In *BP Exploration Co v Hunt (No 2)*[138] a currency-of-judgment issue arose before Robert Goff J, who as trial judge in *The Folias* had already played a role in extending *Miliangos* and as one of the authors of the leading text on the English law of restitution was an acknowledged expert in the type of claim that arose in that case.[139] He also had the benefit of the example set in *The Despina R* and *The Folias*, where the House of Lords had extended *Miliangos* to tort and contract respectively. Under such circumstances it is hardly startling that the court held that foreign currency awards might also be given in claims governed by the principle of unjust enrichment. It would have been shocking had he ruled otherwise, and the result and reasoning of the trial judge were embraced by a unanimous Court of Appeal, though without much elaboration or addition.[140] A further appeal to the House of Lords was also dismissed,[141] although the currency-of-judgment issue was not one of the grounds of that appeal.

Although, given *Miliangos*, it was unremarkable to see English courts conclude that in a restitution claim judgment might be given in something other than sterling, the resultant question that we encountered in the previous two sections obviously arises: what determines the appropriate currency of judgment in such a claim? Goff J spent several pages addressing this issue and his reasoning is clear and cogent. The rule that emerges, however, does not appear to provide any greater level of certainty on the currency question than does the rule regarding contracts that is found in *The Folias* or tort in *The Despina R*. Goff J reasoned that, while a loss to the plaintiff might be a necessary element of the action in restitution, it is not the plaintiff's loss but rather the defendant's enrichment which is the key to the amount of the award. Accordingly, when a currency-of-judgment question arises the award should be assessed 'in the money in which the defendant's benefit can be most fairly and appropriately valued'.[142] Where restitution is being

uncertainties that arise from the approach in *The Despina R*. See especially J Knott, 'Foreign Currency Judgments in Tort: An Illustration of the Wealth-Time Continuum' (1980) 43 *MLR* 18.

[138] *BP Exploration Co v Hunt (No 2)* [1979] 1 WLR 783 (QB) (*BP Exploration*). The claim arose out of a frustrated contract and was authorised by the Law Reform (Frustrated Contracts) Act 1943, but was in essence a claim for restitution and was regarded that way by the court.

[139] The current edition is G Jones (ed), *Goff and Jones: The Law of Restitution*, 7th edn (London, Sweet & Maxwell, 2007). And of course Robert Goff J would go on to become Lord Goff and deliver the lead judgment for the House of Lords in *The Texaco Melbourne*.

[140] [1982] 2 WLR 232 (CA) 245.

[141] [1982] 2 WLR 253, [1983] 2 AC 352.

[142] *BP Exploration*, above n 138, 840. An interesting question, and one on which I know of no judicial authority, is what should be the currency of judgment when a gained-based remedy, sometimes referred to as disgorgement and sometimes (confusingly) as restitution, is awarded for a wrong—breach of contract, for instance. Such remedies are not usual, but as the House of Lords reminded us

sought in respect of a payment of money made pursuant to a contract that is later found to be void—a pre-payment for instance—then the currency of payment in the contract will obviously be the currency of judgment. Moreover, since it was necessary to the resolution of the case before him, Goff J went on to say that where the money of account and the money of payment under such a contract were different then it was the money of account that governed.[143]

However, a claim in restitution is not always for money paid. It could be a claim for the value of services rendered, in which case the judicial award is assessed on quantum meruit basis. Goff J thought that where such services were rendered in connection with a contract then the currency of account in the contract, if there was such a currency, would be a strong contender to be the currency of judgment. However, though he was unwilling to go as far as to say there should be a presumption to that effect, so the currency of judgment in such cases should simply be the one in which the court concludes the defendant felt its enrichment.[144] Not all restitution claims arise out of a contract, and in such cases *BP Exploration* offers no more guidance to determining the currency of the award than that it should be the money in which the defendant could be said to have felt its gain. Accordingly, where a defendant received a money payment in a currency that was not its normal operating currency the selection of the correct currency of judgment could involve the same sort of inquiries—and the same unpredictability of result—that we saw in contract cases such as *The Folias*, *The Texaco Melbourne* and *Barings plc v Coopers & Lybrand*.

Although the judgment of Goff J acknowledged that there was a measure of doubt arising from this new rule, there was no suggestion in his reasons, or in the Court of Appeal's confirmation of his approach, that this new uncertainty was in any way problematic. That is, the judicial innovation in *BP Exploration* was one that appears to have been regarded in a wholly positive light by the judges who brought it about. Since then there have not been a large number of cases where, in a cause of action based on restitution judgment has been awarded in a foreign currency, and none that has sorted out the problem outlined above.[145]

in *Attorney General v Blake* [2000] UKHL 45, on occasion they may be granted. Presumably, since the defendant's gain is the measure of damages in such cases the currency of judgment is the same there as in *BP Exploration*—viz, the money in which the defendant felt its gain. This would raise an interesting prospect in those tort or contract cases where a court might be contemplating granting a gained-based remedy: if the measure of damages were the claimant's loss then the currency of damages would be that in which the plaintiff felt its loss, but if instead the measure were the defendant's gain then the currency of damages would be that in which that gain was felt.

[143] Ibid, 841.

[144] Ibid, 840.

[145] In *Papamichael v National Westminster Bank plc* [2003] 1 Lloyd's Rep 341 (QB) there was an award of 2 billion drachmas as money paid under mistake of fact, but the currency of that judgment was ascertained simply by reference to the money that in fact had been paid. The same was true in *Universe Tankships Inc of Monrovia v International Transport Workers*, above n 107 and *Gloyne v Richardson* [2002] EWCA Civ 166 (CA). In *Niru Battery Manufacturing Co v Milestone Trading Ltd (No 2)* [2004] EWCA Civ 487, [2004] 2 Lloyd's Rep 319 the Court of Appeal upheld a trial judgment

D. Insolvency

Not unexpectedly, the abandonment of the forum-currency/breach-date rule was swiftly extended to insolvency claims. Before *Miliangos*, the old approach applied in insolvency cases as it did elsewhere.[146] In his speech in *Miliangos* Lord Wilberforce had ventured some views on foreign currency claims in this insolvency context; consistent with his wish to push the conversion date to the latest practical time, he thought they should be converted into sterling as of the date the creditor's claim was admitted by the liquidator.[147] However, when the matter fell to be decided by the Chancery Division the following month, the judge there took the view that the *Miliangos* passages dealing with insolvency were mere obiter dicta and the *Miliangos* view did not prevail. This was in spite of the fact that the creditors who asserted claims in US dollars would have benefited from—and accordingly argued for—a late exchange date. Instead, the court in this case of a compulsory winding-up of a corporation selected the date of the winding-up order. This had the simplifying, though arguably Procrustean, advantage of subjecting all creditors to the same date, and moreover a date much earlier that the payment date would be if *Miliangos* applied. However, this seemed to be a practical necessity when those creditors were to share in a fixed fund and do so in some fixed and pre-determined ratio.[148] Thus the court followed *Miliangos* to the extent of abandoning the breach-date/sterling rule, but stopped short of replacing it with the payment-date solution. It opted instead for what it saw as a more practical result which seemed to accord better with insolvency legislation, though it had the effect of subjecting creditors to the risk of a fall in sterling between the liquidation and the time of eventual payment—a risk that *Miliangos* thought that creditors should not have to run.

In another case in 1983 the Court of Appeal agreed that in the insolvency situation a single conversion date—that of liquidation[149]—should be imposed on all creditors, which accorded with the general view in insolvency legislation that creditors' claims should be valued as of that date, which should be regarded as coincident with distribution. In addition to according with the general legislative approach to insolvency, this result had a practical advantage. In insolvency

([2002] EWHC (Comm) 1425) which had awarded judgment in restitution of over US$ 5 million. But that was the amount that had been paid under a letter of credit drawn in US dollars so the case did not address the quantum meruit problem.

146 *In re Russian Commercial and Industrial Bank* [1955] Ch 148 (Ch).

147 *Miliangos*, above n 3, 469. Lord Cross agreed: ibid, 498.

148 *In re Dynamics Corporation of America* [1976] 1 WLR 757 (Ch D) (*Dynamics Corp*), followed in *Re Amalgamated Investment & Property Co* [1985] Ch 349 (Ch). FA Mann was of the view that this was a 'much more acceptable and practicable rate': Case note on *Miliangos*, above n 29, 165. For an opposing view see S Stern, 'The Courts and Foreign Currency Obligations' [1995] *Lloyd's Maritime and Commercial Law Quarterly* 494, 515–17. The holding in the case has now been adopted by statute, with some fine-tuning: Insolvency Act 1986, c 45, s 322, and Insolvency Rules 1986, r 4.91 and r 6.111.

149 *In re Lines Bros Ltd* [1983] Ch D 1 (CA) (*Lines*).

and winding-up cases there is generally a fixed pool of assets to be distributed among more than one creditor, and only rarely enough to go around. Different of those creditors may have claims in different foreign currencies but the insolvency process presents the need to be able to compare like with like on a given day. In such circumstances a payment-date rule poses complex and perhaps insuperable administrative difficulties in dividing up the pie. A single conversion date that will apply to all creditors greatly simplifies matters, and the date at which the insolvency or winding-up process is officially commenced is an obvious candidate—even at the cost of some deviation from the principles otherwise forwarded by the *Miliangos* rule. Arguably a risk of some injustice would arise in a case where there was a surplus of assets over debts, with the result that all creditors would be paid in full. There the deviation from the payment-date rule to an earlier conversion date might disadvantage creditors whose claims were in a currency that was generally appreciating, but such insolvencies must be rare indeed.

E. Interest

A final and subsidiary question concerns the rate at which interest should be calculated in cases where a court awards judgment in a currency other than its own. Should an English court which elects to award damages in Swiss francs assess pre-judgment interest with reference to the interest rates that obtained in England between the contractual breach and the date of trial? Or, in the alternative, should it look to the rates that were in effect in Switzerland during that same period? The House of Lords in *Miliangos* did not rule on this point, though a comment on *Miliangos* published just a couple of months after that judgment made the point that the fall of sterling was accompanied by considerably higher English interest rates than were in effect in Switzerland (with its rising franc) during that same period.[150]

The point fell for resolution some months later in the lower court to which *Miliangos* was remitted for decision on this question.[151] The court in *Miliangos (No 2)* approached the matter by attempting to pursue *Miliangos*'s general goal of promoting *restitutio in integrum*—the purpose of pre-judgment interest being to compensate a successful plaintiff for being kept out of the use of money (or money's worth) between the time of breach and the time of judgment. The first step was to hold that, where damages were assessed in a foreign currency, pre-judgment interest might be awarded at a rate different from that which would be awarded in a case where damages were assessed in English pounds. Since common law courts generally have some discretion in the selection of the appropriate rate, that step seems unremarkable. The next move was to

[150] RA Bowles and J Phillips, 'Judgments in Foreign Currencies—An Economist's View' (1976) 39 *MLR* 196, 197–98.

[151] *Miliangos v George Frank (Textiles) Ltd (No 2)* [1976] 3 All ER 599 (QB) (*Miliangos (No 2)*).

hold that availability of pre-judgment interest under a contract was governed by the proper law of the contract, so if no pre-judgment interest could be awarded under the contract then an English court should not award any. (Presumably the same would apply to tort—the governing law determines the availability of pre-judgment interest.) Assuming that such interest was available under the governing substantive law, the next question that arises is that of the applicable rate. That matter was one of procedure, and thus before an English court was governed by English law, under which the principle of *restitutio in integrum* led to the following resolution:

> A Swiss creditor, kept out of money he ought to get in Swiss francs, would reasonably borrow in Switzerland his replacement Swiss francs pending judgment. What he would have to pay to borrow them would have nothing whatever to do with the English sterling bank rate or the basic English lending rate. … [T]he approach of English law should be: if you opt for a judgment in foreign currency, for better or worse you commit yourself to whatever rate of interest obtains in the context of the currency.[152]

Although the decision contained little in the way of reference to macroeconomic principles, it did appear to recognise that there is likely to be a relationship—an inverse one—between exchange rates and interest rates. A central bank in a country with a declining currency—or, more accurately, a currency which is generally expected to decline internationally—is likely to use its control over the money supply to engineer a higher interest rate in order to attract investors to that currency.[153] In the context of a case like *Miliangos* then, one would predict that in the period between breach and judgment the declining English pound would be accompanied by higher domestic interest rates than would the ascending Swiss franc. And this was in fact the case.[154] Accordingly, to allow the plaintiff to collect damages in Swiss francs (as *Miliangos* did) and then turn around and claim pre-judgment interest at the domestic English interest rate, would amount to overcompensation. The ruling in *Miliangos (No 2)* avoided this result, and although it has not invariably been followed it is the prevailing standard.[155]

152 Ibid, 602.

153 For further discussion of this point see RA Bowles and CJ Whelan 'The Currency of Suit in Actions for Damages' (1980) 25 *McGill Law Journal* 236, 238. Of course other factors will enter into a central bank's calculations as well, in particular its desire, or lack of it, to avoid inflation. However, the discipline imposed by the market for government bonds will place a limit on this and insure that normally the relationship described in the text will prevail.

154 As documented by Bowles & Whelan, 'Judicial Responses' above n 29, 262.

155 In *Helmsing Schiffahrts GmbH & Co KG v Malta Drydocks Corp* [1977] 2 Lloyd's Rep 144 (QB), the court awarded damages in Maltese pounds but thought that the interest rate should not be that of Malta but rather of Germany, which was the proper law of the contract. However, it is the approach of *Miliangos (No 2)*, that has most commonly found favour. It was implemented by the Court of Appeal in *Shell Tankers (UK) Ltd v Astro Comino Armadora SA* [1986] 2 Lloyd's Rep 40 and the Private International Law (Miscellaneous Provisions) Act 1995, s 1(1) confirmed that the interest rate need not be the same as the English statutory rate. This confirmed a recommendation of the Law Commission: *Private International Law: Foreign Money Liabilities*, Law Com No 124 (London, HMSO, 1983) [4.15]. The point was later picked up by the Law Reform Commission of British Columbia, *Report on the Foreign Money Claims Act Regulations* (Vancouver, 1991) 2.

An elaboration of a subsidiary point was made in *The Lu Shan*.[156] Two ships had collided and each brought actions for the repair costs. It was agreed between the parties that they were equally to blame and that their respective repair costs, which were in Australian and US dollars respectively, were the currencies which should be set off against one another to produce a final judgment. But what should be the date from which pre-judgment interest should run? The answer to that question was worth litigating, since Australian dollars, as a weak currency at the time of the repairs and litigation in question, had a much higher interest rate than did American ones. That is, if interest should run from the date of the repairs then by the time of set-off the claim in Australian dollars would be much larger in relation to the claim in US dollars than would be the case if interest was not considered until after the set-off. In a decision which accords with the principle in *Miliangos (No 2)* and which has been called 'a victory for common sense'[157] the court opted for the former view: 'in principle interest should be added to each claim before the balance is struck'.[158]

The same thinking applies to post-judgment interest. Recall that *Miliangos* requires a payment-date conversion, and a considerable period may pass between the granting of judgment and the eventual payment. To the extent that post-judgment interest is intended to fulfill the compensation principle by awarding the judgment creditor commercially realist interest rates on the money it is being kept out of, those rates should be determined by reference to the currency of judgment. This is now permitted and encouraged by statute.[159]

F. The Current Scene

Today, thirty-five years after *Miliangos*, it has become completely routine for English courts to render judgment in foreign currency—indeed they sometimes do it in more than one.[160] In doing so they rarely feel the need to refer to *Miliangos*, *The Folias* or any of the other appellate authorities discussed above. In the commercial courts it has become as common to see judgment awarded in US dollars as it is to see an award in sterling, and this is the case regardless of whether the claim lies in contract, tort, or is for the enforcement of an arbitral

[156] Above n 135.

[157] Knott, above n 56, 7.

[158] *The Lu Shan*, above n 135, 261.

[159] Private International Law (Miscellaneous Provisions) Act 1995, 1995 c 42, s 1. This inserts a new s 44A into the Administration of Justice Act 1970, 1970 c 31, stating that when a judgment is given for a sum expressed in a currency other than sterling the court may order that the post-judgment interest shall run at the rate the court thinks fit. It was enacted pursuant to a recommendation of The Law Commission: *Private International Law: Foreign Money Liabilities*, Cmnd 9064 (London, HMSO, 1981) 49.

[160] For instance in *Morgan Grenfell & Co v Sace—Istituto per i Servizi Assicurativi del Commercio*, unreported (19 December 2001) [2001] EWCA Civ 1932 the Court of Appeal upheld a trial judgment which had held the defendant liable to the claimant for US$ 20,326,232.93 and DM 177,293,981.21.

award or foreign judgment.[161] The uncertainties attendant on the new feeling-the-loss rule remain but do not give rise to appellate wrangling.

V. Damages for Foreign-Exchange Losses

As noted near the end of the introduction, in addition to the currency-of-judgment question there is another matter pertaining to the assessment of damages where foreign currencies are involved. The question of recovery of foreign-exchange losses was identified in the early pages of this book but has not been touched on in the discussion until now. Such claims might conceivably arise in tort but most commonly present themselves where, in respect of a claim for breach of a contractual obligation to satisfy a debt in one currency (usually but not necessarily the money of the forum), the disappointed creditor points out that had it been paid on time it would soon thereafter have converted that payment currency into some other.[162] Such claimants next proceed to argue that, because the money into which they claim they would have converted the currency of the debt has since appreciated as against that in which the debt was to have been satisfied, confining them to a remedy based on the currency of the debt (and limited to the amount of

[161] Some recent examples: *Soico Saci v Novokuznetsk Aluminum Plant* [1998] 2 Lloyd's Rep 337 (CA); *Cil v Owners of the Ship 'Turiddu'*, unreported (29 June 1999) [1999] EWCA Civ 1705 (CA); *Mamidoil-Jetoil Greek Petroleum Co SA v Okta Crude Oil Refinery AD* [2002] 2 Lloyd's Rep 645 (CA); *Kuwait Oil Tanker Co SAK v Al Bader*, unreported (18 May 2002) A3/1998/1625 (CA); *Good Challenger Navegante SA v MetalExport Import SA* [2003] EWCA Civ 1668, [2004] 1 Lloyd's 67 (CA); *Maintop Shipping Co v Bulkindo Lines Pte* [2003] EWHC 1894 (Admlty), [2003] 2 Lloyd's Rep 655 (QB (Admlty)); *Kastor Navigation Co v AGF MAT* [2004] 2 Lloyd's Rep 119 CA); *Saudi Arabian Monetary Agency v Dresdner Bank AG* [2004] EWCA Civ 1074, [2005] 1 Lloyd's Rep 12 (CA); *Contigroup Companies Inc v Glencore AG* [2004] EWHC 2750 (Comm), [2005] 1 Lloyd's Rep 241 (QB (Com Ct)); *Continuity Promotions Ltd v O'Connor's Nenagh Shopping Centre Ltd* [2006] EWHC 3462 (QB); *Tavouareas v Tsavliris* [2006] EWHC 414 9 (Com); *Heidland Werres Diederichs v Flexiquip Hydraulics Ltd* [2006] NIQB 100 (QB); *Uzinterimpex JSC v Standard Bank plc* [2007] 2 Lloyd's Rep 187, aff'd [2008] 2 Lloyd's Rep 456 (CA); *The Vicky 1* [2008] EWCA Civ 101, [2008] 2 Lloyd's Rep 45; *Attorney General of Zambia v Meer Care & Desai (a firm)* [2007] EWHC 952 (Ch), rev'd on other grounds [2008] EWCA Civ 1007; *Antiparos Ene v SK Shipping Co*, [2008] EWHC 1139, [2008] 2 Lloyd's Rep 237 (Com); *PT Berlian Laju Tanker TBK v Nuse Shipping Ltd* [2008] EWHC 1130, [2008] 2 Lloyd's Rep 246 (Com); *Gater Assets Ltd v Nak Naftogaz Ukrainiy* [2008] 1108 (comm) (Com); *Transafrik International Ltd v Venus Corp* [2008] EWHC 1721 (TCC) (QB (TCC)); *Allianz Insurance Co Egypt v Aigaion* [2008] EWHC 1127 (Com); *Statoil ASA v Louis Dreyfus Energy Services LP* [2008] EWHC 2257 (Com); *Nigerian National Petroleum Corp v IPCI (Nigeria) Ltd (No 2)* [2008] EWCA Civ 1157; *R v V* [2008] EWHC 1531 (Com); *Westbrook Resources Ltd v Globe Metallurgical Inc* [2009] EXCA Civ 310. None of these cases mentioned *Miliangos* or any other authority on point; they simply proceeded to pronounce judgment in a foreign currency (usually US dollars) as uncontroversially as in pre-*Miliangos* days they had delivered judgment in sterling.

[162] Typically this latter currency is the plaintiff's home, or normal operating currency. But it need not be so; it could be any money into which the plaintiff claims it would have converted the contracted-for payment. See, eg: *Re Griffiths* [2004] FCAFC 102 (Fed Ct Aust), discussed in the next chapter.

that debt plus interest) fails fully to compensate them. They demand an additional head of damages to make up the difference.

Miliangos did not deal with this sort of argument. Its focus was on situations where the original obligation that was breached was regarded as being in some foreign currency, and the follow-on question of what currency should be used to compensate for the debtor's failure to satisfy that core obligation.[163] It did not deal with claims for consequential losses. Moreover, it should be noted that the remedy authorised by *Miliangos*—assessment of damages in some currency other than English pounds—is in no way required in order to fully compensate a plaintiff advancing an argument of the sort sketched in the preceding paragraph. That is, although the argument for compensation for foreign exchange losses obviously involves some *mention* of a foreign currency and of changing rates of exchange, all that is needed by way of remedy is a component in the damages award which will compensate such a plaintiff for its claimed foreign-exchange loss. Such a component might easily be awarded in the money of the forum.

Despite that difference, many scholars who have wrestled with these two sorts of claims have regarded them as intimately related. These include FA Mann, Charles Proctor (the current editor of Mann's *The Legal Aspect of Money*) and Ronald Brand, the American academic who has most frequently and comprehensively addressed these issues. Each of them has taken the position that *Miliangos*'s new approach to the currency-of-judgment question entails, or at least argues strongly for, a corresponding pro-plaintiff re-configuration of the judicial treatment of exchange losses.[164] In support of this view it must be noted that, at least in some cases, a creditor's argument to be compensated for exchange losses may be a substitute means for it to recover losses thought to result from the application of a currency-of-judgment rule that, in a particular case, operates to its disadvantage. Such a plaintiff can simply reframe its claim. It can shift from the procedural framework of the *Miliangos* rule to the substantive ground of consequential loss, abandoning dispute over what yardstick should be employed to measure its loss and focussing instead on identification of that loss. To illustrate, rather than claiming, as the *Miliangos* plaintiff did, that its losses should be denominated in some foreign money since that was how the *original* loss was felt, the plaintiff advancing a claim for foreign exchange losses might admit that its initial loss

[163] Admittedly, there is room to argue with the words 'regarded as' in the text. That is, one might insist that, in *Miliangos*, the original obligation was not simply *regarded as* being in Swiss francs, but was actually so. After all, that is what the contract that was being sued on said. That may be so, but this way of looking at the matter minimises the effect of the pre-*Miliangos* breach-date rule which said that, at least as far as the English law of judicial remedies was concerned, such losses were remedied only by (and thus in one sense regarded as being in) sterling. The effect of the *Miliangos* change was thus genuinely to regard foreign currency obligations as such.

[164] R Brand, Exchange Loss Damages and the Uniform Foreign-Money Claims Act: The Emperor Hasn't All His Clothes' (1991) 23 *Law and Policy in International Business* 1; FA Mann, 'Recovering Currency Exchange Losses' (1988) 104 *LQR* 3; Mann, *The Legal Aspect of Money*, 5th edn, above n 43, 293; Proctor, 'Changes in Monetary Value', in D Saidov & R Cunnington (eds), *Contract Damages: Domestic and International Perspectives* (Oxford, Hart, 2008) 488–90.

must be expressed in the currency of the forum. However, it could then proceed to claim an additional *consequential* loss for the inability to convert the forum currency (because the defendant failed to pay it) into some other one. Should such an argument prevail it would produce a result equivalent to a successful *Miliangos*-style claim. Note, however, that this new argument takes a slightly different form than the *Miliangos* claimant made. A claimant for foreign exchange losses is arguing that *if* it had been paid in the contracted-for currency, then it *would have* effected a certain currency conversion; it is making a claim about what it would have done had the defendant paid on time. In contrast, a *Miliangos*-type argument requires no speculation about consequential losses; the plaintiff simply claims that the metric the judge should use to evaluate its primary loss at the date of breach should be a specific foreign currency.

Whether the differences in the phrasings of these arguments is significant is an important point, one to which we will return. However, there is no question that the two arguments have much in common. The notion that the shortcomings of the forum-currency/breach-date rule might be remedied by a separate additional component in a damages award was appreciated as long ago as 1920. It was voiced by Scrutton LJ in *Di Ferdinando v Simon, Smits & Co*, a case which confirmed the sterling/breach-date rule as mandatory in English courts.[165] There, having concluded that the forum-currency/breach-date rule had to apply in the case before him, Scrutton LJ speculated as to whether the unfairness to the plaintiff resulting from that rule could be patched up by an additional award of damages: 'It occurred to me that it might possibly be that the subsequent variation in the exchange could be included in the damages, in the nature of interest'.[166] Despite this speculation, however, Scrutton LJ concluded that there was no authority for such a component in a damages award, and for good reason. Such a harm, he thought, was too remote: 'The variation of exchange is not sufficiently connected with the breach as to be within the contemplation of the parties'.[167] Significantly, he did not simply mean that the loss was, on the facts of the case before him, too remote. Rather he meant that as a general rule it be viewed and invariably treated as such.

The connection between the two types of claim was also observed by Otto Kahn-Freund when he investigated the currency-of-judgment question in 1940. Kahn-Freund noted that the forum-currency/breach-date rule did justice between the parties when the pound was appreciating. He went on to observe, however,

[165] Above n 20. See also the judgment of Mocatta J in *Barclays Bank International Ltd v Levin Brothers (Bradford) Ltd*, above n 3. There, at 283, he responded to an argument about the possible injustice of denying judgment in foreign money in a given situation by noting that an equivalent result might be reached by awarding exchange loss damages: 'I need only say that in certain circumstances it is possible to recover as unliquidated damages a currency loss due to the change in the relevant rates of exchange occurring subsequently to a failure to make payment on the due date'. A similar point was made by the Queensland Court of Appeal in *State of Queensland v Northaus Trading Co* (unreported 13 August 1999) Appeal No 6299 of 1998 [3].

[166] *Di Ferdinando*, ibid, 416.

[167] Ibid.

that it did not seem to do so if sterling declined during litigation. He proceeded to argue that the breach-date rule might be abandoned, but if that could not be done then he acknowledged that a claim for foreign-currency losses might get to the same result by different means, or at least different words:

> If the Courts are ever faced with the opposite situation [*ie*, sterling's fall (as would be the case in *Miliangos*)], the rule might be revised or the power of giving judgment in foreign currency might be introduced by legislation. Another possibility would be to give the creditors the hitherto unknown claim for damages on the ground of delay of payment.[168]

The close connection between the conversion-date question and the question of awarding damages for foreign exchange losses requires some exploration of the precise relationship between the two. Specifically, what, if any, effect should *Miliangos*'s adoption of a payment-date conversion rule have on the availability, or otherwise, of a claim for foreign exchange losses such as that described above? Should a so-called revolution on the currency-of-judgment question have any consequences for a claim for a component in a damages award to compensate for forgone foreign exchange gains?

Until recently, the doctrinal obstacle which confronted any plaintiff advancing a claim of the sort just described was the 1893 House of Lords ruling in *London, Chatham and Dover Railway v South Eastern Railway*.[169] That decision held that damages might not be recovered for late payment of a debt. A plaintiff debtor might recover the debt itself but, apart from nominal damages, other claims—even for interest (which was the matter in respect of which damages were claimed in that case)—might not be compensated. Since interest could not be recouped in its own right, allowing a plaintiff to do so as an element of damages would be doing indirectly that which might not be done directly.

Insofar as interest is concerned, that matter has been taken care of by statute and need not be addressed here.[170] In addition, both before and after *Miliangos* some other inroads into the general rule have made in some other areas.[171] However, at the time of *Miliangos* the *Dover Railway* ruling still stood in the way of any attempt to recover damages for foreign exchange losses as described above.

The claim has been made that the new rule enunciated in *Miliangos* is merely a procedural one (or, alternatively, an aspect of English private international law),

[168] Kahn-Freund, above n 17, 231. Presumably the damages for delay would be granted only in the cases where foreign currency was involved, so it was a species of foreign exchange loss.

[169] *London, Chatham and Dover Railway v South Eastern Railway* [1893] AC 429 (HL) (*Dover Railway*).

[170] Late Payment of Commercial Debts (Interest) Act 1998, c 20.

[171] Again Lord Denning was a prominent actor in chipping away at the old rule. In *Trans Trust SPRL v Danubian Trading Co* [1952] 2 QB 297 (CA) (*Trans Trust*) he distinguished the rule on the dubious basis that it did not apply where the obligation breached was one to open a letter of credit rather than to pay money. A more significant inroad on the *Dover Railway* rule occurred in *Wadsworth v Lydall* [1981] 1 WLR 598, where the Court of Appeal ruled that the limitation applied only to claims for general damages and not to those for special damages.

while the question of foreign exchange losses is a matter of remedial or substantive law.[172] Consequently, *Miliangos* was not construed as having any direct and binding effect on the law with respect to claims for foreign exchange losses. However, as the following account of English judicial treatment of the exchange loss question shows, there has been a connection of sorts between the two. At the very least, the modernising effect of *Miliangos*—the assertion that late-twentieth-century commerce required a fresh approach to the law's treatment of foreign currency—appears to have authorised judicial reformulation of the rules regarding foreign exchange losses.

A key decision here is the 1979 decision in *Ozalid Group (Export) Ltd v African Continental Bank*.[173] There the contractual obligation breached was one to pay a foreign currency on a certain date. That money had in fact been paid, but nine weeks late. Damages were claimed in respect of losses said to follow from the fact that the plaintiff, had it received that foreign money on the due date, would promptly have converted it to English pounds, and furthermore that the defendant knew this. Since pounds had appreciated in relation to the foreign currency in the period between breach and the date the payment was eventually made, the plaintiff advanced a claim for the loss it suffered by not being able to convert the payment into pounds at the earlier date.

As just described, *Ozalid* appears to be a classic instance of a claim for foreign exchange losses. As treated and resolved by the court, however, it is no easy matter to tell whether the case was regarded an exchange-loss case or a currency-of-judgment one. Despite the fact that the plaintiff asked for damages for late payment, the judgment of Donaldson J made no reference to *Dover Railway*, to any of the modern cases that addressed the scope of the *Dover Railway* rule (such as *Trans Trust*[174]), or to authorities on the broader question of consequential losses and remoteness, such as *Hadley v Baxendale*.[175] Rather, he drew all his inspiration and guidance from recent changes on the law respecting the currency of judgment. He noted that everything had changed since 1975: 'The law on claims which involve foreign currency was revolutionised by the decision of the House of Lords in *Miliangos*… '.[176] Further, he took note of *The Folias* and *The Despina R* and the

[172] Goode, above n 92, 138–43.

[173] Above n 3 (*Ozalid*). Another case that relied on the modernising effect of *Miliangos* to bring about a change in an area of law other than the currency-of-judgment question was *Choice Investments Ltd v Jeromnimon Midland Bank Ltd* [1981] 1 QB 149 (CA). The case presented a question of statutory construction: was a US dollar account in an English bank a 'debt' for the purposes of a given statute? Lord Denning, with whom the other members of the court agreed noted that prior to *Miliangos* it might not have been so regarded, but in light of *Miliangos* it should be.

[174] Above n 171. Arguably this is explicable by Donaldson J's thinking that, even though the contract before him was governed by English law, the ruling in *Dover Railway* was confined to claims where the original debt was in sterling.

[175] *Hadley v Baxendale* (1854) 9 Ex 341 (Ex Ch).

[176] Above n 3, 233. Despite his admiration for *Miliangos*, the reasons of Donaldson J suggest at times that he had not read that decision very closely. He twice stated that *Miliangos* had imposed a judgment-day conversion date (233, 234) and he treated the claim before him as one for damages, not debt. For this latter error, which led him into thinking that the currency of judgment should be

feeling-the-loss rule that came out of those two cases, and concluded that in light of those authorities this was a case where the plaintiff had felt its loss in sterling. The value he put on that loss, however, was simply the diminution of wealth that the plaintiff claimed to have suffered when the defendant's late payment of the foreign currency deprived it of the chance to convert that money into sterling:

> Once it is proved that the plaintiff's true loss is to be measured in sterling, any payment made on account in a different currency falls to be credited against that sterling loss at the rate of exchange ruling at the date of payment.[177]

In short, the court's reasoning appears to be that, since the law as developed in *Miliangos*, *The Folias* and the *Despina R* indicated that sterling should be the currency of judgment in this case, the plaintiff's claim for exchange losses should be granted, and moreover nothing in either the *Dover Railway* line of cases nor the general law of foreseeability stood in the way of the plaintiff's recovery.[178] The effect of this was to blur considerably that already uncertain line between exchange-loss cases and currency-of-judgment cases; somehow *Miliangos*, *The Folias* and *The Despina R* had become crucial authorities for deciding when a claim for exchange losses would be permitted to succeed.

If *Ozalid* was representative of all post-*Miliangos* cases on this point then for practical purposes there would no longer be a meaningful distinction between the currency-of-judgment problem and claims for foreign-exchange losses; the two would have effectively merged and, by way of interpretation, *Miliangos* would have eliminated the barrier to recovery posed by *Dover Railway*. However, not all post-*Miliangos* cases awarding damages for foreign-exchange losses relied on *Miliangos* and the currency-of-judgment cases as support for this result. In *International Minerals & Chemical Corp v Karl O Helm AG*,[179] decided a few years after *Ozalid*, the court dealt with a claim for late payment of Belgian francs. Hobhouse J held for the plaintiff and gave judgment in debt for the francs. He saw no need to cite *Miliangos* or any other authority in support of this, since by this time, nine years after *Miliangos*, such judgments were commonplace. However, the plaintiff also requested an additional damages award, to be assessed in US dollars, to compensate it for the fact that had it received timeous payment of the francs it would have promptly have swapped that payment for dollars. The plaintiff further noted that the defendant had knowledge that the plaintiff

pounds, he was criticised by Hobhouse J in *International Minerals & Chemical Corp v Karl O Helm AG* [1986] 1 Lloyd's Rep 81 (QB) 105.

[177] Ibid, 234. Of course there would be no 'sterling loss' to compensate for unless one first decided, contrary to *Dover Railway*, that damages could be awarded for late payment of a debt, but the effective conflation of the currency-of-judgment and damages-for-late-payment issues nicely allows this point to be skipped over.

[178] For criticism of the reasoning and result in *Ozalid* on the grounds that the plaintiff should have taken steps to prevent the sort of loss it claimed to have suffered, see FM Ventris, *Banker's Documentary Credits*, 3rd edn (London, Lloyd's of London Press, 1990) 248–49.

[179] *International Minerals & Chemical Corp v Karl O Helm AG*, above n 176.

would have acted in this fashion, and that since the Belgian franc had fallen against the dollar in the post-breach period compensatory damages should be awarded to address this loss. In siding with the plaintiff on this point the court did not, as the *Ozalid* court did, make the finding that the currency of judgment was US dollars; indeed, as noted, on the main claim the currency of judgment was Belgian francs. Rather, Hobhouse J's focus was on the scope of the bar against such claims (*Dover Railway*), the growing exceptions to that bar (*Trans Trust*) and the general authorities on remoteness (*Hadley v Baxendale*, *Czarnikow (C) Ltd v Koufos*[180] and *Victoria Laundry (Windsor) Ltd v Newman*[181]). In short, he saw the plaintiff's claim as one for consequential damages, the result of which was in no way directly influenced by the currency-of-judgment cases—apart from the fact that those cases now entitled him to award those compensatory damages in dollars.

Much the same approach was evident in 1987 when the House of Lords had the opportunity to consider liability for foreign exchange losses in *President of India v Lips Maritime Corp*.[182] In holding that such losses might be awarded in an appropriate case, though not in the case before it, their Lordships regarded the question principally as one in which there was a clash between the bar to such damages in the *Dover Railway* case and the general principles of remoteness emerging from *Hadley v Baxendale*. Although the extracts from counsel's argument that are reported in the Appeal Cases show attempts to draw support from *Miliangos* and *The Despina R*,[183] the speeches of their Lordships in *The Lips* do not seek to forge links between the exchange-loss question and the currency-of-judgment question. The *Miliangos* revolution provided no authority for extending the traditional bar to recovery of such losses and the House of Lords did not allow them in this case because the plaintiff's basic claim was not for debt but for damages and because there 'is no such thing as a cause of action in damages for late payment of damages'.[184] For this approach, however, the judgment in *The Lips* has come in for academic criticism for disregarding the logic of *Miliangos*:

> The holding in *The Lips* ... impedes the further development of the *Miliangos* rationale favoring consideration of transnational commercial concerns when a foreign currency obligation is involved. The failure to relate the issue in *The Lips* to *Miliangos* leaves uncertain the future development of the *Miliangos* rule.[185]

[180] *Czarnikow (C) Ltd v Koufos* [1969] AC 361 (HL).

[181] *Victoria Laundry (Windsor) Ltd v Newman* [1949] 2 KB 528 (CA).

[182] *President of India v Lips Maritime Corp* [1988] AC 395 (HL) (*The Lips*); followed on this point in *Ventouris v Mountain (The 'Italia Express' (No 2))* [1992] 2 Lloyd's Rep 281 (QB).

[183] Ibid, 417.

[184] Ibid, 425.

[185] Brand, above n 164, 37-38. See also the comment by FA Mann, 'Recovering Currency Exchange Losses' above n 164. Mann thought the decision in *The Lips* was tragic and called this 'the most conceptualistic reasoning ... which one has had to read for a long time'. (ibid, 4.) He included that same criticism in his text, the bible of monetary law: Mann, *The Legal Aspect of Money*, 5th edn, above n 43, 293. Similar but more temperately expressed criticism was offered by Charles Proctor, above n 164, 490.

The latest chapter in this story is *Travelers Casualty and Surety Co of Canada v Sun Life Assurance Co of Canada (UK)*.[186] There the claimants sought a declaration that they were not liable to the defendants under a series of insurance policies. While the claimants were successful, the court went on to deal with what their liability under those policies would be in the event the defendant was successful on appeal. The policies called for indemnification in US dollars for amounts the defendant might have to pay out. The defendant had made such payments and had made them in sterling. At the time the defendant made those payments the exchange rate of dollars to pounds was in the region of 1.4/1. By the time of trial, however, the dollar had appreciated and the exchange rate was around 1.8 or 1.9/1, and given the amounts in issue the value at stake in the selection of the exchange date was in the neighbourhood of $5,000,000.

The court held that the contracts in issue had provided for a conversion at the date of payment—effectively a breach-date conversion (which meant that, given the subsequent fall in the dollar, the insured would endure the same sort of loss that the plaintiff seller in *Miliangos* would supposedly have suffered). That is, for every £1 it paid out, the insured would be indemnified to the tune of $1.4. But then the court noted that this would not amount to full indemnification, since it now took around $1.9 to purchase £1:

> Such a payment will not put Sun Life [the insured] into the position it would have been in if timely payment had been made in accordance with the policy, and will not provide it with a full indemnity against its insured losses. Those losses were all incurred in sterling.[187]

However, the court then went on to note the holding of the House of Lords in *The Lips* provided the remedy for this perceived injustice. The award could be topped up by the addition of an additional amount for exchange losses—the amount that the insured would have lost by not converting the indemnifying payment in US$ into sterling back when the US$ was strong. Note that the effect of this is the equivalent of awarding damages at the rate of exchange in effect at the time of judgment (despite the fact that the contract effectively provided for breach-date conversion).

The question of whether exchange loss claims of the sort described here are justified is one to which I will return. It should be noted at this point, however, that the claim is one which seems to operate as a one-way street in favour of plaintiffs. That is, if in a case such as *Travelers Casualty* the US dollar had appreciated vis-a-vis sterling the insured would have made no reference to the fact that, had it received its dollar payment on time, it would promptly have converted those dollars into (now depreciated pounds), so that its award should be less in light of the loss that the late payment had caused it to avoid. And a defendant who advanced

[186] *Travelers Casualty and Surety Co of Canada v Sun Life Assurance Co of Canada (UK)* [2006] EWHC 2716 (Com) (*Travelers Casualty*).

[187] Ibid [427].

an argument that it should be required to pay less because the late payment permitted the claimant to realise 'foreign exchange gains' would not find that argument warmly received. Whether the one-sided nature of the damages claim for foreign exchange losses due to late payment is something that should concern us, and the separate issue of whether the ruling and reasoning in *Miliangos* should be regarded as having any consequence for that matter, are matters to which I will return after we examine the law on this foreign currency claims in certain other jurisdictions.[188] More recently still, the House of Lords has swept away *Dover Railway* as a general rule precluding the awarding of interest for late payment of a debt; the matter is now entirely a question of foreseeability.[189]

The role that *Miliangos* has to play in sorting out claims for exchange losses remains uncertain. Its ruling, or at least its rhetoric, casts a long shadow and the case has had an influence well beyond the narrow point of law that it decided. That effect was to eliminate, or at least play a role in eliminating, long-standing barriers to other types of claims that contained a foreign currency element. Its concern with novel fiscal circumstances and the need to start afresh and craft new rules for new times has prompted subsequent English courts to decentre sterling's role in judicial awards. This was not limited to broadening the payment date rule to cover claims for damages and restitution. It went beyond that and influenced handing of claims for consequential losses—at least where the consequence in question involved currency exchange. The question of whether this is a good or a bad thing will be taken up in later chapters.

[188] Though it should be noted that *Travelers Casualty* has met with a positive reception from only person who has commented on it: C Proctor, 'Changes in Monetary Value and the Assessment of Damages', above n 7, 489–90.

[189] *Sempra Metals Ltd v Inland Revenue Commissioners* [2007] UKHL 34, [2008] 1 AC 561. The case itself did not concern late payment of a debt but was rather a claim in restitution. However, the interest question arose and in the course of addressing it the House of Lords decided that both *Dover Railway* and *The Lips* were no longer good law and that interest might be recovered for late payment of a debt when such losses were shown to be foreseeable.

2

Damages Assessment Problems and Foreign Currency

We are now in a position to say what justice is.

Aristotle
Nicomachean Ethics, V, v

The epigraph from *The Ethics* probably strikes the reader as opaque, or at least misplaced. It is worth taking note, however, of the order of the things that Aristotle considers when, in Book V, he embarks on his celebrated inquiry, what is justice? He deals first with various human faculties (the sound body, the healthy mind), then with injustice and how justice differs from virtue. Next he draws the distinction between distributive and corrective justice, and proceeds to discourse on the nature of these two conceptions. He then turns to reciprocity, and then finally, of all things, he discusses the function of money. Only after he has finished explaining what currency is and how it stands in relation to other commodities does Aristotle declare, 'We are now in a position to say what justice is'. In a list of subjects that includes virtue, the healthy mind and corrective justice, mention of lucre seems a little out of place. Yet for Aristotle, it seems that something about money is a precondition to understanding justice.

While the scope of this book is a thousand times narrower than Book V of *The Ethics*, it is still possible that an investigation into the role that currency—and, in particular, curren*cies*—has to play in remedying torts and breaches of contract will be the source of broader lessons about private law generally. At any rate, the time has come to launch an investigation into whether the legal changes set out in the previous chapter are satisfactory.

Chapter one was almost entirely descriptive, perhaps ploddingly so. As the presence of some dissenting judgments in the English cases bears out, there is room for debate about the virtues and defects of various legal approaches to foreign currency obligations. But in the last chapter I did not seek to take sides between the dissenters and those in the majority. It was helpful at this early stage to proceed by offering a mostly unadorned account of the sorts of questions that had been presented to English courts and the general nature of the solutions that judges devised to respond to them. However, we can no longer defer evaluation of these doctrinal developments. The goal of this chapter will be to venture some preliminary assessments of the role of currency, or rather of multiple oscillating currencies, in the awarding of damages. No final pronouncements will be made. It would be premature to do so before we look at the problem more broadly—in particular at how it has been handled in the courts of some other common law countries, and also at some legislative initiatives and some provisions in international conventions. So the goal here is not to venture final conclusions about how the currency-of-judgment question should be settled. It is simply to take some first steps in a normative inquiry so that we can make tentative assessments about the developments to be examined in the following chapters. From such a position we can assess how other common law courts have wrestled with the currency-of-judgment problem and perhaps eventually arrive at an optimal approach.

I. The Currency of Judgment

One position on which almost everyone seems agreed, at least in post-*Miliangos* times, is that the chief function of legal rules concerning the currency of judgment should be to conduce to fair and accurate compensation. Arguably that is the *sole* goal of such rules and no other consideration is even pertinent[1]—apart, of course, from such adjustments as might arise from a prudential requirement to articulate legal rules in a manner that conduces to making them understandable and amenable to easy and regular administration.

This was not always the case. As we will see in later chapters, some countries have, or used to have, statutes which appear to require courts to render judgment only in the local money. This legislation seems to stand in the way of those countries adopting *Miliangos*. Such statutes seek to protect and promote the currency of the forum, and thus the local mint and maybe even local sovereignty, even if that protection comes at the expense of accurate compensation. We will consider some of those statutes later.

Even in England, however, which has not had such legislation, compensation has in the past sometimes been subordinated to other concerns. For instance in *Havana Railways*—the 1960 House of Lords decision that affirmed the old forum-currency/breach-date rule—there are passages that concede that that rule might not be ideal in terms of exact compensation. There, however, it was thought that insurmountable practical and procedural difficulties standing in the way of awarding judgment in foreign money precluded an English court's departing from that rule.[2] That is, the speeches in *Havana Railways* took no issue with the claim that, other things being equal, accurate compensation should be the aim of rules governing foreign money claims. The problem was that in their Lordships' views other things were *not* equal. It was virtually a presupposition in that case

[1] At least this is true in those cases where the general goal of the remedy the court is applying is compensation. Where the remedial goal is something else—unravelling unjust enrichment, for example—then the arrangements for selecting the currency of judgment should promote that other goal.

[2] *Re United Railways of Havana and Regla Warehouses Ltd* [1961] AC 1007 (HL) 1044, 1051–52 (Lord Reid) (*Havana Railways*).

that the breach-date rule was the only workable one, or at least that judgment in an English court could only be given in sterling, largely because it could only be enforced in sterling.[3] If in some cases injustice flowed from that then there was really little that could be done about it and English courts need have no special shame about that state of affairs since the same thing happened in the courts of all countries, or at least so it was thought.[4]

In *Miliangos*, as we have seen, the House of Lords reconsidered the matter in light of the trail blazed by arbitrators and judicial enforcement of arbitral awards. It discovered that the practicalities of awarding damages in a foreign currency were perhaps not so great after all, so that there was no longer any need to subordinate the goal of accurate compensation, which the majority thought the payment-date rule seemed better suited to fulfill. That is the view that prevails now. These days, with the exception of insolvency cases, where the need to divide up a fixed fund still dictates a necessary divergence from the objective of precise compensation, it is a shared starting point that the rules on foreign currency claims should facilitate realisation of the broader aims of private law remedies. In most cases that aim is fair compensation: putting the wronged party in the position they would have occupied had they not been wronged, so far as money can ever be thought to do that.

Perhaps this point seems so obvious as not to be worth dwelling on. It is helpful to note, however, that it is entirely possible for judges to bring other sorts of considerations into play. For instance, macroeconomic or political concerns might be taken into account in selecting a rule to govern the currency of judgment. These might include benefitting the local economy by adopting the rule most likely to encourage parties to maintain their wealth in the forum currency; having a rule that, on the whole, benefits locals over foreigners; or, conversely, maintaining a reputation as being an appealing country in which to litigate by selecting a rule which would, on the whole, favour foreign litigants over resident ones.[5] All of these might point to currency-of-judgment rules which would deviate from exact compensation. As noted above, however, such considerations performed no significant role in *Miliangos* or the cases that came after it.[6] At least

[3] Lord Denning was most explicit on this point: *Havana Railways*, ibid at 1068–69. To the same effect see the words of Scrutton LJ in *Di Ferdinando v Simon, Smits & Co* [1920] 3 KB 409 (CA) 415 (*Di Ferdinando*).

[4] *Havana Railways*, ibid, 1068–69 (Lord Denning), 1043 (Viscount Simonds), 1059 (Lord Radcliffe).

[5] In the next chapter we will encounter a decision of the Supreme Court of India where, albeit only in passing, the court seems to take such macroeconomic considerations into account in articulating an approach to the currency-of-judgment problem. In that case the court said that in addition to the goal of accurate compensation, decision makers faced with foreign currency claims should also keep in mind the economic situation of the country. The court did not elaborate on how this consideration should be assessed but the context suggests that it thought it was important to keep hard foreign currencies such as dollars and francs from leaving the country. See the discussion of *Standard Chartered Bank v Raman* (2006) 5 SCC 727 (SC India) at p 138 n 200.

[6] See the discussion above at pp 30–31. The only significant appearance of this sort of discourse in *Miliangos* appeared in the dissenting speech of Lord Simon. There, in a list of questions designed

in England, such concerns have played almost no part in judicial analysis of the currency-of-judgment question.

Another source of non-compensatory considerations that might be called into play on the currency question comes to light if we briefly consider the law relating to costs and interest (both pre- and post-judgment). First costs. Courts in private law cases have a measure of power to order one party to litigation to pay the other party money to reimburse the latter for all or some portion of its expenses in conducting that litigation. Lawyers' fees are the largest portion of such outlays, but there can also be disbursements, experts' fees, travel and other expenditure. Rules regarding costs vary, but the general directive in the Commonwealth (but not the United States) is that costs follow the event. This means that the judge orders the losing party to pay the winner's expenses, or at least some substantial portion of them.[7] The obvious goal of this is compensation: a successful plaintiff who receives an award of damages in recompense for the violation of some right is not made fully whole if it still has to bear the cost of filing the court action, paying a lawyer to assist in the vindication of that right, and so on. An award of costs on top of the damages award indemnifies that claimant for the outlay made in enforcing its right. Where it is the defendant who prevails, an award of costs in its favour performs a similar compensatory role. In practice, awards of costs rarely amount to full compensation—probably something more like two-thirds. However, despite that systematic shortfall the underlying rationale for granting a winning litigant costs remains that of compensation.

However, courts possess some discretion when it comes to awarding costs. The general rule need not be applied if there is good cause not to. A lengthy exploration of what amounts to good cause—that is, of the sorts of elements that may be taken into account in the exercise of the judicial discretion as to costs—is beyond the needs or scope of this work. It varies among jurisdictions. Broadly speaking, however, the following sorts of factors might be looked at: whether a party's conduct during the court case tended to lengthen the litigation unnecessarily, whether a party refused to admit something that should have been admitted, whether a party was vexatious in its conduct of the proceedings, and finally the principle of access to justice, which might prompt a court not to award costs against an impecunious litigant in circumstances where such an award would work a hardship on that party.[8]

Much the same can be said for the law relating to interest, a subject that bears some kinship with the currency-of-judgment question. The prime aim of awarding a successful litigant interest at a commercially realistic rate on top of damages

to show why the doctrinal change proposed by the majority should only be effected, if at all, by Parliament, he asked, 'Would the reversal of the *Havana* rule . . . have any significant effect on this country's balance of payments?': *Miliangos v George Frank (Textiles) Ltd* [1976] AC 443 (HL) 481 (*Miliangos*).

[7] In England and Wales this rule is now found in Civil Procedure Rule 44.3(2)(a).

[8] M Orkin, *The Law of Costs*, 2nd edn (Aurora, Ont, Canada Law Book, 2008) ch 2.

is to achieve fuller, more accurate compensation.[9] However, courts have the power in certain circumstances to make an award of interest that either under- or over-compensates the successful litigant, for instance, by varying the rate or the period in which interest will be allowed, or even by disallowing it entirely. They may do so in light of factors relating to the parties' conduct in the litigation—for example, punishing a party who raised and persisted in a frivolous defence and thus protracted the proceedings.

Not surprisingly, the extent to which judicial discretion over costs and interest may legitimately be employed to promote goals other than compensation is a contested matter. In particular, using interest awards to advance goals such as access to justice or minimising the time and expense of litigation is controversial. The point here, however, is that when it comes to the question under consideration in this book—the currency of judgment—there is no comparable controversy. There is no strain of judicial analysis of the currency-of-judgment question that contends that the money of judgment should be selected so as to punish a party who has improperly protracted the litigation, or to go lightly on one who is impecunious. These days, selection of that currency proceeds entirely on the basis that the rules regarding that matter should be ones which conduce to fair compensation.

Of course it would be entirely feasible to employ currency conversion dates for the same ends as courts sometimes use costs and interest awards—to punish and thus anticipatorily influence conduct during litigation. Conversion dates could equally be used to redistribute wealth or (in less controversial terms) promote access to justice. If judges were in need of such tools then currency conversion dates would be a handy one, though of course, unlike costs and interest, they would have the drawback of being available only in a subset of decided cases. However, neither the cases we have seen so far nor those we will encounter in ensuing chapters offer any suggestion that conversion dates and currency selection should be deployed for such purposes.

There is a potential qualification to this. In some court decisions and statutes we will encounter it is stated that judges should select a conversion date that is just in all the circumstances. Sometimes this is phrased as a requirement to select the currency or conversion date that is equitable. Such broad, open-ended standards might conceivably authorise using currency conversion dates to penalise undesirable litigation conduct. As we will see, there are decisions where judges proclaim that they are selecting a given currency conversion date because it is equitable and yet offer no explanation as to why that is the case. In such instances it is certainly possible that among the unstated factors influencing the resolution of the currency question were the sorts of non-compensatory considerations sometimes taken into account when awarding or withholding costs. However, even there judges do not openly claim (or admit) that this is the case. That is, we will

[9] In England see *Sempra Metals Ltd v Inland Revenue Commissioners* [2007] UKHL 34, [2008] 1 AC 561 (HL); and in Canada, *Bank of America Canada v Mutual Trust Co* 2002 SCC 43, [2002] 2 SCR 601 [36–38].

encounter no case where the judge has said that he is selecting a given money to be the currency-of-judgment because that selection punishes one of the litigants for dilatory litigation tactics or the like. So in the absence of *express* dissent from the dominant sentiment that the goal of selecting the currency of judgment is to realise the greater good of accurate compensation it seems safe to evaluate the law on the basis of how well it realises that function.

Of course even in cases that do not present the currency-of-judgment question the question of what constitutes fair reparation is often fraught with contention. Persons can contend that the compensation principle dictates a breach-date conversion, a payment-date-conversion, or even a wait and see approach. Agreeing that compensation is the proper guiding principle for the currency-of-judgment question is no more than a first step, but at least it constitutes a framework for analysis and debate.

Against that background then, how do the rules on the currency of judgment fare? First note that when more than one currency is involved in a claim for compensation only one can serve as the measure of that compensation.[10] As we have seen, traditionally in English courts the unit of measure was sterling, with all other obligations, including ones in other moneys, assessed by that yardstick, and at least since the 1920s this evaluation was consistently effected as of the date of breach. According to *Miliangos*, the defect of that rule was that it led to departures from correct compensation. While there are passages in that seminal decision that convey the sense that under-compensation of plaintiffs is a greater mischief than its opposite,[11] for the most part the Law Lords' *summon bonum* in *Miliangos* was simply *accuracy* of compensation; plaintiffs should neither be under- nor over-compensated:

> The relevant certainty which the rule ought to achieve is that which gives the creditor neither more nor less than he bargained for. He bargained for 415,522.45 Swiss francs; . . . whichever way the exchange into those currencies may go, he should get 415,522.45 Swiss francs or as nearly as can be brought about.[12]

[10] At least this is so where the two moneys have fluctuated in value against one another during litigation or may do so pending payment of the judgment; if one is pegged to the other this stricture will not apply. J Gidding expanded on this point in 'The Measurement of Foreign Money Obligations' (1950) 36 *Virginia Law Review* 215, 220 (footnote omitted): 'Two kinds of money, varying in their exchange ratio to one another, cannot both be nominal units, or units of measure. Only one can be the money of account or measure, the other will be for all practical purposes, a commodity. One, in effect, will have a price in terms of the other'. Of course this does not mean that within one law suit different heads of damage might be assessed in different currencies. However, for obvious reasons we do not see courts saying that, under a given head of damages, the defendant must pay the plaintiff 'either a million euros or a million and a half dollars'.

[11] *Miliangos*, above n 6. Lord Wilberforce wrote that 'justice demands that the *creditor* not suffer from fluctuations in the value of sterling' (465, emphasis added). In a similar vein he went on to observe, 'it must surely be wrong in principle to allow procedure to affect, detrimentally, the substance of the creditor's rights' (ibid).

[12] Ibid, 466 (Lord Wilberforce). On that same page he also wrote that for the creditor 'what matters is that a Swiss franc for good or ill should remain a Swiss franc'. This aspect of the reasoning in *Miliangos* was emphasised with approval by Mocatta J in *Barclays Bank International Ltd v Levin Brothers (Bradford) Ltd* [1977] 1 QB 270 (QB).

In cases like *Miliangos*, where the money of the forum had fallen against that of the debt, the breach-date rule supposedly operated to shortchange plaintiffs. In situations where the fluctuation went the other way the old rule would seem to benefit them, but this would still be a departure from faithful compensation and therefore to be avoided. Any fluctuation between the currency of the debt and that of the forum in the post-breach period would, it seemed, lead to a deviation from precise compensation.

At this point it will be helpful to look a little more closely at the reasoning (and the rhetoric) in *Miliangos*, which was described in the previous chapter but not scrutinised. It is worth pausing to note that in the view of Lord Wilberforce in *Miliangos* the old breach-date rule that led to this inaccuracy was supported not only by the now overthrown notion that for practical considerations judgment had to be rendered in sterling, but also by a fallacy called nominalism.[13] A classic expression of monetary nominalism is the following statement by Denning LJ: 'Sterling is the constant unit of value by which in the eye of the law everything else is measured. Prices of commodities may go up or down, other currencies may go up and down, but sterling remains the same'.[14] In the view of their Lordships in *Miliangos*, monetary nominalism, which had by then been disavowed by Lord Denning, was no longer tenable.[15]

Arguably, however, *Miliangos*'s rejection of nominalism plays no more than a rhetorical function in the reasoning in that case. It is not defined there and may be no more than a vague pejorative—a close kin to 'formalism'—that is used to denigrate the approach of an earlier age as unsophisticated and parochial, especially now that the long-overvalued pound was falling.

Likewise when Lord Wilberforce noted that the breach-date rule might possibly extend 'back to the Year Books'[16] he was not praising it as fundamental. Rather, he was setting it up as a sort of pre-Copernican relic in which, instead of the centre of the universe being occupied by the earth, that place was taken by sterling. That this supposedly benighted view could persist until the 1960 decision in *Havana Railways* was due, in the opinion of Lord Wilberforce in *Miliangos*, only to the relative lack of fluctuation of the relevant currencies, which minimised the ill effects of having selected an unfair rule. But that situation, he claimed, had changed in the 15 years since *Havana Railways*:

> The situation as regards currency stability has substantially changed even since 1961. Instead of the main world currencies being fixed and fairly stable in value, subject to the risk of periodic re- or devaluations, many of them are now 'floating,' i.e., they have no fixed exchange value even from day to day. This is true of sterling.[17]

[13] *Miliangos*, ibid, 466.
[14] *Treseder-Griffen v Co-operative Insurance Society* [1956] 2 QB 127 (CA) 144.
[15] *Miliangos*, above n 6, 466.
[16] Ibid, 459.
[17] Ibid, 463.

If all of this seems something of a digression from analysis of the question of how to achieve faithful compensation in the face of oscillating currencies, the point is that that is largely how it functioned in *Miliangos*—as a diversion. While the reasoning in that case emphasised the crucial goal of accurate compensation, its insistence that the existing rule was ancient, was fatally infected by something called monetary nominalism, and had been crafted before the period of the daily rise and fall of currencies, operated to relieve the majority in *Miliangos* from any fully elaborated account of exactly why and how the breach-date rule was productive of inaccurate compensation.

Perhaps that conclusion may seem so obvious as not to need articulation, but in order to understand why the payment-date rule operates as an improvement over the breach-date rule it supplanted it is necessary to be clearer about the *way* in which the traditional breach-date rule might be said to have departed from or undermined accurate compensation. In this connection it is worth noting that under the pre-*Miliangos* regime a plaintiff in the position of the unpaid seller Miliangos could without much effort take steps to avoid the risks cast upon it by the forum-currency/breach-date rule. Application of the rule has both downside and upside risks, of course. But to the extent that an unpaid seller does not want to live with the hazards inflicted on it by the breach-date rule it could purchase a futures contract to shift its risk away from English pounds and back into francs[18]—a point Lord Denning had made in the course of defending the breach-date rule in *Havana Railways*.[19] In fact for all we know the plaintiff seller in *Miliangos* did exactly this; it had originally pleaded its claim in sterling and surely would have known about the breach-date rule. Before *Miliangos* that rule was both widely-known and uniformly applied; its initial effects in terms of risk distribution, whatever we might think of their fairness, were both obvious and easily dodged. Moreover, proper hedging by a claimant could not only escape the risks that the forum-currency/breach-date rule subjects it to, but, if the claimant so preferred, substitute the risks associated with the payment-date rule. That is, it could without great effort achieve a result that replicated that which would follow from *Miliangos*.

[18] Alternatively it might simply do the following: on the date that it was supposed to receive payment of Swiss francs from the defendant it could borrow from a bank the number of pounds sterling required to purchase those francs on that day. It could then turn around and exchange those pounds for francs. When it was successful in collecting its pounds from the defendant then, at least provided interest was awarded at a commercially reasonable rate, it should have sufficient sterling to pay off that loan. Of course this would not permit the creditor to avoid all risk. It would merely be exchanging the risks associated with fluctuation of pounds sterling for those associated with fluctuations of the Swiss franc. That, however, was the risk it contracted for. In addition, it is worth noting that the negative effects of the breach-date rule may have been taken into account in the terms of the original bargain struck by the parties. That is, a seller like the plaintiff in *Miliangos* may well have charged a higher price for its goods because it knew at the time of contracting that if it had to sue in England to recover the price it would be subjected to the breach-date rule.

[19] Above n 2, 1070. Lord Reid made the same point at 1051.

It is important not to forget that *any* rule on the currency of judgment, even *Miliangos*'s new payment-date rule, subjects claimants to some financial perils.[20] Just as there is no risk-free form in which to retain one's wealth, there is no commodity in which compensation can be awarded that does not carry with it the hazard that its value vis-a-vis other commodities will decline over the course of litigation—and of course also the chance that it will rise. However, a firm conversion-date rule like the breach-date rule does tell civil litigants what risks they are running.

To all of that it may be objected that we should not trivialise the effort required to acquire knowledge of the operative standard affecting the currency of judgment and then take steps to avoid the negative consequences of that rule's operation. With respect to the former, however—the costs of acquiring the knowledge of which risks are imposed on litigants by the operative remedial rules of the forum in which they have chosen to litigate—there will always be costs to plaintiffs (and defendants too, for that matter) in finding out what that rule is. That is, whether the rule on foreign currency involves a breach-date or a payment-date conversion, plaintiffs who are unfamiliar with the rules will incur the bother of discovering them.

At various points in this book we will encounter courts and commentators asserting that one of a variety of conversion dates—that of breach, of judgment, or of the losing party's eventual payment of the judgment debt—fulfills the goal of accurate compensation. (*Miliangos*, for instance, made this claim for payment-date conversion.) In light of the foregoing it might be said that they are all wrong, or all right. Any conversion date a court picks will necessarily impose on claimants some risk they would not have had to run had the defendant not breached its obligation. To that extent they all deviate at least a little from exact compensation. Still, so does a judgment for debt or an award of damages in a purely domestic case. To the extent that a claimant has to accept money in recompense for some other obligation or wait until the outcome of litigation before it can collect its debt it will be subject to possible outcomes, upside and downside, it had not initially agreed to run—and necessarily so, since no court can turn the clock back and make it as if the obligation had never been breached. Any sort of judicial compensation places on claimants the risk that the commodity used to effect that compensation will fluctuate in value during the course of settling the grievance. Despite these deviations from perfect compensation, however, sublunary analysts are commonly content to describe these rules as fulfilling the compensation principle. We do not regard such rules as particularly unjust to claimants since when they can identify in advance the metric by which compensation will be meted out then if they do not care to run the accompanying risks they can take steps to alter them. In any event it is the best we can do to set things right, and despite

[20] Courts often fail to note this. For a judgment that does see *The Amoco Cadiz*, 954 F 2d 1279 (7th Cir 1992) 1329.

the risks and costs it inevitably inflicts on claimants we are prepared to call it fair compensation.

In this respect, although it may be no more than a convention to call our accepted approach to damages fair compensation, any conversion date from the time of breach to the day of ultimate payment might fairly be said to accord with the compensation principle. So those, like Megarry J for instance, who claim that breach-date conversion instantiates the compensation principle, are on defensible ground.[21] However, so are those, like Lord Wilberforce in *Miliangos*, who make the same claim for payment-date conversion, and similarly those who make the claim for a judgment-date conversion.[22] Such claims are incomplete only insofar as they imply, as they typically do, that other candidate conversion dates do *not* accord with the goal of accurate compensation. They are misleading only when (as *Miliangos* did) they point out and disparage the fluctuation risks that *other* conversion dates entail for plaintiffs, while at the same time omitting to acknowledge that their own preferred solution inevitably inflicts hazards too, even if they are different ones. The resolution of the currency-of-judgment problem cannot be achieved by doing no more than pointing to a given conversion date, noting that it satisfies the compensation standard and claiming the matter is therefore settled—since other dates satisfy the standard too. More nuanced inquiries are required.

When the operative rule is breach-date conversion, this still leaves plaintiffs who do not wish to chance that risk with the cost of taking steps to avoid it. The fact that the contract in *Miliangos* stipulated payment in Swiss francs indicated that, in terms of the perils of currency fluctuation after the completion of the contract, most likely the seller was content to chance the possibilities, at least until the time stipulated for contractual payment, of the franc's rise or fall.[23] So requiring it to hedge against a drop in sterling would thus likely involve making it take steps it was not otherwise planning to make. However, while we should not underrate the effort required to (1) appreciate the need to hedge against sterling's fall and (2) do so, it nevertheless bears noting that this effort is no greater—indeed no different—from what is required of the non-breaching party in a purely domestic contract dispute involving non-delivery of goods or non-performance of services. There the general rule of contract damages stipulates that the wrongfully withheld performance is evaluated, in the currency of the forum, as of the date of breach. So the innocent party, if it does not wish to suffer the ill consequences of the fall of the forum currency vis-a-vis the contracted-for performance, is in effect required to purchase substitute performance at the date of breach. When we return to reconsider the position of the foreign-currency creditor it might seem, then, that the unfairness, if indeed there was any, of the old breach-date rule was simply to

[21] *Hawkins v Hawkins* [1972] 1 Ch 714 (Ch D) 720.

[22] For example the British Columbia Supreme Court in *Banque Indosuez v Canadian Overseas Airlines Ltd* (1990) 40 CPC (2d) 33 (BCSC) 35, aff'd on appeal. Its reasoning on this point was approved in *Albionex (Overseas) Ltd v Conagra Ltd* 2009 MBQB 200.

[23] SA Rea, 'Inflation and the Law of Contracts and Torts' (1982) 14 *Ottawa Law Review* 465, 474.

treat foreign currency creditors the same way the law of damages treats domestic (indeed all) buyers of goods or services.[24]

Of course in this respect the old breach-date rule still treated foreign currency creditors differently, and arguably worse, than it did creditors whose claims were in sterling. This latter group did not need not mitigate in this sense at all. They had bargained for sterling (and the attendant risks of that currency's rise or fall pending payment), and for the duration of their claim the law preserved that risk. However, it is important to observe that even such entirely domestic creditors may only have planned to run the risks of fluctuations in sterling up to the time they were entitled to be paid. These creditors for domestic currencies might well have counted on using the money they were entitled to receive to purchase some other commodity. Just because someone bargains to accept payment in pounds does not mean they will preserve those pounds for years; they might spend them. When they are not paid in a timely fashion then they may have to borrow money with which to acquire that commodity, since normally (at least in the absence of special circumstances) they would not be able to claim for their losses flowing from not acquiring that commodity. In short, in practical terms even domestic creditors—that is, creditors in entirely domestic cases, cases with no foreign currency element—who are not timeously paid may find that the remedies the common law standardly provides subject them to fluctuation risks they had not planned to run. If they want to avoid those risks they will have to take positive steps to do so. (Likewise, even under the *Miliangos* payment-date rule, unpaid creditors in foreign currencies are not *necessarily* relieved from the obligation to make risk-shifting moves, since they too may have intended to use the bargained-for payment to acquire some other commodity.)[25]

So compensation, as it is effected through the standard judicial remedies for unpaid debts and breach of contract is a rough concept indeed. Creditors are made whole but litigation takes time, and during that time they are also subjected to risks they had not bargained for. The law does not cushion them against all

[24] There is a passage in *Miliangos* where Lord Wilberforce suggests that the foreign creditor would find this situation more burdensome than a domestic party would. In the course of explaining why he would confine the ruling in that case to actions in debt, and leave the case of damages for another day, he noted that damages cases raised issues not raised by debt claims, especially as regards mitigation: 'Whereas in the case of the inevitable contract to supply a foreign cow, the intending purchaser has to be treated as going into the market to buy one at the date of breach, this doctrine cannot be applied to a foreign money obligation, for the intending creditor has nothing to buy his own currency with—except his own currency', (468). This seems flatly wrong: parties may find it difficult to acquire substitute performance if they are impecunious, but for a solvent party and a fungible commodity the difficulties of acquiring substitute performance do not vary with respect to the foreignness or otherwise of the commodity contracted for.

[25] To expand, a creditor in the position of Miliangos might have planned to use the Swiss francs in which the price of the goods was to be paid to acquire some new commodity, more raw materials for instance. The payment-date rule which emerges from *Miliangos* does not effectively relieve that creditor from the need to acquire (for instance by borrowing) more Swiss francs to exchange for those raw materials during the pendency of the litigation. The more one picks at the threads of *Miliangos* the more the skein unravels.

those risks. Rather, it gives them information about what the risks are and leaves them to their own devices as to whether they want to take steps to substitute different risks.

On the analysis thus far, it is less than obvious how *Miliangos*'s shift from the forum-currency/breach-date rule to a payment-date rule amounts to a great leap forward. All it does is to alter the nature of the risks that foreign-currency creditors must run during litigation. True, in most (but not all) cases the fluctuation risks that the payment-date rule imposes on creditors will be more to their liking than will the risks following from the breach-date rule. So a payment-date rule is less likely than a breach-date rule to put foreign currency creditors to the bother of taking steps to avoid those risks and substitute the ones they prefer. To the extent this new distribution of risks seems fairer in that it effectively treats creditors for foreign currency obligations just as the law treats creditors for local money obligations, it seems like a step in the right direction. However, it is a small step—hardly the move from gross injustice to perfect fairness that it might appear to be at first glance, and that Lord Wilberforce implied it was. Like some other revolutions, the *Miliangos* one may not have amounted to quite the transformation that its proponents claimed it was.

Shortly I will offer another reason why the *Miliangos* payment-date rule operates as an improvement over the old law.[26] It is helpful first to point to another consequence arising from that new rule: reduced uncertainty, at least in some cases. Under the forum-currency/breach-date rule, parties at least knew for sure what the currency of judgment would be: it would be the national money of the forum. Any obligations that might be thought to be initially expressed in other currencies, or most justly compensated by an award in some other currency, would—just like obligations to deliver commodities or services—effectively be converted to the money of the forum on a date which would, in almost all cases, be ascertainable in advance by both parties will little doubt—the date of breach. As we have seen, the rule might be sub-optimal in what it required claimants to do by way of guarding against fluctuation risks during litigation, but any such unfairness was not great.

In actions brought to collect a debt, like *Miliangos*, the new payment-date rule gives rise to no diminution of that certitude. In such claims there will almost never be doubt as to what the money of the debt is, and that money becomes the currency of judgment for the plaintiff's claim. In debt actions the parties can have as much confidence in what the currency of judgment will be as they did under the old breach-date rule; the accuracy of the information about what risks they are running during the course of litigation and the subsequent collection process is not attenuated.

[26] A reason not offered by any of their Lordships in *Miliangos*. It is an admittedly quirky feature of my analysis that I think the best reason for adopting the rule in that case is one that was not advanced by any members of the court.

As the last chapter showed, however, *Miliangos* was not the end of the story. The *Miliangos* approach of permitting courts in debt claims to order judgment in a foreign currency was within a couple of years extended with almost no hesitation to actions in damages. Courts thought that to confine *Miliangos* to debt claims would be to betray its modernising spirit. In damages claims, however, the payment-date rule operates quite differently from the way it did in debt cases. In damages claims, permitting a court to deliver judgment in a foreign currency does not, as in debt claims, tell the claimant that provided that it is successful it will get the performance it contracted for. When damages are awarded to a plaintiff who did not receive some contracted-for goods or services, or whose person or property was tortiously injured, that plaintiff is still required to accept money in substitution for the violated right. Accordingly such a plaintiff will still normally be expected to mitigate by purchasing substitute performance. At least it will generally treated as if it did so. In that sense, and unlike the situation with the switch to a payment-date rule in debt claims, the developments in cases such as *The Folias* and *The Despina R* do not have the effect of lessening the likelihood that the plaintiff will want to take steps during litigation to alter the fluctuation risks thrown upon it by such litigation. The nature of damages as a substitutionary remedy, in combination with the duty to mitigate, effectively subjects all plaintiffs to currency-fluctuation risks that they did not bargain for, even plaintiffs in entirely domestic cases. The only difference arising from *Miliangos* and the post-*Miliangos* development is that the money offered as compensatory substitution for the violated right is not necessarily that of the forum.

The problem is, of course, that in the wake of the post-*Miliangos* cases there is now, at least in some instances, doubt about what the currency of judgment will be.[27] In cases of contract damages (as in *The Folias*) or tort (as in *The Despina R*) the new feeling-the-loss rule offers substantially less certainty than did the old breach-date one. Litigants are effectively told that, if the claimant is successful in establishing its claim the remedy will be the value of the violated right in money—but they are not necessarily provided with information to let them know *which* money. That is a question may not be resolved until the date of judgment when the judge arrives at a decision as to the currency in which the claimant will be regarded as having felt its loss. To the extent that there is indecision about which metric a court will select for the currency of judgment—the money of account, the money the claimant expended to cure the breach, the money in which transactions in the underlying commodity are normally carried out, the money in which the claimant normally operates, and so on—neither the claimant

[27] One of the handful of commentaries to identify this new uncertainty as a problem with the *Miliangos* revolution is RA Bowles and CJ Whelan, 'Judicial Responses to Exchange Rate Instability', in Burrows, P and Veljanovski CG (eds), *The Economic Approach to Law* (London, Butterworths, 1981) 253, 265. The same two authors had previously made the point in a short comment on *The Folias* and *The Despina R*: 'Judgments in Foreign Currencies: Extension of the *Miliangos* Rule' (1979) 42 *MLR* 452, 457. They reiterated it in 'Exchange Rate Instability and the Law' (1983) 133 *New Law Journal* 28: 'the new rules give rise to an uncertainty that was previously absent'.

nor the defendant has information to enable it to avoid with certainty the risks of fluctuation in the currency of judgment. So, to the extent that it is useful that the law on the assessment of damages provides litigants with unambiguous information about which money will be awarded in substitution for the right violated by the defendant then, at least to the extent there is doubt about what the currency of judgment will be, the new rule is not an improvement.[28] In this respect the can of worms prised open by the House of Lords in *Miliangos* is a little bigger than it is sometimes acknowledged to be. Of course certainty is not the only goal of the law of damages. There are aspects of that law—the foreseeability requirement for instance—that in the service of other principles introduce elements of uncertainty that can make it difficult for parties to predict in advance the amount of damages that will be awarded as compensation for a given wrong. Possibly the most we can say is that it would be a bad idea to introduce uncertainty into the law of damages without some good reason.

On the analysis so far it seems like the question of whether *Miliangos* brought about improved fidelity to the compensation principle depends on whether one regards the greater fairness of the mildly plaintiff-favouring redistributed risks of currency fluctuation during litigation as being worth the price of the increased uncertainty imposed, at least in some cases, on both parties as to what the currency of judgment will be. Persons might differ in their assessments of this. While certainly is no doubt one goal of the law of damages it is hardly the only one, as the rules regarding remoteness illustrate. Those turn on whether a given loss is to be judged reasonably foreseeable, and that is a matter which may easily remain in doubt until judgment is granted.

However, there are other factors we have not yet taken into account. In particular, it is necessary to revisit the claim made above that the old breach-date rule provided the parties with a high level of certainty as to what the currency of judgment will be. Looked at from the point of view of a single jurisdiction the forum-currency/breach-date rule undoubtedly had the virtue of certainty on this question. Parties knew from the outset which currency would be used to effect compensation and which conversion date would be employed. In some cases, however, there is more than one jurisdiction in play. Because of the way that rules of court jurisdiction are structured, in some disputes there may be two or more places where the non-breaching party might bring an action for compensation. When each of those potential fora applies the breach-date rule there is no certainty about the currency of judgment—at least in the time between breach and the time when the ultimate forum is selected. For example, if both England and New York apply the forum-currency/breach-date rule, and if a claimant can

[28] Moreover, in addition to the reduction in certainty there are the added costs, court time and (sometimes) appeals that must, at least in some cases, be devoted to arguing over and selecting the currency of judgment. This is not to suggest that the state of affairs that existed in English courts before *Miliangos*, *The Despina R* and *The Folias* was any prelapsarian Eden, only that something was lost with the switch to the payment-date rule.

bring its action in either of those two places, then at least for a period following the accrual of the cause of action there will be uncertainty as to what the currency of judgment will be. Moreover, this is an uncertainty which systematically operates to the advantage of the claimant creditor, since it is generally that party which has the choice of forum. That is, where there are two national courts available, each of which applies a breach-date conversion from foreign currencies to that of the forum, then between the time of breach and the time when the creditor must commence its action the creditor has the beneficial option of selecting the forum whose currency has done the best during that period.[29]

There is a second way in which the existence of multiple fora may operate in combination with the forum-currency/breach-date rule to produce unfairness to defendants. Consider *Competex SA v Labow*.[30] There the creditor obtained a sterling judgment in England and promptly sued on it in the United States. A court in New York recognised the English decision and accordingly gave judgment for the creditor. However, since the American court applied the breach-date rule it converted the pounds of the original English judgment to American dollars as of the date of the English judgment.[31] The debtor then satisfied the judgment in England by payment in pounds sterling. By this time, however, the pound had fallen vis-a-vis the dollar and the creditor sought to enforce the now more valuable judgment in the US, in US dollars. The American court permitted this, and although it was prepared to give credit for the sterling payment at the then prevailing rate of exchange, it still held that the creditor was able to collect the remaining portion in US dollars.

Note that, like the circumstances just discussed where the plaintiff has the choice of more than one forum in which to bring its original action, here the breach-date rule operates as a sort of one-way street for the creditor: if the pound appreciates as against the dollar the creditor can enforce in England in sterling. But if the pound falls and the dollar rises then the creditor can enforce in the US. In effect there are two breach dates: the original forum considers the initial failure to perform the substantive obligation as the date of breach; the enforcing court considers the first court's judgment to be the date of breach. In some cases, though obviously not all, the plaintiff may be in a position to take its pick.[32]

[29] Of course this does not mean that this currency will come out on top at the end of the day, when payment is made. But if it is the currency that has been the strongest in the interval between breach and commencing the action then in most cases it will end up being the currency that is strongest in the period between breach and ultimate payment. In effect, it has a head start on the others. It will not necessarily win the race, but other things being equal it is the one to bet on.

[30] *Competex SA v Labow* 783 F 2d 333 (2d Cir 1986) (*Competex*). For negative commentary on the decision along the lines I pursue in the text see M Leigh, Case Comment (1986) 80 *American Journal of International Law* 1958; F Leary & M Casey, 'Fluctuating Currencies: Obligations Payable in Foreign Moneys' (1988) 60(1) *New York State Bar Journal* 16, 18–19.

[31] The first-instance judgment is reported at 613 F Supp 332 (SDNY 1985).

[32] A similar, though not identical, English decision, with Canada as the original forum, is *Yorkshire Insurance Co v Nisbet Shipping Co* [1962] 2 QB 330 (QB); and in the Ghanaian case of *Broderick v Northern Engineering Product* [1991] 2 GLR 88 (HC) the court took note of a comparable problem.

A payment-date rule avoids all of this. In cases where there is more than one national forum where a claimant can launch its original action, if both of them apply the *Miliangos* payment-date rule then the currency of judgment will be the same, regardless of where the suit is brought. In the judgment-enforcement illustrated by *Competex* the English judgment would remain an obligation in sterling, even when converted to a US court judgment, so payment in pounds, regardless of which country it was made in, would satisfy both judgments. Both of these situations illustrate limitations on the claim that the old breach-date rule provided for certainty and show how, at least in some cases, the new payment-date rule eliminates some uncertainties.

It may be helpful to pause again to sum up the pros and cons of the contending rules on the analysis so far. From the point of view of accuracy of compensation, the advantages of a payment-date rule are not, as is sometimes suggested, that during litigation it invariably avoids subjecting a plaintiff to a currency fluctuation risk that the plaintiff never bargained for. Rather the payment-date rule's virtue is simply that it diminishes the number of cases in which such a foreign-currency creditor will during litigation be subjected to a currency-fluctuation different from that it bargained for. Consequently it reduces the situations in which those creditors will want to enter into transactions to hedge those risks. It is thus fairer to claimants and no less fair to defendants. Bolstering this is that fact that reduction brings those risks into line with those that a creditor in domestic currency is typically forced to confront, so foreign creditors are treated the same as domestic ones. To this can now be added the increased fairness (due to increased certainty) to defendants in multi-forum cases, where in effect the old breach date rule gave some creditors the advantage of selecting their currency of judgment in light of post-breach fluctuations.[33]

Against these two advantages, however, must be weighed the uncertainties inflicted on both plaintiffs and defendants in cases where the remedy is not an award for payment of a debt but rather damages. There it is less obvious that the payment-date rule lessens the plaintiff's incentives to take steps during mitigation to alter the fluctuation risks that litigation forces on it. Of course, in this regard the payment-date rule does not make the plaintiff worse off; it simply does not amount to an improvement. There is, however, the added problem that, at least in some cases, neither the plaintiff nor the defendant knows until judgment what the currency of judgment will be. Both sides to litigation are deprived of the information they would need in order to assess and, if they so wished, alter litigation's currency fluctuation risks. This was information that the pre-*Miliangos* breach-date rule provided with some degree of certainty. To the extent that courts will

[33] It is noteworthy that in *Miliangos* the House of Lords never considers the claim that one advantage of the new payment-date rule it adopted in that case was increased fairness to *defendants*. *Miliangos* is invariably regarded as a legal change brought about to provide better justice to claimants. Yet, if the arguments about the multi-forum and judgment-enforcement (*Competex*) situations are sound then one advantage of the payment-date rule is increased fairness to defendants, at least in actions in debt.

side with plaintiffs in their choice of the currency of judgment then plaintiffs may not object to this new measure of uncertainty, though defendants certainly will.[34] To the extent, however, that plaintiffs will not invariably have their way with the currency of judgment—as in *The Texaco Melbourne*—the increased uncertainty will be welcome to no litigants.

Although none of the above resolves the currency-of-judgment question it should at least provide the basis for suspicion of arguments that some courts have, perhaps too facilely, relied on. It may additionally provide some basis for pointing out advantages and disadvantages of judicial decisions, statutes and multilateral conventions we will encounter in the next three chapters.

II. Foreign-Exchange Losses

What about so-called claims for foreign-exchange losses—creditors' arguments that they should be made whole for losses traceable to the fact that late- or non-payment of a debt[35] in one currency has deprived them of the chance to convert that currency into another, which has since appreciated? As noted, there are affinities between such claims and the currency-of-judgment question. The most obvious is that the currency-of-judgment and the foreign-exchange loss questions are both matters of damages assessment and involve foreign money. This association is reinforced by that fact that, at least until relatively recently, in each instance the governing rule was one that could easily be castigated as archaic and unresponsive to the purportedly new realities of daily currency fluctuation. In the case of the currency-of-judgment question the doctrine in question was the pre-*Miliangos* forum-currency/breach-date standard. As we have seen, that rule was seen to be out of touch with the new financial realities of the post-Bretton Woods era. In the case of foreign-exchange losses the old rule was that which came from the nineteenth-century House of Lords case *London, Chatham and Dover Railway v South Eastern Railway*.[36] That rule stipulated there could be no damages for late

[34] Recall the cases discussed at pp 42–47.

[35] Nearly all the cases involving claims for foreign-exchange losses arise from late- or non-payment of a debt. However, such claims could also arise in cases where the breached obligation is not for payment of money but for the delivery of some other commodity. By way of example, in the next chapter we will encounter a decision of the Queensland Court of Appeal where the claimant argues that the defendant's late delivery of cattle deprived it of the opportunity to turn around and sell those cattle and consequently that he has lost an anticipated profit for which he seeks damages. That is a common enough sort of claim, but in this case the claimant adds the twist that, had the contracted-for cattle been delivered on time, he would have turned around and sold them for a given *foreign* currency—one which during litigation turns out to have appreciated against the Australian dollar: *State of Queensland v Northaus Trading Co* (unreported 13 August 1999) Appeal No 6299 of 1998. The plaintiff's claim for additional compensation in the amount of that fluctuation is one for foreign-exchange loss, but not one arising from a debt claim.

[36] *London, Chatham and Dover Railway v South Eastern Railway* [1893] AC 429 (HL) (*Dover Railway*). See the discussion in ch 1 at pp 58–66. One thing that made this rule appear particularly

payment of a debt. By the 1970s each of these doctrines had come to seem antiquated, and they were further linked by the fact that both seemed to favour debtors over creditors by producing awards which were likely to be undercompensatory.

There is yet a further affinity between the two questions. In a given piece of litigation the same result—as measured by the exchange value of the ultimate award—can often be arrived at under either rule. Sometimes a court feels it cannot do justice to a plaintiff because the rules governing the currency in which damages must be awarded do not permit it to grant a remedy in the money it would like. A court in that position may be able to arrive at the result it prefers by first granting its award in the money it feels compelled to employ and then awarding additional compensation under the heading foreign-exchange losses.[37]

Given all these points of contact, it was not surprising that the perceived pro-plaintiff revolution in *Miliangos* would end up influencing doctrinal development on the question of foreign-exchange losses. We saw at the end of the last chapter that in England this did occur: some post-*Miliangos* courts relied on *Miliangos* to justify shifting the rules on exchange-loss damages in a plaintiff-favouring direction.[38] We will see in the next chapter that courts in some Commonwealth countries have done the same, and in the chapter after that we will see that there are connections in the United States as well.

However, these similarities may just be superficial features that mask deep-seated differences between exchange-loss damages and the currency-of-judgment question. While both deal with compensation—with ascertaining a sum of money that will put a claimant in the position it would have occupied had an agreement had not been breached—claims for foreign-exchange losses involve *consequential* losses, and that entails an inquiry not present in the currency-of-judgment question. Exchange-loss claims require an investigation into what a plaintiff *would have done* subsequent to contractual performance had the contract been performed. In addition to this counterfactual speculation about causation—did the breach really disable the plaintiff from following a given course of action?—exchange-loss claims further require a judgment about whether that loss, if it existed, was within the scope of the risk that it is fair to impose on the defendant.

In addition to the links between the currency-of-judgment problem and the question of exchange-loss damages there is an obvious need for the latter to be

antiquated was that, as originally articulated, it even barred claims for interest to compensate for late payment of a debt, and that seemed to have a consistently under-compensatory effect. The interest question had been taken care of by statute, but that aspect of the *Dover Railway* ruling continued to taint it and render it suspect to modern eyes.

[37] See ch 1 at pp 62–66.

[38] Above, ch 1 at pp 62–66. Admittedly it is difficult to gauge the precise effect of *Miliangos* here. This is so because at the same time that its impact was being felt in the foreign-exchange loss cases the courts were abandoning some of the rigid pro-defendant rules that had been in place for certain types of consequential losses and saying that such claims should just be assessed under the general rules governing foreseeability and remoteness.

consistent with the general law on consequential damages. That is, there is a close connection between a case where a claimant says (1) had I been paid on time I would have taken that payment and converted it into euros, and one where the claimant says (2) had I been paid on time I would have taken that payment and bought land with it. Unless some reason could be found for treating currency differently from all other commodities then any difference in treatment between those two cases would be unjustifiable. As Charles Rickett noted in commenting on a decision where a court, relying on *Miliangos*, had awarded exchange-loss damages, 'why stop at exchange losses?'[39] We could always imagine a disappointed creditor in a debt case arguing that had the contracted for money been paid on time she would promptly have converted it not into foreign currency but into some other commodity, and that her losses should be measured by reference to that other form of wealth.[40] A problem, therefore, with associating exchange-loss claims too closely with the currency-of-judgment question is that this threatens to drive a wedge between exchange loss cases and cases where the debtor wants compensation for harm allegedly flowing from not being able to acquire some commodity other than money.

An obvious difficulty with accepting arguments for consequential losses flowing from late payment of a debt (and a justification for the *Dover Railway* rule), is that they give an unjustified advantage to plaintiffs. Allowing such claims to prevail does not seem evenhanded, since unpaid debtors will advance them only where the commodity into which they say they would have converted the contractual benefit has increased in value in comparison with the original benefit in the post-breach period. Where the situation is otherwise—where the commodity they would have acquired with the money they were to have been paid has fallen in value—plaintiffs will keep quiet and seek damages measured by reference solely to the original debt. Such a one-way result seems antithetical to general principles of damages law in that it effectively permits claimants to exercise risk-free speculation at defendants' expense: if the currency or commodity into which they would have converted the contracted-for currency goes up then they will claim for the resulting loss, but if it goes down they will remain silent.

Of course, one might temper the consequences of such a course of action by allowing defaulting debtors to maintain that if they had paid on time the plaintiff would have converted the contractual obligation into the now devalued commodity, and that damages should be assessed by reference to that commodity. Put another way, it could permit defendant non-paying debtors to contend that judgments against them should not be for the full amount of the original debt, since had they paid the creditor would promptly have turned around and made a losing

[39] CEF Rickett, 'Contract Damages for Exchange Losses—a New Zealand Development' [1982] *Lloyd's Maritime and Commercial Law Quarterly* 566, 571.

[40] In fact such arguments need not be limited to claims for breach of contract. A plaintiff who had a tort claim for destruction of its property might easily contend that, had the property not been destroyed, she would soon thereafter have exchanged it for some other resource—one which has subsequently grown in value at a rate greater than the destroyed property.

investment with that money. The debtors' late (or non-) payment has saved the creditor from the consequences of that bad investment so the principle of compensation requires that the savings are taken into account by, in effect, deducting them from what would otherwise be a judgment in the amount of the original debt. It might be thought that if we allowed debtors to prevail in such arguments there would be symmetry with allowing a plaintiff's claim for foreign exchange losses, and the law on this point could be regarded as fairly balanced between the two parties to a debt: plaintiff creditors could claim consequential damages for foreign-exchange gains the debtor's default made them unable to realise, and in appropriate cases defendant debtors will not have to pay the full amount of the debt because their earlier default turns out to have kept their creditor from entering into a losing investment.

There are problems with this, however. While there are instances of creditors claiming exchange-loss damages the reported cases do not reveal defendant debtors making claims like those described in the previous paragraph. This is hardly surprising. Defendant debtors will only rarely have access to the sort of information on which such a claim might be based. At least they will lack the means to offer convincing proof on the point. Even if we acknowledge that, in theory, defendants should be able to assert a defence based on the argument that their late payment preserved their creditor from an unwise use of the money that should have been paid, such defences will almost never succeed. So recognising plaintiffs' claims for foreign-exchange losses seems inevitably to produce a situation where, in effect, unpaid creditors can engage in what amounts to risk-free speculation at the expense of their debtors.

A further basis for judicial wariness of granting claims for foreign-exchange losses, and yet another justification of the *Dover Railways* rule insofar as it applied to such claims, is that they run counter to the general principle that plaintiffs should not be compensated for losses they should be expected to have avoided by means of reasonable, post-breach mitigative behaviour. Where the breached obligation was one to have paid a given sum of money on a given date, normally an unpaid creditor would be expected to acquire the equivalent sum elsewhere, perhaps by borrowing it, and use that money to avert any consequential losses flowing from the breach. This should never have stood in the way of claims for pre-judgment interest, which explains why that aspect of the *Dover Railway* rule has been over-ruled. However, it should apply to claims for foreign-exchange losses. That does not mean that such claims should never be awarded, only that before they are granted some reason should be found for excusing the plaintiff from the obligation to mitigate in that case—impecuniosity, for instance.[41]

Despite these differences between the currency-of-judgment question and exchange loss claims, the previously-mentioned affinities between such claims have sometimes prevailed. The result, as we have seen in the last chapter and

[41] Impecuniosity, or at least the plaintiff's inability to come up with the required mitigating resources in the short time available to it, explains the exception to the *Dover Railway* rule created by the Court of Appeal in *Trans Trust SPRL v Danubian Trading Co* [1952] 2 QB 297 (CA), mentioned in ch 1 at pp 61–62.

will see again in later ones, is that judges have on occasion treated developments on the currency-of-judgment front—*Miliangos* in particular—as support for acceding to a plaintiff's demands for compensation for foreign-exchange losses. In some cases it is understandable that this should be so. Claims for this sort of consequential loss can on occasion seem especially strong. With currencies we can sometimes have a high degree of confidence in a claimant's argument that, had it been paid on time, it would have converted the payment into another currency. For instance, some legal rule might require contracting parties to deal in a given currency, but there may be clear evidence that the plaintiff does not otherwise retain its wealth in that money. In such circumstances it is easy to believe a plaintiff creditor who claims that had it received the contracted-for payment it would immediately have converted that money into its home currency. Even in the absence of such legal requirements to deal in a given money there may be situations where all trading in a certain commodity takes place in a given currency, but where the plaintiff can show that while it uses that currency for such trading it does not otherwise keep any of its wealth in that money, and moreover that the defendant knows that. In situations where we credit the plaintiff's assertion that, had it been paid it would have exchanged that payment for some other given currency, claims for losses in the amount of forgone gains from that currency's appreciation seem especially appealing.

However courts' historical reluctance to grant exchange-loss damages is also understandable.[42] Because they are a type of consequential loss, claims for exchange-loss damages are analytically distinct from the currency-of-judgment question. They raise issues of causation, foreseeability[43] and mitigation that currency-of-judgment disputes do not present and they have a strong claim to be treated in the same way that other claims for consequential loss are treated—namely, with a scrutiny informed by a concern to see that the loss in question, if proven, is within the scope of a risk fairly imposed on the defendant. The fact that in a given case the granting of exchange-loss damages may operate to generate a result that is financially identical to selecting a given currency as one in which to render damages does not render the two questions identical. In particular, it does not mean that switching the currency-of-judgment rule from a breach-date conversion to a payment-date conversion, as *Miliangos* did, entails any adjustment to the handling of the exchange-loss problem.

[42] Of course for more than a century that reluctance did not have to be articulated in the terms I have set out. It was a consequence of the broader *Dover Railways* ban on damages for late payment of a debt.

[43] In the words of Djakhongir Saidov, discussing this sort of claim in *The Law of Damages in International Sales* (Oxford, Hart Publishing, 2008) 254: 'The foreseeability rule is of particular importance here and in awarding damages, judges and arbitrators need to ensure that the breaching party foresaw or was in a position to foresee that the injured party would exchange its domestic currency for a foreign one and this may often not be the case'.

3

The Commonwealth

We are engaged in settling the law upon a question in which any rule is artificial and to some extent arbitrary.

Viscount Simonds[1]

When *Miliangos* appeared in 1975 the forum-currency/breach-date rule was firmly ensconced throughout the Commonwealth. At least this was so in those jurisdictions that had any decisional law on the currency-of-judgment question. Prior to *Miliangos* there does not appear to be any significant record of Commonwealth courts adopting a practice of awarding damages in anything other than their own national currency, at least in the twentieth century. A couple of departures from breach-date conversion can be found, but they are so few and far between that we may regard them as anomalies.[2] Moreover, in the pre-*Miliangos* period there appears to be little evidence of chafing at the forum-currency/breach-date rule, at least nothing corresponding with Lord Denning's activity in the English Court of Appeal[3] or the scholarly grumblings of Mann, Morris or Kahn-Freund. Within the Commonwealth legal system, the matter of foreign currency obligations is not one of those instances where legal change originated in the courts of the former colonies and then became adopted in the metropole. Rather, the shift, at least initially, was led by the commercially sophisticated courts in London.

Despite the absence of express displeasure with the pre-*Miliangos* situation in Commonwealth courts or academic writing, the change brought by the House of Lords judgment in *Miliangos* was warmly embraced throughout the Commonwealth legal system. As we will see repeatedly in this chapter, it was welcomed nearly without reservation by Commonwealth courts, scholars, law reform commissions and in some cases by legislative bodies. Any hesitation or refusal to implement the shift from a breach-date to a payment-date conversion has been attributable either to legislation which seemed to stand in the way of that development or the typical delays attendant on overruling or finding ways to distinguish old precedents.

[1] *Re United Railways of Havana and Regla Warehouses* [1961] AC 1007 (HL) 1048 (*Havana Railways*).

[2] In Canada there was *Quartier v Farah* (1921) 49 OLR 186, 64 DLR 37 (CA) (judgment-date conversion) and in Australia there was *Re Dawson* (1966) 2 NSWLR 211 (SC) (same).

[3] *The Teh Hu* [1970] P 106 (CA); *Jugoslavenska Oceanska Plovibda v Castle Investment Co* [1973] 3 WLR 847 (CA); *Schorsch Meier GmbH v Hennin* [1975] 1 QB 416 (CA).

This welcoming of *Miliangos* should come as no surprise. Many of the pre-*Miliangos* Commonwealth decisions implementing the forum-currency/breach-date rule had done so in express reliance on English decisions such as *The Volturno*[4] or *Havana Railways*[5]—authorities which had been rejected by *Miliangos*. That might not have been sufficient to bring about change in Commonwealth courts if *Miliangos* had been regarded as badly reasoned. But it was not. Rather, *Miliangos* was regarded by Commonwealth judges not only as authoritative but as being correctly decided and for the right reasons; it was read as revealing the unsuitable nature of the old rule in current conditions.

However, although the courts of Commonwealth countries were imitators rather than innovators when it came to abandoning the forum-currency/breach-date rule, an account of *Miliangos*'s reception in the Commonwealth reveals a variety of instructive sidelights on the matter of foreign currency obligations. Questions have arisen in Commonwealth courtrooms that have not yet presented themselves in English ones. In addition, there are instances where Commonwealth courts, operating with *Miliangos* in mind, appear to have forged ahead of their English counterparts. Finally, some Commonwealth courts appear to have grasped *Miliangos* in a manner quite contrary to the way it has been understood in England. In particular, the case and its English progeny have sometimes been read as paving the way for a flexible, case-by-case approach to the currency-of-judgment question, rather than as replacing one fixed rule with another. The result is that, although almost all Commonwealth courts purport to follow the English lead, they have sometimes implemented solutions to the currency-of-judgment problem which are in fact entirely different from that described in chapter one.

In some Commonwealth countries the volume of high-stakes commercial litigation is low and the currency-of-judgment question arises only infrequently. For instance, in the High Court of Barbados a foreign currency case arose just a year and a half after *Miliangos*. The High Court had little hesitation in rejecting the old *Havana Railways* approach and following the new *Miliangos* rule.[6] However, the case offers little discussion of the problem and since then little has happened on this front in the courts of that country. Much the same may be said about the first Bahamian appellate case to consider the question in the post-*Miliangos* era.[7] That was a contracts case and the appeal court affirmed that damages might be awarded in a foreign currency. It further followed the English lead on the question of whether pre-judgment interest should then be calculated with reference to local interest rates or those prevailing in the country in whose currency damages were chosen.[8] However, although there was much pertinent quotation from English

[4] *Celia (Owners) v SS Volturno (Owners)* [1921] 2 AC 544 (HL) (*The Volturno*).

[5] Above, n 1.

[6] *Sardinha v Johnson* (1977) 30 West Indian Reports 1 (High Ct Barbados).

[7] *Bayview Holdings Ltd v Kosinski* [1987] BHS J No 99, 1986 No 7. The Privy Council also declared the *Miliangos* approach to be the law of Trinidad and Tobago: *Trinidad Homes Developers Ltd v IMH Investments Ltd* [2003] UKPC 85.

[8] *Miliangos v George Frank (Textiles) Ltd (No 2)* [1977] 1 QB 489 (QB) (*Miliangos (No 2)*).

cases and texts, the court did not go beyond that. *Miliangos* was also welcomed in Papua New Guinea, and in 1992 the High Court of Guyana took the same approach, awarding judgment in US dollars, quoting from Lord Wilberforce's judgment in *Miliangos* and then saying, '[t]he learned Law Lord has expressed in eloquent language my own considered opinion on this aspect of the law, and in the circumstances the plaintiff is entitled to judgment [in US dollars]'.[9]

However, some Commonwealth courts that have claimed to follow *Miliangos* appear to have imperfectly grasped its holding. The Eastern Caribbean Supreme Court professed to follow *Miliangos* in a contract case, but appears to have misunderstood the House of Lords decision as holding that, while damages might be assessed in a foreign currency, they should be converted into the local currency at 'the due date, or the transaction date'.[10] This is a misreading of *Miliangos* we will encounter again. It is a remarkable one. *Miliangos* is famed for imposing a payment-date conversion. A problem might arise from the fact that 'payment-date' is potentially ambiguous: it might mean the date that a payment *should* have been made (under a contract, for instance), or it might mean the date that the judgment debtor eventually *does* pay the creditor. However that is a problem which disappears as soon as it is stated, for any reading of *Miliangos* that ventures beyond the headnote quickly dispels that ambiguity. After all, the former of those meanings—the date that payment should have been paid but was not—is just another way of describing the date of breach, and that was precisely the rule that was so comprehensively and emphatically rejected in *Miliangos*, so there is little excuse for this misinterpretation. Nevertheless, we will see other courts falling into it, as the Eastern Caribbean Supreme Court seems to have done when it claimed that *Miliangos*

> affirms, subject to the narrow exception, the 'long accepted and authoritatively reiterated rule' as stated *in Re United Railways of the [sic] Havana and Regla Warehouses Ltd* ... that a money judgment by an English court could only be given in sterling...[11]

There was no reference to subsequent expansion of the *Miliangos* decision by later English decisions such as *The Folias*.[12]

I. Africa

African courts should provide fertile ground for decisions on the currency-of-judgment question since in the post-*Miliangos* period many African countries

[9] *Martindale v Guyana National Co-operative Bank* [1992] GUY J No 1, 1117/91 (Guyana High Ct). The Papua New Guinea decision welcoming *Miliangos* was *Vevehupa v Motor Vehicles (PNG) Trust* [1983] PNGLR 343 (NCJ).

[10] *Dabreo v Dolland* (2000) ECSCJ No 55, Civil Suit No 81 of 1995 [11]. For Canadian examples of a comparable error see n 84 below.

[11] Ibid [7].

[12] There was a reference to *Barclays Bank International Ltd v Levin Brothers (Bradford) Ltd* [1977] 1 QB 270 (QB), but it involved a misunderstanding of what that case held.

have experienced more extreme currency fluctuation than England or the other major western trading nations have—commonly the steep decline of their national money against the hard-currencies of the west. Indeed in some instances this has given rise to the question whether, in assessing damages, courts should convert from the foreign to the national currency at the real rate or some unrealistic official rate imposed by government regulation.[13] That is a different question to that pursued here, which focuses on selecting among national currencies.[14]

The Supreme Court of Zimbabwe, although emphasising that it was not bound by English cases, readily followed *Miliangos*, which it declared to be an innovative decision that embodied 'a more realistic approach to modern economic conditions'.[15] The Supreme Court of Ghana did the same,[16] as did courts in Kenya,[17] Tanzania[18] and Nigeria.[19] The only impediment to full implementation of the payment-date rule in common law Africa would seem to be the persistence of a number of statutes dealing with enforcement of foreign court judgments. These statutes, which pre-date *Miliangos*, contain provisions requiring conversion into the money of the forum and do so in accordance with the breach-date rule, which in the judgment-enforcement situation is the date of the original judgment.[20]

[13] The courts of Zimbabwe have wrestled with this: for a decision adopting the real rate see *Meristem Investments (Pvt) Ltd v NMB Bank Ltd* [2002] ZWHHC 211, 2002 (2) ZLR 729, and for one using the official rate see *Echodelta Ltd v Kerr & Down Safaris (Pvt) Ltd* 2004 (1) SA 508 at 514 (HC Z), where the judge described the official rate as 'removed from reality' but felt constrained to apply it. For discussion of these cases see R Oppong, 'A Decade of Private International Law in African Courts 1997–2007 (Part I)' (2007) 9 *Yearbook of Private International Law* 223, 251–52. In addition, some African courts still have to wrestle with the effects of exchange-control legislation, as in *Takoradi Flour Mills v Samir Faris* [2005–2006] SCGLR 882. India has had this problem as well, and for discussion of its effect on the currency-of-judgment question see below at pp 136–37.

[14] American courts dealt with the problems arising from official rates of exchange which differed from the rates actually in effect in the market: see ch 4 at p 148.

[15] *Makwindi Oil Procurement (Pvt) Ltd v National Oil Co of Zimbabwe* 1988 (2) ZLR 482, 1989 (3) SA 191, [1989] LRC (Comm) 806 (SC Z), 813. This was followed by the Harare High Court in *Chiraga v Msimuko* 2002 (2) ZLR 368, 2004 (1) SA 98. In the remainder of this chapter I deal with separate jurisdictions—Scotland, Singapore, New Zealand and so on. Yet here I group all of Commonwealth Africa together, without distinguishing separate countries or even placing them in regional groups such as southern Africa, east Africa and west Africa. The explanation for this is the same one that caused me to deal so briefly with the Caribbean and Papua New Guinea: availability, or rather non-availability, of materials. For many of these countries I have found just one or two cases on point, perhaps because that is all there is or perhaps due to the fact that judgments can be difficult to access.

[16] *Royal Dutch Airlines (KLM) v Farmex Ltd (No2)* [1989–90] 2 GLR 623 (SC). This case also held that the applicable pre-judgment interest rate should be that of the currency in which judgment was awarded, and was approved on this point in *Butt v Chapel Hill Properties Ltd* [2003–2004] SCGLR 636 (SC) 668 and *National Investment Bank v Silver Peak Ltd* [2003–2004] SCGLR 1008 (SC) 1010.

[17] *Ingra v National Construction Corp* [1987] KLR 652 (HC); *Beluf Establishment v Attorney-General* (23 September 1993) Civil Appeal no 134 of 1986 (Kenya CA).

[18] *Transport Equipment Ltd v Valambhia* 1993 TLR 91 (CA); *Attorney General v Sisi Enterprises Ltd* [2005] TZCA 2.

[19] *Metronex Nigeria Ltd v Griffen & George Ltd* [1991] 1 NWLR 651 (HC); *Erik Emborg Export A/S v Jos International Breweries plc* [2003] 5 NWLR 505 (CA).

[20] Ghana: Courts Act 1996 Act 459, s 82(7); Uganda: Foreign Judgments (Reciprocal Enforcement) Act, 1991 c 9 s 3(2); Botswana: Judgments (International Enforcement) Act, 1981 c 11:04, s 5(5); Nigeria: Foreign Judgments (Reciprocal Enforcement) Act 1990, c F35 LFN, s 4(3); Zambia: Foreign Judgments (Reciprocal Enforcement) Act 1958, c 76, s 4(3); Namibia: Enforcement of Foreign Civil

In the wake of *Miliangos* there has been some judicial criticism of this rule, but to date legislative reforms have not been forthcoming.[21]

The African decisions embracing *Miliangos* have also taken note of the post-*Miliangos* developments in *The Despina R* and *The Folias* and have adopted the view that the currency of judgment should be the one that best expresses the plaintiff's loss. This means that, as in England, plaintiffs requesting judgment in a foreign currency do not invariably get their way.[22] However, a number of these cases seem to be good illustrations of the uncertainty that comes from the feeling-the-loss rule. In a critical assessment of the adoption of the *Miliangos* rule by Ghanaian courts one commentator rightly pointed out that the reasoning of the Supreme Court of Ghana on the currency point was not well supported by the English cases and demonstrated considerable 'lack of care and close examination of the legal issues'.[23] The court had awarded judgment for £23,800 on the basis of the plaintiff's claim that sterling was the currency of the contract, despite the fact, pointed out by the dissenting judge, that the documentary evidence showed that the currency of the contract was the plaintiff's home currency (cedis) and despite there being any factors which showed that the plaintiff had felt its loss in sterling.

As is the case with most other legal issues, the continent's richest body of case law on the currency-of-judgment question is that of South Africa, and while it too demonstrates the easy triumph of *Miliangos* it also features the most probing judicial expression of disagreement with the rule that emerged in England in

Judgments Act 1994, Act 28 of 1994, s 3(4); Tanzania: Foreign Judgments (Reciprocal Enforcement) Ordinance 1935, s 4(3). Here is the Botswana version: 'Where the sum payable under a judgment which is to be registered is expressed in a currency other than the currency of Botswana the judgment shall be registered as if it were a judgment for such sum in the currency of Botswana as, on the basis of the rate of exchange prevailing at the date of the judgment of the original court, is equivalent to the sum so payable'. Kenya has a differently worded statutory provision which uses permissive language: Foreign Judgments (Reciprocal Enforcement) Act 1984, c 43, s 7(1). However, the High Court has interpreted it as requiring conversion into Kenyan shillings at the date the foreign judgment is registered: *Ssebaggala & Sons Electric Centre Ltd v Kenya National Shipping Line Ltd* [2000] LLR 931 (HCK). For discussion see R Oppong, 'A Decade of Private International Law in African Courts 1997–2007 (Part II)' (2008) 10 *Yearbook of Private International Law* 367, 375–76.

[21] In *Broderick v Northern Engineering Product* [1991] 2 GLR 88 the High Court called for reform of the Ghanaian provision in force at that time (the Courts Act, 1971 (Act 372), s 77(5)) as giving rise to injustice. But when the legislation was updated giving rise to the provision quoted in the preceding footnote this call was not heeded. With respect to enforcement of arbitration awards a Kenyan court has held that the conversion date should be the date of the award: *Universal TPT Co v Tzortzis* [1973] 1 EA 310 (HCK).

[22] As in *Thys v Steyn* [2006] eKLR (where the High Court at Nairobi insisted on granting judgment in Kenyan shillings since it regarded the plaintiff's claim for judgment in dollars as giving the plaintiff a 'supranormal profit') and *Delmas America Africa Line Inc v Kisko Products Ghana Ltd* [2005–2006] SCGLR 75 (where the plaintiff asked for judgment in US dollars but the Supreme Court upheld judgment in Canadian dollars). In Ghana, Amua-Sakyi J suggested in *Mensah v National Savings Bank* [1989–1990] 1 GLR 620 (SC) 625 that it was wrong to give judgment in a foreign currency when the parties had not conducted their transactions with each other in that money.

[23] RE Bannerman, 'Award of Damages in Foreign Currency: A Critical Look at the Judgments' (1993–95) 19 *Review of Ghana Law* 231, 234.

post-*Miliangos* developments. In the immediate wake of *Miliangos* there were a couple of South African decisions that resisted changing the breach-date rule.[24] Those, however, were soon overcome by judgments that regarded *Miliangos* as a salutary development and adopted its result, awarding judgment in a foreign currency but giving the judgment debtor the option of satisfying that judgment in the rand equivalent at the date payment was eventually made.[25] Most of these claimed to be following the reasoning offered by the House of Lords. However one, *Barclays Bank of Swaziland v Mnyeketi*, also found support for the payment-date solution in South Africa's Roman-Dutch legal tradition. There the judge concluded that the pre-*Miliangos* forum-currency/breach date rule had manifested a parochial English attitude alien to South Africa's tradition in that it had represented a 'chauvinistic approach to foreign currency'[26]—an approach at odds to that found in Roman-Dutch law.

The currency-of-judgment question reached South Africa's highest judicial body in 1994 when the Appellate Division of the Supreme Court of South Africa approved judgment in US dollars in a torts case.[27] While the court both affirmed the *Miliangos* payment-date rule and the feeling-the-loss approach of *The Folias* and *The Despina R*, it is perhaps most notable for a vigorous dissent. Harms JA expressed the view that post-*Miliangos* developments in England were problematic and not to be followed in South Africa. His judgment is a rare judicial expression of the notion expressed in the last chapter that while *Miliangos* was rightly decided—that is, it was entirely correct to award judgment in foreign currencies in cases of debt and enforcement of foreign-country judgments—the feeling-the-loss rule that grew out of the extension of *Miliangos* to damages claims for tort or breach of contract was not an unqualified good. Harms JA decried the uncertainty associated

[24] *Malilang v MV Houda Pearl* 1986 (2) SA 714 (A) and *Voest Alpine Intertrading Gesellschaft mbH v Burwill and Co* 1985 (2) SA 149 (W). In the former case the court held that it was statutorily required to apply English admiralty law as administered by the English High Court in 1890. Accordingly it concluded that, *Miliangos* notwithstanding, that law required application of the old breach-date conversion rule.

[25] *Murata Machinery Ltd v Capelon Yarns (Pty) Ltd* 1986 (4) SA 671 (C); *Elgin Brown and Hamer (Pty) Ltd v Dampskibsselkabt Torm Ltd* [1988] 4 SA 671 (N); *Mediterranean Shipping Co Ltd v Speedwell Shipping Co Ltd* [1989] 1 SALR 164 (D); *Eden v Pienaar* 2001 (1) SA 158 (W). In *Society of Lloyd's v Price; Society of Lloyd's v Lee* [2006] SCA 87 (RSA) the court did not even afford the parties a choice. It simply gave judgment in sterling.

[26] *Barclays Bank of Swaziland v Mnyeketi* 1992 (3) SA 425 (W), 435. For an approving case comment see L Nieuwoudt, 'The Power of a South African Court to Give Judgment in Foreign Currency' (1992) 18 *South African Yearbook of International Law* 147. An analysis of the early post-*Miliangos* South African cases is in SH High and D Pickering, 'Determination of Damages Awards under Conditions of Exchange-Rate Fluctuations: Problems and (Some) Solutions' (1994) 111 *South African Law Journal* 270, 277–79.

[27] *Standard Chartered Bank of Canada v Nedperm Bank Ltd* 1994 (4) SA 747 (AD). This was an action for negligent misrepresentation. The following year the Supreme Court of Appeal dealt with a negligence action for personal injury and unanimously followed the route England had taken in *Hoffman v Sofaer* [1982] 1 WLR 1350 (QB), discussed in ch 1 at p 51. It awarded the plaintiff's future loss of earnings damages and future medical expenses in his home currency (US dollars), but damages for pain and suffering in rand: *Radell v Multilateral Motor Vehicle Accident Fund* 1995 (4) SA 24 (AD).

with the feeling-the-loss rule and took the position that it deviated from normal principles of damages which required all plaintiffs, regardless of what currency they might operate in, to have their loss measured in the currency of the forum:

> I fail to see why, simply because the plaintiff is a foreign plaintiff, these basic principles do not apply and why he should be treated differently. The argument that to do otherwise would mean that the plaintiff may be denied the amount of his actual loss … misses the point—it is inherent in the law of delict and the principle of nominalism that a plaintiff may, at the end of the day, be out of pocket. In any event, any loss flowing from the depreciation of the local currency is not caused by the wrong…[28]

The position that *Miliangos* should be confined to actions in debt, or even the milder claim that its extension to damages necessarily gives rise to unwelcome uncertainty in the assessment of damages, is an exceptional one. No other judge joined Harms JA in his dissent. Moreover, no court outside Africa has taken cognisance of his arguments.[29]

II. Scotland

The Scottish legal system is intimately connected with the English one, with a common final appellate court, plenty of co-extensive legislation and many shared legal traditions. Accordingly, when in *Commerzbank AG v Large*[30] the Inner House of the Court of Session encountered a foreign currency case just a year and a half after *Miliangos* and reached a similar result, citing *Miliangos* in support, it is not surprising that the case would come to be regarded simply as the Scottish *Miliangos*. It is tempting simply to conclude that *Miliangos* was promptly imported from England into Scotland and that little more needs to be said. However, the process by which Scots law abandoned the sterling/breach-date rule and accepted that judgments might be given in foreign currency is more nuanced and more interesting than that. It reveals a legal system struggling to adapt to modern commercial needs while asserting its own individuality and uniqueness.

No Scottish cases had been cited to the lower courts or the House of Lords in *Miliangos*. However, Lord Fraser, the sole Scottish judge to sit on the *Miliangos* appeal in the House of Lords, did locate a Scottish case apparently on point and

[28] *Standard Chartered Bank of Canada v Nedperm Bank Ltd*, ibid at [9] of the reasons of Harms JA.

[29] For that matter, it appears that no court outside Africa has taken notice of *any* of the judgments of any African courts on the currency question. This is a familiar one-way street: courts in common law Africa routinely take notice of judicial developments in the UK and elsewhere in the Commonwealth, but the reverse is not often the case.

[30] *Commerzbank AG v Large*, 1977 Scots Law Times 219 (*Commerzbank*). Similarly *Miliangos* was welcomed in Ireland, which previously followed the forum-currency/breach-date rule: *Damen & Zonen v O'Shea* (1977), unreported (High Ct 1977-414); *Northern Bank Ltd v Edwards* [1984] IR 284 (Sup Ct). See W Binchy, *Irish Conflicts of Law* (Dublin, Butterworths, 1988) 649 ff.

made mention of it in his brief speech in that case.[31] The decision cited by Lord Fraser was the 1824 judgment of the House of Lords in *Hyslops v Gordon*.[32] Lord Fraser advanced *Hyslops* for the proposition that, at least insofar as Scots law was concerned, judgment could only be given in sterling. In *Hyslops*, the House of Lords had granted an appeal from a Court of Session decree where judgment had been pronounced for a sum of US dollars. It held that the conversion date should be the time of the raising of the action. Lord Gifford's speech was the only one to be reported. He wrote that

> undoubtedly the Court of Session should have done that in this case, which it is the habit of this country to do when an action is brought for a sum of money recovered in foreign money—they should have ascertained what is to be paid in this country; and therefore undoubtedly, this House must remit the case back, in order that that sum may be ascertained in British money which is due from one party to the other.[33]

However, just as the majority in *Miliangos* ruled that it need not follow *Havana Railways* since things had changed since 1960, Lord Fraser found that *Hyslops* need not be followed since, in his opinion, the reason for mandating sterling judgment in that case was the difficulty in establishing the relevant rate of exchange, a consideration which no longer obtained in the 1970s.[34] Thus, in *Miliangos* at least, *Hyslops* could be disregarded and doubts could be expressed about its present authority.

However, Lord Fraser was the only member of the *Miliangos* court to mention *Hyslops*. Lord Wilberforce did not attempt to overrule *Hyslops* as he had done with *Havana Railways*. Moreover, as a strict matter of *stare decisis*, the House of Lords probably cannot overrule one of its own Scottish decisions in an English appeal (or vice versa).[35] Thus *Miliangos* could not overrule *Hyslops* and when the foreign currency matter next came before a Scottish court that court would be faced with the interesting decision of whether to follow *Hyslops* or *Miliangos*. *Commerzbank* was made more interesting by the fact that in *Miliangos* the House of Lords had reminded lower courts that only it could overrule a House of Lords decision. That is, *Miliangos* had the curious dual character of the House of Lords taking the radical step of overruling one of its own recent decisions and bringing English law into supposed conformity with the needs of the commercial community, while at the same time reminding lower courts (and perhaps Lord Denning in particular) that they should themselves be dutiful followers of precedent. That second aspect of *Miliangos* would thus seem to indicate that lower Scottish courts must follow *Hyslops* and adhere to the forum-currency/breach-date rule—leaving it to the

[31] *Miliangos v George Frank (Textiles) Ltd* [1976] AC 443 (HL) 502 (*Miliangos*).

[32] *Hyslops v Gordon* (1824) 2 Shaw's Appeals 451 (HL) (*Hyslops*). The case was not a well known one, but it was mentioned in the principal Scottish text on conflict of laws: A Anton, *Private International Law: A Treatise from the Standpoint of Scots Law* (Edinburgh, Green, 1967) 550–51.

[33] *Hyslops*, ibid, 458. The court held that the conversion date should be the date of the raising of the action.

[34] *Miliangos*, above n 31, 502.

[35] *The Laws of Scotland, Stair Memorial Encyclopaedia* (Edinburgh, Butterworths, 1987) vol 22 [277].

House of Lords sitting on appeal from such a Scottish case to overrule *Hyslops*. Moreover this should be the case notwithstanding the fact that twentieth-century Scottish courts confronted with conversion-date issues had not mentioned *Hyslops* but instead had relied on the (now rejected) English decision in *The Volturno* as authority for a mandatory sterling/breach-date rule.[36]

As noted above, in *Commerzbank* the Scottish Inner House adopted the *Miliangos* result, or something close to it. In a case which was notably similar to *Miliangos* on the facts, it held that a Scottish court might grant a decree in German marks, to be converted into sterling either at the date of voluntary payment or at the date of the extract (the latest date at which a Scottish court is involved in a legal action), whichever is earlier. In *Commerzbank*, the Inner House began its reasoning by agreeing with the view of *Hyslops* which had been expressed by Lord Fraser in *Miliangos*, namely that *Hyslops*'s apparent invocation of the sterling rule was based on conditions that no longer obtained—the difficulty in ascertaining the exchange rate at the relevant time—and thus need not be followed. About this conclusion, two observations may be made. The first is, as mentioned above, it is generally thought that only the House of Lords can overrule a House of Lords decision, and since *Miliangos* did not overrule *Hyslops* the Inner House should have followed the latter, regardless of any claimed change of circumstances. This aspect of *Hyslops* caused consternation in several quarters, since it appeared to depart from established judicial method. It caused one Scottish commentator to write that the reasoning in *Commerzbank* involved 'lighting a brush fire in the jurisprudence of legal precedent'.[37] Secondly, there is good reason to doubt that either Lord Fraser (in *Miliangos*) or the Inner House (in *Commerzbank*) was correct in saying that the result in *Hyslops* had been dictated by difficulties in establishing the exchange rate. As two Scottish commentators on *Commerzbank* have pointed out, no such claim can be found in *Hyslops*, which was based on different reasoning altogether and in fact contradicts Lord Fraser's claim.[38] (In fact it is interesting to note in passing that there was a House of Lords decision just two years after *Hyslops* in which Lord Gifford was content to apply the judgment date as the time of conversion.[39] However, this case was mentioned in neither *Miliangos* nor *Commerzbank*.)

Be that as it may, in *Commerzbank* the Inner House, having by perhaps dubious means freed itself from the sterling breach-date rule, did not base its support for the *Miliangos* result in Lord Wilberforce style reasoning about the needs of commerce and the just result. Rather, it dug back into one of the

[36] *Macfie's Judicial Factor v Macfie*, 1932 Scots Law Times 460, 462 (Outer House).

[37] AF Rodger, 'The Strange Demise of *Hyslops v Gordon*' in AJ Gamble (ed), *Obligations in Context: Essays in Honour of Professor DM Walker* (Edinburgh, W Green, 1990), 2.

[38] Rodger, ibid, 2; G Maher, 'Foreign Currency Judgments: The Scottish Experience' (1995) 44 *ICLQ* 72, 77. See also *Hyslops* itself, above n 25, 460. The conclusion reached by these scholars is not that *Hyslops* was not binding on the court in *Commerzbank*, but rather that it could very easily have been distinguished.

[39] *McBraire v Hamiltons* (1926) 2 Wilson and Shaw's Scots Appeals 66 (HL).

earliest institutional writers of Scottish law, Sir Thomas Craig of Riccarton (1538–1608). It quoted Craig's Latin language *Jus Feudale*, which it described as a late sixteenth-century work,[40] on the matter of contractual payment, and came to the conclusion the principles to be found there 'appear to us to be the same as the objectives of the law of England recently declared by the House of Lords in *Miliangos*'.[41]

The cited passages in Craig's *Jus Feudale* do not in fact deal with court judgments at all. Rather they address the matter of payments made pursuant to a contract.[42] In that respect they are flimsy authority for the matter before the Inner House in *Commerzbank*. However, they allowed the court to claim—as a South African court would[43]—that the result dictated by the pragmatic, commercially-orientated reasoning in *Miliangos* is in fact the result that follows from an investigation into one's own national legal tradition. This prompted one Scots commentator on *Commerzbank* to claim it as an instance of the 'sturdy independence'[44] of Scottish judicial decision making: the Scots, it seems, had the currency issue sorted out centuries ago and had only been led into the (now exposed) error of the breach-date rule by the House of Lords in *Hyslops*. Now that the House of Lords in *Miliangos* had discovered the error of its ways it was open for Scottish courts to rediscover and re-impose the right answer.

Of course a disadvantage of this method of judicial reasoning is that it may provide a less-that-optimal amount of guidance to subsequent lower courts as they proceed to work out the ramifications of a new approach to assessment of damages. As we have seen, the English courts in the years following *Miliangos* encountered a number of problems not dealt with in that case. Nevertheless they were able to rely on the reasons offered in *Miliangos*, especially those of Lord Wilberforce, to assist them in working out those problems. Insofar as *Commerzbank* may be viewed as Scotland's *Miliangos*, its quaint invocation of a sixteenth-century text—while perhaps useful in fanning the flames of a native commercial law tradition—provided no such guidance.

In the years following *Commerzbank* the courts of Scotland have on a number of occasions been confronted with damages cases raising foreign currency issues, and, as might be expected, they display a general willingness to apply *Commerzbank* expansively and abandon the old sterling/breach-date rule in a variety of

[40] It appears that *Jus Feudale* was in fact a seventeenth-century publication: *The Laws of Scotland, Stair Memorial Encyclopaedia* (Edinburgh, Butterworths, 1987), vol 22 [534]. This lists the publication date of *Jus Feudale* as 1655 but states that it was in fact completed in the first decade of the seventeenth century.

[41] *Commerzbank*, above n 30, 382.

[42] As pointed out by Maher, above n 38, 76.

[43] See above at n 26.

[44] EA Marshall, 'Decrees in Foreign Currency: Following Craig—or *Miliangos*?' [1978] *Scots Law Times* (News) 77, 78.

circumstances.[45] However, they have not invariably done so.[46] Moreover, although these cases have cited *Commerzbank*, and sometimes also made reference to *Miliangos* and *The Despina R*, on the whole they have failed to articulate a generalised theory or rule on the question of foreign currency damages that is anywhere as comprehensive as that which has emerged in England after *Miliangos*. Clearly Craig's *Jus Feudale*, while useful for reinforcing the sturdy independence of Hibernian legal tradition, has not yet provided the resources necessary for fleshing out the details. *Commerzbank*, in failing to come to grips with the currency question in modern terms, provided no groundwork for lower courts to grapple with the complexities of the later issues which might arise. This has led one Scottish analyst to remark that 'it is far from clear whether Scots law has any independent doctrines on foreign currency judgments or, alternatively, whether Scots law completely accepts the approach of English law on this subject'.[47]

III. Canada

At the time *Miliangos* appeared courts in Canada were solidly and it would seem quite comfortably in the grip of the forum-currency/breach-date rule. There had been a couple of nineteenth-century cases that had applied other conversion dates.[48] There was even an Ontario Court of Appeal judgment as late as 1921 which had pondered the matter at some length and, following an examination of English, Canadian and American decisions and the texts of Westlake and Story, imposed a judgment-date conversion.[49] These older cases are described and discussed in

[45] See, eg: *Wimpey Construction (UK) Ltd v Martin Black & Co Wire Ropes) Ltd* 1882 SLT 239 (Outer House) (conversion at date of payment or extract); *Worf v Western SMT Co* 1987 SLT 317 (Outer House) (judgment date conversion); *Bhatia v Tribax Ltd* 1994 SLT 1201 (Outer House) (conversion at date of payment or extract); *Bank of Scotland v Junior* 1999 SCLR 284; *China National Star Petroleum Co v Tor Drilling (UK) Ltd* [2002] Scot CS 86 (Outer House); *Brackencroft Ltd v Silvers Marine Ltd* 2006 SC 633 (Inner House); *Fullemann v McInnes's Executors* 1993 SLT 259 (Outer House) (conversion at date of payment or extract). In this last-mentioned case, however, the award for solatium was given in sterling. That is, without mentioning the English case of *Hoffman v Sofaer* (ch 1, n 136) the court in this personal injury case reached the same result—awarding damages for lost wages in the currency in which those wages would have been earned, but reverting to the forum currency for the award for pain and suffering. Canadian courts have done the same: *Prasad v Frandsen* (1985) 60 BCLR 343 (BCSC); *Bonham v Weir* 2009 BCSC 1080.

[46] *Alberta Distillers Ltd v Matthew Gloag (Overseas) Ltd*, 23 Dec 1992 (Outer House).

[47] Maher, above n 38, 89. A similar complaint about the reasoning in *Commerzbank* is voiced by DJ Cusine, 'More Fair Exchange' (1978) 23 *Journal of the Law Society of Scotland* 136, 137.

[48] *Campbell v Wilson* (1838) 2 NBR (Berton) 416 (Sup Ct New Brunswick) (time of trial); *Morell v Ward* (1863) 10 Grant's Chancery Cases 231 (Upper Canada, Chancery) (Vankoughnet C expressed the view (at 233) that the conversion date might be either the date of breach or some subsequent time, at the plaintiff's option).

[49] *Quartier v Farah*, above n 2. The court applied the date of the judgment at trial, not its own. There was also a 1963 personal injury case where the court awarded damages for loss of earnings in the money of the country in which the plaintiff was resident: *Smith v Canadian Pacific Railway* (1963)

a 1932 article in the Canadian Bar Review.[50] I will not rehearse the early history of Canadian law on this point, since following the 1921 decision of the House of Lords in *The Volturno*[51] Canadian courts dutifully fell into line with the English lead and imposed the forum-currency/breach-date rule.

The Supreme Court of Canada led the way with two decisions, one from 1927 and the other from 1945. The first of these was *Custodian v Blucher*.[52] Although *Custodian* arguably remains the leading Canadian case on foreign currency obligations, that was not the reason the case went to the Supreme Court. The currency question was a subsidiary aspect of the litigation and the Supreme Court's discussion of it was not lengthy. Its unanimous reasons on the currency issue mainly observed that English courts had adopted the breach-date rule in cases such as *Manners v Pearson*, *Di Ferdinando v Simon, Smits & Co* and most recently *The Volturno*, and that Canadian judges should follow suit. However, obeying English precedent was not the only element of the Supreme Court's reasoning in *Custodian*. The Court also voiced the view that these English breach-date cases were 'right in principle'.[53] Nevertheless, as is typical of Canadian judge-made law from that period, the main explanation offered for the holding was that since English courts had settled the matter Canadian courts should follow them.

The second Supreme Court of Canada case on the matter, the 1945 decision in *Gatineau Power Co v Crown Life Insurance Co*,[54] offered an even more cursory analysis. Again the conversion-date question was not the main point behind the appeal to the Supreme Court and in dealing with it the Court did no more than confirm that English courts persisted in following the breach-date rule and that its own decision 18 years before in *Custodian* should continue to represent Canadian law.

The Supreme Court of Canada has not spoken on this matter since 1945. Prior to *Miliangos* that silence was not surprising. In light of English judges' unwavering support for the breach-date rule in the mid-twentieth century, as evidenced most strongly by the 1960 decision in *Havana Railways*, and in the absence of any signs of rebellion in the lower courts, there was little need for Canada's highest court to revisit the question. Even though the Supreme Court of Canada became the country's final appellate court for civil matters in 1949,[55] and was thus in theory

41 DLR (2d) 249 (Sask QB). No authorities were cited on the point and the decision must be regarded as *per incuriam*.

[50] J Denison, 'Fluctuations in Exchange in the Courts' (1932) 10 *Canadian Bar Review* 134.

[51] Above n 3.

[52] *Custodian v Blucher* [1927] SCR 420, [1927] 3 DLR 40 (*Custodian*).

[53] Ibid, 426 SCR.

[54] *Gatineau Power Co v Crown Life Insurance Co* [1945] SCR 655, [1945] 4 DLR 1 (*Gatineau Power*).

[55] The superintending authority of the Judicial Committee of Privy Council did not end abruptly. The 1949 abolition of appeals to the Privy Council from civil matters heard by Canadian courts only applied to actions launched after that date. The last Canadian case to be decided by the Privy Council was decided in 1959: *Ponoka-Calmar Oils Ltd v Earl F Wakefield Co* [1960] AC 18. It was not until 1978 that the Supreme Court of Canada declared it would not feel bound to follow Privy Council precedents: *Re Agricultural Products Marketing Act* [1978] 2 SCR 1.

free to chart its own course in this area and depart from the breach-date rule laid down in *The Volturno*, in practice Canadian courts were slow to strike out on their own, especially in private law matters.

However, after the 1975 decision in *Miliangos* circumstances were ripe for the Supreme Court of Canada to revisit the currency question. After all, the chief case on which the Supreme Court had based its approach to the issue in 1927, *The Volturno*, though not technically overruled in *Miliangos*, had certainly been undermined there; it had been declared to be out of touch with modern circumstances. However, the Supreme Court of Canada has declined to take up the challenge. There have been six invitations for that court to revisit the issue in the post-*Miliangos* era but it has declined every one, and this despite the fact—which we will explore below—that the decisions appealed from had by no means arrived at a uniform solution to the conversion-date problem.[56]

That does not mean, however, that *Miliangos* has been without effect in Canada. On the contrary, many lower courts and some provincial legislatures have been attracted by the reasoning and result in that case, and they have contrived to push Canadian law towards later conversion dates. However, some courts, regarding themselves as fettered by the old Supreme Court breach-date cases, have been unwilling to make this response. As a result Canadian law on foreign currency obligations has become a tangled garden, much more difficult to summarise than that in England. There are four reasons for this confusion and complexity. One is a federal statute which some (but not all) courts interpret as bearing on the issue.

[56] In *Williams & Glyn's Bank Ltd v Belkin Packaging Ltd* [1983] 1 SCR 661 the currency of judgment issue had engaged and divided the courts below. The trial judge had employed a judgment-date conversion: (1979) 17 BCLR 153 (SC). The one judge of the appeal court who considered the matter thought that the breach-date rule should govern: (1981) 28 BCLR 96 (CA). The Supreme Court of Canada held that there was no liability, so it did not have to resolve the issue. It might conceivably have offered some clarifying obiter but it elected not to—except to wrongly claim (at 672) that *Miliangos* had applied a judgment-date conversion. The currency issue arose a couple of years later in *NV Bocimar SA v Century Insurance of Canada* 53 NR 383 (Fed Ct App), but the Supreme Court of Canada reversed the lower courts on the finding of liability: [1987] 1 SCR 1247. Having found that the defendants should succeed, the Supreme Court did not have to face issues related to damages; again it might well have elected to do so by way of obiter, but as with the previous case it did not. The following year there was *Stott v Merit Investment Corp* (1988) 63 OR (2d) 545, 48 DLR (4th) 288 (CA), where leave to appeal to the Supreme Court of Canada was refused: 49 DLR (4th) vii. That case imposed a date-of-breach conversion to Canadian dollars. More recently, there was an application for leave to appeal the 2004 decision of the Manitoba Court of Appeal in *Kellogg Brown & Root Inc v Aerotech Herman Nelson Inc* 2004 MBCA 63, 238 DLR (4th) 594 (Man CA). The provincial appeal court had split on the appropriate conversion date and an application for leave to appeal was made to the Supreme Court of Canada. However, that was dismissed, [2004] SCCA no 244. Then there was *Nelson Marketing International Inc v Royal and Sun Alliance Insurance Co of Canada*, 2005 BCSC 772, 27 CCLI (4th) 57. There the currency-of-judgment issue arose at trial but the provincial appeal court allowed the defendant's appeal on grounds of liability so did not have to address damages (2006 BCCA 327 57 BCLR (4th) 27). The Supreme Court of Canada dismissed an application for leave to appeal: [2006] SCCA No 370. The following year the top court refused leave in an Ontario case that would have presented a currency-of-judgment issue: *Bank of Montreal v Woldegabriel* [2007] OJ No 1305 (SCJ) [73], aff'd 2008 ONCA 71, application for leave to appeal to the Supreme Court of Canada dismissed [2008] SCCA No 119 (SCC). The Supreme Court of Canada never gives reasons for its decisions on applications for leave to appeal.

This statute was irrelevant so long as the breach-date rule predominated, but it arguably comes into play where a payment-date conversion is sought, so Canadian courts seeking to follow *Miliangos* have had to grapple with it. The second complicating factor is that three of Canada's ten provinces have passed legislation effectively overruling both the old breach-date rule and the federal statute just mentioned. Two of those statutes are identical to one another but the third takes another tack. In addition, two other provinces have legislation dealing with the recognition of foreign-country judgments, and those enactments address the conversion-date issue in that context, though in different ways.

The third source of complexity does not arise from statutes but rather unresolved disagreement over whether the Supreme Court of Canada's old breach-date cases—*Custodian* and *Gatineau Power*, both of which followed *The Volturno*—continue to represent Canadian law in the wake of *Miliangos*. Some courts see the old breach-date authorities as still operative until such time as the Supreme Court of Canada should expressly overrule them. They might prefer the reasoning and result in *Miliangos* but they consider themselves precluded from following it. However, other courts do not regard themselves as so constrained—either because they hold that times have changed sufficiently to make the old Supreme Court authorities irrelevant, or because they are able to distinguish the old authorities on some other ground—for instance that they apply to some causes of action but not all. The fourth source of confusion and complexity in Canadian law flows from the fact that among those lower Canadian courts inclined and prepared to follow *Miliangos* there is disagreement—and I will argue misunderstanding—about the holding in that case. In particular, in Canada *Miliangos* is most commonly read as affording courts generous flexibility in selecting the best conversion date for each individual case, and doing so in light of currency fluctuations during the litigation. In view of all of that, Canadian law on the foreign-currency question cannot be summed up briefly. Nevertheless, the remainder of this section offers further details on Canadian responses to the currency-of-judgment question.

There was, and still is, a venerable piece of Canadian federal legislation which appears to bar that country's judges from ever awarding judgment in foreign money. Section 12 of Canada's Currency Act has no equivalent in the United Kingdom (though it does have an American counterpart that will be examined in the next chapter). It dates to 1871, the fourth year of Canada's existence of a sovereign state:

> All public accounts established or maintained in Canada shall be in the currency of Canada, *and any reference to money* or monetary value *in any* indictment or other *legal proceedings shall be stated in the currency of Canada*.[57] (emphasis added)

[57] Currency Act, RSC 1985, c C-52, s 12. The original was An Act to Establish One Uniform Currency for the Dominion of Canada, 34 Vict c 4. As we shall see with a nearly identical federal legislative provision in the United States, to be examined in the next chapter, it is far from certain that this section was intended to prevent a court giving a judgment in a foreign currency. Like the United Kingdom (see ch 1, n 72), Canada has a couple of pre-*Miliangos* statutes that, for the purposes of establishing

The meaning, purpose and scope of this are unclear. When it first appeared it evidently had the goal of promoting the monopoly, or at least the predominance, of the new Canadian currency against other competitor currencies that would have been circulating in the young country immediately before the introduction of the Canadian dollar. Read literally, however, the requirement that any reference to money in a Canadian legal proceeding must be to Canadian dollars is remarkably broad. It would prevent a witness in a Canadian criminal prosecution from testifying, 'The accused stole my purse which contained 100 euros'. After all, that is a reference to money in a legal proceeding, and as such might arguably be required to be stated in the currency of Canada. Not surprisingly, there is no record of anyone maintaining that section 12 of the Currency Act has this sort of effect. And of course Canadian courts, including the Supreme Court of Canada, have routinely been willing to make passing reference to foreign currencies in their judgments.[58] However, some litigants have taken positions that contend for a broad interpretation of section 12. For instance, there are cases where parties to Canadian civil actions have claimed that offers to settle expressed in a foreign currency do not comport with section 12 of the Currency Act and thus fail to amount to valid settlement offers.[59] Not surprisingly, judges have had little truck

limits on damages, mandate certain conversion dates in certain narrowly defined instances: Canada Shipping Act, RSC 1985, c S-9, s 84; Carriage by Air Act, RSC 1985, c C-26, s 2(6) (giving effect to the Warsaw Convention of 1929, as amended at The Hague in 1955). In the post-*Miliangos* era the federal government also amended its bankruptcy and insolvency legislation to deal with international bankruptcies and it adopted the conversion-date rule reached by the English courts in the insolvency context in *Lines* and *Dynamics Corp* decisions, ch 1, pp 54–55 (a date-of-bankruptcy conversion). This was done in 1997 when it passed the Bankruptcy and Insolvency Act, RSC 1985, c B-3, s 275 and the Companies' Creditors Arrangement Act, RSC 1985, c C-36, s 18.6(8). Canada has also passed a statute effectively implementing the UNCITRAL Model Law on cross-border insolvencies: SC 2005, c 47 and making other changes to the Bankruptcy and Insolvency Act. That statute, which has not yet been proclaimed, has a provision on foreign currency conversions similar to the one in the existing legislation. However, in apparent recognition that foreign currency issues can arise in domestic bankruptcies as well as cross-border ones it relocated the currency provision to the general part of the statute. When that statute is proclaimed it will replace the provisions on international insolvencies in the current Bankruptcy and Insolvency Act. In addition, a 2001 federal statute deals with registration and enforcement of foreign court judgments in marine pollution matters and stipulates a conversion from the foreign currency to Canadian dollars as of the rate prevailing on date of the foreign judgment: Marine Liability Act, SC 2001, c 6, s 67(1).

[58] For instance, *Citadel General Insurance Co v Vytlingham* [2007] 3 SCR 373 [3]; *Beals v Saldanha* [2003] 3 SCR 416 [3]; *Holt Cargo Systems Inc v ABC Containerline NV* [2001] 3 SCR 907 [31]. None of these cases dealt with the conversion-date issue. They and others like them are simply cases where the Supreme Court of Canada, usually in the course of recounting the facts of a case, made reference to some foreign currency and gave no hint that doing so ran afoul of the Currency Act.

[59] *Champion International Corp v The Sabina*, 2003 FCT 39, 227 FCR 107, appeal dismissed [2003] FCJ No 1479 (Fed CA), application for leave to appeal to Supreme Court of Canada dismissed, [2003] SCCA No 519; *Trans North Turbo Air Ltd v North 60 Petro Ltd*, 2003 YKSC 18, appeal dismissed 2004 YKCA 9 (without mentioning this point). More closely akin to the purse example in the text, one Canadian judge has taken the view that s 12 does apply to references to money in affidavits submitted in Canadian proceedings, at least in some circumstances: *Levine v Pacific International Securities Inc* (1998) 46 BCLR (3d) 110, 16 CPC (4th) 334 (SC) [58]. There has also been inconclusive litigation over whether, in light of s 12, a garnishment order expressed in a foreign currency is valid: *Exquisite Excavation Corp v Exchequer Energy Resources Ltd* (1985) 63 BCLR 273 (CA).

with these arguments for broad, literal but impractical, application of the statute. However, questions as to its scope remain. Fortunately, an exhaustive inquiry into the reach of section 12 of Canada's Currency Act is not required here. For our purposes all that needs to be addressed is what effect, if any, that section might have on judgments based on foreign currency obligations. First, nothing in the Currency Act requires Canadian courts to apply a breach-date conversion in judgments based on foreign currency obligations. The legislation mandates only that statements about money in Canadian legal proceedings be expressed in Canadian dollars. Canadian courts converting from a foreign currency to the local one at any date up to and including judgment would thus conform to section 12. The Currency Act only begins to raise problems for Canadian judges when they want to accept the *Miliangos* solution and issue judgments in foreign money. Doing so would appear to require them to issue a judgment that referred to a currency other than the Canadian dollar.

But how substantial an obstacle is this? It will be recalled that in England after *Miliangos*, the new payment-date rule is implemented by a court's issuing relief in a form that affords the judgment debtor its option of fulfilling the judgment in either of two ways: (1) the debtor can satisfy the judgment in the foreign money, or (2) it can pay in the sterling equivalent of that foreign currency on the date of payment. In Canada, a judicial ruling in form (1) would seem to violate section 12 of the Currency Act, at least if we read that statute as governing the words a judge must employ when delivering a judgment, which is the way most Canadian courts have read it. When, four years before *Miliangos*, a Canadian trial judge awarded judgment in a contract case in US dollars, apparently oblivious to the long-standing Supreme Court of Canada cases mandating the breach-date rule, the appeal court promptly overturned that decision. It did so on the basis on that the Currency Act did not permit a judge to do such a thing.[60] That is, however anachronistic such a constraint might seem today, arguably section 12 means that Canadian courts are not entitled to issue orders in the form 'the defendant shall pay the plaintiff 50,000 euros'. So option (1) does not seem to be available.

It should be noted in passing that not all Canadian courts judges felt so constrained by the federal statute. A couple, namely the Saskatchewan Court of Appeal and the Yukon Supreme Court, have simply ignored it, following *Miliangos*

[60] *Baumgartner v Carsley Silk Co* (1971) 23 DLR (3d) 255 (Que CA). Like *Miliangos*, this was an action by a seller for the purchase price of textiles which had been delivered to the defendant and which had not been paid for due to the defendant's assertion that the cloth was defective in quality. The appeal court did not conclude that the result reached by the trial court was unfair or out of line with authority, only that it was not permitted by s 12 of the Currency Act, or rather its predecessor equivalent: s 11 of the Currency, Mint and Exchange Fund Act, RSC 1952, c 315. In fact the appeal court did not even think a litigant could, in its pleadings, ask for judgment in foreign money. The plaintiff had asked for judgment in US dollars and the appeal court thought that even that request violated the federal statute, so it dismissed the action. Since the dismissal was on a pleadings point, the plaintiff seller could refile.

and awarding judgment in US dollars.[61] Those judgments are in a minority, however; most Canadian courts think that they cannot simply decree judgment in foreign money.

What is less clear, however, is whether section 12 stands in the way of option (2). That is, does it preclude a Canadian court from handing down an order in the form 'the defendant will pay the plaintiff whatever amount of Canadian dollars is equivalent to 50,000 euros on the date that payment is made'? Unless one reads the Currency Act so strictly as to forbid a judge from so much as *mentioning* a foreign currency, a judgment in form (2) does not appear to run afoul of the Currency Act. It is still a judgment in Canadian dollars. Thus it might appear open to Canadian courts inclined to implement *Miliangos*'s payment-date rule not to worry about the Currency Act so long as they confine themselves to requiring judgment debtors to pay in the Canadian equivalent of the foreign currency at the date of payment.[62]

However, when we turn to the decided cases we find that judicial responses to the problem just described have been varied. Despite unanimous approval of *Miliangos* by Canadian courts, the majority of Canadian judges in the post-*Miliangos* era have held that, due to the Currency Act, judgment in form (2) is not available to them and that accordingly the latest conversion date they can adopt is one as of the date of their judgment. Their reasoning seems to be that the common law requires money judgments to specify some precise amount of a given currency to be paid—an exact integer and not an amount in Canadian dollars to be determined at a later date by reference to some other variable.[63] Since by virtue of the Currency Act that amount must be expressed in Canadian dollars, it seems to follow that courts cannot issue judgment in an amount of Canadian dollars to be determined by reference to the value in those dollars of some foreign currency at some time in the future. As a consequence, such courts can accompany *Miliangos* only as far as the judgment date, at which point the underlying obligation must be converted to Canadian dollars.

The position is illustrated by the first Canadian judgment to consider *Miliangos*. *Batavia Times Publishing Co v Davis*[64] is the Canadian case that has pondered the

[61] *Sandy Frank Film Syndication Inc v CFQC Broadcasting Ltd* (1983) 23 Sask R 241 (CA); *Trans North Turbo Air Ltd v North 60 Petro Ltd* [2003] YJ No 60 (SC). A third court to do this was the Supreme Court of Prince Edward Island in *Aluminio Paderno SpA v Paderno Canada Ltd* (1985) 52 Nfld & PEIR 292 (though another decision of that same court that year found that it was constrained to apply the breach-date rule: *Presse v Serra* (1985) 52 Nfld & PEIR 97 (PEISC)). This result is now permitted by statute in that province, but at the time of this decision that legislation had not been passed. Canadian courts have also embraced the idea that when interest is awarded it should be at the market rate of the currency in which damages are given: *Reading and Bates Construction Co v Baker Energy Resources Corp* [1995] 1 FC 483 (Fed CA), leave to appeal to SCC refused [1994] SCCA No 532.

[62] Of course one imagines that in such situation the payment might well be in the foreign currency itself, since the parties would be indifferent.

[63] No authority is ever cited for this proposition. However, the decisions can best (and perhaps only) be understood by reading them to be based on some such claim.

[64] *Batavia Times Publishing Co v Davis* (1978) 20 OR (2d) 437, 88 DLR (3d) 144 (HC) 153–54; aff'd 26 OR (2d) 249n and 800n (CA) (*Batavia Times*).

foreign currency obligation question at greatest length. It was an action to enforce an American court judgment which had been rendered in US dollars. The Ontario judge expressed a liking for the modernising result the House of Lords had reached in *Miliangos*, a payment-date conversion. Nevertheless, he did not think that the Currency Act permitted him to impose that solution:

> I do not believe that the Courts of Canada are able to move to the date of effective payment as providing the rate of exchange as the English Courts have now done in cases involving circumstances similar to those outlined in *Miliangos*...
>
> If I could be satisfied that there are no procedural or practical problems and that the *Currency and Exchange Act* either did not apply to judgments or did not prevent a judgment being given for a sum of foreign currency and its equivalent in Canadian dollars, as the English Courts are now doing, I would adopt the effective date of payment as being the date for determining the rate of exchange. Because I am not certain that there are no problems and because I assume that the *Currency and Exchange Act* does not permit judgments to be given as they are now being given in England, I will use the rate of exchange as prevailing at the date of the second judgment herein, the date of my judgment....[65]

The court concluded that the conversion date in such cases was not governed by the old Supreme Court of Canada breach-date authorities, since those cases had dealt with different causes of action. Accordingly, the judge followed *Miliangos* as far as he thought the statute permitted. He converted into Canadian currency as of the date of his judgment. Other Canadian courts have held themselves similarly bound by the Currency Act, including the Federal Court of Appeal and, most recently, the Manitoba Court of Appeal in a case in which the Supreme Court of Canada refused leave to appeal.[66]

Curiously, although most Canadian courts have concluded that the Currency Act limits the form in which they can proclaim judgment, many do not think it is wrong to write reasons for judgment that refer throughout only to foreign currencies and then at the last minute, as little more than an afterthought, tack on a judgment-date conversion to the local currency. For example, in *Halla Merchant Co v Portserv Ltd* the court noted at the beginning of its judgment that currency references through its reasons would be to US dollars.[67] After numerous references to money throughout those reasons, always in US dollars, the court gave judgment for US$133,950 and then concluded by remarking that the Currency Act required that to be converted to its Canadian currency equivalent. It did not even bother to say what that Canadian equivalent was.[68] It seems curious to conclude that compliance with the Currency Act can be satisfied by this sort of lip service but that the statute does not permit judges to order conversion from the foreign money

[65] Ibid, 446–47. The Currency and Exchange Act was the then current name for the Currency Act. The provision in question was identical to that quoted above at n 57.

[66] *Atlantic Lines & Navigation Co v The Didymi* [1988] 1 FC 3 (CA); *Kellogg*, above n 56 [77].

[67] *Halla Merchant Co v Portserv Ltd* [1997] FCJ No 219, 126 FTR 300 [1].

[68] Ibid [32].

into Canadian dollars at the rate that is found to exist at some future time, such as the date of payment. However, that is precisely where most Canadian judges have drawn the line. In effect, for many courts the Currency Act permits only a partial implementation of *Miliangos*: the conversion-date can be moved from the date of breach to the date of judgment, but no later.

These problems arising from the Currency Act might be considerable were it not now the case that most Canadian litigation that raises a currency-of-judgment question now takes place in a province that, in an effort to mimic *Miliangos*, has brought in legislation to skirt any effect which that federal statute might have on the question. Three of Canada's ten provinces, including the two most populous common law jurisdictions, convinced of the soundness of *Miliangos* and dissatisfied with the effect of the federal statute which seemed to limit the full implementation of *Miliangos* in Canada, have enacted legislation to finesse the effect of the Currency Act. Although valid federal legislation prevails over valid provincial statutes in the event of a direct clash, the provinces which opted effectively to reverse the effect of section 12 of the Currency Act managed to do it without purporting to overrule directly the federal statute's requirement that court judgments be expressed in Canadian dollars. They simply brought in legislation which permits courts in those provinces to render awards in the form 'the defendant shall pay the plaintiff the amount in Canadian dollars equivalent to X amount of [the relevant foreign currency] at the date the payment is eventually made'.[69] That is, rather than try to overrule the federal legislation directly—which constitutionally they could not do[70]—they opted to change the common law rule that required judgments to be rendered in a definite sum and not by reference to some other variable. (This raises the question of whether there was such a common law rule. As we have seen, however, most Canadian courts have acted as though there was.) The resulting payment-date conversion is the functional equivalent of awarding damages in the foreign currency. In fact it is one of the two options authorised by *Miliangos* itself, which recommended giving judgment in a form which gave the

[69] Courts of Justice Act, RSO 1990, c C.43, s 121 (Ontario, in force since 1984); Supreme Court Act, RSPEI 1988, c S-10, Sec 46 (Prince Edward Island, in force since 1989); and Foreign Money Claims Act, RSBC 1996, c 154 (British Columbia, in force since 1996). The origins of the last mentioned can be traced to a thoughtful report of the Law Reform Commission of British Columbia: *Report on Foreign Money Liabilities*, Report No 65 (Vancouver, Queen's Printer for British Columbia, 1983).

[70] Assuming, that is, that s 12 of the Currency Act is valid federal legislation in the first place. The Government of Canada has express constitutional authority to pass laws in relation to 'Currency and Coinage': Constitution Act, 1867, (UK) 1867, c 3, s 91 (14). This grant of legislation authority is clearly sufficient to support most of the provisions in the Currency Act, a statute that deals mainly with establishing the Canadian dollar as the official money of the country. Arguably, however, it might not give the federal government the right to legislate with respect to the currency of court judgments, at least in the courts of the provinces (as opposed to the federal courts), which might be thought to be the exclusive right of the provinces under their power to legislate with respect to the administration of justice in the province. The argument that s 12 of the Currency Act is ultra vires the federal government was advanced in B Riorden, 'The Currency of Suit in Actions for Foreign Debts' (1978) 24 *McGill Law Journal* 438 and his arguments were approved by the Law Reform Commission of British Columbia, above n 69 at 49. However, the point does not appear to have been argued at length before a court.

defendant the option of satisfying the judgment either in the foreign currency or its equivalent in sterling at the payment date.

These three provincial statutes may appear to do little more than to authorise courts in those provinces to, in effect, follow *Miliangos* and impose a payment-date conversion. However, a tour of the cases decided pursuant to these statutes shows that there is more than one way to interpret *Miliangos* and illustrates some of the difficulties in trying to codify it. The first legislative change was section 121 of Ontario's Courts of Justice Act, enacted nine years after *Miliangos*. In the period immediately following *Miliangos* a couple of Ontario judges had held themselves still bound to apply the breach-date conversion rule adopted by the Supreme Court of Canada in 1927,[71] but like the court in *Batavia Times* most Ontario judges confronted with the issue managed to distinguish the old Supreme Court precedents and select another date, albeit not one past the date of judgment.[72] Then in 1984 Ontario's provincial legislature stepped in and provided for a payment-date conversion rule:

> where a person obtains an order to enforce an obligation in a foreign currency, the order shall require payment of an amount in Canadian currency sufficient to purchase the amount of the obligation in the foreign currency at a bank in Ontario listed in Schedule I to the Bank Act (Canada) at the close of business on the first day on which the bank quotes a Canadian dollar rate for purchase of the foreign currency before the day payment of the obligation is received by the creditor.[73]

Although the statute specifies payment-date conversion, many Ontario courts applying it have simply treated it as simply permitting judgment to be issued in a foreign currency. For instance, in one case the Ontario Court of Appeal dealt with the conversion-date issue in one sentence: 'The appeal is allowed and it is ordered that the respondent pay the appellant the $100,000 US she received from Huppe in 1998 in accordance with s 121 of the Courts of Justice Act'.[74] Similarly, even

[71] *Oshawa Group Ltd v Great American Insurance Co* (1982) 132 DLR (3d) 453 (Ont CA) 467.

[72] *Batavia Times*, above n 64.

[73] Courts of Justice Act, above n 69, s 121(1). For the sake of convenience and the elimination of disputes about what the applicable conversion rate is at the precise moment when the judgment debtor pays the creditor, the statute selects the conversion date as of one day *before* the actual payment. For practical purposes, however, this is little different from a payment-date conversion, so for brevity's sake I will refer to it as a payment-date conversion.

[74] *Highland Nursing Home Employee Pension Plan Trust v Aldridge* (2004) 46 CBR (4th) 298 (Ont CA) [11]. To similar effect see *MacMillan v White*, [1991] OJ No 2143 (Gen Div); *Abrasive Engineering & Manufacturing, Inc v Cowan & Stevens Machinery Sales, Ltd*, [2003] OJ No 2037, 33 CPC (5th) 195 (SCJ) [30]; *Bates v Island Cove Development Ltd*, [2003] OJ No 4868, 18 RPR (4th) 129 (Ont SCJ) [38]; *Reichman v Vered* (2003) 33 BLR (3d) 245 (Ont SCJ); *United States v Shield Development Co* (2004) 74 OR 583 (SC) [45], aff'd (2005) 74 OR (3d) 595 (CA); *Sun Hung Kai Investment Services Ltd v Sung*, [2005] OJ No 5761 (SCJ) [66]; *Forewell v Savoia Canada Inc*, [2005] OJ No 2126 (SCJ, Master) [5]; *Moritex Europe Ltd v Oz Optics Ltd*, [2005] OJ No 5525 (SCJ) [21]; *Disney Enterprises Inc v Click Enterprises Inc* (2006) 267 DLR (4th) 291 (Ont SCJ); *Stel-Van Homes v Fortini* (2006) 21 BLR (4th) 78 (Ont SCJ) and *Bank of Montreal v Woldegabriel*, above n 56; *Bush v Mereshensky* (2008) RFL (6th) 450 (Ont SCJ); *Bachi Corp v ThinkFilm Inc* [2009] OJ No 2686 (SCJ); *Cimmaster v Piccione*, 2010 ONSC 96 (SCJ). Not all of these cases even bother to mention the statute; some simply grant judgment in the foreign currency.

where there is a set-off between different currencies there is no need to convert to a common one; an Ontario court can simply issue judgment in the form

> there will be judgment for the defendant/plaintiff by counterclaim in an amount equal to the difference between the counterclaim of $36,683.43 and the Canadian dollar equivalent of 28,835,800 Italian lire, calculated pursuant to Section 121 of the *Courts of Justice Act*...[75]

Courts rendering judgment in this form are clearly only offering the most token obedience to the federal Currency Act's requirement that they must render judgment in Canadian dollars. They are in fact rendering judgment in foreign currencies and then simply tacking on a mention of the provision in the provincial legislation that provides for a payment-date conversion of that foreign money into Canadian dollars. However, perhaps as evidence that the Currency Act was never intended to apply to this problem in the first place, no one has quarrelled with it.

Setting aside this procedural dance, the interesting question is how Ontario courts have resolved the tough currency-of-judgment questions that have arisen in the English courts in cases such as *The Folias*, *The Despina R* and *The Texaco Melbourne*. The Ontario statute does not seek to address those hard questions. It leaves them in judges' hands. While the statute says that the conversion date shall be the day before payment, that only applies where a party gets judgment 'to enforce an obligation in a foreign currency'. Nothing in the legislation provides the least guidance as to when that condition is met or, more generally, how a judge determines the currency of the underlying obligation. Its focus is to permit courts to follow *Miliangos*, without saying when they should do so, apart from directing them to an inquiry into when the right being sued on may properly be labelled a foreign currency obligation.

Of course there will be some easy cases on this question, as *Miliangos* itself was. Where a party seeks to enforce a foreign-country court judgment expressed in that foreign country's currency then clearly that qualifies as an obligation to enforce a foreign currency. Ontario courts have been consistent in concluding that the triggering provisions of section 121 are met in those circumstances.[76] The same would be true of a claim for some contractual debt where the underlying debt was expressed in some foreign currency,[77] or where the defendant wrongfully appropriated the contents of a bank account in a given foreign currency.[78]

However, as *The Folias* and the uncertainties of the English feeling-the-loss test discussed in chapter one illustrate, not all cases will be so free from dispute.

[75] *Pastorelli Ceramiche Spa v O'Gaudet Sales Inc* [1995] OJ No 1117 (CJ).

[76] *Girsberger v Kresz* (2000) 47 OR (3d) 145 (SCJ), aff'd 50 OR (3d) 157 (CA) (US judgment in US$); *United States v Shield Development Co*, above n 56 (US judgment in US$); *John Wood & Co (Residential and Agricultural) Ltd v Science*, 2005 WL 2143278 (Ont SCJ) (UK judgment in sterling).

[77] Such as the claims in *Softrade Inc v United Republic of Tanzania* (2003) WL 22204619 (Ont SCJ) and *Good One Express Canada Ltd v 1355930 Ontario Inc* [2004] OJ No 4111 (SCJ), where the defendants did not pay the purchase price (which had been expressed in a foreign currency) of goods that had been delivered to them.

[78] As in *Sun Hung Kai Investment Services Ltd v Sung* [2005] OJ No 5761 (SCJ).

However, although Ontario cases applying the statute have been prepared to acknowledge that the legislation's inspiration was the payment-date conversion date adopted by the House of Lords in *Miliangos*,[79] they have not gone further and wrestled with either the pre- or post-*Miliangos* case law in an effort to clarify and specify when the statute is engaged.[80] Indeed, only a couple of cases have expressly acknowledged the issue. One is *General Refractories Co of Canada v Venturdyne Ltd*,[81] where the defendant, having been held liable for breach of a contract for the sale of goods, argued that section 121 was not applicable. It maintained that the provision should be limited to actions for enforcement of a foreign judgment or for debts in a foreign currency, but not for damages for breach of contract, which was what it was being held liable for. The court rejected these arguments and held that section 121 applied to damages claims. However, not unlike *Miliangos* itself, it did not clearly state what it was about this contract that made the provision pertinent. Was it the fact that a foreign currency was the money of account specified in the contract, that the defendant was a foreign resident, that the plaintiff's expenditure had in fact been made in a foreign currency, or some combination of those factors? That the obligation in question qualified as a foreign currency evidently did not depend on the proper law of the contract, for the court in *General Refractories* found that the contract was governed by the law of Ontario. Apart from that, however, it is not clear what the court thought were the factors that made section 121 applicable; it simply found that it was.

Only marginally more informative is the second Ontario case in which the interpretative point was raised. In *Ticketnet Corp v Air Canada*[82] the currency question arose from a claim for lost profits resulting from a breach of contract and the amount at stake in selecting the conversion date was $1.35 million Cdn. The profits would have been made in the United States and the evidence as to what they would have been had been offered in US dollars. The court held that the statue did not apply since it

> addresses conversion to Canadian currency of *orders* to enforce an obligation in foreign currency. Section 121 does not directly apply here because no *order* was made requiring payment in foreign currency.[83]

That left the court free to adopt a conversion date different from that prescribed by the statute, which it did. The court appeared to think that section 121 applied only when the Ontario court dealt with some *pre-existing* order to enforce foreign

[79] For instance, *Governor and Co of the Bank of Ireland v Canada* [1989] OJ No 269 (HCJ).

[80] Parties have mentioned the old Canadian breach-date cases, such as *Gatineau Power*, above n 54, as part of an argument that the breach-date rule is the just one and the payment-date rule in the statute should not be applied against them—for example, *Moritex Europe Ltd v Oz Optics Ltd*, above n 74. This is not an argument that the statute does not apply because the obligation in question is a foreign-currency one.

[81] *General Refractories Co of Canada v Venturdyne Ltd*, [2002] OJ No 54, [2002] Ont Trial Cases 10 (SCJ) (*General Refractories*).

[82] *Ticketnet Corp v Air Canada* (1997) 154 DLR (4th) 271, 105 OAC 87 (CA) (*Ticketnet*).

[83] Ibid, [158] (emphasis added).

currency, which would seem to apply only in the situation where an Ontario court was asked to recognise a foreign-country judgment, or perhaps an arbitral award. But of course that is not what section 121 says. It applies 'where a person obtains an order to enforce an obligation in a foreign currency'—that is, where an Ontario court makes an order to enforce an obligation (not an order) in a foreign currency. It is not surprising that later Ontario cases have not followed, or even mentioned *Ticketnet* on this point.

Putting aside *General Refractories*, which makes an obvious point, and *Ticketnet*, which is obviously wrong, there is little in the Ontario cases to answer the question of what the result would be if *The Folias* were to be litigated in that jurisdiction. Would a damages claim qualify 'a foreign currency obligation' simply because it was under a contract where the money of account was a foreign currency? If so, would the foreign currency obligation be in the money of account, the money that had been expended to repair the ship (as the Court of Appeal held in *The Folias*), or the money in which the plaintiff felt its loss (as the House of Lords finally decided in that case)? The Ontario statute, as noted, does not address this but rather leaves it up to the courts, but to date the courts have not been helpful.

This failure to wrestle with the currency-of-judgment question in the explicit way in which English judges have done is not due to the fact that no Ontario cases have raised the issue. Such cases inescapably do: in damages claims choices are inevitably made to prefer, say, the currency of the contract over the currency used to cure the breach, and that is true even when those choices are not expressly recognised. So Ontario courts applying the Courts of Justice Act have decided cases which shed some light on what those courts regard as amounting to a foreign currency obligation, even if those cases do now acknowledge the issue in the way that *The Folias* did. For instance, in one case the money used to cure the effects of the defendant's tort qualified as the currency of judgment,[84]

[84] *Itamunoala v Pierce* 2004 WL 3167084, 2004 CarswellOnt 6070 (SCJ). This case is interesting because it illustrates a potential misreading of the statute. The court, at [121], applied a conversion date as of the date the plaintiff paid out funds to a third party. Apparently it did so thinking that this was the 'payment date' referred to in s 121(1). Similar judicial errors appear to have been made in *Doerr Electric Corp v Phelan Brothers Electrical Distributors Ltd* [1986] OJ No 1815 (Dist Ct); *Muske v Blocher*, [1989] OJ No 1316 (Dist Ct) and *Corporate Bank and Trust Co v Toronto-Dominion Bank*, [1987] OJ No 418 (HC). There is a British Columbia case which makes a similar mistake with respect to that province's similarly-worded statute: *Refco Futures (Canada) v SYB Holdings Corp*, 2001 BCSC 1037, 16 BLR (3d) 243 (SC) [35–36], aff'd on this point 2004 BCCA 15, 23 BCLR (3d) 309, 40 BLR (3d) 130 (CA) [119]. There are also cases that appear to have misread s 121 as requiring conversion as of the last day of the trial: *Boardwalk Realty v Maalouf* (1992) 6 OR (3d) 737 (CA) [19]; *La San Giuseppe v Forti Moulding Ltd* [1999] OJ No 3352 (SC); *Cogemar SRL Marble & Granite v Stone Top Factory Inc* [2003] OJ No 4263 (SC); *Lynch v Segal* [2007] OJ No 4983, 48 RFL (6th) 397 (SCJ) [42]; *Bailey v Cintas Corp* [2008] OJ No 1112 (SCJ) [84]. Or, as in *Esses v Friedberg & Co* [2007] OJ No 3029 (SCJ) [5], the day before judgment. Indeed, a variety of conversion dates have been applied in Ontario courts, and not always due to the exercise of the equitable power. For instance in *Groupe Atlantus v Benmoise*, [2007] OJ No 4674, the court applied the rate as of the last day of the hearing of the case. In addition, there are also a couple of cases where the courts simply seemed unaware of the provincial statute's existence and proceeded as though the matter was governed only by the Currency Act and the common law: *Dunning v Dunning* [2006] O J No 1927 (SCJ); *Smart v Guerster* 2005 BCSC 792.

even though the plaintiff's home currency might have been some other money. Similarly, another case held that lost profits that would have been made in a foreign currency should be awarded in that currency, even though the money of the account was a different currency.[85] At times Ontario cases have resulted in judgments in foreign currencies in cases where English courts would have been unlikely to do so. For instance, a plaintiff who lost valuable personal property due to the defendant's negligence was permitted to claim the value of that property in US dollars for no reason other than that she had originally paid for that property in that currency—a fact which falls considerably short of proving that the plaintiff felt the loss in that money.[86]

There is an explanation for the Ontario courts' failure to address the currency-of-judgment question in the way English judges have done in cases like *The Folias*, *The Despina R* and the lower-court cases that have wrestled with applying those appellate decisions. In addition to the provision quoted above, the Ontario statute contains a subsection permitting courts to depart from the payment-date conversion rule where the effects of applying that general rule 'would be inequitable to any party'. Where that condition is satisfied the statute expressly authorises courts to set the conversion date 'on such other day as the court considers equitable in the circumstances'.[87] In short, where either party discharges the onus[88] of showing that a payment-date conversion is inequitable, a judge applying the Ontario statue can select another date. Since the ability to select whatever conversion date a court considers equitable can have an effect comparable to that of the ability to choose among competing currencies of judgment, the currency-of-judgment question in Ontario courts is reframed as an inquiry into the equitable conversion date.

It might be thought that the obligation to articulate what amounts to an inequitable result and the consequential need to justify some alternative conversion date would prompt Ontario courts to engage both with general principles and with case law such as *The Folias*. Both inquiries are ways of wrestling with what amounts to fair compensation. In practice, however, judicial inquiries under the flexible conversion date provision in the Ontario statute have not given rise to illuminating inquiries as to what amounts to a equitable conversion date and hence a fair award. There does not seem to be a leading case on point. Courts applying this provision have only infrequently bothered to make an express finding that application of the general rule would lead to inequity. Instead they have been content to proceed as though the statutory provision confers on them a

[85] *Venture Capital USA Inc v Yorkton Securities Inc* (2003) 66 OR (3d) 760 (SCJ).

[86] *Shams v Dalvid*, [2000] OJ No 2856, 97-CV-2951 (Ont SCJ). There was no evidence of any American connection in the case apart from the fact that the invoices the plaintiff produced as evidence of the value of the property were in US dollars.

[87] Courts of Justice Act, above n 69, s 121 (3).

[88] Few courts dealing with s 121(3) have dealt explicitly with the burden of proof. Those which have, however, have placed the onus of proving the inequity of the default payment-date conversion rule on the party who argues for some other date: *Moritex Europe Ltd v Oz Optics Ltd*, above n 74 [8], and *Esses v Friedberg & Co*, above n 84 [5]. The courts which have not expressly mentioned the burden of proof have appeared, not surprisingly, to take a similar approach.

broad and unfettered discretion to select whatever conversion date seems proper, a discretion whose exercise need not be justified or explained at length. Moreover, in contrast to the English courts Ontario judges have commonly been willing to select the fair conversion date in light of the direction in which the relevant currencies have fluctuated during litigation.[89] In short, neither in judicial discussion of the features which make a payment-date conversion generally applicable, nor in judicial invocations of the clause that allows them to escape the general conversion date and impose some other, have Ontario courts demonstrated much liking for the notion that the compensation principle requires some fixed principles for dealing with foreign currency.

Canada's smallest province, Prince Edward Island, has a statutory provision identical to Ontario's.[90] However, there is relatively little litigation there and the cases that have been decided under that statute add little to those decided under its Ontario model.[91]

The third Canadian province with legislation on the currency question is British Columbia, which in 1996 enacted a short stand-alone statute dealing with the subject; the Foreign Money Claims Act. Like the Ontario and Prince Edward Island statutes, the British Columbia legislation has the effect of circumventing the federal Currency Act and sanctioning a payment-date conversion. However, its approach as to when such a conversion-date should be reached differs from that in the Ontario and Prince Edward Island legislation. Rather than authorising payment-date conversion when the underlying obligation is designated as 'an obligation in a foreign currency', the British Columbia act authorises a court to do so where it reaches the conclusion that doing so will achieve true and accurate compensation of the plaintiff:

> 1(1) If, before making an order for the payment of money arising out of a claim or loss, the court considers that the person in whose favour the order will be made will be most truly and exactly compensated if all or part of the money payable under the order is measured in a currency other than the currency of Canada, the court must order that the money payable under the order will be that amount of Canadian currency that is necessary to purchase the equivalent amount of the other currency at a chartered bank located in British Columbia at the close of business on the conversion date.

[89] See *Stott v Merit Investment Corp*, above n 56; *Good One Express Canada Ltd v 1355930 Ontario Inc*, 2004 WL 2201655 (Ont SCJ), 2004 CarswellOnt 4054; *Itamunoala v Pierce*, above n 84. For cases that expressly state that the requirement for the operation of the exception in s 121(3) is that the result produced by the general rule must be 'inequitable' see *Yordanes v Bank of Nova Scotia* (2006) 78 OR (3d) 590, 23 BLR (4th) 220 (SCJ) [141], *Buchanan v Geotel Communications Corp* [2002] OJ No 2083, 18 CCEL (3d) 17 (SCJ) [184] and *Bailey v Cintas Corp*, above n 84 [85], *Orr v Magna Entertainment Corp*, [2008] OJ No 116, 63 CCEL (3d) 132 (SCJ) [221]. However, none of those decisions provides much assistance as to why conversion at payment date would be 'inequitable', apart from the fact that payment-date conversion would be less beneficial to the plaintiff than the date the court prefers to select.

[90] Supreme Court Act, above n 69, in force since 1996.

[91] *Lotito v Scantlebury* (1995), 129 Nfld & PEIR 58 (PEISC), rev'd 146 Nfld & PEIR 337 (CA); *Society of Lloyd's v McNeill* (2003), 2003 PEISCTD 88, 233 Nfld & PEIR 37.

(2) The conversion date is the last day, before the day on which a payment under the order is made by the judgment debtor to the judgment creditor, that the bank referred to in subsection (1) quotes a Canadian dollar equivalent to the other currency.[92]

Unlike the Ontario and Prince Edward Island provisions, there is no power under the British Columbia statute to order a different conversion date if the result of payment-date conversion is unjust.[93] Arguably, however, no such power is needed, since a measure of flexibility infused into the statute by its triggering provision—viz, that an order in foreign currency achieves the most true and exact compensation. That is, a court applying the British Columbia statute and wishing to effect a conversion at, say, the breach date or the date of judgment, might simply reach the conclusion that the plaintiff is *not* most truly and exactly compensated by an order in a currency other than that of Canada.[94] Where that is the case the statute has nothing to say on the currency matter; nothing in it operates to constrain the court's selection of the conversion date.

One might hope that that the effect of statute, in freeing courts from the effect both of the Currency Act and the breach-date rule in the old Supreme Court of Canada cases,[95] would enable them to engage in the sorts of inquiry and deliberations that the English courts wrestled with in *Miliangos* and *The Folias*. However, as with decisions in those other two provinces, that hope has not been realised. Certainly after the statute came into effect the judges of British Columbia have not hesitated to change their practice and award damages in foreign currencies. In that province's courts that practice is now commonplace. [96] But their reasons

[92] Foreign Money Claims Act, above n 69 (in force since 1996).

[93] And this is the way the courts of that province have interpreted it: see *Litecubes LLC v Northern Light Products Inc*, 2009 BCSC 427 [13], where the court made it clear that s 1 of the statute was not discretionary.

[94] The court in *Sports Pool Distributors Inc v Dangerfield*, 2008 BCSC 9 contemplated doing this, but in the end concluded that the plaintiff was best compensated by an award in US dollars, so it applied the statute.

[95] Before the British Columbia statute came into force in August 1996 that province's courts held that the Currency Act constrained them from adopting a payment-date conversion: *Am-Pac Forest Products Inc v Phoenix Doors Ltd* (1979) 14 BCLR 63, 12 CPC 97 (SC); *Williams & Glyn's Bank v Belkin Packaging Ltd* (BCCA) above n 56; *Worthen v Brink, Hudson & Lefever Ltd* [1990] BCJ No 2029 (SC); *Banque Indosuez v Canadian Overseas Airlines Ltd* (1990) 40 Carswells Practice Cases (2d) 33 (BCSC), aff'd without reference to this point, [1992] BCJ No 578 (CA); *S&S Seafood Co v Toronto-Dominion Bank* [1993] BCJ No 375 (BCSC). However, some of them had abandoned the breach-date rule and imposed a date later than breach: *Worthen v Brink, Hudson & Lefever Ltd*, [1990] BCJ No 2029 (BCSC) (date at which plaintiff should have spent money in mitigation); *Banque Indosuez* (judgment date); *Prasad v Frandsen*, above n 45 (judgment date); *Salzburger Sparkasse v Total Plastics Service Inc* (1988) 50 DLR (4th) 639 (BCSC) (judgment date). One recent case seems to have overlooked the existence of the statute and felt itself constrained to apply a judgment-date conversion: *Smart v Guerster*, above n 84. And another imposed a trial-date conversion rate from US$, again without mention of the statute: *Powers v Mesaros*, 2007 BCSC 694, 37 BCLR (4th) 119.

[96] *Stanton v Gudbranson* (1999) 45 RFL (4th) 85 (BCSC); *Zaidenburg v Hamouth*, 2003 BCSC 671, aff'd 2005 BCCA 356, 42 BCLR (4th) 303; *British Columbia v Biond Fury* 2004 BCSC 796; *Fraser v Houston* 2005 BCSC 1781; *Carpenter v Whistler Air Services Ltd* 2005 BCSC 296; *Cabaniss v Cabaniss* 2006 BCSC 1522; *Skippings Rutley v Darragh* 2008 BCSC 159; *Catalyst Pulp & Paper Sales Inc v Universal Paper Export Co* 2008 BCSC 515; *Roberts v Horizon FX Limited Partnership* 2009 BCSC 304; *XY Inc v IND Lifetech Inc* 2009 BCSC 453; *Lang v Lapp* 2009 BCSC 638. As with the Ontario provision,

for doing so have often amounted to no more than an unexplained finding that the claimant would, in the words of the legislation, be most truly and exactly compensated if damages were awarded in a currency other than Canadian dollars.[97] In contract cases where the money of account is a foreign currency then the British Columbia courts seem inclined to find that awarding damages in that foreign currency most exactly compensates the claimant.[98] However, this seems partly due to the fact that arguments that might indicate some other currency of judgment, such as the feeling-the-loss test from *The Folias* and *The Despina R*, are not advanced.

This is not to suggest that the British Columbia statute invariably results in a foreign currency award every time it is pleaded. It does not. However, even where the statute has been found inapplicable the courts' reasoning has not been illuminating. In *John James Rickard Noble Second Generation Family Trust v Heuson Pharmaceutical Corp* the court rejected a claim that damages be awarded in US dollars, but offered no reasons other than that it was not 'of the view that the plaintiffs would be "most truly and exactly" compensated if the judgment were in an amount equal to the Canadian dollar equivalent of the US dollar investment converted as of the day before the order'.[99] There was no hint as to what justified this conclusion.

No more illuminating is *Han v Cho*, a claim brought in respect of a fraud perpetrated in Korea in which the plaintiffs had been deceived into giving the defendant billions of Korean won.[100] The plaintiffs succeeded in their claim in a

some British Columbia courts making orders under the statute do not even mention the conversion-date issue. They recognise that the underlying reality of the statute, if it applies, is that damages are awarded in the foreign currency. For instance, the form of judgment in *Sports Pool Distributors Inc v Dangerfield*, 2008 BCSC 9 [133] was simply 'I find that the appropriate order is that the amount of US$254,046 is payable, together with interest, in accordance with the Foreign Money Claims Act and the Foreign Money Claims Regulation, BC Reg 165/96'.

[97] The most detailed and thoughtful analysis of the triggering provision of the statute to date appeared in *Litecubes LLC v Northern Light Products Inc*, above n 93. There the court spent several paragraphs considering the defendant's argument that the plaintiff would not be most truly and exactly compensated if judgment was awarded in US dollars, as the plaintiff had requested. However, the claim was not a complex one like *The Folias*, but rather was one for enforcement of a Missouri judgment that had been rendered in US dollars. It was hardly surprising that the court concluded by rejecting the defendant's argument and issuing judgment in US dollars, and the reasoning sheds little light on how the British Columbia statute should be applied to cases outside the foreign-judgment enforcement context.

[98] As in *Cargo Dynamics Logistic Inc v Apex Micro Manufacturing* 2009 BCSC 832.

[99] *John James Rickard Noble Second Generation Family Trust v Heuson Pharmaceutical Corp* 2004 BCSC 482, 47 CPC (5th) 107 [47]. A different reason for not applying the statute was offered in *Nelson Marketing International Inc v Royal and Sun Alliance Insurance Co of Canada*, 2005 BCSC 772. There Cullen J concluded that the action before him was one involving marine insurance, which was part of Canadian maritime law and thus not affected by provincial statutes. Accordingly he considered himself bound by the old Supreme Court of Canada cases and applied a breach-date conversion. The British Columbia Court of Appeal allowed the appeal on grounds of liability and did not mention the currency issue: 2006 BCCA 327, 57 BCLR (4th) 27. The Supreme Court of Canada dismissed an application for leave to appeal: [2006] SCCA No 370.

[100] *Han v Cho* 2009 BCSC 458.

British Columbia court, but the judge found that the provincial statute did not apply because this was not a case in which the plaintiff would not be most truly compensated by an award in the foreign currency. This holding seems hard to justify. The claim arose out of a transaction carried out in Korea in the currency of that country. However, the won had depreciated as against the Canadian dollar in the years following the breach. The court reasoned that the penalty in a case of this sort should deprive the wrongdoer of the benefits of the fraud and it found that it could do this by holding that this was not the sort of case where the plaintiff would be most truly and exactly compensated by an order in foreign currency. That left the judge free to select a conversion date that seemed equitable in the circumstances and he selected one near the date of breach, a date which benefitted the plaintiffs. There was no judicial inquiry into the precise award that the disgorgement measure of damages would produce, perhaps because the evidence did not make such an inquiry easy. Instead the court seems to have effected a sort of rough approximation of the disgorgement measure by the proxy of (1) first finding that the provincial statute did not apply, so that the court was not required to give judgment in a foreign currency, and then (2) rendering judgment in Canadian dollars and in so doing selecting the most plaintiff-favouring conversion date.[101] In the face of judicial desire to deprive the defendant of all benefits of her fraudulent behaviour, combined with lack of evidence of what those benefits were, the approach in *Han v Cho* is understandable. However, it contributes to a situation where the British Columbia courts seem required to give little explanation for when their currency-of-judgment legislation applies and consequently leaves them relatively unfettered to select conversion dates based on their view of what is equitable in light of fluctuations between the relevant currencies during the course of litigation. Like the Ontario statute, the British Columbia one has been applied in a manner which effectively allows judges to use the currency-of-judgment factor as a tool to permit them to achieve a variety of ends that might be difficult to achieve if they were pursued by other, more direct routes.

None of the seven other Canadian provinces has a general statute dealing with foreign currency obligations. Two, however, have limited legislative provisions that specify the conversion-date issue when foreign-country money judgments are enforced. Article 3161 of Quebec's Civil Code, in force since 1991, opts for the date of the original foreign court order:

> Where a foreign decision orders a debtor to pay a sum of money expressed in foreign currency, a Quebec authority converts the sum into Canadian currency at the rate of exchange prevailing on the day the decision became enforceable at the place where it was rendered.[102]

[101] The court also awarded substantial punitive damages, also in Canadian dollars. Ibid [123].

[102] Art 3161 goes on to address the interest question: 'The determination of interest payable under a foreign decision is governed by the law of the authority that rendered the decision until its conversion'. The article has been overlooked: in *VJ v P-L S* [2006] QJ No 9265 the judge, without reference to the Civil Code, converted a French judgment for euros into Canadian dollars at the exchange rate in force shortly before his judgment—not the French one, which was more than a year earlier. The Federal

This provision appears to permit of no exceptions, though curiously it has been held not to apply to recognition of foreign arbitral awards.[103] Saskatchewan's provision on this same subject, in force since 2006, mandates a different result. In line with *Miliangos*, it requires a payment-date conversion and likewise does not allow for any exceptions.[104] This variety could give rise to strategic behaviour on the part of foreign judgment creditors who have the option of enforcing their judgments in more than one province. Since Quebec legislation mandates conversion at the date of the original foreign judgment, and Ontario, Prince Edward Island, British Columbia and Saskatchewan opt for conversion at the date the judgment is eventually paid, where the foreign currency in question has fluctuated vis-a-vis the Canadian dollar between the time it was granted and when enforcement is sought, the judgment creditor will have an opportunity to select the province for enforcement accordingly.[105]

Where the foregoing statutes do not apply, the currency question in Canada, like that in England, is a matter of judge-made law. There is a good deal of Canadian case law dealing with the conversion-date issue from jurisdictions that have no statute on the matter. At first glance these decisions may seem to have little in common with cases decided under the various statutes just dealt with, since such a large variety of different conversion dates are found in them. Some courts continue to apply the forum-currency/breach-date rule.[106] They do so because they regard themselves as bound by the old Supreme Court of Canada decisions on this point. Some such courts expressly admit that they prefer the

Court of Canada also converts at the date of the foreign judgment, but allows courts free rein to select another date: Federal Court Rule 331 (SOR 98/106) reads: 'Unless the Court orders otherwise, an amount payable under a foreign judgment shall be converted into the equivalent amount in Canadian currency on the basis of the rate of exchange, ascertained from a chartered bank in Canada, that was prevailing on the day on which the foreign judgment was rendered'.

[103] *Varma-Sampo v Beninco Holdings Canada Inc* [2001] JQ No 6011 (CS) [41]. Having held that the Civil Code was silent on the conversion date for arbitral awards the court then followed the decision of the Quebec Court of Appeal in *Cohen v Hill Samuel & Co* [1989] RJQ 2078 [*Cohen v Hill*] and allowed the judgment creditor its choice of conversion dates. See the discussion below at n 130.

[104] Enforcement of Foreign Judgments Act, SS 2005, E-9.121, s 13(1). This statute is based on a 2003 model act of the Uniform Law Conference of Canada. It seems likely that some other Canadian provinces will enact similar statutes before long. The Alberta Law Reform Institute has recommended that that province do so: Alberta Law Reform Institute, *Final Report No 94: Enforcement of Judgments* (Edmonton, Alta, Alberta Law Reform Institute, 2008) 37.

[105] Or even initially to enforce the foreign judgment in one province (say Quebec) and then enforce that judgment in a second (say, Ontario).

[106] *NV Bocimar SA v Century Insurance of Canada*, above n 56; *Dollina Enterprises Ltd v Wilson Haffenden* [1977] 1 FC 169 (TD), aff'd [1977] 2 FC 73 (CA); *Schweizeriche Metallwerke Selve & Co v Atlantic Container Line* (1985) 63 NR 104 (CA); *Capitol Life Insurance Co v Canada* [1988] 2 CTC 101, 87 NR 153 (Fed Ct App); *Kruger Inc v Baltic Shipping Co* [1988] 1 FC 262 (Fed Ct); *Lee S Wilbur & Co v The Martha Ingraham* [1989] FCJ No 427 (TD) (though here, since no evidence was led as to the conversion rate at the date of breach, the court applied the rate in effect at the time of its judgment); *Shibamoto & Co v Western Fish Producers Inc* (1991), 48 FTR 176 (TD), var'd 145 NR 106 (CA); *Kiat v Ng* (1992) 128 NBR (2d) 374 (QB). When that involves enforcement of a foreign-country judgment the date of breach is the date the foreign court issued its judgment: *Morgan v Guimond Boats Ltd* (2006) 357 NR 190 (Fed CA).

reasoning in *Miliangos* but do not feel free to follow it.[107] The majority, however, have found a way to avoid regarding themselves as bound to apply the old rule. They have most commonly done this by distinguishing the old Supreme Court of Canada cases—for example, by finding that the cause of action before them differs in some respect from those in which the Supreme Court affirmed the breach-date rule. This leaves them free to adopt some other conversion date. The dates adopted have not *necessarily* been later than the breach-date; that is, it is possible for a court to conclude that it has the discretion to select a conversion date later than the breach date but that justice is done in the case before it by applying a breach-date conversion.[108] In practice a variety of other conversion dates has been imposed. These include the date costs were incurred to cure the breach,[109] the date of the commencement of the action,[110] the date on which the defendant filed its statement of defence,[111] the date of the hearing,[112] the date of judgment,[113] the date the taxing officer submitted his report as to costs,[114] a specified post-judgment date (eg three months after the judgment),[115] the date of payment,[116] the date of the bankruptcy petition (in some insolvency proceedings),[117] and a

[107] *Farmer's National Bank and Trust Co of Ashtabula v Coles* (1981) 33 NBR (2d) 248 (QB); *Kruger Inc v Baltic Shipping Co* (1988) 11 FTR 80 (TD) 105, aff'd 57 DLR (4th) 498 (CA).

[108] As in *Seafood Exporters Corp of Newfoundland & Labrador v Donnelly Farms Ltd* (1989) 81 Nfld & PEI R 173 (Nfld SC) and *Stendel v Edelman* [1990] JQ No 1065, 30 QAC 202 (CA).

[109] *Santa Marina Shipping Co SA v Madeg Holdings Inc* (1986) 6 FTR 269 (Fed Ct Can).

[110] In *Airtemp Corp v Chrysler Airtemp Ltd* (1981), 121 DLR (3d) 236 (Ont High Ct) this was regarded as the date the plaintiff issued the writ, while in *Clinton v Ford* (1982), 137 DLR (3rd) 281 (Ont Ct Ap) it was taken to be the date the statement of claim was issued. Also *Équipments Stosik Inc v Hock Seng Lee Heavy Industries Sdn Bhd*, 2007 QCCA 1531; *Armtec Ltd v Canada Export Development Corp* 2007 QCCA 99.

[111] *Promech Sorting Systems BV v Bronco Rentals & Leasing Ltd* (1994) 93 Man R (2d) 36 (QB). The case was reversed (123 DLR (4th) 111 (Man CA)), but not on grounds that involved foreign currency.

[112] *Ripulone v Pontecorvo* (1989), 98 NBR (2d) 267 (QB), var'd 104 NBR (2d) 56 (CA).

[113] *Srl Rolimex v McCormack, Zatzman Ltd* (1979) 32 NBR (2d) 436 (QB); *American Savings and Loan Assn v Stechishin* (1993) 14 Alta LR (3d) 255 (QB); *Minkler v Sheppard* (1991) 60 BCLR (2d) 360 (SC); *Salzburger Sparkasse v Total Plastic Services Inc* (1988) 50 DLR 639 (BCSC); *Beukeveld Import-Export Agriculture Machines v Agricultural and Industrial Representatives Ltd* (1988) 75 Nfld & PEIR 156 (PEI SC); *Dino Music AG v Quality Dino Entertainment Ltd* (1994) 94 Man R (2d) 46, [1994] 9 WWR 137 (Man QB); *Alliedsignal Inc v DuPont Canada Inc* [1999] FCJ No 38, 86 Carswells Practice Cases (3d) 324 (Fed Ct App); *PLB Holdings v Gehring* 2002 ABQB 594, 322 AR 205 (QB); *Proctor v Schellenberg* 2002 MBQB 135, [2002] 7 WWR 287, 164 Man Rep (2d) 188, aff'd without reference to this point, 2002 MBCA 170, 30 CPC (5th) 89 (Man Ct App); *PLB Holdings Corp v Gehring*, 2002 ABQB 594, 322 AR 205 (Alta QB); *Lloyd's v Berezowski* 2006 AMQM 625, 63 Alta L R (4th) 169 (QB).

[114] *Dillingham Corp Canada Ltd v The Ship Shinyu Maru* [1980] 1 FC 303 (Fed Ct Canada). Obviously this was not a claim for damages. It was, however, closely analogous to that since it involved a claim for disbursement on behalf of the successful defendant. The taxing officer had decided that the conversion from the currency of expenditure into Canadian dollars should be made at the rate prevailing on the day the action was discontinued. The court held that it should be the date of the taxing officer's report.

[115] *Skaggs Companies Inc v Mega Technical Holdings Inc* [2001] 1 WWR 359 (Alta QB).

[116] *Ferris v Welsh* [1985] BCJ No 128 (Co Ct) (QL).

[117] *Re Canadian Vinyl Industries Inc* (1978) 29 CBR (NS) 112 (Que SC); *Re Olympia & York Developments Ltd* (1997) 45 CBR (3d) 100 (Ont Ct Gen Div)). These cases were decided before the 1997 amendments to federal bankruptcy legislation that mandated a date-of-bankruptcy conversion

combination of different dates.[118] Still other Canadian judges (again, expressly relying on *Miliangos*, and ignoring the Currency Act) have simply given judgment in a foreign currency,[119] the equivalent of a payment-date conversion.

A further source of uncertainty arises within Canada from the fact that in some instances plaintiffs may have a choice of which province to bring their action in, or the choice of bringing a suit in either a federal or a provincial court. In such instances, even if the case law within a given judicial system seems to display some consistency of approach to the currency-of-judgment/conversion-date issue, that does not guarantee certainty with respect to a given dispute, at least not until the plaintiff commences its action. In short, Canada experiences the problem of forum shopping between provinces and between provincial and federal courts with respect to the conversion-date question.

If all of this seems little short of chaos it may be helpful to note that this variety of conversion dates does not arise from judges who have arrived at the conclusion that a given conversion date is the logically correct one and should be applied in all cases. Rather, although they generally purport to approve of and follow *Miliangos*, they tend to take the view that flexibility is the prime virtue and that courts should have the power to select among a range of possible conversion dates. Thus a court which applies a judgment-date conversion one day may find itself applying a breach-date conversion the next. *Miliangos* is thus generally understood not as substituting one firm date (that of payment) for another (the breach-date). Rather, it is read as overturning an out-of-date regime in which judges were constrained to apply a given conversion date and setting them free to select a date that is fair. In the words of a typical Canadian judgment:

> I take the position that I have the discretion to choose a currency conversion rate which best promotes equity between the parties based on the particular circumstances of the case before me. This is all the more important in times of dramatically fluctuating currency rates in which we find ourselves in this time. The courts should not be hampered by a rigid rule which does not allow equity to be done in the circumstances of each individual case.[120]

Moreover, that discretion is generally understood in Canada as one that should be exercised in favour of the plaintiff. That is, if the foreign currency has appreciated vis-a-vis the Canadian dollar during the course of litigation, then a late

date: above n 57. For a full discussion of Canadian case law on this point before the 1997 amendment see J Honsberger, 'Foreign Currency Problems in Canadian Proposals' (1983) 1 *National Insolvency Review* 12.

[118] *Agrex SA v Canadian Dairy Commission* (1984) 24 BLR 206 (Fed Ct); *McCutcheon v McCutcheon* (1989) 102 NBR 271 (QB). In *Prasad v Frandsen*, above n 45, a personal injury case, the court awarded damages for lost wages in sterling (the money in which those wages would have been earned), with a conversion to dollars as of the judgment day, but awarded damages for pain and suffering in the money of the forum. Canadian courts seem generally to have understood that the rate of pre-judgment interest should be that of the currency in which judgment is effectively awarded: *Reading and Bates Construction Co v Baker Energy Resources* [1995] 1 FC 483 (CA) 506.

[119] See the three cases cited in n 61.

[120] *Alpine Canada Alpin v Non-Marine Underwriters, Lloyd's London* (1999) 245 Alta Rep 252 [1999] 1 WWR 359 (QB) [35].

conversion date should be chosen—that of judgment or payment. The express reasoning in such cases is that such a result prevents a windfall to the defendant.[121] On the other hand, if the Canadian dollar rises during the course of litigation, then an early conversion date is perceived as fairer—perhaps the breach date or the date on which the plaintiff launched its action. Some courts have even permitted the plaintiff, during the course of litigation, to modify the conversion date it is requesting, and to do so in express response to currency fluctuations during litigation—again stating that such an approach is fair.[122]

The judgment that has spelled out in the most detail the rationale for judicial choice in selection of the conversion date is the 2004 decision of the Manitoba Court of Appeal in *Kellogg Brown & Root Inc v Aerotech Herman Nelson Inc*,[123] a sale of goods case. *Kellogg* is among the lengthiest Canadian considerations of the conversion date question, including the two Supreme Court of Canada cases on the subject,[124] and one of few in which there was a dissent. In his dissenting judgment Twaddle JA, while expressing some sympathy for *Miliangos*, thought that precedent did not permit Canadian lower courts to depart from the breach-date rule laid down long ago in *Custodian* and *Gatineau Power*. To him it was open for the Supreme Court of Canada to revisit the issue, and indeed high time for it to do so, but until such time as the Supreme Court should overrule its own pre-*Miliangos* breach-date decisions it was improper for any other Canadian courts to ignore those authorities. He noted that several Canadian lower courts had thought otherwise and he pointed out the resulting confusion. In parts, Twaddle JA's reasons read as a plea for a fixed, mandatory conversion date. His main thrust however, is simply to decry the fact that those Canadian courts which in the period after *Miliangos* had concluded that they were not bound by the breach-date rule had been anything but unanimous in settling on what new rule should apply. That is, he was not necessarily arguing against a rule that afforded judges a measure of choice in selecting the conversion date.

In response, the majority spent some time concluding that they were not bound by the old breach-date cases from the Supreme Court of Canada, both because those cases were based on English authority that had since been rejected by the House of Lords in *Miliangos* and because they had been decided against a background of stable currencies that no longer characterised international money markets.[125] Having freed itself from the shackles of precedent the majority felt free to craft a new approach. In doing so it emphasised the importance of full compensation for the 'innocent plaintiff' and the ability of the party in breach to hedge against the possibility of currency fluctuations by buying an appropriate amount of Canadian dollars. Since the Canadian dollar had fallen vis-a-vis the

121 *Stevenson Estate v Siewert* (2000) 191 DLR (4th) 151 (Alta CA).
122 *C-L Associates Inc v Airside Equipment Sales* (2000) 151 Man R (2d) 200 (QB).
123 Above n 56.
124 *Custodian*, above n 52.
125 *Kellogg*, above n 56 [89–103].

relevant foreign currency between the date of breach and the trial judgment and then risen again between the trial judgment and the appeal, the court selected the higher of those two dates—the trial judgment—as the appropriate conversion date. No reference was made to the fact that this solution did *not* achieve the court's stated goal of allowing the defendant to hedge against fluctuation by purchasing Canadian dollars as of the breach date.[126] The court emphasised judicial flexibility in selecting the appropriate conversion date in light of the 'equities' of the case, and while it did not go so far as to say that invariably involved selecting the most plaintiff-favouring date, that's where it came down in this case.

The courts that have gone the furthest in formalising this creditor-favouring position are those of Quebec. Indeed no jurisdiction in the world appears to have gone farther. As noted and discussed above, Quebec has a mandatory statutory conversion date that applies to enforcement of foreign judgments.[127] However, it has no comparable provisions bearing on other foreign currency obligations, leaving judges free to craft their own. *Miliangos* was favourably received in Quebec courts but, unlike the courts of some other Canadian provinces, Quebec judges held that the requirement in the federal Currency Act to deliver judgment only in Canadian dollars meant that the latest conversion date they could select was that prevailing at judgment.[128] However, in 1989 the Quebec Court of Appeal held that, as a general rule fairness required that the successful plaintiff be able to select its preferred conversion date, and moreover to wait until trial to do so. *Cohen v Hill* continues to be the touchstone of Quebec law on foreign currency obligations and its reasons deserve to be quoted at some length:

> Without proof of negligence, the interests of the creditor should be preferred over those of the debtor when considering choice of conversion date. His title is established. … If he deems a certain date of conversion to adequately protect his interests, then this date should be accepted and evidence of the exchange rate should be sufficient for the Quebec tribunal to make a judgment.…
>
> The creditor, in a given situation, must produce evidence of the exchange rate. If his claim is justified, he can benefit from his preferred choice of conversion date. After all, the debtor can always pay earlier. One exception would be a case where the creditor's

[126] At risk of unnecessary repetition, the reason for that is as follows: A defendant who at the date of breach purchases sufficient forum currency to cover any eventual judgment will not be able to protect itself from a court which selects as the conversion date the time when the forum currency was at its peak. In *Kellogg*, Canadian currency had gone up between breach and trial, but at that time the defendant would have had no way of knowing which way it was going to go in the future. If it had purchased the Canadian currency at the breach date and then held onto it until the appeal judgment, it would not have had enough to satisfy the judgment the appeal court imposed, since it imposed a judgment which converted from the foreign currency obligation to Canadian dollars as of the higher value of the Canadian dollar which existed at the date of trial.

[127] Above n 102.

[128] That was the position in Quebec before *Miliangos*: *Carsley Silk*, above n 60. It continued to be the position after: *AeroThrust Corp v Québecair* [1989] QJ No 1212 (SC); *Cohen v Hill*, above n 103; *Stendel v Edelman* [1990] JQ No 1065, 30 QAC 202 (Que CA); *Universal Paper Export Co v Tembec Inc* [2001] QJ No 5227 (SC); *Armtec Ltd v Canada Export Development Corp*, 2007 QCCA 99 (Que CA).

> inaction or negligence results in a conversion date which prejudices the debtor due to a fluctuating exchange rate.
>
> A creditor may not speculate at the expense of a debtor. However, if the debtor hasn't paid in an expeditious manner, he can't complain about the creditor's choice of conversion date. The respondent thus has the right to choose the exchange rate at the date of the foreign judgment, and to provide evidence, and the lower court judge has the right to decide on the basis of this rate.[129]

Since then the typical Quebec case dealing with a foreign currency obligation has been resolved by a brief reference to *Cohen v Hill* followed by the court allowing the successful plaintiff to select its preferred conversion date, up to and including the date of judgment.[130]

Cohen v Hill does not go quite so far as to give the successful plaintiff an untrammelled choice of conversion dates. First, plaintiffs cannot simply select any date in history for the conversion from the foreign money. Rather, the date must be no earlier than when the cause of action arose and no later than the date of judgment, and must moreover be a date upon which something relevant to the action happened—that is, the date of breach, of the plaintiff sending a demand for payment, of launching the action, of trial, but not simply a date plucked from the calendar.[131] There are additional limitations. *Cohen v Hill* said that the plaintiff cannot speculate at the expense of the defendant and that to exercise its choice of conversion dates the plaintiff must not have been negligent. It did not elaborate on these requirements but later cases have dealt

[129] Ibid at p 2083. The case dealt with enforcement of a UK judgment rendered in sterling. At that time the new *Civil Code* had not yet come into effect so art 3161, discussed above at n 102, did not yet govern the conversion date in such situations. Conversion of foreign court judgments is now a matter for art 3161, but *Cohen v Hill Samuel & Co* has been held to apply to foreign currency obligations generally.

[130] But not up to the date of payment, for the Currency Act is regarded as precluding that: *Melrose International Trading Ltd v IMP Inc* [1998] QJ No 398 (QC); *Kroll Associates Inc v Calvi* [1999] QJ No 1348 (SC); *Hohe-Modell M Hohe GmbH & Co KG v Jocami International Inc* [1999] QJ No 2081 (SC); *Lebedev v Papa* [1999] QJ No 4251; *Dallaire v Kirouac* [1999] QJ No 6807 (SC); *173384 Canada Inc v Jubinville* [1999] QJ No 5637 (SC); *Newfoundland Ltd v Wrebbit Toys and Games Manufacturers Inc* [2000] JQ 1643 (SC); *Gérald Abelson Holdings Inc v Platinum Equity Holding Inc* [2002] QJ No 2691 (SC), aff'd [2004] QJ No 6827 (CA); *Universal Paper Export Co v Tembec Inc*, above n 82; *Morris Asset Management Inc v Telistics Software Inc* [2005] QJ No 1966 (SC); *Van der Heyden v Bell Canada International Inc* [2005] JQ No 12726 (SC); *Nottingham Builders Ltd v Location de Motoneiges Haute Matawinie Inc* 2006 QCCQ; *Iron Ore Company of Canada v Export Development Canada* 2007 QCCS 4296 (SC); and *Équipements Stosik Inc v Hock Seng Lee Heavy Industries Sdn Bhd* 2007 QCCA 1531. However, when a plaintiff wanted to rely on the rule in *Cohen v Hill* to sustain a claim for foreign exchange losses the court would not allow it: in *Le Portz v Ethypharm* QCCS 2703 the plaintiff wanted to augment its claim by saying that late payment of a debt deprived it of its chance to exchange the expected payment for euros, and that euros having appreciated against the dollar during litigation the rule in *Cohen v Hill* required that compensation be awarded for the resulting loss. The court rejected that.

[131] This is confirmed in *Sanchez v Ayraud* 2008 QCCQ 1279. There the court acknowledged that the plaintiff should get its choice of conversion dates but did not allow the plaintiff to backdate that choice to a date before the breach.

with them. In *Tradex Ltd v Laframboise Monetary Services International Inc*[132] the court—motivated by the fact that the defendant had not been at fault but was simply being required to repay funds under a contract that was being held ineffective—decided that it would be inequitable to allow the plaintiff either of its preferred conversion dates (the date the defendant received payment from the plaintiff or the date of the institution of the action) and imposed instead a judgment-date conversion. While the case is encouraging in its recognition that the interests of the defendant must play some role in the selection of the appropriate conversion date, its reasoning is brief and unconvincing. The defendant had received an advance under a contract. The advance was in US dollars at a time when that currency was very strong as against the Canadian dollar. At trial it was held that, through no fault of the defendant, the contract had become largely ineffective and that a portion of the advance should be repaid. By this time the Canadian and US dollars were close to par, so the plaintiff not surprisingly argued for conversion from US to Canadian dollars at the time it had originally paid the defendant, which would have the effect of giving it a lot more Canadian dollars. The court thought that this would be 'inequitable' to the defendant, but there was no consideration of the plaintiff's position. In short, the judgment offers little helpful guidance on when a plaintiff's choice of conversion date will be rejected as unfair to the defendant.

Canadian courts taking the generally plaintiff-favouring route exemplified in *Cohen v Hill* sometimes rely on the passages in *Miliangos* that point to the injustice of under-compensating the plaintiff by selecting a conversion date that fails to meet the standards of *restitutio in integrum*. As noted in the previous chapter, such passages certainly exist; Lord Wilberforce was concerned to avoid under-compensation in the case before him. However, in *Miliangos* he was also concerned with the possibility of overcompensation, and his solution was one which required the plaintiff to take the risks of fluctuations of the currency in which it would feel the loss, and to take those for good or ill—a solution promoted by a payment-date conversion in all cases.

That the current Canadian approach would claim support from *Miliangos*, then, is curious. *Miliangos* provides a certain—some even call it rigid—conversion date. While it is true that in *The Despina R* Lord Wilberforce acknowledged that there could be dangers in approving a hard and fast rule,[133] that was in the context of trying to lay down a sub-rule for determining the single currency which most truly expresses the plaintiff's loss. *The Despina R* says that judgment must be awarded in the currency in which the plaintiff felt its loss, and then goes on to admit that in some cases there may be difficulty in determining just what that currency is. However, it never approves an approach that grants a judge discretion in the matter.

[132] *Tradex Ltd v Laframboise Monetary Services International Inc* 2008 QCCS 3299.

[133] *Owners of MV Eleftherotria v Owners of MV Despina R* [1979] AC 685, [1979] 1 Lloyd's Law Rep 1(HL) (*The Despina R*) 698–99 (AC).

The odd Canadian reading of *Miliangos* is evident both in the courts of the provinces where the currency-of-judgment problem is left entirely to judges and in those that have statutes on the matter, for the statutes are principally concerned to free judges from the breach-date rule and the need to grant judgment only in Canadian dollars and do not go further and attempt to define when an obligation must be vindicated by a judgment in foreign money. In both instances it as if Canadian courts had only read the first part of *Miliangos*—the part that castigated the breach-date rule—and had read neither the second half of *Miliangos* nor any of the post-*Miliangos* House of Lords cases which strove to sort out the consequence of the new payment-date rule. It is no easy matter to account for this, though as we will see both in some later sections of this chapter and in the following chapter's exploration of American law, Canadian judges are not entirely alone in their interpretation of *Miliangos*. Moreover Canada's most authoritative academic writer on the law of damages, Stephen Waddams, is in favour of a measure of flexibility in selecting the conversion date, and his work is sometimes cited by Canadian courts who favour this approach.[134] Another explanation for the unusual Canadian construal of *Miliangos* may simply be that in the private law of Canada flexibility is an especially prized virtue. In crafting a private law which departs from its English parent, Canadian judges seem frequently to have taken the view that a one-size-fits-all rule is rigid, mechanical, old-fashioned and, most importantly, productive of injustice. They view the English emphasis on certainty as misguided—as a willingness to sacrifice fair results in the individual case for the benefits of bright-line rules. Thus, despite their shared legal heritage, there are many tests and standards in Canadian private law that are more open-ended and flexible than their counterparts in England—for instance the test for unconscionability,[135] determining the scope of the duty of care in the tort of negligence,[136] exceptions to the general rule against third-party beneficiaries,[137] the test for unjust enrichment[138] and the test for who may owe a fiduciary duty.

This, however, seems woefully insufficient to explain what after all amounts to a plain misreading of a House of Lords judgment. We will see, however, that it is a not a misreading that is confined to Canada.

[134] S Waddams, *The Law of Damages*, looseleaf edn (Aurora, Ont, Canada Law Book, 2008) [7.300].

[135] Compare *Hunter Engineering Co v Syncrude Canada Ltd* (1989) 57 DLR (4th) 385 (Sup Ct Can) (especially its use of the open-ended concept of inequality of bargaining power) with *National Westminster Bank plc v Morgan* [1985] AC 686 (HL).

[136] Compare *Cooper v Hobart* [2001] 3 SCR 537 (with its focus on foreseeability and policy) with the more categorical approach in *Caparo Industries v Dickman* [1990] 1 All ER 568 (HL) and *Murphy v Brentwood District Council* [1990] 2 All ER 908 (HL).

[137] In Canada the Supreme Court discovered a flexible exception to the strict third-party beneficiary rule in *Fraser River Pile & Dredge Ltd v Can-Dive Services Ltd* [1999] SCR 108 (Sup Ct Can). English courts found no such exception, so eventually Parliament had to step in: Contracts (Rights of Third Parties) Act 1991, c 31.

[138] Compare *Pettkus v Becker* [1980] 2 SCR 834 with *Kleinwort Benson Ltd v Lincoln City Council* [1999] 2 AC 349 (HL).

IV. Australia

The Australian story is in most ways similar to the Canadian. On the eve of *Miliangos* the breach-date rule seemed securely in place, supported by a decision of the country's top court. In the wake of *Miliangos* we still have no comprehensive analysis of the matter from the highest appellate court. But the country's lower courts, convinced that *Miliangos* was correctly decided, have found ways to move to a payment-date conversion. However, as in Canada they have not read *Miliangos* as requiring that result, but only as permitting it when circumstances justify it, and that justification is generally found only where such a conversion date benefits the plaintiff. The Australian scene differs from the Canadian one in that Australia has no legislation which seeks comprehensively to address the currency-of-judgment question, but apart from that the two countries' responses to foreign currency obligations are remarkably similar.

The extension of *Miliangos* to the Australian legal system seems to have proceeded nearly without impediment. There is no record of any Australian judge expressing the view that *Miliangos* was wrongly decided. Rather, the general response was that the House of Lords had made a timely adaptation of the law to the demands of commercial reality and that Australian courts should take the same route. Still, as with Canada, Australian decisions on the currency-of-judgment rule reveal that there is more than one way to understand *Miliangos*. Let us examine the Australian developments in more detail.

Before *Miliangos* Australian courts had followed English authority and applied the forum-currency/breach-date rule. In 1931 the High Court of Australia had quoted English authority for the proposition that 'in translating damages from foreign currency into sterling, the date at which that process has to be effected is the date of the breach of contract'.[139] It went on to hold that 'the rule must be the same between the currencies of the Dominions'.[140] This principle was applied as recently as the year before *Miliangos*, when the Supreme Court of Victoria refused to register a mortgage in which all money sums were expressed in US dollars.[141]

In these decisions there was no sense that there was anything inappropriate or unjust in the application of the forum-currency/breach-date rule; its operation was mandated not only by the authority of English precedent but by the dictates of common sense. There was one notable pre-*Miliangos* case in which an Australian judge had, in effect, applied a judgment-date rule.[142] However, that was not a claim for damages. Rather, the action was one for breach of trust, where

[139] *AH McDonald and Co Pty v Wells* (1931) 45 CLR 506, 515, quoting *In re British American Continental Bank: Goldzieher & Penso's Claim* (1922) 2 Ch 575 (CA) 587.
[140] Ibid.
[141] *Bando Trading Co v Registrar of Titles* [1975] VR 353 (SC). There is a statutory exception imposing a judgment-date conversion in limited circumstances: Civil Aviation (Carriers Liability) Act 1959 (Cth), s 23.
[142] *Re Dawson*, above n 2.

the court viewed the underlying legal obligation on the defendant as being to effect compensation *in specie*. Apart from that there is no record of pre-*Miliangos* departure from the forum-currency/breach date rule.

Then came *Miliangos*, which presented Australian judges with the same tension between the demands of stare decisis and those of commercial good sense that we have seen in the courts of Scotland and Canada. Early in the post-*Miliangos* era the President of the New South Wales Court of Appeal expressed the view this dilemma should be resolved in favour of following precedent. He stated that if an Australian judge at first instance were to follow *Miliangos* and award damages in a foreign currency, such a decision 'would be found erroneous, and corrected on appeal'.[143] This was not because *Miliangos* was thought to be wrong, but because, in light of existing authorities on the subject, such a change in the law should not be brought about by a judge of first instance. This reflects a view that Lord Wilberforce has expressed in *Miliangos* itself in commenting on the decision of the Court of Appeal in that case—namely that, since the forum-currency/breach-date rule had been confirmed by decisions of final appeal courts, changes to that should be brought about only by those same courts.

Despite this view, however, imposition of the payment-date rule in Australia did not await intervention by final appellate court. Rather it was implemented by first-instance decisions. For instance, in a collision case the Admiralty Division of the Supreme Court of New South Wales was prepared to apply *The Despina R* and award damages in Japanese yen (which had recently appreciated as against the Australian dollar) based on no more than an 'inference … that it conducted its operations in yen and that it had expended its normal currency to meet the expenditure on the repairs which were carried out'.[144] This decision was approved the following year, where the judge noted that in the years immediately following *Miliangos* the commercial judges of New South Wales had, after some initial difficulties, 'regularly entered judgments for plaintiffs in foreign currency'.[145] The year after that the abandonment of the forum-currency/breach-date rule was extended

[143] *Johnco Nominees Pty v Albury-Wondonga (New South Wales) Corp* [1977] 1 NSWLR 43 (CA), 56. To similar effect see *Proctor v Jetway Aviation Pty* [1984] 1 NSWLR 166, 171 and 179 (New South Wales, Ct App). It should be noted that, unlike Canada, Australia has no statutory provision which might be construed to stand in the way of granting judgments expressed in foreign currencies.

[144] *Mitsui Osk Lines Ltd v The Mineral Transporter* [1983] 2 NSWLR 564 (SC, Adm). The judge then went on to calculate pre-judgment interest with reference to Australian rather than Japanese rates. This is contrary to the more common and more sensible practice of employing the interest rates applicable to the currency in question, but it appears that neither party suggested that the court do otherwise. An appeal to the Privy Council was allowed in part ([1986] AC 1) on the question of liability, but the currency issue was not addressed and the JCPC confirmed, at least in part, an Australian judgment in yen.

[145] *Maschinenfabrik Augsburg-Nurenburg AG v Altikar Pty* [1984] 3 NSWLR 152 (Comm List) 153; *Aldridge Electrical Industries Pty v Mobitec Ab* (20 Sept 2001), [2001] NSWSC 823. In addition, the *Miliangos (No 2)* (above n 8) approach to the appropriate interest rate on judgments in foreign currencies now seems firmly entrenched in Australia: *State Bank of New South Wales Ltd v Swiss Bank Corp* (1995) 39 NSWLR 350 (CA); *Westpac Banking Corp v Stone Gemini* [1999] FCA 917; *New Cap Reinsurance Corp v Grant* [2009] NSWSC 662.

to the bankruptcy context.[146] In addition, in 1988 the Australian Law Reform Commission issued a report, the General Insolvency Inquiry, which addressed the conversion-date question. It recommended legislative adoption of the solution that had been reached in England in the *Dynamics Corp* and *Lines* decisions, namely that all such claims be should converted on the same date—the date of the insolvency.[147] This eventually found its way into Commonwealth legislation dealing with the winding up of corporations.[148] That did not extend to bankruptcies of individuals, but the same result was reached there by judicial decision.[149]

The general approach of the Australian courts in their abandonment of the forum-currency/breach-date approach was to echo the observations in *Miliangos* that changes in the commercial world—specifically the increase in dealings in foreign currency and the recent prevalence of daily currency fluctuation—had brought about a situation where justice demanded that judges be able to award damages in foreign currencies, and that, given *Miliangos*, there was no impediment to Australian judges following that route.[150] For example, in *David Securities Pty v Commonwealth Bank of Australia* the Federal Court noted that departure from the forum-currency/breach-date rule was justified by *Miliangos* 'in the

[146] *Re Ikin; ex parte Lamborghini Tractors of Australia Pty* (1985) 58 ALR 759 (Fed Ct). In December 1985 there were legislative amendments to Australian bankruptcy legislation which addressed the foreign currency issue. The Statute Law (Miscellaneous Provisions) Act (No 2) 1985 revised s 41 of the Bankruptcy Act to provide that bankruptcy notices shall be issued in a form which permits the debtor to pay either in a foreign currency or in Australian dollars, as converted from the relevant foreign currency the rate prevailing two days before the bankruptcy notice. As noted in *Bond v HongkongBank of Australia* (1992) 106 ALR 273, 277 (Fed Ct), this gives the debtor 'the advantage of being able to select, at the time he effects payment, that which then is the more favourable course'. Near the end of 1996 a minor alteration to this provision was brought into force by the Bankruptcy Legislation Amendment Act 1996 (Cth), No 44 1996. This provision and the general issue of the conversion date in bankruptcy are discussed in *Parianos v Lymlid Pty Ltd* (28 June 1999) [1999] FCA 684 (Fed Ct Aust), a case which decided that a bankruptcy notice that did not employ the conversion date set out in the rules was a nullity.

[147] The Law Reform Commission, *Report No 45: General Insolvency Inquiry* (Canberra, Australian Government Publishing Service, 1988) vol 1, 328.

[148] Corporations Act 2001, s 554C, which was added by 2001 No 50. That section, which is in the portion of the statute dealing with winding up of corporations, provides that the conversion takes place on the relevant date, and the definition of 'relevant date' indicates that it is the date on which the winding up is taken to have begun. Even before the legislation came into effect courts had reached the same result: *Re Gresham Corp Pty* [1990] 1 Qd R 306 (SC).

[149] *Re Griffiths* [2004] FCAFC 102 (Fed Ct Aust) (16 August 2004). That unanimous decision did go on to say, in [74], that there might be exceptions to this rule 'in an unusual case'. The Court of Appeal of the New South Wales Supreme Court took a similar approach with receiverships: *Fisher v Madden* (2002) 54 NSWLR 179.

[150] These are substantially the reasons offered by the Supreme Court of Queensland in *Australian and New Zealand Banking Group Ltd v Cawood* [1987] 1 Qd R 131 (SC) 133–34, where contract damages in Swiss francs were authorised, a decision which was followed the next year in *European Asian Bank AG v Katsikalis* [1988] 1 Qd R 45 (SC). The view taken in the Supreme Court of South Australia was remarkably similar: *Foti v Banque Nationale de Paris (No 1)* (1989) 54 SASR 354 (SC) 430–32. And the same result was reached in the State of Victoria, *ITC Distribution Ltd v Filmpac Holdings Ltd*, unreported (SC Vict) No 4787 of 1990, (6 March 1990), where Fullagar J wondered whether it was proper for a single judge at first instance to depart from older authority and follow *Miliangos*, but decided to do so because he thought the result was desirable.

present state of currency upheaval'.[151] As in *Miliangos* itself, such references to a present supposedly unprecedented state of currency fluctuation (generally unsubstantiated by any evidence that the present is in truth a time of particularly violent fluctuations) served to cast doubt on the breach-date rule and to dispel any obligation to state in detail what is wrong with such a rule. Opposition to the *Miliangos* payment-date rule is thus made to appear obsolete and oblivious to the reality of the modern commercial world.

There have been some peripheral limitations to the triumph of *Miliangos* in Australia. For instance there have been split decisions on whether the Corporations Law[152] requires that statutory demands brought under that statute be phrased in Australian dollars, even if the underlying currency is a foreign one.[153] Similarly it has been held that income tax assessments must be made only in Australian dollars[154] and occasionally a trial judge will decide that the old breach-date rule still applies.[155] However, in the field of pure private law there was no notable resistance to *Miliangos*. Moreover, Commonwealth legislation passed in 1991 dealing with enforcement of some foreign-country court judgments confirms that when those judgments are in a foreign currency, as of course they typically are,[156] they may be registered in that currency.[157]

[151] *David Securities Pty v Commonwealth Bank of Australia* No G234 of 1988 (6 June 1989) 25. Another Victorian case which refers to the regular practice of entering judgments in foreign currencies is *MEC Import Sales Pty v Iozelli SRL*, unreported (SC Vict) No 6361 of 1998 (25 Sept 1998). Comparable Federal Court decisions are *Ly v Jenkins* [2001] FCA 1640 (Fed Ct Aust) [155] and *Marketforce Advertising Ltd v Stadium Events Pty* [2009] WADC 126.

[152] S 459E(2)(e).

[153] See, eg: *Vehicle Wash Systems Pty v Mark VII Equipment Inc* (1997) 150 ALR 261 (Fed Ct Aust) (must be in Australian dollars); *Daewoo Australia Pty v Suncorp-Metway Ltd* [2000] NSWSC 35 (Sup Ct 11 February 2000) (may be in forum currency).

[154] *Conley v Deputy Commissioner of Taxation* (1998) 152 ALR 467 (Fed Ct Aust).

[155] *Glen King Marine & Trading Services v Owners of the Ship Armada Ternak* (26 June 1998) QG 82 of 1997 (Fed Ct Aus). The court held that *Miliangos* was confined to claims in debt and did not apply to damages. No mention was made of *The Despina R* or *The Folias*.

[156] Of course these days foreign judgments are not necessarily in the national money of the original forum. For instance, in *Jenton Overseas Pte Ltd v Townsing* [2008] VSC 470 the Supreme Court of Victoria confirmed the enforcement of a Singapore judgment that had been rendered in New Zealand dollars.

[157] Foreign Judgments Act 1991 (Cth), s 6(11)(a). Section 6(11)(b) gives the judgment creditor the option of converting from the foreign currency to Australian dollars at the time of registration. This does not seem an unfair instance of plaintiff choice; since the selection is not retroactive and since the judgment debtor is given notice of the registration the judgment debtor always knows which currency the judgment must be paid in. It has been held that when a foreign judgment is registered with the currency of the original judgment and is converted into Australian dollars as of the date of the original judgment the registration is a nullity and must be set aside: *Lewis v Beck*, unreported 12 May 1998 BC9802042 (Sup Ct Victoria). An interesting case arose under the statute in *Re SA Cryonic Medical*, unreported 22 August 2002 BC200204891 (Sup Ct Victoria) where a judgment debtor sought to register a foreign judgment for the sum of 158,000 French francs—a currency that no longer existed at the time of registration. The creditor wanted that converted to Australian dollars and the statute required that conversion to be carried out as of the time of registration. The court solved the problem by first converting from francs at the official conversion date in force when the euro took over from the franc, and then from euros to Australian dollars at the rate in effect as of the time of the registration of the judgment under the act.

When the matter finally arose for consideration by an appellate court, the *Miliangos* principle was, unsurprisingly, approved, and thus it now appears there is little doubt that it is part of the law of Australia. However that case—the decision of the Court of Appeal of New South Wales in *Brown Boveri (Australia) Pty v Baltic Shipping Co*[158]—arguably promulgates a misunderstanding of *Miliangos*. *Brown Boveri* in fact had little to do with *Miliangos*, since it concerned the liability limitation in The Hague Rules of 1924. Specifically the case was concerned with whether that cap on damages should be determined with respect to 1924 values or current ones. The court held in favour of the former, which benefitted the plaintiff. The defendant advanced an argument based on *Miliangos*, and on a statement from the post-*Miliangos* English case of *Barclays Bank International Ltd v Levin Brothers (Bradford) Ltd*[159] where Mocatta J had expressed the view that the *Miliangos* rule was an optional one (a view that had subsequently been rejected in England). The court in *Brown Boveri* distinguished the application of *Barclay's Bank* to the issue before it (where the *defendant* sought the option of paying in the currency of its choice), but appeared to adopt the view that the plaintiff retained that option when it brought suit. In other words, in its view nothing flowing from *Miliangos* ever required a plaintiff to express its claim in a foreign currency:

> Each country is entitled to expect that, special provision apart, a debt for civil wrong will be settled in that country, at least if a party entitled to sue there so claims. The currency of Australia is Australian dollars. The [plaintiff] has lawfully sued it in the Supreme Court of this State of Australia claiming a judgment expressed in that currency. There is nothing to require it to accept payment in pounds sterling in this country.[160]

Brown Boveri has been followed on this point,[161] and this approach even appears to have been approved by the High Court of Australia, though that was only in a passing comment.[162] Thus it appears that in Australia the *Miliangos* rule payment-date rule functions as an optional one—a rule that plaintiffs can invoke or not, as they see fit. This differs a little from the Canadian position in that the Australian cases display little of that commitment to a flexible, equitable approach which, in an effort to forestall so-called windfalls, expressly takes account of the ways in

[158] (1989) 15 NSWLR 448 (CA) (*Brown Boveri*).

[159] *Barclays Bank International Ltd v Levin Brothers (Bradford) Ltd* [1977] 1 QB 270 (QB).

[160] *Brown Boveri*, above n 158, 464.

[161] *Vlasons Shipping, Inc v Neuchatel Swiss General Insurance Co Ltd (No 2)* [1998] VSC 135 (20 Nov 1998). The court in *Vlasons* also followed *ITC Distribution Ltd*, above n 150, on this same point. For a recent case that appears to confirm that the payment-date rule is one that plaintiffs may invoke at their option see *Norsemeter Holdings AS v Pieter Boele (No 3)* [2002] NSWSC 390. *Trainor Asia Ltd v Calverley* [2007] WADC 124 (Dist Ct West Aus) is another case where the court claims a discretion to award damages in foreign currencies or convert to Australian dollars at a date of its choosing.

[162] As with Canada, Australia's highest court has not considered the currency-of-judgment question in the post-*Miliangos* era. However, in one case dealing with another aspect of the law of damages one judge of the High Court of Australia made a brief approving reference to *Miliangos* and seemed to suggest that its rule was an optional one: *Johnson v Perez* (1988) 166 CLR 351, 387. The High Court also made passing reference to *Miliangos* in *Public Service Board of New South Wales v Osmond* (1986) 159 CLR 656 and *Commonwealth v Amann Aviation Pty* (1991) 174 CLR 64, but those were not foreign currency cases either.

which the relevant currencies have fared against one another during litigation. Rather, the Australian view seems simply to be that the right of a plaintiff before an Australian court to demand payment in Australian dollars was a longstanding one, and that *Miliangos* should be understood as *supplementing* that right (by adding the option of seeking judgment in a foreign currency) but not as taking it away. This appears to represent a notable departure from *Miliangos*, however comparable to the situation we have seen in Canada, it does not seem to have been acknowledged as such.

Finally, the Australian courts have on a few occasions engaged with the question of recovery for foreign exchange losses. Their response, at least as reflected in the current leading case, has been that *Miliangos* and the general revolution on the currency-of-damages question have no direct application here. Accordingly the question should simply be approached as an instance of a claim for consequential loss and thus subject to limitation on the ground of foreseeability.[163] Moreover it would seem that in the normal case losses of this sort would generally be regarded as too remote.[164] Losses said to accrue to a creditor on the basis that the creditor, if paid on time, would have taken that money and engaged in profitable foreign currency speculation, are simply not within the scope of the risk that the debtor agrees to cover. Moreover recovery for such losses may be denied simply on the basis that they were not caused by the breach.[165] In this respect, unlike the situation in England, in Australia *Miliangos* has not given birth to any pro-plaintiff shift in the assessment of foreign-exchange losses. Such claims continue to fall into the general category of consequential losses and in the absence of special circumstances will be difficult for the plaintiff to establish.

V. Singapore

After Canada and Australia, the foreign-currency claim scene in Singapore presents a simpler and prettier picture—simpler because in the absence of inconsistent

[163] *Evans v European Bank Associates* [2009] NSWCA 67. The authority of the case is somewhat complicated by the fact that it was not a claim for damages but rather for compensation arising from the plaintiff's undertaking with respect to some money paid into court. Much of the case is taken up with discussion of how the principles for awarding recovery under such an undertaking are not identical with the principles for calculating damages for breach of contract. However, although the court concluded that there are important differences between these two situations, at the end of the day the *Hadley v Baxendale* foreseeability test seemed to apply to both.

[164] *State of Queensland v Northaus Trading Co*, unreported 13 August 1999 Appeal No 6299 of 1998 (Qld CA).

[165] *Evans v European Bank Associates*, above n 163. The causation point was articulated by Gyles JA [129]: 'Properly analyzed, [the creditor] did not need this particular parcel of money to speculate in currencies .... There is no principled basis upon which [the creditor] should be underwritten in placing a hypothetical bet on a hazardous enterprise because it can show in retrospect that the bet would have been successful. There is no reason for earmarking this particular money for making that particular bet.'

approaches of state and federal courts, clashing federal and provincial statutes, or indeed applicable statutes of any sort, the relevant law may be described in relatively short compass. And prettier because the Singapore judges appear to have studied *Miliangos* and its English progeny with considerable care and to have been persuaded by its deep rationale, and in particular its argument for certainty.

Like almost all courts faced with *Miliangos*, those of Singapore were of the view that it was a laudable judgment that deserved to be imitated.[166] They were convinced by the reasoning that the old breach-date rule, while it might once have been defensible, was out of touch in a world of rapidly fluctuating currencies. Indeed one Singapore case is notable for one of the more extreme statements of this form. In *Wardley Ltd v Tunku Adnan*, an action on a guarantee, the Singapore High Court was happy to follow *Miliangos* and give judgment in Swiss francs on the basis that the breach-date rule was wholly unrealistic in modern days when wild fluctuations became a daily or hourly event.[167] The courts of Singapore have likewise been prepared to follow the reasoning of *Miliangos (No 2)* and hold that where damages are awarded in a foreign currency the appropriate interest rate on the judgment is the relevant interest rate for that currency for the period in question.[168] They also follow *Lines* and hold that where the claim was in bankruptcy an exception should be made to the payment-date rule.[169] In one respect the Singapore courts have pushed beyond *Miliangos*; they have been willing to order judgment in the relevant foreign currency, without necessarily giving the judgment debtor the option of discharging the judgment in Singapore dollars.[170]

Most notably, especially in contrast with the treatment of the problem in Canada and Australia, Singapore judges have been consistent in regarding the *Miliangos* payment-date standard as a mandatory one; they do not view it is as a rule to be applied only when it favours plaintiffs or as giving rise to a judicial discretion or an opportunity for judges to pursue an ill-defined equity. The first Singapore judgment to consider this issue was *Sarathi Co v The Vishva Pratibha*,[171] a contract damages case decided four and a half years after *Miliangos*. Application of the new payment-date rule was disadvantageous to the plaintiffs, but the court,

[166] *Ooi Han Sun v Bee Han Meng* [1991] SLR 824, [1991] 3 MLJ 219 (High Ct); *Tatung Electronics (S) Pte Ltd v Binatone International Ltd* [1991] 1 SLR 204, [1991] 3 MLJ 212 (CA). At the time *Miliangos* was handed down and for fourteen years thereafter the Privy Council was the final appellate court for Singapore. Since the Privy Council is basically the House of Lords sitting in another place, Singapore judges' deference to *Miliangos* was to be expected.

[167] *Wardley Ltd v Tunku Adnan* [1991] 1 SLR 721 (HC) 724. The court also made the interesting observation that the result of *Miliangos* was to give effect to the principle of nominalism. Traditionally it has been taken to be the case that the old breach-date rule was an instantiation of nominalism.

[168] *TKM (Singapore) Pte Ltd v Export Credit Insurance Corp of Singapore* [1993] 1 SLR 1041 (High Ct Sing), aff'd [1994] 2 SLR 137 (CA), sub nom *Ecics Holdings Ltd v TKM (Singapore) Pte Ltd*.

[169] *Re Mohamed Yunus Valibhoy, ex p Bank of Credit and Commerce Hong Kong* [1995] 1 SLR 601. Instead the court opted for conversion as of the date the receiving orders were made.

[170] Some Singapore judgments imitate the English format and issue in a form which gives the debtor its option, but some—such as *Comboni Vincenzo v Shankar's Emporium (Pte) Ltd* [2007] SGHC 55, [2007] 2 SLR 1020—simply issue judgment for an amount expressed in foreign currency.

[171] *Sarathi Co v The Vishva Pratibha* [1980] 2 MLJ 265 (High Ct Sing).

referring with approval on this point to both *The Maratha Envoy* and *The Folias*, concluded that what is sauce for the goose is sauce for the gander and gave judgment in sterling, as the defendant had requested. Twelve years later, in one of the most detailed and helpful judgments ever delivered on this point, the court in *Indo Commercial Society (Pte) Ltd v Ebrahim*[172] reached the same result. The court quoted the crucial passage from Lord Wilberforce's speech in *Miliangos* that the creditor 'has no concern with pounds sterling; for him what matters is that a Swiss franc *for good or ill* should remain a Swiss franc'.[173] It also drew support for this point with quotations from Roy Goode, the English Law Commission, *Cheshire and North on Private International Law*, *Dicey and Morris on the Conflict of Laws*, *McGregor on Damages*, and FA Mann's *The Legal Aspect of Money* and concluded that the fact 'that some plaintiffs may suffer loss from the strict application of *Miliangos* should not be allowed to detract from its logic'.[174]

Indeed the Singapore courts have been willing simply to order damages in the appropriate foreign currency even when neither of the parties adverted to the currency issue in its pleadings or argument. This was the result in the 1993 judgment *Chinsim Trading (Pte) Ltd v Indian Bank*, an action on a letter of credit in US dollars, where the court noted that

> the parties focused their energies on the issues of liability and left the issues of the proper currency and sum of claim unaddressed. I will not go into the issue beyond referring to the House of Lords decision in *Miliangos v George Frank (Textiles) Ltd* … and say that the proper currency for this judgment should be the American currency.[175]

A similar case decided the same year was *Thai Kenaf Co v Keck Seng*,[176] where the plaintiff in a contract case requested a breach-date conversion and the defendant made no representations on the currency issue. The court held that the *Miliangos* rule was mandatory and ordered judgment for US dollars or its equivalent in Singapore dollars at the time of payment.

In short, unlike Canada and Australia, which have claimed to admire *Miliangos* but have in fact departed significantly from it, the judges in Singapore have followed a line very similar to their counterparts in England.

VI. Malaysia

Across the causeway the story is much the same. Although there was pre-*Miliangos* case law holding that the forum-currency/breach-date rule was mandatory,[177]

172 *Indo Commercial Society (Pte) Ltd v Ebrahim* [1992] 2 SLR 1041, [1992] SGHC 230 (HC).
173 Ibid at [36], quoting *Miliangos*, above n 8, 466 (emphasis added by the High Court of Singapore).
174 Ibid.
175 *Chinsim Trading (Pte) Ltd v Indian Bank* [1993] 2 SLR 144 (HC) 153–54.
176 [1993] 2 SLR 92 (HC).
177 *Overseas Chinese Banking Corp v Firm of Yaik Joo Ann* [1936] MLJ 88 (HC).

and although that decision was followed in a couple of early post-*Miliangos* decisions,[178] on the whole *Miliangos* was greeted as a sensible, modernising change in the law and implemented by the courts.[179] Again, the times-have-changed rationale has been enthusiastically embraced:

> The realization that currency stability is a thing of the past prompted the English Court of Appeal and the House of Lords to change the English jurisprudence as early as 1975. We in Malaysia must not be left behind....
>
> The English judges were bold enough to hold that if an amount due under a contract was in a foreign currency, the courts have the power to give judgment in that foreign currency. In Malaysia the time has come to be progressive and pragmatic in thought and action. Malaysian judges must be bold and be brave enough to hand out judgments in foreign currencies.[180]

As in Singapore, Malaysian courts have been prepared simply to issue judgment in the relevant foreign currency, without always expressly giving the judgment debtor the option of paying the equivalent in ringgits. More importantly, as in the UK and Singapore (and unlike Canada and Australia), Malaysian cases bear no trace of the notion that the *Miliangos* result is to be imposed only when it favours the plaintiff. Rather, it is a mandatory rule. Although Malaysian judges do not seem to have gone as far as the Singapore courts in implementing the *Miliangos* solution even when neither of the parties has requested it, they have not required that it be pleaded at the outset. In *Owners of Cargo Carried in the Ship 'GangChen' v The Ship 'Gang Chen'*[181] the plaintiff cargo owners had given evidence that the currency of the contract of carriage was US dollars but had made no submissions as to the currency in which judgment should be ordered. Currency fluctuation did not seem to be an issue and the court initially gave judgment in US dollars or its equivalent in Malaysian ringgits at the date of judgment. Before that order

[178] *Re Kang Chong Yeow; ex p Mivan Far East Sdn Bhd* [2001] 3 MLJ 98 (High Ct (Kuala Lumpur)); *Ascot International Pte Ltd v Elevic Trading Sdn Bhd* [1996] MLJU 98 (High Ct (Kuala Lumpur)). Neither court made mention of *Miliangos* or any of the other modern case law on point. In addition, there is one Malaysian case that declined to apply *Miliangos* to enforcement of a foreign judgment when the relevant reciprocal enforcement legislation (with Brunei) appeared to require judgment to be entered in Malaysian currency: *Hua Daily News Bhd v Tan Thein Chin* [1986] 2 MLJ 107 (Sup Ct Civ App). The court opted for conversion as of the date of its (that is, the Malaysian) judgment.

[179] *New Kok Ann Realty Sdn Bhd v Development & Commercial Bank Ltd New Hebrides* [1987] 2 MLJ 57 (Sup Ct Kuala Lumpur); *Re P Suppiah* [1989] 2 MLJ 479 (High Ct (Johor Bahru)); *PT Anekapangan Dwitama v Far East Food Industries Sdn Bhd* [1998] 7 MLJ 270 (High Ct Kuala Lumpur); *Megah Sakati Sdn Bhd v Oversea-Chinese Banking Corp* [2005] MLJU 358 (High Ct (Johor Bahru)); *Inter Diam Pte Ltd v PJ Diamond Centre Sdn Bhd* [2007] 7 MLJ 189 (High Ct (Shah Alam)). The foregoing cases dealt with original causes of action, but the *Miliangos* payment-date rule has also been enforced when Malaysian courts enforce foreign judgments: *Prestige Manufacturing Sdn Bhd v Genericx Marketing Sdn Bhd* [2001] MLJU 755 (High Ct (Kuala Lumpur)). At the time *Miliangos* appeared and for a decade after that the final appellate body for Malaysia was the Privy Council.

[180] *Den Norske Bank Asa v Owners of the Ship 'Forum Alasaka'* [1998] MLJU 55 (High Ct (Johor Bahru)) [39] and [49].

[181] *Owners of Cargo Carried in the Ship Gang Chen v The Ship Gang Chen* [1998] 6 MLJ 492, varying [1998] 6 MLJ 468 (High Ct (Kuala Lumpur)).

could be formalised currency fluctuation did become an issue: the ringgit fell sharply as against the dollar. The plaintiffs returned to court asking that judgment be modified so that it was only in dollars. The court, citing *Miliangos* and *The Despina R*, varied its original judgment accordingly on the grounds that US dollars were the currency of the contract and the just measure of the plaintiffs' loss, and that their failure to plead that point in a timely fashion or raise it in argument should not prejudice them.

There is even a decision of the Malaysian High Court, unique to the common law, which holds that when damages have not been proven and the plaintiff must be content with only a nominal award, the *Miliangos* principle requires that nominal damages should be awarded in the money that would have been the currency of judgment had damages been proven.[182] While that result is unimportant from a commercial point of view it still amounts to a revealing instance of pushing *Miliangos* beyond its original confines. Since nominal damages are a symbol, as opposed to compensation, it is far from obvious that the principle in *Miliangos* extends to nominal damages. The Malaysian view, however, is that if a foreign currency is the money of the claim then it is also the proper currency in which to award nominal damages.

VII. Hong Kong

Hong Kong was the only Commonwealth jurisdiction to hesitate on principled grounds before embracing *Miliangos*. Some Canadian courts have not yet abandoned the forum-currency/breach-date rule, only because they regard themselves as hobbled by old Supreme Court of Canada decisions that accepted that rule and which have not yet been reconsidered by that court. But, at least for a while, Hong Kong took the view that the reasoning in *Miliangos* did not apply to it. In the first Hong Kong case to consider *Miliangos* the District Court took the view that the principal justification for the holding in that case was that the English pound was generally declining and in such circumstances the breach-date rule unfairly prejudiced plaintiffs.[183] Since that was not the case with Hong Kong's currency, the underlying justification for *Miliangos* arguably did not apply and the breach-date rule should continue to be the law of Hong Kong. This is an unusual interpretation of *Miliangos*. While commentators have suggested that the fall in sterling was what prompted the decision in that case, as has been noted many times in this book, the rationale of the case was that the new rule should operate for good or ill. But that was not how it was read in Hong Kong, at least initially.

However, that unusual interpretation did not survive the appearance in England of the feeling-the-loss rule in *The Despina R* and *The Folias*. That rule,

[182] *Popular Industries Ltd v Eastern Garment Manufacturing Sdn Bhd* [1989] 3 MLJ 360 (High Ct Penang) 369.

[183] *Stibbe (Burtotex) Ltd v Bayman* (1975) unreported DCCJ005215/1976 (DC HK).

with all its attendant uncertainties, soon became part of Hong Kong law,[184] as did the rule in *Miliangos (No 2)* that provided that when judgment was awarded in a foreign currency the applicable interest rate should be the one for that currency.[185] The Hong Kong courts are now governed by a practice direction similar to the one that appeared in the UK following *Miliangos* stating that when a court allows a claim in a foreign currency it should do so in the following form: 'It is adjudged that the Defendant do pay to the Plaintiff (state the sum in foreign currency for which Judgment has been order) or the Hong Kong dollar equivalent at the time of payment'.[186]

VIII. Cyprus

Cypriot courts had uncomplainingly followed the forum-currency/breach date rule right up until the eve of *Miliangos*.[187] However, when *Miliangos* arrived they acknowledged it as a revolutionary and radical[188] decision that should be implemented without delay or reservation.[189] The Supreme Court was even willing to adopt the English practice direction as to how foreign currency judgments should be quantified in local currency when they had to be enforced by the issue of a writ of *fieri facias*.[190]

[184] *Balasing Guring v Ng Lay* (1986) unreported HCA004587/1985 (HC HK); *Chak Kak v Pacrim International Capital Inc* (2008) unreported CACV 366/2007 (CA HK). An illustration of the uncertainties that accompany the feeling-the-loss rule can be seen in the first Hong Kong decision to follow *The Despina R* and *The Folias*: *Sabah Shipbuilding, Repairing and Engineering Sdn Bhd v Houston Engineering and Equipment Ltd* (1978) unreported HCA001810/1976 (CFI HK). There the court stated that it found the currency point 'an extremely difficult matter to decide' but in the end decided that the currency of judgment should be that in which the contractual payment should have been made rather than the plaintiff's 'natural and proper currency'.

[185] *Fargo Shipping Co v Hwa Haur Trading (Hong Kong) Co* (1979) unreported HCA0011959/1978 (HC HK), following *Miliangos (No 2)*, above n 8.

[186] Practice Direction of the Government of Hong Kong Special Administrative Region of the Peoples Republic of China, PD 16.2.

[187] *Papavassilou v East Mediterranean Line* (1974) 1 CLR 183 (DC). Loizou J's judgment in that case betrays no sign of dissatisfaction with the breach-date rule. He wrote, at 188: 'It seems to me that the principle of law applicable to a case where there is a claim for damages for breach of contract or for tort in terms of foreign currency [the claim] must be converted into Cyprus Pounds at the rate prevailing at the date of the breach or tortious act. Furthermore, when a plaintiff sues in the Courts of Cyprus, the claim and judgment must be in terms of Cyprus Pounds'.

[188] This was how *Miliangos* was described by Savvides J in *Koulombis v The Ship 'Maria'* (1984) 1 CLR 285 (DC) 289.

[189] *Trade Development Bank v The Ship Ariadni PA* (1981) 1 CLR 653 (DC); *Linmare Shipping Co v Boustani* (1981) 1 CLR 386 (DC); *Lamaignere v Selene Shipping Agencies Ltd* (1982) 1 CLR 227 (DC); *Etaireia v Always Travel Holidays Ltd* (1990) unreported Ap 211/89 (DC). In *Pafitis v Bonifacio* (1983) 1 CLR 883 (DC), a road accident case, the court employed a breach-date conversion, but only because both parties agreed it should.

[190] *Williams & Glyns Bank plc v The Ship Maria* (1986) 1 CLR 627 (SC) 631–33. This was an appeal of the case cited at n 187. The currency of judgment was not an issue in the appeal but the Supreme Court took the occasion to provide instructions as to how the new payment-date rule should

The rationale that the Cyprus courts most emphasised for the switch to the payment-date rule was that world currencies were no longer stable, as they seem to have been before the 1970s, and that England's move to the payment-date rule

> was dictated not by any problems peculiar to English society but by the need to facilitate international trade and keep the avenues of commerce open, considerations relevant to the policy of the law in every country. The solution is a just one ....[191]

Unlike the courts of some countries, Canada for instance, those of Cyprus have been alive to the fact that the feeling-the-loss test which emerged from the extension of *Miliangos* to damages cases can lead to uncertainty and present difficult decisions as to what the currency of judgment should be in any given case. Possibly this arises from the fact that the majority of Cyprus cases raising the currency of judgment-issue have been admiralty decisions where several moneys are in play. However the Supreme Court of Cyprus has not regarded this new uncertainty as cause for concern, noting simply that as a result of such cases as *The Despina R* 'there is discretion in an appropriate case to select the foreign currency in which judgment should be given in the interest of effective restitution.[192]

IX. India

In its broad contours the reception of *Miliangos* in India followed a now familiar pattern: the revolution in English practice was admired and imitated, with the result that the old forum-currency/breach-date rule was swiftly abandoned and courts moved towards either granting judgments in foreign currency or at least adopting later conversion dates. However, due partly to legislation and partly to an unusual interpretation of English case law the situation in India is unique. The matter first came before the Delhi High Court about 20 months after *Miliangos* in a case involving enforcement of an arbitral award arising out of an oil exploration agreement between a French company and an arm of the government of India. The award had been given in French francs and had been made a decree of the court six months before *Miliangos* was decided, but not enforced. Some months after *Miliangos* the plaintiff brought an application for execution and the question of the conversion date arose. The court took note of the new reality of fluctuating currencies and praised *Miliangos* in florid language:

> The decision of the House of Lords in *Miliangos* ... is a landmark in the Conflict of Laws. It is a striking example of judicial activism as it represents a progressive and reforming spirit in the field of international commerce which for many decades had been burdened

be implemented where the defendant did not voluntarily pay the judgment in the foreign currency. The English practice direction was the one published at [1976] 1 All ER 669, noted in ch 1 at __.

[191] *Lamaignere v Selene Shipping Agencies Ltd*, above n 189 at 235.

[192] *Williams & Glyns Bank plc v The Ship Maria*, above n 190, 633.

> by poorly reasoned precedent. This important decision marks the culmination of trail-blazing opinion expressed by Lord Denning in the Court of Appeal successively in three cases … .[193]

Unfortunately, for all its enthusiasm for *Miliangos*, the court seems to have misread that case. *Miliangos* had held that where the judgment debtor refused to pay then, in an effort to get as close as possible to a payment-date conversion, conversion should be as of the day the court authorised enforcement. The Delhi High Court interpreted this as meaning the date that the arbitral award had been entered in the court rolls, which was a year and a half before its own judgment.

The case went on appeal to the Supreme Court of India which produced the decision that continues to set the tone in India today. The Supreme Court's unanimous judgment in *Forasol v Oil & Natural Gas Commission* is perhaps the lengthiest analysis of the currency-of-judgment issue in any jurisdiction.[194] Madon J took note of the starting position in the *Havana Railways* case and then of the Court of Appeal decisions in which Lord Denning began to undermine it: *Jugoslavenska* and *Schorsch Meier*. He discussed the two lower-court judgments in *Miliangos* and then the decision of the House of Lords. Unlike some judges looking at the English position he did not stop with *Miliangos* but went on to consider the ensuing developments in *The Despina R*, *The Folias* and the practice direction that sought to regularise matters in England. He concluded that a breach-date conversion 'does not have the effect of putting the plaintiff in the same position in which he would have been had the defendant discharged his obligation when he should have done'.[195] All of this seemed to be a prelude to adopting *Miliangos* as the law of India.

However, then two things happened. The first was that Madon J had regard to a couple of statutes that seemed to stand in the way of bringing *Miliangos* to India. One was the Foreign Exchange Regulation Act 1973.[196] Since this legislation required the permission of an administrative body before debts could be settled in foreign currencies there was an obvious problem in courts ordering such payment. The Supreme Court decided this might be dealt with by ordering payment in the foreign currency subject to such permission being granted, and failing that in the equivalent in rupees. The other piece of legislation, which posed more of an

[193] *Forasol v Oil & Natural Gas Commission* (1977) EFA (OS) No 5 of 1977 (Delhi HC) [33].

[194] *Forasol v Oil & Natural Gas Commission* [1983] INSC 162, 1984 AIR 241 (*Forasol*).

[195] Ibid at 260 (AIR). Madon J claimed this was the case because during the suit the rupee might decline to the plaintiff's prejudice.

[196] Foreign Exchange Regulation Act 1973 (Act 46 of 1973). In 2000 this product of the Indira Ghandi government was repealed and replaced by the Foreign Exchange Management Act 1999 (Act 42 of 1999). Although this new statute was part of a trade liberalisation package it did not entirely eliminate exchange controls and courts deciding currency-of-judgment cases in the post-2000 period have not abandoned the approach laid down in *Forasol*: see *Standard Chartered Bank v Raman* (2006) 5 SCC 727 (SC India); *MMTC v M/S Bamar Co Ltd* (2009) FAO(OS) 124/2006 (Delhi HC), where the lower court had awarded judgment in US dollars but in confirming it the High Court noted that, due to continuing legal restrictions, the plaintiff should be entitled to judgment in the *Forasol* format.

impediment, was a statute dealing with the payment of court fees.[197] This required a plaintiff to pay fees according to the amount it was claiming, and such fees had to be paid in rupees. India has a large number of courts with different monetary jurisdictions and plaintiffs are required to bring their grievances before the court with the lowest such jurisdiction that fits their claim, and to pay fees accordingly in the currency of India. As the Supreme Court noted, advancing a claim for a foreign currency, or even the rupee equivalent at date of payment, thus presented the problem that 'the value of the suit for the purposes of court-fees would be incapable of computation for it would not be possible to say what the rate of exchange on that date would be'.[198] For that reason the Supreme Court held that it was not possible for India to accept the payment-date conversion rule adopted in England. Curiously, however, the Supreme Court was prepared to accept a judgment-day conversion, permitting plaintiffs to value their claim for costs purposes as of the date of filing the suit.

It seemed then that India has followed *Miliangos* only as far as a judgment-date conversion from the foreign currency, with the additional wrinkle that in issuing judgment courts should take care to note that the payment should be made in the foreign currency only if the concerned authorities permitted it, and in the absence of such permission payment should be in the rupee equivalent as of the date of judgment. However, in a remarkable closing passage where the court summed up its ruling it also added that, in addition to the new judgment-day conversion rule, plaintiffs retained the option to convert their claim to rupees

> either at the rate of exchange prevailing on the date when the amount became payable for he was entitled to receive that amount on that date or, at his option, at the rate of exchange prevailing on the date of filing the suit because that is the date on which he is seeking the assistance of the court for recovering the amount due to him.[199]

This represents an unexpected shift from everything that had preceded it in the judgment. There is nothing in the earlier passages of the Supreme Court's reasoning that paves the way for granting plaintiffs an option of this sort. Moreover, despite the Supreme Court's lengthy and thoroughly approving account of English developments, there is nothing in *Miliangos* or the subsequent English cases that authorises such a choice. In effect the Supreme Court's judgment first expresses admiration for *Miliangos*, then finds that due to legislation it cannot impose a payment-date conversion but must settle for judgment-date, and then almost as an afterthought adds that plaintiffs always have the option of asking for conversion at the date they launch their suit. A later Supreme Court of India decision departed even more markedly from the English approach by allowing a plaintiff to modify his pleadings years after he first made them in order to avoid the negative effects of a currency fluctuation that occurred during the

[197] Court-Fees Act 1870 (VII of 1870).
[198] *Forasol*, above n 194, 262 (AIR).
[199] Ibid, 270 (AIR).

course of litigation.[200] The judicial attitude toward foreign currency obligations, then, is much like that in Canada and Australia, and unlike that in Hong Kong, Singapore and Malaysia.

X. New Zealand

Proceedings in the courts of New Zealand add yet another twist to the story of the judicial treatment of foreign money obligations. When issue of the exchange date for foreign currency obligations first arose in that country in the post-*Miliangos* era, the High Court had no qualms about following the House of Lords and assessing damages in a foreign currency.[201] That court, like others in the Commonwealth, was of the view that *Miliangos* was a salutary and commercially progressive development, and was prepared to abide by it and impose a payment-date conversion. In addition, in 1992 the government amended the Reciprocal Enforcement of Judgments Act 1934 to allow judgments registered pursuant to it to be registered in the currency in which the original judgment was expressed.[202] The same result follows in judgments enforced at common law, outside the statute.[203]

While assessment of damages in foreign currency may have become a commonplace practice in New Zealand courts there is little sign of any discussion in those cases of the sorts of questions that vexed English judges in *The Folias*,

[200] *Punjab National Bank v Indian Bank* [2003] 2 LRI 562 (SC). In addition, in *Standard Chartered Bank v Raman*, above n 196, the court wrote, at [7], that in addition to keeping in mind the goal of accurate compensation, judges deciding foreign currency claims 'should also keep in mind the economic situation of the country'. Kapedia J went on to note that '[e]ncashment of dollar denominated deposits have [*sic*] certain economic implications'. The court did not elaborate further on how this non-compensatory consideration should come into play.

[201] *Marr v Arabco Traders Ltd* (1987) 1 NZBLC 102 (HC); *American Express Europe Ltd v Bishop* (1987) 1 PRNZ 635 (HC). The latter was followed in *Brintons Ltd v Feltex Furnishings of New Zealand Ltd (No 2)* [1991] 2 NZLR 683 (HC). Other cases illustrating the willingness of New Zealand courts to award judgment in foreign currency are *ABC Shipbrokers v The Ship Offi Gloria* [1993] 3 NZLR 576 (HC); *Air New Zealand Ltd v Nippon Credit Bank Ltd* [1997] 1 NZLR 218 (Ct App NZ) (though the trial judgment in $US was overturned on grounds not pertinent to the currency question); *International Factors Marine (Singapore) Pte Ltd v The Ship Komtek II* [1998] 2 NZLR 108 (HC); and *Airwork (NZ) Ltd v Vertical Flight Management Ltd* [1999] 1 NZLR 641 (CA); *Yang v Ko* [2007] NZHC 729. However, in *ASB Securities Ltd v Geurts* [2005] 1 NZLR 484 (HC) the court, without discussion of the point, converted from the currency of the claim to New Zealand dollars at the rate in effect on the opening day of the hearing.

[202] Reciprocal Enforcement of Judgments Amendment Act 1992, (1992 No 10) s 5(4). Like the 1991 Australian legislation mentioned above at n 157, the New Zealand statute gives the foreign judgment creditor the option of converting to the local currency as of the date of registration. Note that the original judgment need not be in the currency of the original forum: in *Questnet Ltd v Lane* [2008] NZAR 495 the High Court confirmed the registration of a Hong Kong judgment that had been given in US$. (The Hong Kong judgment is *Questnet Ltd v Lane* (2008) No 1475 of 2006 (HC).) Similarly, in *Bolton v Marine Services Ltd* [1996] 2 NZLR 15 the Court of Appeal confirmed the registration of a decision from the Solomon Islands that had been rendered in Australian dollars.

[203] *Commonwealth Reserves I v Chodar* [2001] 2 NZLR 374 (High Ct); *Reeves v One World Challenge LLC* [2006] 2 NZLR 184 (NZ Ct App); and see *Hada v Neal* [2005] NZFLR 567 (High Ct).

The Despina R and *The Texaco Melbourne*. As in Canada and Australia, New Zealand cases display little discussion of when it is appropriate to award damages in a currency other than that of the forum. Again, this is not to say that the issues are not there. For instance, in a recent case plaintiffs brought suit in respect of fraudulently-caused losses in an investment scheme.[204] They succeeded against a director of the bankrupt investment company for breach of his statutory duties. Venner J held that the defendant should be liable for half of the plaintiffs' losses and noted she had the power to grant judgment in the currency that best reflected the loss. The plaintiffs' investments had been in New Zealand dollars but the bankrupt company's investments had been conducted in US dollars. The court, at the plaintiffs' request, gave the bulk of its judgment in US dollars, which had appreciated against the New Zealand dollar in the period in question—a move which appears to have had the effect not just of giving the plaintiffs their investment back but allowing them some measure of profit on their investment. The court's justification for this was just a brief assertion that since the underlying investments were conducted in US dollars that was a sufficient basis for assessing damages in that currency.[205] One cannot help but speculate that had the New Zealand dollar risen against the American one the plaintiffs would have asked for compensation in the former and the court would have granted it. However, the stated reasoning—that the plaintiffs suffered their loss not in the currency of the money they originally invested but rather in the currency in which the investment company unsuccessfully dabbled—leaves one unsure about this.

A rare recognition that the currency-of-judgment question is difficult and cannot fairly be resolved by one-sentence assertions that the claimant felt its loss in a given money is the decision of the Court of Appeal in *Scales Trading Ltd v Far Eastern Shipping Co*.[206] Even there, however, the analysis was not extensive, which was unfortunate since the issue was a novel one. The claim was one on a guaranty and the US dollar was the currency of that debt. However, the greenback having appreciated as against the New Zealand dollar, the defendant argued that allowing the claim in the former money would produce a windfall for the plaintiff since, when the primary obligation was not performed the plaintiff had taken steps to cure that loss and had done so by (at least in effect and in part) acquiring New Zealand dollars to satisfy that obligation. In short, despite the fact that the currency of account in the underlying contract was a foreign one, in the post-breach period the creditor had hedged against that loss by taking steps to convert its risk to the currency of the forum. Thus the plaintiff's post-breach mitigative behaviour had demonstrated that the New Zealand dollar was the currency in which it felt its loss, or so the defendant argued, and in such circumstances the plaintiff could not turn around and claim in the currency of account of the contract. The Court of Appeal rejected that argument, in part on the ground that it

204 *FXHT Fund Managers Ltd (in liquidation) v Oberholster* [2009] NZHC 435.
205 Ibid [121].
206 *Scales Trading Ltd v Far Eastern Shipping Co* [1999] 3 NZLR 26 (CA).

was not proven that the plaintiff had felt its loss in New Zealand dollars but also on the grounds that US dollars were the currency of the guaranty so *Miliangos* made it the applicable currency of judgment.[207] In short, the court seemed convinced of the argument the English courts had accepted in cases like *The Maratha Envoy* that the currency of account should be the currency of judgment in contract cases, and not inclined to reject that clear and certain standard in favour of *The Folias*'s search for the money in which the claimant truly felt its loss.

The most interesting effect of *Miliangos* in New Zealand courts, however, has not been their willingness to rely on *Miliangos* and jettison the breach-date rule, or their possible reluctance to engage in the vagaries of the feeling-the-loss inquiry. Rather, it has been the effect of *Miliangos* on the related question of damages for foreign-exchange losses. At the end of chapter one we saw the part *Miliangos* played in opening up this new head of loss in England in cases such as *Ozalid*, *The Lips* and *Travelers Casualty*. Although nothing in *Miliangos* purported to address this issue directly, somehow the 'spirit' of *Miliangos*—understood as a willingness to reject old (purportedly) pro-defendant rules regarding foreign money and replace them with new (purportedly) plaintiff-friendly ones—had the effect of convincing English courts to become more welcoming to such claims. As we have seen, Australia seems to have rejected this and taken the position that exchange loss damages are a different issue from the currency-judgment question and that therefore *Miliangos* has no bearing on the former.[208]

The New Zealand courts taken the opposite tack. In *Isaac Naylor and Sons Ltd v New Zealand Co-operative Wool Marketing Association Ltd*[209] the plaintiff was a New Zealand seller who suffered late payment at the hands of an English buyer. Under the terms of the contract the payment was to be made in sterling. The buyer's claim before the New Zealand court was for losses said to follow from the fact that, had it timeously received that sterling payment, it would then have converted it into New Zealand dollars. The New Zealand dollar had of course risen against the pound in the interval between when payment should have been made and when it was in fact made.[210] The plaintiff argued that the loss resulting from the inability to translate the contractual payment into its home currency was one for which it deserved to be compensated. Although this was a novel sort of claim

[207] Ibid, at 46. The matter went to the Judicial Committee of the Privy Council ([2001] 1 NZLR 513) which differed from the Court of Appeal on the substantive question of liability, but the currency question was not in issue before the JCPC.

[208] *Evans v European Bank Associates*, above n 163.

[209] *Isaac Naylor and Sons Ltd v New Zealand Co-operative Wool Marketing Association Ltd* [1981] 1 NZLR 361 (CA) (*Naylor*).

[210] I write 'of course', of course, only to draw attention to the fact that, had the fluctuation between New Zealand and UK currency gone the other way, the plaintiff would never have advanced such a claim. This is the one-way street effect noted in the previous chapter at pp 85–86. It should also be observed how the claim in *Naylor* might theoretically have been phrased, not as one for exchange losses, but as a currency-of-judgment claim. That is, the plaintiff buyer might simply have said that the proper currency of judgment was that in which it truly felt its loss—which was not the money stipulated in the contract, but rather (along the lines of *The Folias*) its home currency, the New Zealand dollar.

in New Zealand, one that had not been recognised before and which had no solid precedent elsewhere in the common law, the New Zealand Court of Appeal was unanimous in holding that henceforth such damages might be claimed. All three judges gave *Miliangos* credit for this development. Cooke J praised the realistic solution reached in that case and went on to note that '*Miliangos* does not directly answer [the question before me] but I think that its emphasis on realism and general principles does afford encouragement'.[211] Richardson J noted that *Miliangos* had recognised that 'the substantial change in the relative stability of exchange rates'[212] in recent years called for a reassessment of traditional approaches to the law of damages. Although he noted that *Miliangos* was 'far removed on its facts from the present case' he also detected a common 'underlying concern' that justified accepting the plaintiff's claim in the case before him.[213]

McMullin J went the farthest in grounding his justification for awarding this novel type of consequential loss squarely on *Miliangos* and its subsequent elaboration in *The Despina R*. He asserted that *Miliangos* stood for the rejection of the nominalistic principle that a plaintiff had to take the pound sterling as he found it, and also for a rejection of the older cases. Accordingly the claimant might be awarded exchange losses, since such an award best gave effect to the compensation principle.[214] What is notable about that claim, of course, is that *Miliangos* had made that argument in support of rejecting the breach-date rule, which required that, even where the plaintiff had contracted for payment in one currency the plaintiff would have to accept judgment in pounds, and moreover in the pound as the plaintiff found it, even if it had fallen in the period before trial. McMullin J used *Miliangos*'s claim about the unfairness of requiring plaintiffs to take the pound as they found it in quite the opposite way—that is, to permit a claimant who had contracted for payment in one currency to say that it should not have to take that currency as it found it. The defendant in *Naylor* was not oblivious to this, and in fact tried to enlist *Miliangos* in its favour by pointing out that the House of Lords in that case had sought to forward the virtue of certainty. It argued that, according to *Miliangos*, 'the parties, having chosen the currency of account, thereby took the risk of a variation in exchange rates'.[215] However the New Zealand Court of Appeal denied that this aspect of *Miliangos* was pertinent to the case before it.

The case has received considerable notice outside New Zealand. Some commentators have lauded it and held it up as a model for courts in their own countries.[216]

[211] *Naylor*, above n 209, 365.
[212] Ibid, 375.
[213] Ibid.
[214] Ibid, 383.
[215] Ibid, 382.
[216] R Brand, 'Exchange Loss Damages and the Uniform Foreign-Money Claims Act: The Emperor Hasn't All His Clothes' (1991) 23 *Law and Policy in International Business* 1, 46–52; C Proctor, 'Changes in Monetary Value and the Assessment of Damages', in D Saidov & R Cunnington (eds), *Contract Damages: Domestic and International Perspectives* (Oxford, Hart, 2008) 482, 488.

Others have been more hesitant, on the grounds laid out in the analysis of this issue at the end of the last chapter. In brief, those grounds were that exchange-loss damages are a species of consequential loss and awarding them requires consideration of the issues of foreseeability and mitigation—issues which are apt to be ignored if *Miliangos* is thought to govern.[217]

However, *Naylor* has been enthusiastically followed.[218] Its scope has even been enlarged so that it is no longer a precondition to the claim that the plaintiff must be someone claiming that his loss is due to the late payment of a contractually-specified money of payment preventing him from converting that money into his home currency. Thus, one New Zealander can now claim against another for losses arising when late payment of New Zealand dollars deprives the claimant of the chance to convert that payment into US dollars.[219] This pushes New Zealand law even further in a pro-plaintiff direction than *The Lips*.[220] Most importantly, this contentious legal development was one that drew considerable support from *Miliangos*, even though the issues in the cases were not analogous. In *Naylor*, references to *Miliangos* seemed to function principally as justifications for sweeping aside old precedents which stood in the way of the plaintiff's claim, and for suggesting that limitations on damages claims articulated in the days before the modern era of fluctuating currencies were bound to be hopelessly obsolete. But in the post-*Naylor* New Zealand case law on exchange-loss damages *Miliangos* is treated as applying directly.

In the words of New Zealand scholar Charles Rickett, '[t]he effects of the *Miliangos* decision continue to be felt in areas not directly on point in the original decision. The emphasis on realism and modernism provides a justification for radical developments'.[221]

XI. Concluding Observations on Commonwealth Developments

Although courts throughout the Commonwealth have expressed agreement with the House of Lords decision in *Miliangos* and its English progeny, that decision has not been uniformly implemented. Canadian courts, for a variety of reasons,

[217] CEF Rickett, 'Contract Damages for Exchange Losses—a New Zealand Development' [1982] *Lloyd's Maritime and Commercial Law Quarterly* 566, 570; V Black, 'Damages for Foreign Exchange Losses in Contract Actions' [1991] *New Zealand Recent Law Review* 190, 197–201.

[218] *Volk v Hirstlens (NZ) Ltd* [1987] 1 NZLR 385 (High Ct).

[219] This was confirmed in what happened in *Rochis Ltd v Chambers* [2007] NZCA 479 when the New Zealand Court of Appeal affirmed the High Court's awarding of foreign exchange losses at trial. The court held that a term of the contract effectively operated to put the buyer on notice that the seller would probably convert the New Zealand dollars into American ones.

[220] *The Lips* [1988] AC 395 (HL).

[221] Rickett, above n 217, 576.

are all over the map on the currency-of-judgment and conversion-date issues. Moreover they seem to have paid little attention to the 'for good or ill' aspect of *Miliangos*, preferring instead to select the conversion date depending on which way the fluctuations have gone during litigation. Their view of *Miliangos* seems to focus on the aspect of the case that released them from an obligation to apply one rule, without quite seeming to appreciate that it laid down another. Australian courts purport to follow *Miliangos* but in practice seem to deviate from it in permitting claimants a greater right of election over the currency of judgment than is accorded in England. New Zealand courts seem to approve of *Miliangos* and have gone on to use it as a springboard to granting damages for foreign exchange losses in situations where they (1) would not have been granted before and (2) are probably still not granted in England.

I conclude this chapter by echoing a sentiment expressed by Steven Stern, namely that, although *Miliangos* was originally intended to prevent uncertainty on the currency-of-judgment issue, when one takes a comparative perspective that decision seems to have had the opposite effect.[222] The homogeneity that once existed throughout the Commonwealth by virtue of the dominance of the forum-currency/breach-date rule is a thing of the past.

[222] S Stern, 'Judgments in Foreign Currencies: A Comparative Analysis' [1997] *Journal of Business Law* 266. Stern's briefer comparative account shares some of the outlines of mine, though we differ on many questions of detail. Most notably, he claims (at 279) that by virtue of the Currency Act Canadian courts are compelled to give judgment only in the currency of Canada and have not employed a payment-day conversion rate. An excellent report of the early reception of *Miliangos* in the Commonwealth may also be found in J Gold, *Legal Effects of Fluctuating Exchange Rates* (Washington, International Monetary Fund, 1990) 290–330, but it is now dated.

4

The United States of America

The type of problem here, because of the time element, has been said to involve a consideration of 'a fourth dimension—namely that of time.' Since it also apparently involves an attempt to coordinate the currencies of two different national systems, a mathematical-minded legal philosopher might suggest the application of the general theory of relativity, which seeks to formulate 'laws' for all coordinate physical systems and thus to attain uniformity.

Jerome Frank[1]

The American legal system approached the currency-of-judgment problem from the same starting point English courts did, and the cases that have come before its judges have presented problems similar to those faced by their English counterparts. Yet the position the US has arrived at today differs from the English one in a number of ways. While English courts appear to have sorted out the problem in a manner that is roughly satisfactory, at least to them, and which does not give rise to calls for legislative intervention, the American situation is by comparison chaotic. A variety of contending solutions is in play, some judge-made and some legislative, and the disagreements among their academic proponents seem intractable.

Examining the question of foreign currency obligations in American law involves wrestling with some complicating factors not present in a study of that matter in the English context. First, there is the fact of the federal system, which we have already encountered with Canada and Australia. Each American state is capable of adopting its own solution to the problems posed by foreign currency obligations, either through state legislation or, in the absence of that, judge-made rules. All of that is subject to any overriding federal legislation, but as we shall see there has been little of that, and none in the modern era. In addition, as with Canada, the federal courts in the United States can adopt a solution of their own. However, unlike the situation in Canada, where the currency-of-judgment issue is generally regarded as procedural—which means that provincial courts apply their own rules to all cases that come before them, regardless of the governing law, and federal courts do the same—in the United States it is generally regarded as substantive. So, in both federal and state courts, the question of what approach will be taken to the currency-of-judgment problem can turn on the not always

[1] In his judgment for the majority in *Shaw, Savill Albion & Co v The Fredericksburg* 189 F 2d 952 (2d Cir 1951) 954 (footnotes, including one to the works of Albert Einstein, omitted).

uncomplicated question of whether the dispute in question is governed by federal or state law. That is, a federal court might end up applying the federal rule on the currency-of-judgment question if federal law governs the claim, but a state currency rule if state law is found to apply. Today, depending on what American court is considering the matter and whether that court is applying federal or state law, there are four different rules that might be applied; (1) a breach-date conversion to American dollars, (2) a judgment-day rule, (3) a payment-day rule (following *Miliangos* and a statute enacted by 22 US states that adopts a *Miliangos*-like solution), and (4) a flexible approach whereby judges select the conversion date, usually in light of the fluctuations during litigation and almost always in a way that favours the plaintiff.

Not surprisingly, this has given rise to calls for a unified approach. That brings into play various institutions whose mandate is to limit or ameliorate the effects of diversity in the American legal system—institutions such as the American Law Institute (ALI) and the National Conference of Commissioners on Uniform State Laws (NCCUSL). They have responded but their proffered solutions—various restatements of the law and a uniform model statute—are not binding on the states. They may be followed by state judges (in the case of the ALI's restatements) or enacted by state legislatures (in the case of NCCUSL model legislation). However, they need not be. There are some areas of the law where restatements and model legislation have been adopted by all, or almost all, American states—thus producing near uniformity in that field where diverse solutions, while constitutionally permissible, are seen as undesirable. But the currency-of-judgment question is not one of these. The principal model statute has been adopted by fewer than half the states. Moreover, the one institution that might be able to impose a common solution, Congress, has not yet been tempted to pass legislation on the matter. As a result, variety persists and seems likely to continue to do so.

The federal factor is not the only thing that distinguishes the American scene from the English. As noted, in the United States the question of foreign currency obligations is generally seen to be a question of substantive law, and more particularly to fall within the province of conflicts of law, and thus to be amenable to the notoriously contentious, and still vigorously contended, theories and approaches which characterise American engagement with that field. That is, unlike the English (and most Commonwealth) cases, where the discourse of private remedial law—and in particular the goal of accurate compensation—dominates the currency-of-judgment question, in the United States the language of private international law plays a significant role. American choice-of-law methodology has at times been highly abstract and conceptualistic, at least in comparison with the typically more pragmatic approach of English judges, and has led to approaches to the currency-of-judgment problem that appear driven more by theoretical consistency with the general approach to choice of law than by a concern to arrive at fair results. The theory in question sometimes owes less to an inquiry into how to bring about accurate compensation for private wrongs against a background of fluctuating currencies than it does to how to reconcile the currency-of-judgment question with the broader theoretical approach to issues of choice of law.

An additional background fact to keep in mind when assessing the American jurisprudence is that in the great majority of American cases, especially those in the twentieth century, the US dollar has been stronger than the relevant foreign currency. In American courts it has been the forum currency that has appreciated in the period between breach and judgment. This was most notably so in a series of important US Supreme Court cases in the 1920s under the Trading with the Enemy Act,[2] where the relevant foreign currencies were those of Germany and Austria-Hungary, which had declined disastrously following the Great War. In the American cases of the 1920s the decline of foreign currencies was so pervasive and so permeated judicial decisions and scholarship that the alternative—a decline in the greenback's strength—seemed almost unimaginable. As a result, an early conversion date to the money of the forum—such as the date of breach—would normally give the plaintiff a greater recovery than a later one. Early conversion would shelter the (often foreign) plaintiff against the effects of the foreign currency's fall.[3] It is a matter of legitimate debate whether the strength (or otherwise) of a country's currency should be pertinent to its treatment of foreign currency obligations; however, demonstrably it has commonly been so. Accordingly it is helpful, when reading American cases in the first three quarters of the last century to recall that the US dollar seemed perpetually on the rise.

I. Early Days

The English rule that courts could give judgment only in pounds sterling was received by the American colonies, which then naturally substituted their own currency for the English pound.[4] However, the eighteenth-century American case law demonstrates little judicial discussion of the currency-of-judgment problem. Rather, early colonial courts in North America seem simply to have assumed that they could render awards only in their own money. This practice was soon cemented in American legal procedure. Indeed support for it was often derived

[2] October 6, 1917, c 106; 40 St 411.

[3] Though not quite invariably: see *Page v Levinson* 281 Fed 555 (D Md 1922); *Sulka & Co v Brandt* 277 NYS 421 (Sup Ct 1935). These judgments remarked on the unfairness to the defendant of the result the breach-date rule produced in those cases, but did not think that amounted to justification for abandoning the rule. The second case arose against the background of the 1934 devaluation of the dollar as against many currencies due to changing practices of the US Federal Reserve as to the role of gold as an anchor for the American monetary system. For analysis of the 1934 devaluation see M Friedman & J Schwartz, *A Monetary History of the United States: 1867–1960* (Princeton, NJ, Princeton U Press, 1962) 469–74.

[4] A Nussbaum, *Money in the Law: National and International* (Brooklyn, Foundation Press, 1950) 365. Each American colony had its own monetary system, with courts generally awarding damages in their own version of the pound.

from an early piece of federal legislation. Paragraph 20 of the Coinage Act of 1792 appeared to speak to the issue of foreign currency obligations. The relevant part of that provision read:

> The money of account of the United States shall be expressed in dollars ... and all accounts in the public offices and all proceedings in the courts shall be kept and had in conformity to this regulation.[5]

A number of American courts read this statute as requiring them to deliver judgment only in US dollars,[6] although two appeal courts have held that where a lower court enters a judgment in a foreign currency that practice, though erroneous, does not render the judgment void. So where a judgment can be overturned only on the basis of voidness, but not on the grounds it was wrong in law, such a judgment expressed in foreign money can stand.[7] Historical studies of the background to the Coinage Act of 1792 have suggested that it may not have been intended to have any such effect, or indeed to speak to the question of court proceedings at all.[8] Be that as it may, there seems little doubt that this early American statute, much like its Canadian counterpart,[9] had the effect of contributing to the view that the national legislature had commanded courts to render judgment expressed only in the national money. When Joseph Story published his influential text on the conflict of laws in 1834, he was able to take it for granted that United States courts lacked the authority to award damages in anything other than the national money. Story's treatise included a seven-page section dealing with agreements payable in foreign currencies, situated in the middle of a chapter headed

[5] An Act Establishing a Mint and Regulating the Coins of the United States of 1792, 1 Stat 246, 250, formerly found codified at 31 USC s 5101 (Coinage Act of 1792). This part was repealed when the Coinage Act of 1792 was re-enacted in 1982, 96 Stat 877, 980, 31 USC s 1501. According to the report of the Judiciary Committee, the relevant passage was omitted as surplus. HR Rept No 97-651, 97th Cong 2d sess, at 146–47 (1982). Note, as seen in the preceding chapter, Canada has parallel federal legislation and its proper construction is every bit as uncertain as that of its American equivalent.

[6] See, eg: *Frontera Transport Co v Abaunza* 271 F 169 (5th Cir 1921) 176; *Shaw, Savill, Albion & Co v The Fredericksburg*, above n 1, 954 and note 5; *International Silk Guild, Inc v Rogers* 262 F 2d 219 (DC Cir 1958) 224; *American National Insurance Co v De Cardenas* 181 So 2d 359 (Florida App 1965); *BV Wijsmuller v United States* 487 F Supp 156 (SDNY 1979), aff'd 633 F 2d 202 (2d Cir 1980); *Jamaica Nutrition Holdings Ltd v United Shipping Co* 643 F 2d 376 (5th Cir 1981); *Bamberger v Clark* 390 F 2d 485 (DC Cir 1968); *Rose Hall Ltd v Chase Manhattan Overseas Banking Corp* 566 F Supp 1558 (D Del 1983). This view has been supported by some scholars, for example PJ Eder, 'Legal Theories of Money' (1934) 20 *Cornell Law Quarterly* 52, 63; SL Cohn, 'Conversion Date of Foreign Money Obligations during the War' (1962) 50 *Georgetown Law Journal* 513, 514; Anon, 'Dollar Damage Awards to Foreign Plaintiffs: Conversion and Revaluation of Foreign Currencies' (1952) 61 *Yale Law Journal* 758, 759, note 4.

[7] *Baumlin & Ernst Ltd v Gemini Ltd* 637 F 2d 238 (4th Cir 1980); *Potenz Corp v Petrozzini* 170 Ill App 3d 617, 525 NE 2d 173 (App Ct Illinois 1988).

[8] JD Becker, 'The Currency of Judgment' (1977) 25 *American Journal of Comparative Law* 152, 158; R Brand, 'Restructuring the US Approach to Judgments on Foreign Currency Liabilities: Building on the English Experience' (1985) 11 *Yale Journal of International Law* 139, 157–59; R Brand, *Fundamentals of International Business Transactions* (The Hague, Kluwer Law International, 2000) 668–71.

[9] See ch 3 at pp 101–106.

'Foreign Contracts'.[10] That section of Story's work began with the starting point, which he never questioned, that American judges could dispense judgment only in dollars. He then proceeded to focus almost exclusively on how those courts might do justice between the parties in such circumstances. Story's main concern was to see that in their application of the forum-currency/breach-date rule American courts looked to the real effective exchange rate between the foreign currency and the American dollar, rather than some legislatively-established nominal par of exchange. He was concerned to see that there was full compensation, though not over-compensation, of plaintiffs in contract matters and that judicial reference to official but commercially unrealistic par exchange rates did not stand in the way of this. However, all of this took place within the unquestioned framework of the forum currency.

This approach did not change in the subsequent editions of Story's book. Moreover, United States Supreme Court decisions of the latter half of the nineteenth century appeared to affirm that American courts should award judgment in US dollars.[11]

However, although American courts throughout the nineteenth century demonstrated almost no sympathy for the argument that they could grant judgment in anything other than the money of the forum, they did not invariably impose breach-date conversions. Rather, it appears that many different conversion dates were at one time or another employed. Monetary scholar Joseph Dach undertook an extensive study of the conversion dates actually used by American courts in the years up to World War I. Dach found that judges had employed a messy variety of such dates, including, in chronological order, the date the contract was made, the date of the breach of the obligation sued upon, the time the suit was launched, the time of the trial, the time the verdict was announced, and the time judgment was granted.[12] Another account of the unruly diversity of conversion times

[10] J Story, *Commentaries on the Conflict of Laws, Foreign and Domestic* (Boston, Hilliard, Gray & Co, 1834) 254–60. Note that at this time the United States had yet to issue paper currency, though some banks did so. A variety of currencies was in regular use and official par values could differ from the exchange rates accepted in practice. In the words of the Supreme Court of the United States, 'the circulating medium consisted almost entirely of bank notes issued by numerous independent corporations variously organized under State legislation. . .': *Veazie Bank v Fenno* 75 US 533 (1869) 536.

[11] *Butler v Horwitz* 74 US 258 (1869); *Bronson v Rodes* 74 US 229 (1869). It is debatable how firmly these two judgments from the greenback period truly stand for the proposition that American courts are absolutely barred from giving judgment in a currency other than dollars. Some commentators believe they do: Anon, 'The Value of Foreign Money for the Purposes of Suit' (1926) 26 *Columbia Law Review* 209; C Maw, 'Fluctuating Rates of Exchange and the Conflict of Laws' (1927) 40 *Harvard Law Review* 618, 620, note 7; RC Effros, 'The Legal Nature of Obligations Payable in Foreign Currencies' (1986) 11 *North Carolina Journal of International Law and Commercial Regulation* 445, 447; AV Levontin, 'Foreign Money Loans: The Rate of Conversion' (1960) 1 *Israel Law Review* 250, 271; Anon, 'Rate of Exchange Applicable to Damages Arising from Maritime Torts' (1952) 52 *Columbia Law Review* 141. However, Ronald Brand has argued that they should not be read as doing so: Brand, 'Restructuring', above n 8, 159–61. However both decisions *did* enter judgment in dollars and they are commonly understood as requiring such a result.

[12] See J Dach, 'Conversion of Foreign Money: A Comparative Study of Changing Rules' (1954) 3 *American Journal of Comparative Law* 155, 158–60, and the many cases cited there. For another account

implemented by American courts in the nineteenth century even lists time of collection as one of the dates employed.[13] In addition there was an 1894 Texas decision that, in an interesting attempt to arrive at an even-handed outcome, opted for the using the average of the exchange rates between the due date and the date the action was launched.[14] Finally, there were also cases where, in the face Story's contentions to the contrary, courts elected to convert at mint par, even though that did not reflect the true rate employed in business.

However, as was the case in England, the early twentieth century, and in particular proceedings in the aftermath of The Great War, tended to bring about a greater degree of uniformity and systemisation on the conversion-date issue. The matter came to be addressed both by appellate courts and legal scholars pursuing the Langdellian agenda of systematising American common law. Some American judgments, even in the post-World War I period, openly acknowledged that a variety of dates had been employed in the past and held that it was desirable to improve the law by finding and instituting the logically correct one, thus imposing some order and regularity on the chaos.[15] Other American courts in this period, like some English ones, moved towards a more orderly approach by promulgating the view that the breach-date rule had been the dominant one in the common law for centuries and had nearly the force of natural law. In any event, the proliferation of conversion dates that had characterised nineteenth-century adjudication tended, in the 1920s, to get replaced by a single, dominant rule. Furthermore, with some academic support[16] and some reference to English decisions, the solution American judges opted for in the early part of the twentieth century was the same one English courts settled on at about that time: the breach-date rule.

The forum-currency/breach-date rule became firmly entrenched in the commercially dominant state of New York in 1923 in *Hoppe v Russo-Asiatic Bank*.[17] *Hoppe* prescribed that rule in very broad terms, as applying to claims for damages (liquidated or unliquidated) in both contract and tort, regardless of the nationality or residence of the parties. It also applied to enforcement of foreign country judgments, though there the date of breach has been held to be not the breach of the underlying contractual or tort obligation but the date at which the foreign court judgment is made.[18]

of the nineteenth-century American cases and the wide variety of conversion dates they employed see J Drake, 'The Reckoning of Damages in Fluctuating Exchange' (1925) 23 *Michigan Law Review* 695, 708 ff.

[13] O Fraenkel, 'Foreign Moneys in Domestic Courts' (1935) 35 *Columbia Law Review* 360, 362.

[14] *Butler v Merchant* 27 SW 193 (Tex Civ App 1894).

[15] See *Liberty National Bank of New York v Burr* 270 F 251 (ED Penn 1921).

[16] E Gluck, 'The Rate of Exchange in the Law of Damages' (1922) 22 *Columbia Law Review* 217.

[17] *Hoppe v Russo-Asiatic Bank* 138 NE 497 (NYCA 1923) (*Hoppe*).

[18] *Indag SA v Irridelco Corp* 658 F Supp 763 (SD NY 1987). This is in accordance with the orthodox common law approach to enforcement of foreign judgments. That approach regards foreign judgments as creating an obligation between the parties—an obligation which, assuming the foreign judgment meets the criteria for recognition in the local forum, is breached when that foreign judgment is handed down and the debtor does not immediately pay. That is, if the debtor has not satisfied the

Although some lower courts initially balked at the imposition of a single, rigid rule, appeal courts in New York applied *Hoppe* and soon brought about a situation where the breach-date rule was uniformly applied to all sorts of claims.[19] New York State was far and away the leading centre for business dispute resolution in the United States at that time, and the New York rule, which was no more than the American label for the breach-date/forum currency rule, soon became adopted by many other American jurisdictions. Thus, by the early 1920s the American solution to the problems posed by foreign currency obligations was identical to the English one confirmed by the House of Lords in 1921 in *The Volturno*:[20] judgment could be rendered only in the forum currency and the pre-existing variety of conversion dates had been replaced by a prescribed one, the breach date, which was broadly viewed as satisfactory.

However, further American developments on the currency question were soon to bring this congruence to an end.

II. The Conflict of Laws Approach

In a series of cases engendered by the extreme monetary fluctuations following World War I, especially those in Germany, the matter of foreign currency obligations came before many American courts, and eventually the Supreme Court of the United States. This monetary instability engendered some academic discussion of the foreign currency question.[21] It also gave rise to an innovation in American law, one that set it apart from the English and Commonwealth approach, and continues to do so. In all of those cases—indeed in American cases until the 1990s—the unquestioned starting point was that American courts could render judgment only in US dollars; thus the only subject remaining before the courts was that of the suitable conversion date. As noted, by the 1920s American decisions had settled on breach-date conversion, but in a trio of cases in the mid-1920s that changed. All three were decisions of the Supreme Court of the

foreign judgment then, in effect, an obligation is breached the day it is created. This applies even if the foreign judgment is appealed; that is, the date of the trial judgment is, for the purposes of the recognising court, the breach date. Note that this creates a potential opportunity for strategic plaintiff choice of conversion dates. If a plaintiff sues to enforce a foreign judgment and the receiving court applies a breach-date rule then the conversion date is that of the foreign court's judgment. If instead that same plaintiff, having obtained the foreign court judgment, elects instead to bring an action in the second forum on the original cause of action and succeeds, then the second forum's breach-date rule would convert at the date the underlying cause of action arose.

[19] For a fuller account of New York cases adopting *Hoppe*'s breach-date rule see Fraenkel, above n 13, 369–77. There is also a detailed discussion of the cases in *De Sayve v De la Valdene* 124 NYS 2d 143 (Sup Ct NY City 1953).

[20] *Celia (Owners) v SS Volturno (Owners)* [1921] 2 AC 544 (HL) (*The Volturno*).

[21] See Maw, Drake and Gluck, above nn 11, 12 and 16 respectively.

United States and in each case the opinion of the Court was a brief opinion written by Oliver Wendell Holmes.

The first was *Guinness v Miller*.[22] In his judgment at first instance, Learned Hand J had viewed the matter as a question of conflict of laws. It was thus to be approached in a conceptualistic fashion focussing on the apparent dictates of sovereignty and vested rights on the currency question. *Guinness* was a case of a debt due in the United States but payable in German marks, a currency which had fallen badly against the dollar between the due date and the time of judgment. Strangely, despite the fact that the case before him was a contract matter, Learned Hand J began his opinion with a discussion of the conversion-date issue in tort. By so doing, he reduced the problem to what he seems to have regarded as its most basic form, unencumbered by considerations of previous party interaction. He began by reasoning that in the case of a cause of action in tort arising in a foreign land, the foreign court would necessarily give damages in its own currency based on the value of the loss at the date of breach.[23] From that starting point, he considered how things should be approached if an American court entertained an original action in respect of that same foreign tort, which, he assumed in light of the then prevailing *lex loci delicti* choice of law rule for tort, would be governed by that foreign law. He next reasoned that an American court could not enforce any law or obligation but that of its own sovereign, but he went on to note that in enforcing American law in such situation, an American judge acting 'under civilized law ... imposes an obligation of its own as nearly homologous as possible to that arising in the place where the tort occurs'.[24] That is, an American court, required by the dictates of comity to focus on replicating the result that would be reached in the courts of the country where the cause of action arose, must accordingly have reference to the currency of the place of the tort. However, since it must give judgment in its own money it should effect a conversion to US dollars at the date of that breach. Learned Hand J noted that the English courts had reached the same result in *The Volturno*. He then went on to hold that things could be no different in contract, and thus that a breach-date rule had to be implemented there too. Because the foreign currency had declined as against the currency of the forum, the effect of the breach-date rule in *Guinness* was to benefit the claimant.

[22] 291 Fed 769 (SDNY 1923), aff'd 299 F 538 (2d Cir 1924); aff'd, *Hicks v Guinness* 299 US 71 (*Guinness*).

[23] It should be noted that in so concluding, Learned Hand J did not appear to contemplate the prospect that the courts of some foreign countries might, in such a situation, give judgment in a currency other than their own, or give judgment in their own currency, but valued at some time other than the breach to take account of fluctuations between their own currency and some other between the breach date and the time of judgment. In other words, the reasoning in *Guinness* assumes that all other foreign courts were constrained by the same initial starting position that American courts were bound by—that is, all courts could give judgment only in their own currency—and additionally all courts, in causes of action governed by their own law, would ignore the relevance of foreign currency and currency fluctuation.

[24] Above n 22, 770.

Guinness imposed a breach-date conversion and in that respect did not depart from the result that had prevailed in most recent cases. All that differed was the reasoning by which that result was reached; not a focus on accurate compensation but rather one on the working out of the vested rights principle. There was little discussion as to whether such an approach was faithful to underlying values of tort or contract or was invariably fair between the parties. It was enough that it seemed to accord with conflict-of-laws theory and to promote the choice-of-law value of uniformity. The judgment of Learned Hand J at first instance was affirmed by the Second Circuit and from there was appealed to the Supreme Court of the United States. There, in a terse unanimous opinion written by Holmes J, the court agreed with Learned Hand J. It likewise had regard to conflicts-of-law philosophy (as opposed to accuracy of compensation), holding that 'the conclusion to which we come seems to us to flow from fundamental theory and not to need other support'.[25]

The real divergence from the English approach came the following year in a second decision of the Supreme Court of the United States, *Deutsche Bank Filiale Nurnberg v Humphrey*.[26] That case picked up the vested rights approach of *Guinness* and used it to arrive at an innovation—and a different conversion date. Like *Guinness*, *Deutsche Bank* dealt with a claim under the US Trading with the Enemy Act[27] concerning a debt originally expressed in German marks, which had recently depreciated sharply with reference to the US dollar. The decision appealed from had applied a breach-date conversion, the rule that had been adopted by the Supreme Court in *Guinness* just the year before. However, in the face of a vigorous four-judge dissent which would have confirmed the judgment under appeal and the uniform application of a breach-date rule, Holmes J wrote another short opinion for himself and four other judges which reversed the judgment in the court below and imposed a judgment-date conversion. He distinguished *Guinness* and its breach-date rule on the basis that in *Guinness* the proper law of the agreement was the law of the United States, whereas in the case before him the agreement was governed by German law. Early in his tenure at the Supreme Court Holmes J had espoused this theory, writing that 'as the only source of [an] obligation is the law of the place of the act, it follows that that law determines not merely the existence of the obligation … but equally determines its extent'.[28] He maintained this vested-rights approach to choice of law throughout his career, according it the

[25] 269 US 71 (1925) 80. The Supreme Court also noted that the result it reached accorded with that recently imposed by the House of Lords in *The Volturno*, above n 20.

[26] 272 US 517, 47 S Ct 46 (1926) [*Deutsche Bank*]. The judgment issued by the Supreme Court in this case was not enforced by the defendant, who, due to the disadvantageous conversion date imposed by the Supreme Court, ended up accepting instead a larger award offered by the United States Foreign-Claim Commission.

[27] October 6, 1917, c 106; 40 St 411.

[28] *Slater v Mexican National Railroad* 194 US 120 (1904) 126. This was not a conversion-date case.

status of an unquestionable a priori assumption,[29] and when the conversion-date issue came before him in *Deutsche Bank* he found that mere breach of an obligation created and thus governed by foreign law would, at the time of breach, create no obligation under American law. In his opinion for the majority, he observed that at the time of the defendant's refusal to pay, the defendant 'owed no duty to the plaintiff under our law'.[30] Since the defendant's breach was only a failure to conform to a duty imposed by German law, it evidently followed that, when the defendant bank initially failed to meet the plaintiff's demand for repayment, the duty became fixed in marks and in addition that it continued to be a liability in marks alone. For that reason, since the vested rights approach to choice of law required that an American court might enforce but should never alter the foreign obligation, it would be wrong for an American court to impose a breach-date conversion. It then followed, evidently, that the obligation became converted into dollars only at some later time.

There is a measure of confusion about the exact conversion date required by the Supreme Court's judgment in *Deutsche Bank*. *Deutsche Bank* was less than clear on that matter, and there is a legitimate question as to whether Holmes J's opinion should be read as authorising a judgment-date conversion or one at the date of the filing of the suit[31] (which was how Lord Simon had understood *Deutsche Bank* in *Miliangos*[32]). In any event, the interpretation put on *Deutsche Bank* in subsequent cases has been that what Holmes J meant, or must be taken to have meant, is the date of judgment.[33] That is, the fact that it is a foreign law which governs the action is taken to mean that—even after the defendant breached the contract

[29] GK Reiblich, 'The Conflict of Laws Philosophy of Justice Holmes' (1939) 28 *Georgetown Law Journal* 1, 8.

[30] *Deutsche Bank*, above n 24, 518–19. Comparable reasoning also justifying a judgment-date conversion had appeared in lower court judgments before *Deutsche Bank*: *The Verdi* 268 F 908 (SDNY 1920); *The Hurona* 268 F 911 (SDNY 1920); *Liberty National Bank of New York v Burr* 270 Fed 251 (ED Penn 1921).

[31] For detailed discussion of this point see W Galleski, 'Conversion of Foreign Money Obligations' (1957) 6 *American Journal of Comparative Law* 111 and H Jones, 'The Spurious Judgment Day Rule for Converting Foreign Currency into Dollars When Suit is Brought Upon an Obligation Governed by Foreign Law' (1968) 3 *International Lawyer* 277. Their view is that Holmes J meant not the date of judgment but rather the date of filing of the suit, and that later cases and scholars have simply misread *Deutsche Bank* on this point. Galleski even adduces some correspondence between Holmes and Sir Frederick Pollock that supports this view. Both Galleski and Jones also think that the date of filing is the better rule. It is difficult to emerge from a reading of Galleski and Jones without being convinced that Holmes J did not intend to adopt a judgment-day conversion. However, for better or worse (and with the exception of one rogue judgment cited by Galleski) Holmes J's reasons in *Deutsche Bank* have been read as though what he meant was a judgment-date conversion. So, despite what he wrote, a date-of-filing conversion plays no part in modern American law.

[32] *Miliangos v George Frank (Textiles) Ltd* [1976] AC 443 (HL) 483 (*Miliangos*). In *Re United Railways of Havana and Regla Warehouses* [1961] AC 1007 (HL) Viscount Simonds expressed the same view (at 1048).

[33] *Thornton v National City Bank* 45 F 2d 127 (2d Cir 1930); *Tillman v Russo Asiatic Bank* 51 F 2d 1023 (2d Cir 1931), cert denied 285 US 539 (1932); *Royal Insurance Co v Compania Transatlantica Espanola* 57 F 2d 288 (EDNY 1932); *Indian Refinery Co v Valvoline Oil Co* 75 F 2d 797 (7th Cir 1935); *Tramontana v SA Empresa de Viacao Aerea Rio Grandense* 350 F 2d 468 (DC Cir 1965), cert denied 383 US 943 (1966).

by failing to make timely payment of the debt—the cause of action and thus the currency of suit remained foreign until such time as they became converted into an American obligation by an American court's pronouncing judgment for the plaintiff.

Any doubt about that was eliminated the following year in the third of the conversion-date cases to come before the Supreme Court, *Zimmermann v Sutherland*.[34] In the view of Holmes J, who delivered yet another succinct opinion for the court, this time unanimous, private international law theory dictated the necessary result and in selecting an exchange date it was not up to the court 'to substitute something else that seemed to them about fair'.[35] To him the matter was not about contract law per se, or the reasonable expectations of the parties, or *restitutio in integrum*. Rather it was about what followed from a decision about which country's law governed. The appropriate currency conversion rule would be derived from choice-of-law theory and no other justification would be required.

Unfortunately there was one passage in *Zimmerman* that generated some additional confusion. Holmes J's judgment on that point may have made it clear that a judgment-date conversion should be applied where the *Deutsche Bank* conditions were satisfied, but it left some doubt as to whether those conditions were met when (1) the underlying claim was governed by foreign law, (2) the debt was payable in a foreign country or (3) both those conditions were met. Here is the ambiguous passage:

> The distinction between *Deutsche Bank* and *Hicks v Guinness* is not … that the plaintiff in *Hicks v Guinness* was in the United States, but that, as the court understood the facts, the debt was payable in New York and subject to American law, so that upon a breach of the contract there arose a present liability in dollars.[36]

The view of the majority of courts that have sought to apply the law emerging from *Deutsche Bank* and *Zimmerman* is that the necessary criterion for invoking a judgment-date conversion is that the obligation in question is governed by foreign law. Place of payment is not decisive.[37] However, the ambiguities in the extract just quoted have been exploited on occasion by courts which sometimes prefer the result dictated by proceeding as though the operative criterion triggering a breach-date conversion is the place of payment.

[34] *Zimmermann v Sutherland* 274 US 253 (1927) (*Zimmermann*). Like *Guinness* and *Deutsche Bank*, *Zimmermann* was a claim under the Trading with the Enemy Act and concerned a European currency that had declined steeply against the American dollar. *Zimmermann* is the last decision of the Supreme Court of the United States to take up the conversion-date question. In this respect the US and Canada are similar: both have Supreme Court decisions on the currency-of-judgment question from the first part of the 20th century, mainly arising out of post World War I cases, and nothing since.

[35] Ibid, 255.

[36] Ibid, 256.

[37] *In re Good Hope Chemical Corp* 747 F 2d 806 (1st Cir 1981), cert denied 471 US 1102; *Jamaica Nutrition Holdings v United Shipping Co*, above n 6.

The best example of this—and a telling instance of result-selective manipulation of conversion-date rules—is the 1968 decision of the Court of Appeals for the District of Columbia Circuit in *Bamberger v Clark*.[38] There the dispute involved a claim under the Trading with the Enemy Act by a man who had worked for IG Farben in Germany in the years preceding World War II. Because he was Jewish, Bamberger was constructively dismissed by Farben in 1939, and in the face of growing Nazi atrocities he fled Germany in the spring of that year, ending up in America two years later. Thirty years later he brought suit on his breached employment contract in the US. The underlying obligation was in reichmarks, which were worth US$172,055 if converted at the time of the pre-war breach, but a mere US$7,824 at the time of judgment. The court's machinations in arriving at the fuller compensation that came from a breach-date conversion are instructive. *Deutsche Bank* and *Zimmerman* were the guiding authorities, and since the claimant's employment contract was obviously governed by German law those authorities pointed to a judgment-date conversion, which would be little help to the claimant. However, without mentioning the dominant governing-law interpretation of those cases, the court held that the place of payment was the operative factor. At first blush that did not appear to assist Bamberger: his employment contract had been for work in Germany. That meant that Germany would have been the agreed place of payment and accordingly a judgment-date conversion would apply. However, the court managed to find that the breach of contract was not complete until after Bamberger had arrived in the US in 1941. It next turned to an interpretation of the law of Nazi Germany at the relevant time, a provision which would permit a court to alter the contractual place of payment in light of equitable concerns, and although that law was uncertain on this point the court concluded that:

> Looking to the language of Section 242 of the German Code, it seems probable that this equity provision, under these compelling circumstances, relieved appellant of the necessity of returning to the land he was forced to flee to collect what was his due.[39]

[38] Above n 6.

[39] Ibid, 488–89. The court's approach to the section seemed to involve interpreting it 'fairly'—that is, fairly from the point of view of an American court in 1968—not interpreting it in the way that a German court would have approached it in 1941. That amounts to a departure from the orthodox solution, which would require a US court purporting to apply German law to reach the conclusion that a German court would have reached at the time. The same result might be reached more forthrightly by invoking the doctrine of public policy. That is, a US court could conclude that a law which required a Jew to return to Germany in 1940 to collect money due to him (which is almost certainly what a German court in 1940 would have required of Bamberger, even assuming it went so far as to conclude that his persecution amounted to constructive dismissal) was, given the consequences of such a return, offensive to deeply-held American values and so should not be implemented in the US court. However, as David Fraser has pointed out in an examination of cases in which US and UK courts had to consider Nazi laws, express reliance on the doctrine of public policy has not been the order of the day where such laws were concerned; rather courts have been able to achieve fair results through manipulation of everyday doctrine: D Fraser, '"This is Not Like Any Other Legal Question": A Brief History of Nazi Law Before UK and US Courts' (2003) 19 *Connecticut Journal of International Law* 59. Presumably the approach of those Canadian judges who opt for the conversion date which is

In the result, this meant that the place of payment of the debt due under Bamberger's employment contract was where Bamberger was located at the date of breach—which happened to be the United States. This step enabled the court to impose a breach-date conversion, concluding 'it follows that under *Hicks v Guinness* ... that the reichmark debt was to be converted into dollars at a 1941 rate of exchange'.[40]

As noted, the place-of-payment interpretation of *Deutsche Bank* and *Zimmerman* is a minority view, though *Bamberger* is not the only instance of a court finding that rule handy in arriving at a desired result.[41] The dominant view, however, is that what triggers the operation of a judgment-date rule was the fact that the obligation was governed by (because it was created by) foreign law—though in admiralty cases arising out of collisions this has been altered to imposing a breach-date conversion when the judgment took place in American waters or the high seas, and a judgment-date conversion when it took place in foreign waters.[42] Thus the breach-date rule would apply where American law created and governed the underlying right, because, under the vested rights approach to choice of law, non-payment of such a debt gave rise to an immediate, present liability under American law (or the law of an American state), and thus, it followed, to a present obligation in dollars. By way of contrast, when the foreign currency obligation was governed by some foreign law, non-payment of such a debt remained an obligation in that foreign law and under that foreign currency until such time as an American court translated it into an American obligation by awarding judgment. So since it was that American judgment which converted the foreign obligation into an American one, it was the time of that judgment which should dictate the date of conversion from the foreign currency to US dollars.

Where the foreign currency had collapsed between the date of breach and the time of judgment the effect of the switch to the breach-date rule would be devastating for the claimant. However, while *Deutsche Bank* and *Zimmerman* were not decided in the context of currencies that had completely collapsed, that has not led

just in all the circumstances would lead to the selection of a judgment-date (or some other late date) conversion without the need either to manipulate contract doctrine, as the *Bamberger* court did, or invoke the public policy rule.

40 Ibid, 489.

41 *Gutu International AG v Raymond Packer Co* 493 F 2d 938 (1st Cir 1974); *Ngoc Quang Trinh v Citibank NA* 623 F Supp 1526 (ED Mich 1985). In addition, some courts have decided that, on the facts of the case before them they need not choose between the country-of-payment rule and the governing-law rule, since both lead to the same result: *Newman-Green Inc v Alfonzo-Larrain R* 612 F Supp 1434 (ND Ill 1985), vacated on other grounds 854 F 2d 915 (2d Cir 1988), rev'd 490 US 826 (1989); *Factofrance Heller v I P M Precision Machinery Co* 627 F Supp 1412 (ND Ill 1986).

42 *The Arkansas* [1929] Am Mar Cas 581 (2d Cir 1929); *The West Arrow* 80 F 2d 853 (2d Cir 1936); *The MacDonaugh v The Werfa* [1934] Am Mar Cas 234 (SDNY 1935); *The Quevilly v The Sampson* [1938] Am Mar Cas 347 (SDNY 1938); *Shaw, Savill, Abion & Co v The Fredericksburg*, above n 1. For criticism of this rule on the ground that what is needed is a flexible approach rather than a rigid one, see Anon 'Rate of Exchange Applicable to Damages arising from Maritime Torts', above n 11, 143–44.

later courts to deviate from those rules when cases presenting such circumstances came before them.[43]

The opinion in *Zimmermann* made no mention of the fact that sometimes some issues in a case are governed by one country's law and others are governed by another's. Which conversion date should apply in that circumstance? Not surprisingly this problem arose in the context of the rule emerging from *Deutsche Bank* and *Zimmerman*. It was generally resolved by holding that only where the *entire* cause of action was governed by foreign law (with the exception of procedural matters, which are always decided according to the law of the forum) would a judgment-date conversion apply. So, for example, in *Gonzalez v Banco de Santander-Puerto Rico*,[44] although the court looked to Spanish law to determine whether a party was a holder in due course, it concluded that the obligation being sued on was governed by local law so that a breach-date conversion was required.

Even putting aside problems arising from the fact different countries' laws can, on occasion, apply to different substantive issues in a case, difficulties can arise from the fact that the question of the governing law is one that sometimes remains unresolved until trial, or that a holding on the governing law can be manipulated in a result-selective fashion by courts. Adopting an approach to the conversion-date problem that makes the date depend on a decision about which country's substantive law provides the *lex causae* produces a situation where the conversion date may remain unresolved until trial, thus undermining the certainty and predictability that obtained under the pre-existing breach-date rule. This was one reason the House of Lords rejected the *Deutsche Bank* approach when it considered the conversion-date question in 1960 in *Havana Railways*. The words of Viscount Simonds on this point show that court's strong preference for certainty: 'It would, in my opinion, introduce the sort of refinement into the law, against which I have striven and shall ever strive, if a different rule were adopted in the case of a foreign debt'.[45] In the 1920s, however, despite the recent developments which had expunged the pre-existing variety of conversion dates in favour of the certainty provided by the breach-date rule, this new uncertainty introduced by the

[43] See *Tillman v Russo Asiatic Bank*, above n 33, and later litigation by the same plaintiff in *Tillman v National City Bank* 118 F 2d 631 (2d Cir 1941), cert denied 314 US 650 (1941). The complete collapse of the czarist ruble combined with the operation of a judgment date-conversion resulted in judgments that were technically in favour of the plaintiff but which in practical terms amounted to discharging the defendants from their obligations. For more detailed discussion of this case and others like it see E Rashba, 'Debts in Collapsed Foreign Currencies' (1944) 54 *Yale Law Journal* 1. Another instance of the collapse of a foreign currency (this time, reichsmarks) combining with the judgment-date rule to result in a worthless judgment is *Sun Insurance Office Ltd v The Arauca Fund* 84 F Supp 516 (SD Fla 1949). Since reichsmarks were at the time of judgment worth nothing, that was what the 'successful' plaintiff got. For criticism of this case, again advocating a flexible conversion-date rule, see J Gidding, 'The Measurement of Foreign Money Obligations' (1950) 36 *Virginia Law Review* 215.

[44] *Gonzalez v Banco de Santander-Puerto Rico* 932 F 2d 999 (1st Cir 1991).

[45] *Havana Railways*, above n 32.

choice-of-law approach was not perceived as problematic by courts. It was enough that it followed from conflicts-of-law abstractions.

Although the rule which emerged from *Deutsche Bank* and *Zimmermann* came in for a measure of criticism at the time—mainly for its reliance on conflicts-of-laws theory at the expense of basic remedial tenets of private law[46]—in practice it met with success.[47] In 1934 in the *Restatement, Conflict of Laws* (the *First Restatement*), the ALI adopted the distinction drawn by the Supreme Court in *Deutsche Bank*, as clarified in *Zimmermann*. This was helpful because *Deutsche Bank* and *Zimmermann* were only binding on federal courts; the fact that they were adopted by the ALI would assist in that rule being espoused by state courts. The ALI promulgated the view that the question of the appropriate exchange rate was to be approached from a conflict-of-laws point of view and resolved by reference to the governing law.[48] As with Story's great text, which had appeared exactly a century earlier, the *First Restatement* was able to take it for granted that American judges could give judgment only in US dollars. It did not advert to the Coinage Act of 1792 as the reason for this constraint. Rather it simply assumed that the limitation must operate, and—like Story before it—it offered no complaint about the justice, or otherwise, of this starting point. The *First Restatement* situated its provisions on the question at the end of its section on damages, rather than in its chapter on contracts, as Story had done, thus acknowledging that the problem was one that might arise in causes of action other than contract and perhaps even aligning itself with the English view that the problem should be viewed as an aspect of private remedial law. It proceeded from the premise that an agreement to deliver a certain amount of a foreign currency was simply an agreement to deliver a commodity, and that the remedial approach presented by the breach of such an agreement was simply one of measuring the value of that commodity. Starting from that position, there seemed little doubt that such a measurement should proceed by the normal approach of valuing the lost commodity at the date of breach. Thus its core provision viewed the problem entirely as one of measurement:

> Damages for breach of a contract to deliver money not the currency of the state where the delivery is to be made are measured in currency of the state of performance at the rate of exchange current at the time of breach.[49]

[46] J Drake, 'The Rule, The Principle, The Standard in Fluctuating Exchange' (1927) 25 *Michigan Law Review* 860, 865 ff; J Drake, 'The Proper Rule in Fluctuating Exchanges' (1930) 28 *Michigan Law Review* 227. But for a contemporary comment championing the conflict-of-laws approach as eminently sound, see C Maw, above n 11, 623.

[47] *Thornton v National City Bank of New York*, above n 33; *Tillman v Russo Asiatic Bank*, above n 33; *Royal Insurance Co v Compania Trasatlantica Espanola* 57 F 2d (EDNY 1932); *Indian Refining Co v Valvoline Oil* 75 F 2d 797 (7th Cir 1935); *The West Arrow*, above n 42.

[48] American Law Institute, *Restatement, Conflict of Laws* (St Paul, Minn, American Law Institute Press, 1934), ss 423, 424. Another contemporary preference for the Federal Court approach, as opposed to the rigid New York rule, appeared in Fraenkel, above n 13, 386.

[49] Ibid, s 423.

However, consistent with the vested rights approach that permeated the *First Restatement*, that breach-date rule would not apply where the cause of action was governed by some foreign law. There the *First Restatement* recommended that American courts should proceed on the basis that the law of the wrong determined the right to damages, and from this it evidently followed that such law also had an effect on which yardstick should be selected to measure damages. This was summarised in the second of the *First Restatement*'s two rules on the matter of damages foreign currency: 'When judgment is rendered on a cause of action for damages created in another state, the rate of exchange adopted is that which exists at the time when the judgment is rendered'.[50]

Thus, in the case of a tort occurring in, say, England, the *First Restatement*'s place-of-the-tort choice of law rule[51] would dictate that an American court apply English tort law to any tort claim brought before it, regardless of other factors that might be thought to bear on choice-of-law in tort, such as the residence of the parties. The vested rights theory then operated to make the currency of the wrong the proper measure of damages between the parties—again, regardless of whether that currency had anything to do with the parties apart from its being the currency of the jurisdiction in which the tort was found to have occurred—and it followed that an American court must award damages measured by that currency. However, the vested rights of the parties did not survive judgment. Or rather, on judgment they were transformed by an American judgment into an American right—a right necessarily formulated in US dollars. That is, since it seemed that an American court could only award damages in US dollars, the currency of the wrong then had to be converted into US dollars at that time of that US judgment. Like *Deutsche Bank* and *Zimmermann*, the *First Restatement* did not advert to drawbacks associated with the uncertainty that might flow from the fact that there could be doubt about whether a given wrong—say, a tort or breach of contract—was governed by some foreign law, so that the conversion date would not be knowable by litigating parties until the judge settled the question of what law governed.

Not all American courts went along with the distinction introduced by the Supreme Court in *Deutsche Bank* and promulgated by the ALI. *Deutsche Bank* only laid down the law for Federal Courts and the *Restatement* was not binding, so state courts remained free to determine their own approach and many stuck to the practice of applying the forum-currency/breach-date rule (the New York rule) in all cases.[52] The New York rule disregards the subtleties—and avoids the uncertainties—of conflict of laws distinctions and always employs a breach-date

[50] Ibid, s 424. In *Deutsche Bank* it was unclear whether the judgment-day rule was applied because American law governed the contract or because the United States was the place of repayment. The *First Restatement* obviously took the view that the former was the correct rule.

[51] Ibid, s 384.

[52] For example, *Dougherty v Equitable Life Assurance Society* 266 NY 71, 193 NE 897 (NYCA 1934); *Richard v American Union Bank* 241 NY 163, 149 NE 338 (NYCA 1925); *Librarie Hachette SA v Paris Book Center Inc*, 62 Misc 2d 873, 309 NYS 2d 701 (Sup Ct NY City 1970); *American National Insurance*

conversion, even when the matter is governed by a foreign law.[53] During this period, when American currency was generally rising against most others, this had the advantage of not resulting in under-compensation of foreign plaintiffs.

The situation changed slightly in 1938 with the decision of the Supreme Court of the United States in *Erie Railroad Co v Tompkins*.[54] *Erie Railroad* was not a foreign-currency case. It was a decision which held that federal courts sitting in diversity jurisdiction must apply the substantive law that the state in which they are sitting would apply. Since the currency question was regarded as substantive law, this holding extended to the rule concerning exchange rate selection.[55] Thus the federal courts would employ the *Guinness/Deutsche Bank* approach when applying federal law, which would lead them to employ a judgment-date conversion in claims where a foreign law was found to govern.[56] However, when exercising their diversity jurisdiction, federal courts would apply the law of the state in which they sat, which for the most part was the New York (breach-date) rule. The effect of *Erie Railroad*, then, was not to alter the fundamental situation in American courts were divided between two principal approaches to the problem posed by foreign currency obligations—the New York rule and the *Guinness/Deutsche Bank* approach. It only altered the scope of operation of each of those rules by confining the latter to cases where the federal courts were applying federal law, or to states which might elect to follow the federal approach rather than the New York rule.

Co v de Cardenas, above n 4; *Rubewa Products Co v Watson's Quality Turkey Products Inc* 242 A 2d 609 (DC Cir 1968); and see the cases discussed by R Brand, 'Restructuring', above n 6, 141.

53 *Parker v Hoppe* 257 NY 333 178 NE 550 (Ct App NY 1931), re-argument denied 258 NY 365, 179 NE 770 (1932); *Simon v Electrospace Corp* 28 NY 2d 136, 269 NE 2d 21 (Ct App NY 1971); *Cunningham v Quaker Oats Co*, 639 F Supp 234 (WDNY 1986). There are a couple of instances where New York courts deviated from this rule: in *Re United Shellac Corp* 97 NYS 2d 817 (Sup Ct App Div 1950) the court thought the breach-date rule would lead to an unfair result and opted instead for converting as of the date of judgment. The so-called New York rule is not confined to that state: in *Compania Engraw Commercial e Industrial v Schenley Distillers Corp* 181 F 2d 876 (9th Cir 1950) the court, sitting in diversity jurisdiction, decided that the New York rule was the law in California.

54 *Erie Railroad Co v Tompkins* 304 US 64 (1938) (*Erie Railroad*).

55 See, eg: *Vishipco Line v Chase Manhattan Bank* 660 F 2d 854 (2d Cir 1981), cert denied 459 US 976, 103 S Ct 313; *Newmont Mines Ltd v Hanover Insurance Co* 784 F 2d 127 (2d Cir 1986).

56 As in *Paris v Central Chiclera, S de RL* 193 F 2d 960 (5th Cir 1952); *Straehler v Brownell* 246 F 2d 675 (DC Cir 1957). Note that this can lead to debates about whether a claim is governed by foreign or US federal law. For instance, in *Skibbs A/S Gylfe v S/T Trujillo* 209 F 2d 386, [1954] AMC 233 (2d Cir 1954), a high seas maritime collision case, the Second Circuit concluded that general maritime law (which was US federal law) governed, so it opted for a breach-date conversion. But in *Conte v Flota Mercante del Estado* 277 F 2d 664 (2d Cir 1960), a personal injury claim on behalf of a seaman injured on the high seas on an Argentine vessel, the same court determined that Argentine law governed and felt constrained to require a judgment-date conversion from pesos to dollars, even though the Argentine peso had fallen drastically against the dollar and this conversion date would disadvantage the injured worker. It can also lead to debates about when judgment is granted. In *Reissner v Rogers* 276 F 2d 506 (DC Cir 1960), a claim under the Trading with the Enemy Act, the court applied this rule but held that the judgment date was the date the Attorney General authorised payment of the plaintiff's claim, not the date when it was later confirmed by a court.

Following those developments, little changed in the American law pertaining to foreign currency obligations until after *Miliangos*. The *Restatement of the Law Second, Conflict of Laws*,[57] adopted and promulgated by the ALI in 1969, largely replicated the *First Restatement*. It had just a single section on the question of damages in foreign currency. Curiously, this was situated at the end of a chapter headed 'Procedure' that also featured provisions on such matters as service of process, notice and proof of foreign law and witnesses. Again the ALI was able to proceed on the stated assumption, which it referred to as fact,[58] that American courts could not grant judgment in anything other than US dollars. Accordingly, its sole provision on the question of foreign currency obligations made no reference to the currency-of-judgment question. Rather, it had the heading 'Time for Converting Foreign Currency into Local Currency'. On this point, the *Second Restatement* maintained the approach of its predecessor and *Deutsche Bank*—namely, that the answer to the conversion-date question should be resolved by determining the governing law. That is, if the law that governed the cause of action was that of the United States (or any one of them) then the breach-date rule applied. But things were different if a foreign law should be found to govern:

> § 144 When in a suit for the recovery of money damages the cause of action is governed by the local law of another state, the forum will convert the currency in which recovery would have been granted in the other state into the local currency as of the date of the award.[59]

Superficially, § 144 of the *Second Restatement* seems the same as its predecessor, § 424 of the *First Restatement*. So, for example, in a tort suit governed by English law it seems that an American court following the *Second Restatement* would assess damages in sterling and convert them into American dollars at the date of judgment.[60] However, there was a small but noteworthy difference between the conversion-date rule in the *First Restatement* and that in the *Second*. The *First Restatement* had proceeded on the assumption that the courts of the governing law would necessarily assess damages in their own currency on the basis of the breach-date rule—as in fact American courts did. However, the *Second Restatement* demonstrated a new awareness of the fact that, elsewhere in the world, courts did not inevitably follow such an approach. Since the courts of some countries were

[57] American Law Institute, *Restatement of the Law, Second, Conflict of Laws* (St Paul, Minn, American Law Institute Publishers, 1971) (the *Second Restatement*).

[58] Ibid, 403: 'The rule of this Section owes its existence to the fact that an Anglo-American court may only render a judgment for money damages in its own local currency'.

[59] *The Second Restatement*, ibid, §144 (p 403).

[60] In passing it should be noted that the choice of law rule in tort was very different in the *Second Restatement* than it was in the *First Restatement*, so that, although the conversion-date rule remained much the same, the way it played out in a given dispute might be very different. That is, under a conflict of laws approach, a change in the rules used to determine the law that governs a given obligation amounts to a change in the rule that determines the currency conversion-date for that obligation. To additionally complicate matters, it could be that a given state court might elect to follow § 144 of the *Second Restatement* on the foreign currency question, but apply a choice of law rule different from that recommended by either the *First* or *Second Restatement*.

prepared to award damages in currencies other than their own, even in cases governed by their own law, uniformity would not be achieved by assuming otherwise. Thus, under the rule in the *Second Restatement* the conversion into US dollars was not a conversion from the currency of the law that governed the underlying obligation but rather a conversion from the currency *in which recovery would have been granted* by the courts of the country whose law governed the cause of action. Moreover the conversion should take place at the time of the American judgment. The *Second Restatement*'s goal in this reformulation was to attempt to preserve and promote uniformity of result and to discourage forum shopping. Plaintiffs should be given no incentive to seek out an American court on the basis that US rules on currency conversion would operate to their advantage.

Of course a moment's reflection reveals that, while the rule in the *Second Restatement* provides for greater uniformity than that in its 1934 predecessor, thanks mainly to its newfound awareness that not all countries' courts approached the problem as American ones did, it still failed to guarantee complete uniformity. There were a couple of reasons for this. First, the *Second Restatement* still required courts to convert to American currency as of the date of the award, rather than, as *Miliangos* would do, the payment date. Thus, to the extent that there is currency fluctuation between the date of the judgment and the date the plaintiff finally collects, uniformity may be defeated. That is, in failing to move to a payment-date conversion it preserves the possibility for the two-forum problem illustrated by *Competex SA v Labow* in chapter two.[61] Further, the *Second Restatement*'s rule turns on an American court imitating the courts of the country that, *under American choice of law rules*, is said to be the country whose law governs the cause of action in question. But of course that country need not necessarily be the one that provides the only alternative forum to the parties. That is, an American court following the *Second Restatement* might well conclude that the case before it was a tort case governed by the law of England, and that English courts would, in such a case, assess damages in sterling. However it is conceivable that the plaintiff in such a case might well have had the option of bringing suit either in France, and that, in that case, French courts would assess damages in francs. In such a case an American court's decision to assess damages initially in sterling would not conduce to uniformity of result.

III. The Influence of *Miliangos*

We have seen that in the mid 1970s English judges, followed promptly thereafter by their counterparts elsewhere in the Commonwealth, undertook fundamental changes to their resolution to the currency-of-judgment problem. The same thing did not happen in the United States at that time. Even after *Miliangos* the US

[61] *Competex SA v Labow* 783 F 2d 333 (2d Cir 1986). See the discussion at pp 81–82.

continued to be divided into courts which clung to the forum-currency/breach-date rule and those which adopted the conflict-of laws laid down by the Supreme Court and espoused by the ALI. There was just one small area in which there was some change in American practice in the 1970s, namely enforcement of arbitral awards in foreign currencies. As we have noted in chapter one, the pre-*Miliangos* decision in *Jugoslavenska*,[62] in which the English Court of Appeal authorised the enforcement of an arbitral award in a foreign currency, might be regarded as a hesitant preliminary step in abandoning the forum-currency rule. In the United States, following that country's 1970 ratification of the *New York Convention*,[63] there was likewise some judicial recognition that arbitral awards requiring payment in foreign currencies might be confirmed by American courts.[64] Apart from that, however, there was little change in American law at the time of *Miliangos.*

Nevertheless, *Miliangos* did eventually have a notable affect on American law with respect to the currency-of-judgment question. As was the case throughout the Commonwealth, *Miliangos* was noticed by American courts, law reformers and scholars, and was generally regarded as a progressive and commercially astute development, one to be imitated. However, unlike the situation in the Commonwealth, where the replication of *Miliangos* occurred almost immediately after it appeared, significant changes in the American position did not begin to take place until the mid and late 1980s—that is, until a decade or more after *Miliangos.* An explanation for this lies in the relative strength of the UK and US currencies at this time. As we have seen, a factor in bringing about the judicial reworking of the foreign money issue in England in the mid-1970s was the fall during that period of the English pound vis-a-vis the currency of many of that country's trading partners—including Germany, Switzerland and the United States. This raised the prospect of under-compensation—or at least apparent under-compensation[65]—of plaintiffs before the English courts if those courts adhered to the forum-currency/breach-date rule. Moreover, many of those plaintiffs would

[62] *Jugoslavenska Oceanska Plovidba v Castle Investment Co* [1974] QB 292, [1973] 3 WLR 847 (CA) (*Jugoslavenska*).

[63] *Convention on the Recognition and Enforcement of Foreign Arbitral Awards*, 10 June 1958, 330 UNTS 3.

[64] *Island Territory of Curacao v Solitron Devices Inc* 356 F Supp 1 (SDNY 1973), aff'd 489 F 2d 1313 (2d Cir 1973, cert denied 416 US 986 (1974); *Waterside Ocean Navigation Co v International Navigation Ltd* 737 F 2d 150 (2d Cir 1984). For approving commentary see H Smit, 'Judgments and Arbitral Awards in a Foreign Currency: A Means of Dealing with Currency Fluctuations in International Adjudication' (1996) 7 *American Review of International Arbitration* 121 and R Brand, 'Restructuring', above n 8, 165. In the wake of *Miliangos* one state, Florida, passed a statute permitting its courts to confirm arbitral awards issued in foreign currencies: Florida Commercial Relations Code § 684.26. However that provision further provides that, upon application of a party, judges must also enter judgment in US dollars as of the date of the arbitral award. The judgment creditor could then, it would seem, enforce either order, which would enable it to reap the benefits of fluctuation either way. As another early breach in the dike of the American rule against entering judgments in anything but dollars, Brand also notes (168) a 1980 case in which an American court permitted a consent judgment to be entered and affirmed in Swiss francs: *Baumlin & Ernst, Ltd v Gemini Ltd* 637 F 2d 238 (4th Cir 1980).

[65] See the discussion above at ch 1, n 55 and accompanying text.

be foreigners whose systematic under-compensation in commercial litigation might detrimentally affect the English judicial system's valued reputation for evenhandedness.

That same situation did not obtain in the United States in the 1970s, when for the most part the dollar remained strong.[66] By the mid 1980s, however, although the US dollar generally continued to appreciate as against the currency of its largest trading partner, Canada, it fell against a number of currencies of western European countries. The first effect of this was the interesting phenomenon of American courts, constrained to apply a breach-date conversion, bending the facts or the rules to find a late breach date so as to minimise under-compensation to the plaintiff.[67] More importantly, in combination with the example offered by *Miliangos*, in due course the dollar's decline gave rise to formal changes in the American position on the currency-of-judgment question.

Of course there is no necessary correlation between a weakening forum currency and the judicial shift to a late conversion date. However, it is an artifact of judicial developments in both England and the United States that the spectre of under-compensation of plaintiffs—particularly, it seems, foreign ones—functions as a stronger catalyst for legal change than the fear of their over-compensation. Indeed some American courts have been quite explicit in claiming that a virtue of the traditional rule was that, in combination with the strong dollar, it had the desirable effect of putting the loss arising from currency fluctuation on the defendant.[68] Of course this would be true only as long as the US dollar continued to rise as against the other currencies in question.

When they at length came, changes in American law took place on three stages. First the ALI—the corporate author of the *Restatements*—took a third look at the currency-of-judgment issue and produced a *Restatement* which authorised judgments in foreign currencies—or at least recommended to judges that they push the common law in that direction. Second, New York State, still an influential centre of commercial litigation, passed legislation influenced by *Miliangos*. Finally, the NCCUSL promulgated a model statute on the matter, one which drew inspiration from *Miliangos* and authorised a payment-date conversion. To date this has been enacted in nearly half the American jurisdictions. I examine these three developments in turn. Although they all acknowledge a debt to *Miliangos*, the solutions they adopted are far from identical, either with the current English position or

[66] In the words of Ronald Brand, discussing the effect of *Miliangos* in the United States, the American move toward the English position was 'retarded by the strong position of the dollar'. R Brand, 'Restructuring', above n 8, 163.

[67] See *In re Good Hope Chemical Corp*, above n 37, where, in a case involving German marks, which had recently appreciated vis-a-vis US dollars, the court, rather unorthodoxly managed to find the date of contractual breach to be the date at which the court allowed the contract to be rejected.

[68] *Skibbs A/S Gylfe v S/T Trujillo*, above n 56; *Jamaica Nutrition Holdings, Ltd v United Shipping Co*, above n 6.

with one another. As we have seen with developments in the Commonwealth, *Miliangos* has been read in different ways.

A. The Third Restatement

The first crack in the wall of the forum-currency rule was the ALI's 1984 *Tentative Draft of the Restatement of Foreign Relations Law*.[69] That document offered only a relatively brief analysis of the problem, but it noted that in *Miliangos* the House of Lords had abandoned the sterling rule as having nothing but precedent to commend it. It went on to assert that experience with the new British rule had been positive.[70]

The *Tentative Draft* proceeded to propose that, in causes of action arising in another country, American courts should have the option of giving judgment either in the currency in which the obligation arose or in US dollars. The scant analysis offered little explanation as to why this option should be confined to situations where the cause of action arose in another country, and indeed the commentary's apparent approval of the English decision in *Hoffman v Sofaer*[71] appears to contradict such a limitation. In that case the cause of action had arisen in England but the English court held that damages might be measured in a foreign currency. It seems that, despite its claimed admiration for the new English approach, the ALI had some initial difficulties in viewing the problem through anything but a conflicts-of-law lens. In addition, the *Tentative Draft* gave little guidance as to which factors should determine which foreign currency should be selected, apart from offering a passing approval of the House of Lords decisions *The Despina R* and *The Folias*, coupled with a description of those cases so skeletal as to be inaccurate.

Nevertheless, the *Tentative Draft* met with a measure of approval. When the *Third Restatement* was adopted and promulgated in May of 1986 it contained a provision which, with several changes in wording, adopted the views of the *Tentative Draft*, even expanding them in some respects. Significantly, the title for that provision was no longer 'Time for Converting Foreign Currency into Local Currency', as it had been in the first two *Restatements*, both of which had assumed that US courts could render judgment only in dollars. Rather it was 'Judgments on Obligations in Foreign Currency':

> § 823 (1) Courts in the United States ordinarily give judgment on causes of action arising in another state, or denominated in a foreign currency, in United States dollars, but they are not precluded from giving judgment in the currency in which the obligation is denominated or the loss was incurred.

[69] American Law Institute, *Restatement of the Law Third, Foreign Relations Law of the United States, Tentative Draft No 5* (St Paul, Minn, American Law Institute Publishers, 1984) (*Tentative Draft*).

[70] Ibid, 156.

[71] *Hoffman v Sofaer* [1982] 1 WLR 1350 (QB). See the discussion of this case at ch 1, n 136.

(2) If, in a case arising out of a foreign currency obligation, the court gives judgment in dollars, the conversion from foreign currency to dollars is to be made at such rate as to make the creditor whole and to avoid rewarding a debtor who has delayed in carrying out the obligation.[72]

Like the post-*Miliangos* Canadian statutes examined in the preceding chapter, this provision is largely directed to loosening the grip of the pre-existing law, without at the same time substituting any specific replacement. Subsection 1 simply negatives the forum currency rule; it authorises American courts to give judgment in foreign currencies, at least for causes of action arising in another state. It says little about the circumstances in which such judgments will be appropriate. Insofar as it claims to restate the law, its assertion that American courts were not precluded from giving judgment in a foreign currency was of debatable accuracy—for the simple reason that at that time almost all American judges who had confronted the question had appeared to believe otherwise. The subsection is perhaps best understood as encouraging American judges to take inspiration from *Miliangos* and consider following the lead of the English courts by casting off the old forum-currency rule. Subsection 2 is likewise partly negative in thrust—telling courts that they are no longer bound by any specific conversion date and that they should now consider themselves free to choose whichever date most effectively fulfills the goal of compensation.

The commentary to § 823 featured reference to *Miliangos* and suggested that the effect of this new provision was to move American law into substantial conformity with the English position.[73] However—although it is far from certain to what extent the drafters of § 823 appreciated this—the commentary to the new provision reveals key differences between its approach and the English one. As noted in chapter one, the English position that emerged from *Miliangos* and its progeny was that there should be a firm rule about which currency should be selected for judgment. To be sure, *The Folias* and *The Despina R*, with their new rule that the currency of judgment should be the one in which the aggrieved party felt the loss, introduced some uncertainty into the process. However, even after those cases the English approach was that there was, at least in theory, one currency which upon proper inquiry would prove to be the metric that best expressed the plaintiff's

[72] American Law Institute, *Restatement of the Law: Foreign Relations Law of the United States* (St Paul, Minn, American Law Institute, 1987) vol 2, 331 (*Third Restatement*). Note that the provisions on the currency question had migrated from the conflict of laws Restatement to the one on Foreign Relations Law. The ALI's earlier *Restatements on Foreign Relations Law of the United States* had not touched on the currency-of-judgment issue. Curiously—as Ron Brand has pointed out ('Restructuring', above n 6)—the *Third Restatement* made no reference to the fact that some American states have statutes which appear to require all judgments to be rendered in US dollars. These tend to be obscure and musty legislative relics, rarely if ever considered by courts, and their application to the foreign currency question is no more certain than was para 20 of the Coinage Act of 1792, discussed above. Nevertheless, some such statutes do exist. Consequently, apart from Federal Courts sitting in non-diversity cases, there is necessarily a measure of doubt about whether judges are free to adopt the approach proposed by the *Third Restatement* in states that have such statutes.

[73] *Third Restatement*, ibid, vol 2, 337.

loss. Moreover, and crucially, identifying that money should not depend on which way the relevant currencies had fluctuated during litigation.

Yet we have seen that some courts in some Commonwealth countries managed to construe *Miliangos* as authorising judges to take a flexible, plaintiff-favouring approach to the currency question. The *Third Restatement* did the same. While the words of § 823 gave only the most general guidance as to when American courts should award damages in a foreign currency, or what conversion date they should select if they elected to give judgment in US dollars, the commentary was more explicit.

> If the court gives judgment in United States dollars ... the date used for conversion should depend on whether the currency of obligation has appreciated or depreciated relative to the dollar. In general, if the foreign currency has depreciated since the injury or breach, judgment should be given at the rate of exchange applicable on the date of injury or breach; if the foreign currency has appreciated since the injury or breach, judgment should be given at the rate of exchange applicable on the date of judgment or the date of payment.[74]

Thus, under the approach of the *Third Restatement*, a key determinant in selecting the currency of judgment is a factor that will not be knowable until trial: the way the relevant currencies have fluctuated with reference to one another. Although the *Third Restatement* does not absolutely require that the plaintiff's choice prevails—since it only states that courts should impose that result 'in general'[75]—the usual result under the *Third Restatement* has been that plaintiffs get the benefit of the fluctuation either way. Unlike claimants in England under the post-*Miliangos* regime, claimants in American courts following the *Third Restatement* cannot lose.

It is essential to note, however, that the *Third Restatement* does not view this as amounting to over-compensation of plaintiffs. That is, rather than view this as a plaintiff-favouring rule—one which consciously punishes defendants for their tort or breach of contract by almost always imposing on them the downside risk of currency fluctuation—the commentary to the *Third Restatement* regards giving the plaintiff the benefit of the more advantageous of two conversion dates as an approach which most consistently enforces the principle of *restitutio in integrum*. That is, just as we have seen courts argue that breach-date conversion or payment-date conversion best implements the compensation principle, The *Third Restatement* makes the same claim for an approach that encourages judges to wait and see how the relevant currencies do vis-a-vis one another during litigation, and then give the plaintiff the benefit of the conversion date that benefits it most. Moreover courts applying the *Third Restatement* agree in regarding its rule in

[74] *Third Restatement*, ibid, vol 2, 332–33. Interestingly, the provision fails to address the important question of pre-judgment interest on awards granted in foreign currencies.

[75] For a rare instance of a court applying the *Third Restatement* yet not allowing the plaintiff the benefit of its preferred conversion date see *SARL Aquatonic—Laboratories PBE v Marie Katelle Inc* 2007 US Dist Lexis 61682 (D Ariz 2007).

this light. For instance, in *El Universal, Compania Periodistica Nacional SA de CV v Phoenician Imports, Inc* the court imposed a breach-date conversion in favour of a foreign creditor whose home currency had dropped between breach and judgment.[76] It quoted the foregoing passage from the commentary to the *Third Restatement* with approval and went on to note that 'these principles should be followed to ensure the only just result: placing the injured party in the position in which he would be had the loss not occurred'.[77]

B. New York State: The City Bar Report and Subsequent Legislation

A development that occurred roughly in tandem with the ALI's *Third Restatement* was a legislative change in New York State. In the immediate post-*Miliangos* era, courts of that jurisdiction continued to apply the forum-currency/breach-date rule, even where the obligation in question was governed by foreign law.[78] In 1985, however, a decade after *Miliangos*, the Committee on Foreign and Comparative Law of the Association of the Bar of New York City published a report on foreign currency judgments.[79] Like the ALI, that Committee was favourably taken with English developments and advanced the view that the 'post-*Miliangos* rules that have evolved in Great Britain can provide US courts with a viable framework upon which a more appropriate compensatory system of awards can be based'.[80]

Although the final draft of the *Third Restatement* had not at this time appeared, the *City Bar Report* took approving note of the 1984 *Tentative Draft*.[81] The Committee recommended that both federal and New York State courts be free to award foreign currency judgments in appropriate cases. Although it was not specific about what should amount to an appropriate case, it did make positive reference to *Miliangos*, *The Despina R* and *The Folias*, and suggest that American courts advance down that road. Significantly, and unlike the *Third Restatement*, the *City Bar Report* took the stance that over-compensation resulting from unrestrained plaintiff choice was a potential problem. It was in favour of accuracy of compensation and accordingly expressed a preference for the English, fixed currency-of-judgment approach over that in the 1984 *Tentative Draft*.

[76] *El Universal, Compania Periodistica Nacional SA de CV v Phoenician Imports, Inc* 802 SW 2d 799 (Tex App—Corpus Christi 1990).

[77] Ibid, 804.

[78] *Weston Banking Corp v Turkiye Garanti Bankasi AS*, 446 NYS 2d 67 (Sup Ct App Div, 1st Div 1982), aff'd 57 NY 2d 315, 442 NE 2d 1195 (Ct App NY, 1982); *Cunningham v Quaker Oats Co*, above n 53 (applying New York law in a diversity jurisdiction case).

[79] Committee on Foreign and Comparative Law, Association of the Bar of New York City, Report on Foreign Currency Judgments (*City Bar Report*). The *City Bar Report* was reprinted in (1986) 18 *New York University Journal of International Law and Politics* 791 and as that is more readily available than the pamphlet published by the Association subsequent page references will be to that journal rather than to the original report.

[80] Ibid, 808.

[81] Above n 69.

Two years later the New York State Legislature followed through by amending that state's law so as to jettison the breach-date rule.[82] The *City Bar Report* was influential in bringing about this statutory change, as was the state bar, which submitted a brief to the New York Legislature pointing out that failing to modernise New York's law on this point 'adversely affects New York's status as a leading center of international finance and commerce'.[83] In fact the New York State Legislature was specifically told that a benefit of changing New York's law in this fashion was that it would then be in conformity with the law of England on this point.[84] It thus appears that, as with *Miliangos* in England, commercial pressures played some part in bringing about a change whereby local courts would be able to grant judgments in foreign currencies. The old breach-date rule was perceived as an obsolete and parochial one, the maintenance of which would put at risk New York's position as the pre-eminent city for international financial transactions.[85]

An examination of the legislation reveals that it has something in common with the *Third Restatement*: while it purports to derive inspiration from *Miliangos* it actually deviates from the English model in a fundamental way. It does not, however, deviate in the way that the *Third Restatement* does. The result the New York statute in brought about is a considerably less radical move than was *Miliangos* in England. For all of the professed admiration for the English ideal in the reports that prompted the legislative change in New York State, a payment-date conversion was not the solution the New York legislature adopted. Indeed, the change to New York law was in some respects more symbolic than real. The statute is a little confusing. It starts off by appearing to follow *Miliangos* and permitting—indeed requiring—New York courts to render judgments in foreign currencies in appropriate cases:

[82] New York State Chapter Law, 20 July 1987, ch 326, codified in New York Judiciary Law, s 27(b). In the previous chapter it was noted that the Ontario and British Columbia legislation dealing with the conversion-date issue had on occasion been overlooked both by litigating parties and the courts. The same seems to have happened with the New York statute on at least one occasion. *Sung Hwan Co v Rite Aid Corp*, 841 NYS 2d 848 (Sup Ct NY 2007) is a New York case where the statute was overlooked, though there the court applied the conflict-of-laws approach which ended up requiring a judgment-date conversion, so the result was the same as if the statute had been applied.

[83] New York State Bar Association Report No 190-A (27 June 1987). The *City Bar Report* had also voiced this argument. It claimed (above n 79, 812) that adopting the *Miliangos* approach would 'contribute to the maintenance of New York State's status as one of the world's financial and commercial centers'.

[84] Letter from LD Rachlin, Chairman of the Committee on International Trade and Transactions of the New York State Bar Association to New York State Legislature (1 July 1987), 1. For an expanded discussion of the passage of this statute see J Freeman, 'Judgments in Foreign Currency—A Little Known Change in New York Law' (1989) 23 *The International Lawyer* 737.

[85] TW Cashel, 'Foreign Currency Judgments: Changing the New York Rule' (1991) 10 *Journal of International Banking Law* 385, 390. There might well have been a corresponding follow-on risk for lawyers which could go some way toward explaining the interests of the city and state bars in changing the New York rule.

> In any case in which the cause of action is based upon an obligation denominated in a currency other than currency of the United States, a court shall render or enter a judgment or decree in the foreign currency of the underlying obligation.[86]

This has allowed at least one American court to cite the New York statute as authority for awarding judgment in yen.[87] That opening sentence appears to adopt the position advocated in the *City Bar Report*.[88] This is deceptive, however, for in its second and concluding sentence the legislation backtrack and opts for judgment-date conversion: 'Such judgment or decree shall be converted into currency of the United States at the rate of exchange prevailing on the date of entry of the judgment or decree'.[89] That is, rather than tracking the payment-date rule that had been implemented in England, the New York statute in fact did no more than to put into place a judgment-date rule, a rule which was already the law in federal courts, at least in actions based on obligations governed by foreign law. To be sure, this was a significant change from the breach-date rule that had generally prevailed in New York up until that time. However it was far from implementing the *Miliangos* payment-date rule recommended in the *City Bar Report* and the *Third Restatement*. In fact, contrary to the assertion in the first sentence of the statute, it does not really amount to awarding damages in a foreign currency at all.[90] Moreover, the New York legislation was confined in its operation to suits based on obligations *denominated* in a foreign currency. The word 'denominated' would appear to limit the statute to cases where the parties, a foreign court or an arbitrator had named some foreign money in connection with some obligation between the parties. In practice that would mean that the legislation is confined to claims for debt and liquidated damages (and possibly some restitutionary actions) and enforcement of foreign court judgments, but evidently not most tort actions.[91] So in a trade mark infringement action where there was no contract between the parties denominating any money owing from one to another the statute did not apply.[92]

[86] New York State Chapter Law, 20 July 1987, above n 82.

[87] *Mitsui & Co v Oceantrawl Corp*, 906 F Supp 202 (SDNY 1995). The court in *Mitsui* did not regard itself as bound by the New York statute as it was applying federal law. It simply cited—or perhaps knowingly misrepresented—the New York statute as authorising the issuing of judgments in yen.

[88] Above n 79, 811.

[89] New York State Chapter Law, 20 July 1987, above n 82.

[90] Two contemporary commentators pointed this out: F Leary & M Casey, 'Fluctuating Currencies: Obligations Payable in Foreign Moneys' (1988) 60(1) *New York State Bar Journal* 16, 20: 'Why enter a judgment in the foreign currency and then instantly convert it into domestic currency when no payment has been made?'

[91] In this connection it is interesting to note that two of the members of the committee that handed down the *City Bar Report*—including the eminent commercial law scholar Allen Farnsworth—partially dissented from that report on the grounds that, while it was roughly correct in principle, it did not offer 'sufficient guidance as to the criteria a court should use when deciding whether [to award damages in a foreign currency]'. Above n 79, 812.

[92] *Aini v Sun Taiyang Co*, 964 F Supp 762 (SDNY 1997). That decision entered judgment for the plaintiff. In a subsequent ruling on damages (*Aini v Sun Taiyang Co*, 96 Civ 7763 (Lak), 1997 US Dist Lexis 9739 (SD NY 1997)) the judge criticised the parties for failing to address the conversion-date

In one vital respect, however, the 1987 New York legislation was closer to the English position than the *Third Restatement*. Within the limited scope of its operation, it is mandatory. It provides that 'a court *shall* render a judgment or decree in the foreign currency'.[93] It declines to accept the plaintiff-favouring approach of the *Third Restatement*. Moreover, that is how New York courts appear to have construed it.[94]

Although confined to one state, the New York statute is an influential one because it is not uncommon for parties to international contracts to elect to be governed by New York law. Thus the Seventh Circuit, applying the law of Illinois in a diversity case, encountered a contractual term in which the parties had agreed that their sale of goods agreement would be governed by the law of New York State.[95] It concluded that such a term should be held to include New York's statute on foreign currency obligations, which was regarded as substantive law, not procedural. Accordingly it imposed the judgment-date conversion that is required by the statute.

Both the new position of the *Third Restatement* and the *City Bar Report* (but, curiously, not the New York statute) were referred to with approval in 1988 in *Teca-Print AG v Amacoil Machinery, Inc*,[96] a breakthrough American case which abandoned the breach-date rule. *Teca-Print*, which may be regarded as the closest United States equivalent to *Miliangos*, was an action on facts that were in many respects similar to those in the House of Lords case. Yet, although *Teca-Print* exhibits some affinities with *Miliangos*, it also displays differences which nicely encapsulate the distinction between the English and American responses to the problem of foreign currency damages. First the similarities. Like *Miliangos*, the *Teca-Print* opinion made much of the currency fluctuations of recent years. In a move which helpfully paved the way for an abandonment of the breach-date rule the court asserted that the US dollar used to be a stable currency but that with 'the dramatic changes which have occurred in the world monetary system over the past 20 years'[97] this was no longer the case. The court then asserted, as had the House of Lords in *Miliangos*, that in a situation where the forum currency has declined in relation to the Swiss franc, the application of the breach-date rule would under-compensate the foreign plaintiff.

question and then went on to quote and apply pre-statute case law for the proposition that New York State applied the breach-date rule.

[93] New York State Chapter Law, 20 July 1987, above n 81 (emphasis added).

[94] See *Dynamic Cassette International Ltd v Mike Lopez & Associates Inc* 923 F Supp 8 (EDNY 1996); *Korea Life Insurance Co v Morgan Guaranty Trust Co of New York* 2004 WL 1858314 (ED NY 2004).

[95] *AGFA-Gevaert v AB Dick* 879 F 2d 1518 (7th Cir 1989) 1525. A recent study establishes the dominance of New York law as the favoured jurisdiction in choice-of-law clauses in commercial agreements in the United States: T Eisenberg & GP Miller, 'The Flight to New York: An Empirical Study of Choice of Law and Choice of Forum Clauses in Publicly-Held Companies' Contracts' (2009) 30 *Cardozo Law Review* 1475.

[96] *Teca-Print AG v Amacoil Machinery Inc* 525 NYS 2d 535 (Sup Ct 1988) (*Teca-Print*).

[97] Ibid, 540.

Now the differences. First, despite the encouragement of the *Third Restatement*, the *Teca-Print* court did not feel permitted to abandon the foundational position that damages must be awarded in dollars. Thus it could not award damages in Swiss francs. It even felt that it could not award a payment-date conversion; rather, it elected a judgment-date exchange, the latest time that it thought permissible. More significantly, the court in *Teca-Print* took the view that the breach-date rule would have produced fair results had the US dollar appreciated against the Swiss franc in the post-breach period. That is, the rule that emerges from *Teca-Print* is like that in the *Third Restatement*, and unlike that in *Miliangos*, in that it opts for a flexible conversion date—a date to be selected by the court in the particular circumstances of the case. Moreover, it seemed that those circumstances should include an inquiry into which way the relevant foreign currency had moved as against the dollar in the period between breach and judgment,[98] so that when the dollar was falling the judgment date was the just one, but that when it was rising the court might return to a breach-date conversion. This is very different from the *Miliangos* position where, from the creditor's view, a Swiss franc must remain a Swiss franc, for good or ill. It is not clear, however, that the court in *Teca-Print* entirely appreciated this, as it seemed to think that its judgment involved moving closer to the English position. Moreover it curiously appeared to approve of the *City Bar Report*, which had given preference to the English, fixed currency-of-judgment position over the *Third Restatement*.

C. The Uniform Foreign-Money Claims Act

Neither the *Third Restatement* nor the New York statute truly brought the American position into line with the post-*Miliangos* situation in England, even if some of their drafters and proponents claimed that was the case. The *Third Restatement* was like *Miliangos* in allowing for a payment-date conversion, but departed from the English model in that it was to be applied in a plaintiff-favouring manner in light of the relevant currencies' oscillations during litigation. The New York legislation was like *Miliangos* in that it was not to be applied in a plaintiff-favouring manner. However, for all the professed admiration for the English model in the reports that led up to it, in the end it opted for a judgment-date conversion.

Even if they had been substantively equivalent to *Miliangos*, neither of those law reform efforts could have amounted to an American *Miliangos* since their scope of operation was more limited: *Miliangos* was binding on all English courts, but the *Third Restatement* and the New York statute had no such country-wide authoritative effect. The *Teca-Print* ruling was closer to *Miliangos* in substantive terms, but it too lacked nationwide effect.

[98] Ibid, 540.

Arguably, the matter of foreign currency obligations might have been viewed as a matter for national legislation. However, apart from the Coinage Act of 1792, which always had an uncertain effect on the matter, and the later ambiguous repealing of a portion of that statute,[99] Congress has never demonstrated interest in the question of foreign currency obligations (or for that matter in private international law generally). Nor, in recent years, has the Supreme Court of the United States, which has not revisited the matter since the three Holmes J opinions of the mid-1920s. As a result, despite modernising initiatives from the ALI and the New York legislature, the American position in the late 1980s remained fragmented, with different rules in the federal and state courts, different rules among the various states and in many cases the result depending on what substantive law the court settled on as the law governing the claim.

Recognising this situation, in 1989 the NCCUSL developed and approved the *Uniform Foreign-Money Claims Act*.[100] Like the *City Bar Report* and the *Third Restatement*, the *UFMCA* aimed to liberate American courts from the clutches of the forum-currency rule. Its prefatory note acknowledged that United States courts treated foreign-money obligations differently from the courts of many of its chief trading partners. And like the *Third Restatement* the *UFMCA* claimed to derive inspiration from the changes brought about in England by *Miliangos*. In addition, like many such reform initiatives in this area, both judicial or legislative, the *UFMCA* preface asserted that currency fluctuations were now more common than was formerly the case,[101] and it proposed changes designed to fulfill more accurately the principle of *restitutio in integrum*.

The *UFMCA* was a model statute recommended to all states for legislative implementation, and its approval by the influential American Bar Association in February 1990 heightened its profile. Moreover, the *UFMCA* is considerably more detailed and comprehensive than either the *Third Restatement* or the 1987 New York statute. Furthermore, despite its obvious affinities with the *Third Restatement* in authorising the granting of judgments in foreign money, the details of the solution offered by the *UFMCA* differ considerably from that advanced by the ALI.

The *UFMCA* begins by making it clear that it applies to foreign-money issues before a court, even if under the choice-of-laws rules of the court hearing the claim some other substantive law governs the proceeding.[102] In short, it adopts the English approach that treats the currency-of-damages approach as procedural and thus eliminates the uncertainty that accompanies any approach that leaves the currency question to be determined by the governing substantive law, which might not be settled until judgment. It then provides that persons may assert claims in foreign currencies and that—except for awards of costs, which must

[99] Above n 5 and accompanying text.

[100] National Conference of Commissioners on Uniform State Laws, *Uniform Foreign-Money Claims Act* (4 August 1989) (*UFMCA*). In 1990 the *UFMCA* was also published at 21 *Journal of Maritime Law and Commerce* 461.

[101] *UFMCA*, ibid, Prefatory Note 5.

[102] *UFMCA*, ibid, s 2(b).

be in US dollars—courts must award judgment in the money of the claim.[103] Judgment debtors are then granted the option of satisfying the judgment by paying, at their election, either in the foreign money or in the dollar equivalent of that foreign money at the time payment is made.[104] In both cases, payment must include any accrued interest. Those rules operate regardless of the substantive law governing the claim.[105] That is, the conflict-of-laws approach associated with *Deutsche Bank*, the *First Restatement* and *Second Restatement* is expressly rejected, though parties to contracts are given the power to vary by agreement the rules that would otherwise apply to them with respect to the currency of judgment.

As described thus far, the *UFMCA* seems not dissimilar to the *Third Restatement*; both allow for a payment-date conversion. There are, however, major differences. The *Third Restatement*, with its focus on the evils of under-compensation of plaintiffs, had allowed for a high degree of plaintiff choice in asserting of the currency of compensation and, if applicable, the conversion date—accompanied by little or no defendant choice. In the final analysis the *Third Restatement* left the decision as to the currency of judgment and conversion date in the hands of the court, not the plaintiff. However, as we have seen, its commentary made it clear that such judicial discretion was, at least in general, to be exercised for the benefit of the plaintiff in light of which way the fluctuations had gone. By way of contrast, like *Miliangos*, the *UFMCA* regarded over-compensation of the aggrieved party as an evil equivalent to that of under-compensation. One of its prime professed goals was to eliminate the 'heads I win, tails you lose'[106] approach of the *Third Restatement*. Indeed in the *UFMCA*'s Prefatory Note its primary illustration of the injustice of the existing American rules was a set of facts which, when adjudicated by those rules would result in *over*-compensation of the claimant.[107]

The *UFMCA* begins by confirming that its provisions are subject to contractual variation. It stipulates that its effects 'may be varied by agreement of the parties made before or after commencement of an action or distribution proceeding or

[103] *UFMCA*, ibid, ss 6 and 7.

[104] Technically, for ease of ascertainment, the exchange rate is the bank-offered rate on the day *before* actual payment is made. In this respect the *UFMCA* is like the Ontario, British Columbia and Prince Edward Island statutes examined in the Canada section of the previous chapter. Typically judgments under the *UFMCA* issue for the amount of foreign currency and then include a sentence like the following: 'At the defendant's option, the defendant may pay the number of United States dollars as will purchase the number of English pounds then owing, with interest due, at the bank-offered spot rate at or near the close of business on the next banking day before the payment': *Society of Lloyd's v Bennett* 2006 WL 1524621 (10th Cir 2006) (applying Utah's Foreign-Money Claims Act to the enforcement of an English court judgment).

[105] *UFMCA*, above n 100, s 2(b).

[106] F Leary & H Rosen, 'The Uniform Foreign-Money Claims Act' (1991) 12 *University of Pennsylvania Journal of International Business Law* 51, 61.

[107] *UFMCA*, above n 100, Prefatory Note 5, using an illustration adapted from the case of *Competex SA v LaBow*, above n 60. See also Leary & Rosen, ibid, 52. There, in giving their account of the situation that led to the promulgation of the *UFMCA*, they point out that 'the mischief to be remedied is the tendency of the common law approach either to overcompensate or under-compensate an aggrieved party'.

the entry of judgment'.[108] However, where there is no such contracting out then the *UFMCA*'s solution takes the form of a virtually mandatory scheme for determining the appropriate currency of a claim. Its key provision is section 4, which deals with determining 'the proper money of the claim':

4 (a) The money in which the parties to a transaction have agreed that payment is to be made is the proper money of the claim for payment.
(b) If the parties to a transaction have not otherwise agreed, the proper money of the claim, as in each case may be appropriate, is the money:
(1) regularly used between the parties as a matter of usage or course of dealing;
(2) used at the time of a transaction in international trade, by trade usage or common practice, for valuing or settling transactions in the particular commodity or service involved; or
(3) in which the loss was ultimately felt or will be incurred by the party claimant.

Although it is a mere definition provision, section 4 is of central importance, for once the proper money of the claim has been identified then, with very few exceptions, judgment must issue in that money. In this respect *UFMCA* is unlike the *Third Restatement* and three Canadian provincial statutes examined in the foregoing chapter. Those acts freed courts from the obligation to issue judgment in forum currency and stipulated a payment-day conversion rule, but they entirely failed to define the situations in which this solution should apply. They simply provided that courts should adopt a payment-date conversion where the underlying claim was a foreign money obligation, or where it was just and proper to issue judgment in a foreign currency. The goal of section 4 of the *UFMCA* is to set out with precision when it was and was not proper for a court to issue such a judgment, and those terms deserve analysis.

The *UFMCA*'s primary rule for determining the proper money of the claim—the currency 'in which parties to a transaction have agreed that payment is to be made'—is one which would apply only to contract claims, since it applies only to claims 'for payment'—that is, not to claims for damages or restitution.[109] Claims for payment would appear to include not only claims for debt, such as for the price of goods, rent, wages, royalties and so on, but also other claims for the transfer of money, such as for liquidated damages. Where there is a currency of payment stipulated under the contract, but the claim is for unliquidated damages, then the proper money of the claim is determined by section 4(b). Those would include (1) claims for damages for breach of contract (other than claims for payment), (2) all claims under contracts where there is not an agreed money of payment, and (3) claims where there is no contract between the parties—tort or restitutionary claims for instance.

The difficulty in selecting an appropriate currency of judgment when the money of account of the contract is not to govern is the same problem as faced the

[108] *UFMCA*, ibid, s 3(a).
[109] *UFMCA*, ibid, s 4(a) and commentary.

House of Lords in *The Folias*, *The Despina R* and *The Texaco Melbourne*. However, rather than simply revert to selecting the currency in which the plaintiff felt its loss, as the House of Lords did in those decisions, the *UFMCA*'s rule strives for a greater degree of certainty: the currency of suit should be the money regularly used between the parties as a matter of usage or course of dealing.[110] If no such currency exists then there is a further default rule: the money employed by common trade usage or common practice for valuing or settling transactions in the particular commodity or service involved.[111] Only where no other rule operates does the *UFMCA* follow the English feeling-the-loss approach: section 4(b)(3) provides that the currency of suit should be the currency 'in which the loss was ultimately felt or will be incurred by the party claimant'.

The *UFMCA* proceeds to say in section 6 that either the plaintiff or the defendant may raise the issue of the proper money of the claim. It does this by providing, first, 'A person may assert a claim in a specified foreign money'. Since the 'may' is permissive this appears to afford claimants their option. Plaintiffs can assert their claim in the foreign currency (and presumably will do so if that benefits them) or say nothing about the currency of the claim in which case it will initially be in US dollars. If the foreign currency has fallen as against the US dollar following the breach one would expect that the claimant would remain silent on the point and hope that the court applies a breach-date conversion. However, the *UFMCA* then goes on to make it clear that defendants have the right to put in issue the question of the money of the claim. It states: 'An opposing party may allege and prove that a claim, in whole or in part, is in a different money than that asserted by the claimant'.

The *UFMCA* makes it clear that the determination of the proper money of the claim is a question of law. It is thus up to a court to identify the appropriate currency of the claim, by the *UFMCA*'s rules for doing so. Once it has identified that currency the court *must* give judgment in it—even where that is not the currency the plaintiff proposed in its original claim. Thus it appears that, contrary to the approach of the *Third Restatement*—which lauded *Miliangos* and other English developments but then went on to provide a quite different solution to that which had been implemented in England—the *UFMCA* praised the English response but then went on to establish a currency of judgment rule that sought to reduce the uncertainty that arose from the English courts' feeling-the-loss rule.

Three additional features of the act may be briefly summarised and commented upon. First, the *UFMCA* regards the question of pre- and post-judgment interest as a matter of substantive state law, and thus has nothing to say on the matter. Although it is generally appreciative of the English approach—and specifically of *Miliangos*, *The Despina R* and *The Folias*—it does not go so far as to commend the solution to the

[110] Ibid, s 4(b)(1).

[111] Ibid, s 4(b)(2). Interestingly, the actual text of the *UFMCA* does not state that the rules in s 4(b) should be applied in the order in which they are stated, but the Comment to that section states that that will normally be the case.

interest issue reached in *Miliangos (No 2)*, which held that the pre-judgment interest rate should be that of the currency of judgment.[112] Although this omission may have made the model statute more attractive to some states, it is an unfortunate one. The interest question is so closely related to the currency question that the exclusion of the former is a mistake. However, leaving it outside the scope of the *UFMCA* probably increased the chances of that model statute's adoption by the states.[113]

Similarly, the *UFMCA* regards the question of exchange-loss damages—that is, the question of claims for consequential losses which we have seen dealt with in cases such as *Isaac Naylor and Sons Ltd v New Zealand Co-operative Wool Marketing Association Ltd*[114]—as a matter of the substantive (or at least remedial) law of the individual states, so it is silent on the matter, leaving it up to state law, which may vary on the question. During the drafting process there was some consideration given to this matter, but ultimately it was decided to leave it to state law.[115] In this respect the *UFMCA* is like the ALI's three restatements, the New York statute and the Canadian legislation discussed in the last chapter. Unlike some attempts to legislate on the currency-of-judgment question that we will encounter in the next chapter, none of those instruments seeks at the same time to deal with the exchange-loss question.

Finally, as with the *Lines* and *General Dynamics* cases in England,[116] the *UFMCA* recognised and accommodated the need for a different rule for insolvency claims and related proceedings. There the policy of finding a single conversion date for a multitude of creditors militates for something other than a payment-date rule (since different creditors might get paid at different times). Accordingly—in line with the English solution—section 8 of the *UFMCA* opts for the date the distribution proceedings are initiated. In cases where there is a fund of money out of which all creditors must be paid, but the fund is inadequate to pay them all, this early conversion date permits the court to determine percentage shares to which each claimant is entitled.

As of the summer of 2009, the *UFMCA* had been adopted by 22 of the 50 American states (including the most populous, California), and by the District of Columbia and the US Virgin Islands.[117]

[112] *Miliangos v George Frank (Textiles) Ltd (No 2)* [1976] 3 All ER 599 (QB).

[113] On this point see F Leary and H Rosen, above n 106, 74–79.

[114] *Isaac Naylor and Sons Ltd v New Zealand Co-operative Wool Marketing Association Ltd* [1981] 1 NZLR 361 (CA). See the discussion in ch 3 at pp 140–42. American courts have been reluctant to see advances on the currency-of-judgment issue as a reason for extending claims for foreign exchange losses. In *Austrian Airlines Oesterreichische Lufverkehrs AG v UT Finance Corp* 2008 US Dist LEXIS 55072 (SD NY) the plaintiff tried to rely on *Teca-Print*, above n 96, in support of a claim for compensation for the fact that non-payment of a contract in US dollars deprived it of the opportunity to convert those dollars to its home currency, euros. The court held that nothing in *Teca-Print*'s doctrinal advance on the currency-of-judgment question authorised a claim for consequential losses of this sort.

[115] *UFMCA*, above n 100, s 13.

[116] See ch 1, n 148 and 149.

[117] See the National Conference of Commissioners on Uniform State Laws web site: www.nccusl.org/Update/uniformact_factsheets/uniformacts-fs-ufmca.asp (accessed 22 February 2010). The states that

It should be noted, however, that a state need not have passed legislation implementing the *UFMCA* for that model statute to guide its courts. For instance, in 1995 the Supreme Court of Massachusetts noted that, while eighteen American jurisdictions had statutorily implemented the *UFMCA*, Massachusetts was not one of them. However, as a matter of common law development the court expressed its approval of the philosophy of the *UFMCA* and also of *Miliangos* and *The Despina R*—especially the emphasis on full compensation, but not over-compensation—and imposed a payment-date conversion.[118]

Not all American commentators have been pleased with the *UFMCA*. In it the NCCUSL opted for certainty over flexibility—not only more certainty than the *Third Restatement* but also more certainty than the English feeling-the-loss approach. Its solution of seeking to define a single money of a claim—a currency which could be identified with a high degree of predictability and which, once ascertained, would become the money in which a court was required to measure and award damages, ran counter to the thinking of those who thought that justice in this area was best achieved by means of an adaptable and generally plaintiff-favouring response. Such critics decried what they called 'the mandatory nature of the *UFMCA*'.[119] They had looked upon *Miliangos* with favour, but only for its role in breaking the stranglehold of the forum-currency rule and thus setting an example for American courts or legislatures to do the same. But insofar as post-*Miliangos* cases in England such as *The Despina R* and *The Folias* had attempted to preserve a measure of certainty and to implement a more nearly neutral regime—they regarded such developments as retrograde and as not to be imitated in the United States.[120] Accordingly, insofar as the *UFMCA* seemed to go even further than the English cases had done in seeking to identify by objective factors a mandatory currency of judgment, that model act was seen as exhibiting the same defects possessed by the old forum-currency/breach-date rule—namely, while offering the benefits of certainty, it did so only at the expense of an unacceptable measure of injustice between the parties.

have adopted it are California, Colorado, Connecticut, Delaware, Hawaii, Idaho, Illinois, Minnesota, Montana, Nevada, New Jersey, New Mexico, North Carolina, North Dakota, Ohio, Oklahoma, Oregon, Rhode Island, Utah, Virginia, Washington and Wisconsin. Some of these adopting states made amendments to the uniform act in the course of enacting it, but all of these were minor. Most of the adoptions were in the period 1989–93 and there have been but two legislative adoptions of the *UFMCA* in the current century: Idaho in 2001 and Rhode Island in 2009.

[118] *Manches & Co v Gilbey* 646 NE 2d 86, 419 Mass 414 (Sup Ct Mass 1995), followed in *Union Camp Chemicals Ltd v State Street Bank and Trust Co* 832 NE 2d 706 (Mass App Ct 2005).

[119] SR Westerheim, 'The Uniform Foreign-Money Claims Act: No Solution to an Old Problem' (1991) 69 *Texas Law Review* 1203, 1221. To similar effect see R Brand, 'Restructuring', above n 8, 57–71.

[120] See P Lion, 'The Need to Retreat from Inflexible Conversion Rules—An Equitable Approach to Judgment in Foreign Currency' (1982) 22 *Santa Clara Law Review* 871; C Beal, 'Foreign Currency Judgments: A New Option for United States Courts' (1998) 19 *University of Pennsylvania Journal of International Economic Law* 101.

IV. An Overview of the Current Scene

In some respects the situation in the United States today resembles that in its neighbour to the north. A generation after *Miliangos*, at a time when the English position with respect to foreign currency obligations seems largely settled, at least in its underlying assumptions and general approach, in the United States debate and diversity remains. There is the occasional case simply granting judgment in a foreign currency, but those are rarities and are mostly confined to actions involving foreign judgments and arbitral awards.[121] This means that the most common question is not that of the appropriate currency of judgment but rather selection of the proper conversion date. While New York has its own statute providing for judgment-day conversion,[122] many other states have enacted the *UFMCA*. In those that have not, judges might still elect as a matter of common law to adopt the approach of the *UFMCA*. But they might equally elect to follow the old breach-date rule,[123] a flexible approach as exemplified by the *Third Restatement*,[124] or the conflict-of-laws approach of the federal courts and the first two *Restatements*.[125] In part, and as noted at the outset, this diversity is due to America's federal nature. If each state has the option of implementing its own approach to the currency of judgment issue then, despite the existence of institutions designed to promote uniformity in those areas of the law where it is deemed desirable, one would expect some variety.

[121] *Waterside Ocean Navigation Co v International Navigation Ltd*, above n 64; *The Amoco Cadiz*, 954 F 2d 1279 (7th Cir 1992); *MTU of North American Inc v Raven Marine Inc* 603 So 2d 803 (Ct App Louisiana 1st Cir 1992); *Mitsui & Co v Oceantrawl Corp*, above n 87.

[122] As in *SAE Sadelmi SpA v Papua New Guinea Electricity Commission* 94 Civ 2959 (SS), 1994 US Dist Lexis 16978 (SD NY 1994); *Weiss v La Suisse, Societé des Assurances sur la Vie* 293 F Supp 2d 397 (SD NY 2003), motion for new trial denied, 313 F Supp 2d 241 (SD NY 2004).

[123] As in *Gathercrest Ltd v First American Bank and Trust* 805 F 2d 995 (11th Cir 1986); *Middle East Banking Co v State Street Bank Int'l* 821 F 2d 897 (2d Cir 1987); *Gonzalez v Banco de Santander-Puerto Rico* 932 F 2d 999 (1st Cir 1991); *Delchi Carrier SpA v Rotorex Corp* 88-CV-1078, Lexis 12820 (N D NY 1994); *Reliastar Life Insurance Co v IOA Inc* 303 F 3d 874 (8th Cir 2002); *Elite Entertainment Corp v Khela Brothers Entertainment Inc* 396 F Supp 2d 680 (ED Virginia 2005); *Ligas v IPD Sales & Marketing LLC* 2007 WL 29008893 (ED Missouri 2007).

[124] *Nikimha Securities Ltd v The Trend Group* 646 F Supp 1211 (ED Penn 1986); *Nimrod Marketing (Overseas) Ltd v Texas Energy Investment Corp* 769 F 2d 1076 (5th Cir 1980); *Sunrise Shipping Ltd v M/V American Chemist* 1999 AMC 2906 (ED Louisiana 1999).

[125] *Laminoirs-Treffileries-Cableries De Lens SA v Southwire Co* (ND Georgia 1980); *Black Sea & Baltic General Insurance Co v Al Nisr Insurance Co* 575 F Supp 685 (SDNY 1983); *Cronel Watch SA v Peterson State Bank* 565 F Supp (ND Ill 1983); *Seguros Banvenez SA v S/S Oliver Drescher* 761 F 2d 855 (2d Cir 1985); *Fils et Cables D'Acier de Lens v Midland Metals Corp* 584 F Supp 240 (SDNY 1984); *La Societé de Diffusion Vinecole SA v Peartree Imports Inc* 1984 US Dist Lexis 17891 (SD NY 1984); *Ingersoll Milling Machine Co v Granger* 833 F 2d 680 (7th Cir 1987) (applying Illinois law); *Pecaflor Construction Inc v Landes* 198 Cal App 3d 342, 243 Cal Rpt 605 (1st Dist 1988); *Budejovicky Budvar NP v Czech Beer Importers Inc* 2006 WL 1980308 (D Conn 2006); *Levis Strauss & Co v Aetna Casualty and Surety Co* 184 Cal App 3d 1479, 237 Cal Rptr 473 (Ct App Cal 1986); *Sembawang Shipyard Ltd v M/V Charger* 955 F 2d 983 (5th Cir 1992); *MacKay v 65248 Canada Ltd* 2007 Bankr 378 BR 448 (MD Penn 2007); *Societé Civile Succession Richard Guino v Redstar Corp* 153 Cal App 4th 697, 63 Cal Rptr 3d 224 (Ct App Cal 2007).

However, there is a difference between the American situation and the Canadian one. Canadian courts, apart from the few that regard themselves as bound by Supreme Court of Canada authority to apply the forum-currency/breach-date rule, appear to adopt a variety of conversion dates because, at least for the most part, they have adopted the view that they must select the conversion-date that does justice in the individual case. Canadian judgments on the matter demonstrate relatively little awareness that the conversion-date issue is a hotly contested one. By way of contrast, in the United States there is a variety of entrenched positions. Many courts have clear stances on what, in their view, the best conversion date should be. American judges demonstrate a good measure of awareness of the contending positions in the conversion-date debate. This situation is fuelled by an ongoing academic debate on the subject. While there are many aspects to this debate, the most contested issue on whether there should be (1) a firm, fixed approach to the conversion-date matter, so as to promote certainty, or (2) whether what is needed is a flexible regime which accords judges a high measure of discretion to either select the currency of judgment, or—if that currency must be US dollars—select the best conversion date.

There are a considerable number of American scholars who are vigorous advocates of a flexible approach to the conversion-date problem. They take the view that 'no easy mechanical formula will provide a fair solution in all cases'.[126] The foremost of these is Ron Brand. It is instructive to examine Brand's position on *Miliangos*. In 1985 he expounded the view that the result in *Miliangos* was driven principally by the desire to do justice at a time when sterling was falling as against other major trading currencies. However, he thought that in its effort to reach that result *Miliangos*, or at least the later English cases that purported to follow and develop *Miliangos*, had erroneously promulgated a rule that would do injustice when sterling appreciated.[127] He favoured the payment-date conversion that was applied in *Miliangos*, but only where the forum's currency had fallen. He thought that the English Law Commission erred when it interpreted *Miliangos* as promulgating a rigid payment-date rule that would operate '*for good or ill*'.[128] He took the stance that in their efforts to establish a mandatory currency of judgment decisions such as *The Despina R* and *The Folias* were betrayals or misunderstandings of *Miliangos*:

> *Miliangos* represented an important departure from the rigid rules of the past in favor of equitable results in the future. Unfortunately, subsequent decisions in the United Kingdom have focused on the payment-date rule rather than the reason for the rule.[129]

[126] P Lion, above n 120, 872.

[127] R Brand, 'Restructuring' above n 8, 180.

[128] Ibid. Brand quotes the Law Commission Report as promulgating a rigid rule that would operate for good or ill. It should be noted that that phrase does not originate with the Law Commission Report, but rather appears in *Miliangos* itself.

[129] R Brand, 'Exchange Loss Damages and the Uniform Foreign-Money Claims Act: The Emperor Hasn't All His Clothes' (1991) 23 *Law and Policy in International Business* 1, 83.

Given that perspective on *Miliangos*, it is not surprising that Brand deplores the approach of the *UFMCA*: 'The Act addresses the problems of a past rigid formula by creating a new mechanical formula'.[130] Brand is not alone among American scholars in thinking that the approach of the *UFMCA* is to adopt a wooden, inflexible and frequently unjust rule.[131]

Given this preference for flexibility one might expect Brand to approve of the approach of the *Third Restatement*. In general he does. However, in his estimation even the considerable flexibility in the *Third Restatement* does not go far enough in allowing courts to protect plaintiffs from the downside risks of currency fluctuation. Brand fears that the *Third Restatement*, although it gives the plaintiff a measure of choice in selecting the currency of judgment, might be interpreted as requiring the plaintiff to exercise that option at the time it starts its action. Such a plaintiff would be likely to select the currency which had appreciated between the accrual of the cause of action and the time the action was commenced and the selection of currency had to be made. But of course that trend might reverse itself before judgment was granted, so that by that time the currency the plaintiff had selected had fallen. In Brand's view a claimant in that position 'should not be held to its best guess at the time initial pleadings are filed as to the foreign currency market over the course of litigation'.[132] Brand would thus modify the *Third Restatement* to give courts the power to award additional damages to the plaintiff for loss caused by the fall, during litigation, of the currency of judgment.[133]

In addition to this wide scholarly support for a flexible approach, there are a number of modern American court decisions which go on at length about the impossibility of doing justice with any rigid rule, the importance of judicial discretion in the selection of the conversion date, and the particular importance of paying attention to what had happened to the exchange rate between the relevant currencies during the course of litigation.[134]

At the other end of the spectrum from the proponents of a flexible, equitable approach to the conversion date problem are those who champion certainty above all other virtues. The *UFMCA* adopts an approach based on the English one but

[130] Ibid, 82.

[131] Westerheim, above n 119; Beal, above n 120. For other American champions of flexibility and doubters of the English approach see M Neus, 'Exchange Rate Selection for Foreign Money Obligations' 25 *Columbia Journal of Transnational Law* (1986) 169, 176–80, 184, *et seq*; Lion, above n 120; TJ Egan, 'Conversion of Judgments Measured in Foreign Currencies' (1982) 39 *Washington and Lee Law Review* 165, 180–84; S Rifkind, 'Money as a Device for Measuring Value' (1926) 26 *Columbia Law Review* 559, 565–67; Anon, 'Conversion Date of Foreign Money Obligations' 65 *Columbia Law Review* (1965) 490, Smit, above n 64, 29.

[132] Brand, 'Restructuring', above n 8, 183.

[133] American courts have been reluctant to see advances on the currency-of-judgment issue as a reason for extending claims for foreign exchange losses. For example, *Austrian Airlines Oesterreichische Luftverkehrs AG v UT Finance Corp* 567 F Supp 2d 579 (SDNY 2008), aff'd 2009 WL 1949715 (2d Cir 2009).

[134] *Aker Verdal A/S v Neil F Lampson, Inc* 828 P 2d 610 (Wash App 1992); *Teca-Print*, above n 96, 538–40; *Jamaica Nutrition Holdings*, above n 6, 381. There are likewise decisions which have felt constrained by precedent to apply a predictable rule, but which have stated that they believe it generates an unjust result: *In re Good Hope Chemical*, above n 37.

seeks to modify it so as to achieve greater certainty in the selection of the currency of judgment. An even more emphatic support of certainty appears in the best-known judicial articulation of this position, the opinion of the Seventh Circuit in *The Amoco Cadiz*.[135] The court was most emphatic and polemical on this point, more so than the *UFMCA* and more so than any English judgment on the matter. In its view predictability was the prime goal and any measure of unpredictability was to be eliminated.

> When all of the transactions occur in dollars, the judgment should be in dollars. Always. When they occur in some other currency, the award should be in that currency. Always. *Certainty* in this practice will enable the parties to hedge against currency risks. Unpredictable currency choices or conversion dates create needless risk. A simple uniform rule that the currency of the judgment matches the currency of the transaction will permit the parties to handle the risks themselves.
>
> [A]ny predictable rule of currency selection is neutral. Although the value of the judgment may fluctuate, the parties' hedging can undo the effect. The highest objective is predictability.[136]

This should be contrasted with the English position that emerges from *The Folias*. Under that approach a contract might be in dollars but a court could conclude that dollars were not the money in which the parties expected damages to be assessed for breach of that contract, and that some other currency more truly expresses the plaintiff's loss. This might be the currency of expenditure or the plaintiff's home currency, and obviously there could be debate and uncertainty in settling the question of which currency really expressed the plaintiff's loss. That uncertainty would not exist under the approach articulated in *The Amoco Cadiz*.[137]

135 Above n 121.

136 Ibid, 1329.

137 Similarly in *Competex, SA v Lebow*, the Second Circuit was forceful in denigrating the extreme plaintiff preference that it perceived in the ALI's *Tentative Draft*. It maintained that there was no justification for a rule that gave the plaintiff its choice of conversion dates, or which permitted a court to select a conversion date based on which way the pertinent currencies had fluctuated, and it preferred instead 'a conversion rule of general application that is neutral between the parties with respect to currency fluctuation'. *Competex, SA v Lebow*, above n 61, 337. There are also American academics who are strong supporters of certainty in the identification of the currency of judgment: see Leary and Rosen, above n 106.

5

International Perspectives

Considering that it is advisable to harmonise certain rules relating to foreign money liabilities …

Preamble to the European Convention
on Foreign Money Liabilities

This study is about the remedial practice of common law courts. By definition, however, the underlying problem has its roots in the international scene, so it may be useful to pay some attention to practice outside the Anglosphere. We have seen that in many common law countries the rules governing the currency-of-judgment question are unsettled. Even if they are settled they are not conducive to certainty and predictability, values which are generally thought to be desirable in the law of judicial remedies. We have further seen that even if the rules on the currency-of-judgment question are rendered clear within a given jurisdiction, the availability of multiple fora, each with its distinct resolution of the problem, will operate to reduce any predictability of result. If a contractual obligation to repay a loan in euros is subject to no conversion to local currency if suit is brought in England, a judgment-day conversion to US dollars if the action is pursued in New York, and a breach-day conversion to Canadian dollars if brought in Canada, then despite the fact that each of those three fora has a clear and certain response to the currency-of-judgment problem there will still be no advance certainty as to what the amount of the judgment will be. There will be even less predictability if the action is brought in a place that employs a wait-and-see approach and selects the conversion date depending on which way the relevant currencies swing during the course of litigation, as some American and Canadian courts do, or allows claimants to elect between a variety of dates. When one considers that the problem may extend beyond the common law world, as it does in many cases, there is the potential for matters to become even more complex.

In light of that, there is a plausible case to be made in favour of international coordination to resolve the currency-of-judgment problem, action which could take the form of a multilateral convention or a model law on the question. More realistically, since the currency question is a narrow one and since such conventions and model laws typically attempt to deal with a broader range of matters, international cooperation on the currency-of-judgment problems might be achieved by provisions on that subject in the context of some convention or model law dealing with some bigger range of cross-border private law concerns.

In the alternative one might hope that an emerging *lex mercatoria* would generate a broadly-shared resolution of the matter.

The goal of this chapter is to canvas what has happened in that regard, and to a lesser extent to point to and consider areas where something might easily be done but where, for whatever reason, nothing has been. It is worth recalling that when common law judges wished to issue judgments that affirmed the forum-currency/breach-date approach they were sometimes prepared to pen remarks that suggested that this rule had uniformly been applied by English judges since time immemorial. They were likewise willing to indicate that courts in other countries necessarily took the same approach and that no other solution was conceivable, or at least practical.[1] In so doing they made the forum-currency/breach-date rule appear to flow from the very nature of having to enforce private obligations in a world of multiple fluctuating national currencies—a situation that was hardly about to disappear. They were thus able to avoid confronting the inconvenient truth that the breach-date rule was in fact neither timeless nor universal.

That it was neither timeless nor universal would not have been hard to find out. In his 1938 book, *The Legal Aspect of Money*, FA Mann had supported his attack on the common law's breach-date rule by listing Austria, Brazil, Denmark, Egypt, Germany, Italy, Norway, Poland and Switzerland as countries willing to issue judgment in currencies other than that of the forum.[2] He named other states that were prepared to do the functional equivalent by ordering a payment-date conversion to the money of the forum. Subsequent editions of his well-known work expanded on this evidence. In light of that, and considering the exalted regard in which Mann's text has long been held, it was curious to see English courts in cases such as *Havana Railways* claim that the forum-currency rule was a practical necessity. The available international evidence simply did not support that. Be that as it may, when in the 1970s the time came for UK courts to abandon the forum-currency/breach-date rule and grant judgments denominated in currencies other than the pound they were quite prepared to change their tune and buttress their decisions by conveying the impression that, elsewhere in the world, judgments in non-forum currencies were an everyday practice. In trying to convince the other members of the English Court of Appeal to abandon the breach-date rule in *The Teh Hu*, Lord Denning made a claim of this sort.[3] Similarly, in the first American appellate level decision to uphold a damages award in a foreign currency, *The Amoco Cadiz*, the Seventh Circuit wrote, 'Courts all over the world enter judgment in currencies other than their own'.[4]

[1] See *Re United Railways of Havana and Regla Warehouses* [1961] AC 1007 (HL) 1051–52 (Lord Reid), 1069–70 (Lord Denning); *Manners v Pearson & Son* [1898] 1 Ch 581 (CA) 587.

[2] FA Mann, *The Legal Aspect of Money* (London, Oxford University Press, 1938) 351. Many continental systems are more favourably disposed to specific performance than the common law is, and in debt cases awarding judgment in the currency of the debt is a lot like specific performance.

[3] *The Teh Hu* [1970] P 106 (CA) 124–25.

[4] *The Amoco Cadiz* 954 F 2d 1279 (7th Cir 1992) 1327. In *Miliangos v George Frank (Textiles) Ltd* [1976] AC 443 (HL) (*Miliangos*), Lord Wilberforce noted (at 464) that arbitral awards in foreign

Not surprisingly, the truth of the matter lies somewhere in-between. As Mann noted 40 years before *Miliangos*, courts in several (though hardly all) non-common-law countries were disposed, in some circumstances, to award judgment in currencies other than their own, or at least to apply payment-day or other late conversion dates. Some civil law countries in Europe permit this, although mainly this seems to be allowed in respect of breach of contractual obligations to pay an amount in foreign currency or when enforcing a foreign court's money judgment—in short, in claims for debt but not damages.[5] However, the correctness of this practice, along with the question of the appropriate conversion date, has long been the subject of scholarly debate, and the practice itself has not been a model of judicial consistency. French courts, for instance, have never in modern times demonstrated that fundamental antipathy to awarding judgments in foreign currencies that characterised pre-*Miliangos* judgments in the common law legal systems. In 1960, at a time when the House of Lords in *Havana Railways* was insisting on the foundational status of the forum-currency/breach-date rule and when American judges were likewise locked into the notion that they could render judgments only in dollars, the Cour de Cassation in *Normand v Buzier* was confirming a judgment for 110,000 Indochinese piastres.[6] Although French judgments denominated in foreign currencies remain unusual[7]—certainly rarer than in some other civil law countries—there have been other instances of such awards.[8] Such decisions seem confined mainly to contract cases where the money of account is a foreign currency, or delictual claims where the plaintiff is a foreigner and has expended foreign currency to remedy the harm of which it complains. They are generally justified by pointing to overwhelming foreign elements in the underlying case. For instance, in *Normand v Buzier* not only had the parties contracted for payment in piastres, the currency of French Indochina, but the court went on to point out that both parties had established commercial operations in Indochina and that payment was to take place there, where both parties had accounts in the same bank.

However, if judgments in foreign currencies remain uncommon in France, what is not rare is their practical equivalent: judgment in French francs with a payment-date conversion from the relevant foreign currency—that is, requiring

currencies were 'honoured all over the world'. (Interestingly, in his dissenting speech seeking to preserve the breach-date rule, Lord Simon observed (at 482) that 'in only nine countries in the world may the writ as well as the judgment be for a sum of money foreign to the forum'.)

[5] JY Gotanda, *Supplemental Damages in Private International Law* (The Hague, Kluwer Law International, 1998) 100–04.

[6] Cour de cassation (Ch, civ, 1re Sect, 1960) 49 *Revue critique de droit international privé* 573. For commentary see L Anselme-Rabinovitch, Note (1960) 49 *Revue critique de droit international privé* 574.

[7] R Libchaber, *Recherches sur la Monnaie en Droit Privé* (Paris, Librairie Générale de Droit et de Jurisprudence, 1992) 130.

[8] *SNCF v Holzer*, Cour d'appel de Paris (5e Ch), 26 Oct 1951 (1953) 42 *Revue critique de droit international privé* 377.

the defendant to pay the amount in francs of the foreign currency on the date the payment is made or the judgment is executed.[9] But if the French legal system did not need a *Miliangos* to bring about a rupture with an outmoded and parochial past, it seems equally true that it has not benefited from the regularising effects of a dominant revolutionary judgment. France continues to demonstrate a certain absence of uniformity and predictability on the conversion-date question. As with Canada (but without the explanation provided by that country's federal system) French courts apply conversion as of the date of breach, the date of the pleadings, the time of judgment and the date of payment. In the estimation of one analyst, French case law 'n'a pas opté pour une solution unique et n'a pas voulu se lier à une règle automatique s'appliquant à tous les cas'.[10] There is more predictability in some areas than in others; in cases where the contractual money of payment is some foreign currency, payment-date conversions appear to predominate.[11] In delictual matters, however, the case law reveals less standardisation.

The lack of consistency in French courts corresponds to a measure of disagreement among that country's scholars as to the appropriate conversion date for foreign currency obligations. In this France seems to resemble the United States. There are those who advocate plaintiff-favouring approaches, either through the method of requiring courts to employ a breach-date conversion where the foreign currency has fallen but a payment-date conversion where it is the forum currency that has dropped,[12] or by simply giving the successful creditor its choice of conversion date, which would effectively amount to the same thing.[13] Others argue for a fixed date, most commonly the date of payment.[14] The arguments for fixed dates do not take the instrumentalist form that they did in *The Amoco Cadiz*, where the goal of certainty is prized above all so that the parties will be able to hedge against that date if they happen not to prefer it. Rather they assume the form that a given date, most commonly that of payment, is the correct, principled conversion date and should be employed because it most accurately fulfills the object of the contract and party autonomy.

[9] Libchaber, above n 7, 130. René Savatier notes one unusual 1920 case which granted judgment in a foreign currency and said that it should be paid in such: R Savatier, 'Questions et Solutions Practiques' (1937) 64 *Clunet* 53, note 1. Many French judgments on foreign currency obligations simply provide for a payment-date conversion into francs or, more recently, euros: *Société Edmond Coignet v Banca Commerciale Italiana* [1990] I L Pr 377 (CA Paris); *Schieffer v Société Jacomo France* [1992] I L Pr 25 (CA Paris); *Société de Transports Internationaux Dehbashi v Gerling Konzern* [1990] I L Pr 104 (CA Poitiers); *Coursier v Fortis Bank SA* [2000] I L Pr 202 (ECJ). The situation in the Netherlands is the same: *Coreck Martime GmbH v Handelsveem BV* [1999] I L Pr 721 (HR).

[10] K Chebil, 'Les Jugements aux Créances Libellées en Monnaie Êtrangère en Droit, Anglais, Français et Canadien' (1982) 27 *McGill Law Journal* 299, 315. Chebil's article provides citations for French cases employing all of the conversion dates mentioned in the text above.

[11] Savatier, above n 9, 54.

[12] NN Penciulescu, *La Monnaie de Paiement Dans les Contracts Internationaux* (Thèse, Paris, 1937) 224–49.

[13] Plaisant, Note, Cass Req, S1951.I33 (3 May 1946).

[14] Savatier, above n 9, 56; Loussouarn, Commentaire, Cass Civ 5e, 20 October 1952, (1953) 80 *Clunet* 384, 390.

It is not the aim of this section to offer any account of currency-of-judgment practice outside the common law world. The goal of this brief and doubtless inadequate glance at France is simply to confirm that the difficulties raised by foreign currency obligations have not been confined to common law courts or common law academic debates. The chief points here are to note that these matters have been contentious elsewhere and that no universal resolution of them has been found; there is no generally-accepted 'civilian solution' to the currency-of-judgment problem that common law courts could, if they were so minded, simply adopt.

This chapter is about the way in which the question is addressed (and often overlooked) in international conventions that seek principally to unify or harmonise the law of cross-border legal relations, or to provide an international or de-localised dispute resolution process for conflicts arising from such relations. As in preceding chapters, its focus is on the remedial practice of courts, not the substantive terms of contractual provisions.[15]

In theory, any international convention dealing with private law matters might choose to address the currency-of-damages question. This is true regardless of whether such convention approached the matter by attempting to unify substantive law principles—for instance those of tort, contract, or just some particular species of contract—or took the alternative route of trying to unify choice of law rules with regard to some class of obligation. In addition, the currency question might be addressed in conventions dealing with the enforcement of foreign judgments.

In practice, however, only a minority of such conventions have sought to grapple with the difficulties arising from foreign currency obligations. Most ignore them. Arguably the drafters of such treaties have not deemed the matter to be of sufficient importance to merit inclusion. An alternative explanation, and a more plausible one, is that commonly such conventions on private law deal solely with what is classified as substantive law; they often say little about *any* remedial matters, and next to nothing about the details of the assessment of damages. This is because many legal systems classify damages questions as falling within the province of localised procedural law, and outside the typical scope of such conventions or other mechanisms for achieving legal uniformity. Some countries even regard damages assessment as lying within the province of juries, and accordingly view such matters as not reducible to precise and particularistic formulations such

[15] For instance, I will not deal here with attempts to create multinational uniformity on the interpretation of currency terms in contracts. To offer an example, UNIDROIT's *Principles of International Commercial Contracts 2004* has a provision dealing with the construction of currency-of-payment terms in contracts. Article 6.1.9 addresses the treatment of a contractual term that calls for payment in a currency other than that of the place of payment. Although provisions of that sort attempt to achieve a uniform interpretation of contracts, they do not purport to bind national courts on the currency-of-judgment question. They set out contractual terms and proffer them to potential contracting parties to adopt if they see fit. They deal with the question of what currencies a contract debtor is entitled to tender payment in, not with the currencies in which courts may or must render judgment in the event of breach of such a contract. They are important initiatives but they fall outside the scope of this study.

as are found in international conventions. While in recent years questions of remedies, damages calculation and procedure have belatedly come to be acknowledged as being of practical importance, they continue to be the elements of national legal systems that are the least amenable to externally-generated change and cross-border standardisation.

Take, for example, the highly successful *United Nations Convention on Contracts for the International Sale of Goods*, adopted in Vienna in 1980.[16] The *CISG* provides uniform substantive rules for agreements for the sale of goods between buyers and sellers whose places of business are in different states—just the sort of contract at issue in *Miliangos*. It features detailed provisions on the obligations of sellers, delivery of goods, taking delivery, passing of risk, anticipatory breach and many other substantive matters. On the currency-of-judgment question, however, it offers not a word. Or at least it offers nothing calculated to produce uniformity of result. The *CISG* does include four short articles dealing with damages. These, however, are cursory and do little more than restate the general principle of compensation and the limiting principles of foreseeability and mitigation. Arguably those articles on damages might be construed by courts as encompassing the currency-of-judgment question. Some scholars have contested as much, claiming that the answer to the currency-of-damages conundrum must be found within the *CISG* and not within the domestic law of the various states parties.[17]

However, they are set forth in such broad language as to provide no answer to competing resolutions of that question. As we have seen, it is possible to argue that any of the common solutions to the currency of judgment problem accord with the compensation principle. Supporters of breach-date, judgment-date and payment-date conversion have all claimed that their solution best fulfills that end. Even those that support a plaintiff-favouring wait-and-see approach have claimed that their solution best achieves the objective of compensation.[18] Thus, even if the *CISG*'s provisions on damages are regarded as addressing, among other things, the currency of judgment question, at most they provide an agreed starting point for analysis—a starting point that has not in the past been shown to lead to any firm result. Accordingly, courts of countries that become parties to the *CISG* will find that they are able to apply *CISG* principles, including the articles on damages, without altering their national practice on foreign currency obligations: either they will view the *CISG* as saying nothing about the problem, or regard it as addressing the issue in terms so general as not to dictate a result

[16] *United Nations Convention on Contracts for the International Sale of Goods*, 11 April 1980, 1489 UNTS 3, (1983) 19 *International Legal Materials* 668 (entered into force 1 January 1988) (*CISG*). When the *CISG* came into force for Japan in August 2009 that brought to 72 the number of contracting countries. The UK, India and Brazil are the only major trading nations that have not joined.

[17] D Saidov, *The Law of Damages in International Sales* (Oxford, Hart Publishing, 2008) 263–66. Saidov rightly admits (264), however, that the challenge 'lies not with the justification of this principle but with its practical application'. That is, nothing in the *CISG*'s text leads ineluctably to any given answer to the currency-of-judgment problem. See also below n 19.

[18] See pp 180–81.

different from existing local practice. As a result, a *CISG* case tried in either of two countries might lead to a very different assessment of damages, even though both were party to the Convention.[19]

It is worthy of note that one area where the uniformity sought by the *CISG* has been threatened by variations in local procedure is that of limitation periods. To the extent that contracting states impose different limitations periods on actions brought under the *CISG* they frustrate the uniformity of result that is the *CISG*'s goal. If one state allows an action to proceed in circumstances where another would dismiss it as being out of time, then uniform treatment of that dispute does not exist. In recognition of that, in 1974 UNCITRAL promulgated the *Convention on the Limitation Period in the International Sale of Goods.*[20] This treaty supplements the *CISG* by imposing a standard four-year limitation period. It recognises the importance of addressing the procedural issues that arise in *CISG* cases in order to produce standardisation of result, and it further demonstrates the practical possibility of doing so. However, nothing comparable has been done for currency of judgment.

There is another UNCITRAL convention—albeit one not in force—that does contain provisions having a more direct effect on the currency-of-judgment question. In December 1988 the General Assembly of the United Nations approved Resolution 43/165 opening for ratification UNCITRAL's *Convention on International Bills of Exchange and International Promissory Notes.*[21] The goal of this instrument was to bring a greater measure of unification to the law of international payments. Like the *CISG*, the *CIBN* created a new type of agreement, or rather two: an international promissory note and an international bill of exchange. These new species of international negotiable instrument would be subject to the substantive law spelled out in the *CIBN*, at least where the parties chose that law.

Unlike the *CISG*, however, the *CIBN* has provisions that sought to address the problems raised by foreign currency obligations. One is an article touching on the question presented in cases such as *The Lips*[22] and *Isaac Naylor and Sons*

[19] Bruno Zeller in *Damages under the Convention on Contracts for the International Sale of Goods*, 2nd edn (Oxford, Oxford University Press, 2009) argues (at 116) that when contracting parties have not stipulated the money in which damages should be awarded then courts or arbiters awarding damages in *CISG* cases should use 'the currency that has the closest relationship to the loss'. Perhaps they should, and Zeller's text might possibly persuade them to do so. However, there is no authority for the proposition that awarding damages in some other money—say, that of the forum—amounts to a failure to conform to the *CISG*. Of course the currency-of-judgment question is not the only one on which differing national approaches to damages assessment will produce different results, even when courts are all applying the *CISG*. For more on this see D Saidov, 'Damages: The Need for Uniformity' (2006) 25 *Journal of Law and Commerce* 393.

[20] www.uncitral.org/pdf/english/texts/sales/limit/limit-conv.pdf.

[21] *Convention on International Bills of Exchange and International Promissory Notes* (1989) 28 *International Legal Materials* 170 (*CIBN*). As of 2010, the *CIBN* is not in force, and it seems unlikely that it ever will be. It attracted a handful of signatures and ratifications in the years immediately following its conclusion, but far short of the number required to bring it into force.

[22] *President of India v Lips Maritime Corp* [1988] AC 395 (HL) (*The Lips*).

Ltd v New Zealand Co-operative Wool Marketing Association Ltd[23]—the matter of damages for foreign-exchange losses. It did not require such damages to be awarded, or even specify the situations in which they might be. However it did make it clear that the *CIBN* did not preclude such losses:

> Art 75(4) Nothing in this article [dealing with dishonour by non-acceptance and non-payment] prevents a court from awarding damages for loss caused to the holder by reason of fluctuations in rates of exchange if such loss is caused by dishonour for non-acceptance or by non-payment.

This provision would permit a court applying a forum-currency/breach-date conversion to award additional damages to an unpaid holder in respect of currency losses resulting from the failure to pay an international negotiable instrument on time. Insofar as the article was not mandatory it did little to promote the *CIBN*'s goal of producing uniformity in the law of international payments. Indeed, it may be regarded as a provision designed to preserve differential treatment at the national level. On the other hand, at least it expressly acknowledges the problem rather than burying it in the general law of damages.

The *CIBN* has a second and more significant provision that appears to touch on the question of currency of judgment. Article 75(3)(d), within the scope of its operation, grants the plaintiff (the unpaid holder of an instrument) the option of selecting either a breach-date or payment-date conversion, at its unfettered discretion:

> 75 (3)(d) If such an instrument [that is, an instrument which states that it must be paid in a currency other than that in which the sum payable is expressed] is dishonoured by non-payment, the amount payable is to be calculated …
>
> (ii) If no rate of exchange is indicated in the instrument, at the option of the holder, according to the rate of exchange on the date of maturity or on the date of actual payment.

As one commentator has observed, this is an approach which is very favourable to lenders.[24] Several things may be noted. The provision does not actually oblige a court to give judgment in the currency in which the note may be payable. However, it does appear to require the functional equivalent. Where it applies, and where a plaintiff so elects, it says that a judge should calculate damages by reference to the date of actual payment. Thus it might require a court of a state party to grant judgment in the form, 'the defendant shall pay the plaintiff the number of units of [forum currency] equivalent to the units of the currency mentioned in the dishonoured instrument on the date of actual payment'.

The provision is remarkably plaintiff-favouring in that it affords the claimant an unfettered choice of conversion dates. Even the *Third Restatement* did not go so far.

[23] *Isaac Naylor and Sons Ltd v New Zealand Co-operative Wool Marketing Association Ltd* [1981] 1 NZLR 361 (CA). See the discussion in ch 3 at pp 140–42.

[24] H Zheng, 'Management of Lenders' Currency Exposure in Multicurrency Financings: Structural Documentation Considerations' (1991) 22 *Law & Policy in International Business* 213, 257.

It suggested that a court should choose between breach-date and payment-date conversion based on the equities of the situation, including which of those dates favoured the claimant. Ultimately, however, it left the matter in the hands of a judge to decide in light of the entirety of circumstances. The *CIBN*, on the other hand, leaves the choice completely up to the plaintiff. A claimant can opt for a breach-date (date of maturity) conversion if it prefers that to a payment-date conversion. Obviously a plaintiff would opt for whichever of the two dates appeared advantageous at the time it was required to exercise that choice. The choice would be exercised in favour of whichever currency (ie, that in which the instrument stated it was to be paid, or the currency of the forum in which the action was brought) had appreciated against the other between the breach date and the date the choice was to be exercised—which appears to be the date of trial.[25]

This plaintiff-favouring aspect of the *CIBN* would override any aspect of local law that attempted to institute a neutral, certain conversion date. Thus, for instance, a court whose domestic law was set by *Miliangos* and its progeny—which would seem, in this instance, to set the contractual currency of payment as the mandatory currency of judgment—would be required to defer to the *CIBN*'s provision and give the claimant its choice.

It seems curious that an international convention would hit on a solution that is more extreme—at least on the pro-defendant/neutral/pro-plaintiff scale—than any domestic treatment of the question. Conceivably banks and other financial institutions, which would generally see themselves as plaintiffs rather than defendants on claims in respect of international bills of exchange, influenced the drafting of this aspect of the *CIBN* in a pro-plaintiff direction. Or perhaps it was just seen as wise policy to promote the negotiability of international promissory notes by instituting—through the currency-conversion provision—a strong (indeed arguably punitive) disincentive to dishonouring such instruments. If that is the case then it remains open to question whether a conversion-date provision of this sort would be a good solution in a convention which dealt with a broader range of contracts, ones where there was no need to create breach disincentives in excess of those which flow from full compensation of the non-breaching party.

Another area which has seen some attempt to regularise the currency-of-judgment question is that of efforts to craft model approaches to contract law, or at least to contracts with some international component. The prime example here is UNIDROIT's Principles of International Commercial Contracts, adopted in 2004.[26] The PICC seeks to provide a platform for harmonisation by setting out a sort of ideal model contract law. The goal is not to supplant domestic contract law, but

[25] Nothing in the *CIBN* addresses when the claimant must exercise the choice given by Art 75(3)(ii). Arguably a court could require such a choice to be exercised in the plaintiff's pleadings, or, alternatively, permit the plaintiff to wait until the end of the trial, or conceivably even later. To the extent that different national courts might arrive at different resolutions of that question there will be a lack of uniformity of result.

[26] Above, n 15 (PICC).

rather to provide a model for international contracts, at least those of a commercial nature, which parties might elect to opt into. Its principal drafter has described it 'as a sort of international "Restatement" of contract law'.[27]

The PICC mainly deal with substantive issues and questions of contractual interpretation, but they also contain provisions on damages, including one on the currency of judgment. That article in question does two things. It acknowledges, at least implicitly, that judgment may be given in a currency other than that of the forum. It then proceeds to give some general guidance as to how the currency of judgment should be selected by a court or arbitrator while at the same time eschewing a firm rule:

> Damages are to be assessed either in the currency in which the monetary obligation was expressed or in the currency in which the harm was suffered, whichever is more appropriate.[28]

A second example of this, at least on a regional level, is the *Principles of European Contract Law*.[29] Prepared in 1999 by the Commission on European Contract Law, the *European Principles* are seen as an important step toward a shared European private law. They contain not only provisions on substantive contract law (formation, validity, interpretation and so on) but also some dealing with remedies, including one on the currency of judgment:

> Damages are to be measured by the currency which most appropriately reflects the aggrieved party's loss.[30]

The official commentary on this article claims that it follows the English and Scottish rule on the currency of damages.[31]

To date neither UNIDROIT's PICC nor the *European Principles* have had a great effect in practice. That may change in time, however. They reflect an encouraging recognition that if true cross-border uniformity is the goal then attention to damages is important. They go beyond that and recognise that if uniformity on the damages question is to be achieved then it will be important to pay attention to the question of the currency in which those damages are assessed, and that this currency will not necessarily, and not always justly, be

[27] MJ Bonnell, 'The UNIDROIT Principles of International Contracts and CISG—Alternatives of Complementary Instruments?'(1996) 26 *Uniform Law Review* 26.

[28] Art 7.4.12. This is identical to the equivalent provision in UNIDROIT's 1994 Principles of International Contracts. There is also a provision that stipulates that interest for late payment of money should be calculated at the commercial rate for that currency: art 7.4.9.

[29] Commission on European Contract Law, *Principles of European Contract Law*, 1998 frontpage. cbs.dk/law/commission_on_european_contract_law/Skabelon/pecl_engelsk.htm (*European Principles*).

[30] *Principles of European Contract Law*, 1998, art 9: 510 www.jus.uio.no/lm/eu.contract.principles.1998/doc.html. Interestingly, the Principles of European Tort Law, a parallel project produced in 2005 by the European Group on Tort Law (www.egtl.org) contain no comparable provision: they state that damages should compensate (art 10.101), but do not go beyond that to address the currency question.

[31] O Lando and H Beale (eds), *Principles of European Contract Law, Parts I and II* (The Hague, Kluwer, 2000) 458.

the currency of the forum. Moreover they go at least a little way in setting out a framework for informing the parties in advance how that currency will be ascertained—it will be the one that appropriately measures the claimant's loss. Compared with the *Uniform Foreign-Money Claims Act* in the United States, which sets out a scheme for determining with a good degree of predictability the proper money of a claim,[32] the approaches in the PICC and the *European Principles* seem open ended. They appear to reflect the principle laid down by the House of Lords in *The Folias* and *The Despina R*—namely that damages should be assessed in the currency in which the injured party felt its loss. However, they give less guidance than those cases do in suggesting how that currency should be ascertained. Arguably, stating that that the currency of judgment should be the one that appropriately compensates the plaintiff for its loss is not going far beyond a statement that damages should be calculated so as to fulfill the principle of compensation—except that the former formulation does acknowledge that courts should not invariably award damages in the national money of the forum. However, unlike the Canadian statutes examined in chapter three, they at least provide a little guidance on the question; they go beyond saying that a court should select the currency which achieves the most equitable result.[33]

Of course even if the parties to a contract stipulate that it is to be interpreted according to the PICC or the *European Principles* there is no guarantee that a court will follow the applicable articles on the currency-of-judgment question. Neither of those documents is designed to be implemented by legislation. So while a court in a case where the parties had stipulated that their agreement was to be governed by the PICC would likely be guided by the parties' clear choice on questions such as contractual interpretation, on the currency-of-judgment question that court might well decide that its own procedural rules governed.

Another area where there is both room and reason to address the currency of judgment question is in international agreements dealing with enforcement of foreign judgments. Such disparity of treatment is the very thing an international agreement on this subject might ideally eliminate, particularly since it would get rid of the problem in cases such as *Competex v LaBow*,[34] where a judgment of one country's courts is granted (in that country's national currency), then accorded recognition in another country (in the enforcing country's money), then subsequently satisfied in the original country, but in an amount which, due to subsequent fluctuations between the two currencies, was not at the time of payment equivalent to the judgment in the second country.

For the most part, however, international treaties on cross-border recognition of court judgments have been content to leave the currency-of-judgment problem unaddressed. The 1971 *Hague Convention on the Recognition and Enforcement*

[32] See ch 4 at p 175.
[33] See pp 111–12.
[34] *Competex SA v LaBow* 783 F 2d 333 (2nd Cir 1986).

of Foreign Judgments in Civil and Commercial Matters was a product of the pre-*Miliangos* era and it contains nothing which addresses the currency issue.[35] States enforcing foreign-country judgments pursuant to their obligations under this convention would be free to treat the currency question in accordance with their national law.[36] A second Hague convention, the 2005 *Convention on Choice of Court Agreements*, also deals, at least in part, with enforcement of foreign court judgments.[37] Although it is obviously a creation of the post-*Miliangos* milieu, it is like the 1971 Convention in declining to tackle the currency-of-judgment question.[38] Like the Hague Conference's *Draft Convention on Jurisdiction and Foreign Judgments in Civil and Commercial Matters*[39] from which it was derived, it does not seek to alter the approach of having the procedural rules of the enforcing court govern. Although neither this draft convention nor its explanatory report deals expressly with the currency question, the latter does suggest that if an enforcing court's rules do not permit it to render judgment in foreign currency then the obligation to enforce a judgment pursuant to the *Choice of Court Convention* would not override that:

> The Convention does not require a Contracting State to grant a remedy that is not available under its law, even when called upon to enforce a foreign judgment in which such a remedy was granted. Contracting States do not have to create new kinds of remedies for the purpose of the Convention.[40]

The explanatory report does go on to note that enforcing courts should give as much effect as possible to a foreign judgment, subject to what local enforcement measures permit.[41] Arguably this obligation might be construed to require a late conversion date into local currency. That is, a creditor enforcing a foreign court judgment pursuant to the *Choice of Court Convention* might conceivably point to this provision in the Explanatory Report to argue that enforcement should be in the currency of the original judgment or, failing that, be converted into local money at a late conversion date. Still, given the lack of specificity in the provision it is difficult to conceive of its having much of a standardising effect on transnational practice, even within its limited sphere of operation.

[35] 1144 UNTS 249; www.hcch.net/index_en.php?act=conventions.text&cid=78 (concluded 1 February 1971). It entered into force on 20 August 1979 but has not been a success. It is in effect in only four places: Cyprus, the Netherlands, Kuwait and Portugal.

[36] Article 14 provides that procedure for the enforcement of foreign judgments is governed by the law of the enforcing state unless the convention provides otherwise. Nothing in the convention provides otherwise on the currency issue.

[37] *Convention of June 30, 2005 on Choice of Court Agreements*, adopted at the 20th Session of the Hague Conference on Private International Law (*Choice of Court Convention*).

[38] Ibid, art 14.

[39] Hague Conference on Private International Law, *Preliminary Draft Convention on Jurisdiction and Foreign Judgments in Civil and Commercial Matters*, adopted by the Special Commission on 30 October 1999, available at on The Hague Conference website at www.hcch.net/upload/wop/jdgmpd11.pdf (Draft Judgments Convention).

[40] *Convention of June 30, 2005 on Choice of Court Agreements, Explanatory Report by Trevor Hartley and Masato Dogauchi* (The Hague, Hague Conference on Private International Law, 2006) [89].

[41] Ibid.

The same thing was done in 1968 in the European Community's well-known judgment enforcement treaty, the *Convention on Jurisdiction and the Recognition and Enforcement of Judgments in Civil and Commercial Matters*,[42] now the *Brussels I Regulation*.[43] UK practice when enforcing foreign money judgments pursuant to the *Brussels I* regime is simply to enforce them in the currency of the original judgment, pursuant to *Miliangos*.[44] Some other countries, such as Ireland and Greece, do the same,[45] and still others, such as France, will convert to local currency but not until the payment date, which is functionally the same as enforcing in the currency of the original award.[46] However others, such as Germany, convert to local currency at the time of the enforcing judgment.[47] Of course this variety of practice is of diminished importance now that so many participants in the *Brussels I* system have adopted the euro, or, as in the case of Denmark, a currency pegged to the euro. However, there are a number of European countries where the euro has not become the national currency.[48] Moreover it should be recalled that the original judgment that is the subject of cross-border enforcement in the *Brussels I* scheme might easily have been in some currency other than euros—American dollars for instance. So even if the currency of the enforcing court is the euro, disparate practice on the conversion date question will remain significant.

Similarly the Organization of American States has a judgment enforcement convention in force between many of its members: the *Inter-American Convention on Extraterritorial Validity of Foreign Judgments and Arbitral Awards*.[49] Concluded in 1979 and in force since 1980, though not north of Mexico), it is like its EC counterpart in saying nothing specific about the currency-of-judgment question. As with the *Brussels I* arrangement, countries recognising foreign judgments pursuant to this convention are free to handle the currency question according to their local preference.

The most notable effort to address the currency question in an international judgment enforcement treaty is found in one that never came into force. In the mid 1970s the United States and the United Kingdom attempted to negotiate a bilateral treaty dealing with the enforcement of final judgments from each other's courts. The United States was not a party to any convention, bilateral or multilateral, dealing with the enforcement of judgments from foreign countries,

[42] *Convention on Jurisdiction and the Recognition and Enforcement of Judgments in Civil and Commercial Matters* 1968, 15 OJ 1998 C 27 (done at Brussels, 27 September 1968) (*Brussels Convention*). The convention was not confined to judgment enforcement; it dealt as well with adjudicatory jurisdiction.

[43] Council Regulation (EC) No 44/2001 (*Brussels I*).

[44] See, eg: *Interdesco SA v Nullifire Ltd* [1992] 1 Lloyd's Rep 180 (QB) (judgment in French francs registered as such).

[45] *Rhatigan v Textiles y Confecciones Europeans SA* [2008] I L Pr 9, IRL900531 (SC); *Re Recognition of an Italian Judgment*, [2002] I L Pr 165 (Thessaloniki CA).

[46] *Ivresse v Societe Tesserlana* [1999] I L Pr 332 (CA Paris).

[47] *Re a Shipowner's Liability* [1996] I L Pr 497 (Hanseatic CA).

[48] The UK, Sweden, Romania, Poland, Hungary and the Czech Republic.

[49] (1979) 18 *International Legal Materials* 1224.

something that remains true today. In the 1970s certain American interests became concerned that while many US courts were relatively generous when it came to enforcing foreign judgments the rulings of American courts were not treated nearly so kindly by other countries.[50] It was thought that a bilateral convention with the UK might be an effective route to approximate equality of treatment, at least between those two jurisdictions. A further American motivation for concluding a bilateral judgment enforcement treaty with the UK can be traced to the UK's 1972 entry into the European Economic Community. That would eventually require the UK to enter into the EEC's *Brussels Convention*.[51] A consequence of that would be that the UK would then have to enforce all judgments of other states party to the *Brussels Convention*, unless it had negotiated a bilateral convention with a third state limiting enforcement of judgments awarded against defendants domiciled or resident in that third state.[52] The United States thus had an incentive to conclude such a treaty so as to preclude such enforcement in the UK of judgments against US residents in the courts of other EEC member countries.

In general, UK courts would not enforce foreign court judgments unless the defendant had either been served while present within the jurisdiction of the foreign court or had submitted to the foreign proceeding, for example in a contractual term or by taking part in the foreign proceedings.[53] This meant that in many instances where American courts had taken jurisdiction over an English defendant under US long-arm jurisdiction the resulting judgment was unenforceable in England. Most American courts, in their foreign-judgment enforcement practice, took a more generous view of what amounted to acceptable exercise of jurisdiction in the court that granted the original judgment. They would commonly enforce UK judgments where the UK court had asserted jurisdiction under its ex juris rules, even where the defendant did not submit to that jurisdiction.

The *United Kingdom-United States Convention on the Reciprocal Recognition and Enforcement of Judgments in Civil Matters*—negotiated and initialled in London on 26 October 1977,[54] nearly a year after *Miliangos*—would have eliminated this asymmetry. It offered a uniform, reciprocal approach through which the UK and US could recognise judgments from each other's courts. However, it was never ratified. Reportedly, UK insurance companies convinced their government that implementation of such a treaty would be antithetical to their and the country's interests.[55] Neither the reasons for that project's failure nor the details of the draft

[50] There is substance to this charge: S Baumgartner, 'How Well Do U.S. Judgments Fare in Europe?' (2009) 40 *George Washington International Law Review* 173.

[51] Above n 42.

[52] Ibid, art 59. For a fuller explanation see P North, 'The Draft U.K./U.S. Judgments Convention: A British Viewpoint' (1979) 1 *Northwestern Journal of International Law and Business* 219.

[53] *Emanuel v Symon* [1908] 1 KB 302; *Henry v Geoprosco International Ltd* [1976] QB 726 (CA).

[54] Cmnd No 6771 (1977), (1977) 16 *International Legal Materials* 71.

[55] Discussion of the English objections to the draft convention, including whether they were well founded, can be found in North, above n 52. Unfortunately North did not comment on the currency provision.

treaty are particularly important here. What is of note for our purposes is the provision on the currency-of-judgment question contained in the draft treaty. It is found in Article 17(5):

> Money judgments entitled to enforcement under this Convention may be enforced by the court addressed either in the currency specified in the judgment or in the local currency at the buying rate in the place where and on the date when enforcement is granted ....

In short, the draft convention adopted the *Miliangos* solution.[56] It recognised that a judgment in a foreign currency constitutes a debt owing in that currency and that the obligation should persist in that currency, even when the judgment is enforced in another country. Like *Miliangos*, it was an approach that opted for certainty. There was no option for the enforcing court to select any other date, even if the result should seem inequitable in light of fluctuations in the relevant currencies following the date of the original judgment. The only option the article offered was one to convert to local currency as of the date of enforcement—that is, a payment-date conversion.

Although the solution offered by Article 17(5) of the draft convention was essentially to embrace the approach the English courts had recently adopted in *Miliangos*, which would mean rejecting the multiplicity of approaches the American courts had accepted, it is interesting to note that had it come into force it might not have been interpreted that way, at least in American courts. The principal American analysis of the draft convention, published in a US law review at a time when the proposed treaty was still under active consideration, took the view that Article 17(5) gave the enforcing court the option between (1) enforcing in the currency of the original judgment and (2) converting to the local currency at the time of the enforcing judgment (not at the time of eventual payment).[57] The authors, Peter Hay and Robert Walker, offered this illustration of how they thought Article 17(5) was supposed to work:

> *P* sues *D* in *F-1* and receives a judgment for 1,000 units of *F-1* currency. *P* subsequently seeks to enforce the judgment in *F-2*, but in the interim the value of *F-2* currency vis-à-vis *F-1* currency has declined from 10/1 to 5/1. How much should the *F-2* court award? The court may award either 1,000 of *F-1* currency (the currency specified in the judgment) or 200 of *F-2* currency ....[58]

[56] I Mathers, 'The UK/US Civil Judgments Convention—I' (1977) 127 *New Law Journal* 777, 779. The claim that the provision quoted in the text mimics *Miliangos* hardly seems to need a supporting footnote. However, since we will shortly see that there have been different readings of art 17(5) I call in Mathers in support.

[57] P Hay & R Walker, 'The Proposed Recognition-of-Judgments Convention between the United States and the United Kingdom' (1976) 11 *Texas International Law Journal* 421, 448.

[58] Ibid. A student comment on the draft convention noted what Hay and Walker had to say about art 17(5) and took no issue with it: MA Alford, 'The Effect of the Proposed U.S.-U.K. Reciprocal Recognition and Enforcement of Civil Judgments Treaty on Current Recognition Practice in the United States' (1979) 18 *Columbia Journal of Transnational Law* 119, 170. Another comment took issue with the provision on the grounds that it was preferable to allow the creditor its election among

This interpretation of Article 17(5) seems to come from treating its final words, 'the date when enforcement is granted', as meaning not the date when money is finally extracted from the judgment debtor, but rather the date when the enforcing court grants a decree recognising the original foreign-court judgment.

This construal of Article 17(5) seems shaky at best. The convention's phrase, 'the date when enforcement is granted' is an echo of the language Lord Wilberforce used in *Miliangos* when he was trying to fine tune what would be the date of payment when a recalcitrant judgment debtor did not pay voluntarily and the post-judgment enforcement mechanism had to be brought to bear—namely, 'the date when leave to enforce in sterling is given'.[59] By this Lord Wilberforce meant conversion at a date as close as practical to actual payment, the closest functional approximation to payment of the debt in the original currency. Yet that is not how Hay and Walker interpreted it; they did not even consider that there was an alternative reading.[60] More importantly, the illustration offered by Hay and Walker is violative of the goal of certainty: the options they think that a court would have on the currency question are decidedly not functional equivalents.

While the understanding of Article 17(5) offered by Hay and Walker seems erroneous, it remains entirely possible that, had the convention come into force, American courts might have espoused that reading of it. In chapter three we saw that the attempts by some Canadian provincial legislatures to offer a statutory version of *Miliangos* have been more than once misinterpreted by courts. Judges have construed 'date of payment' to mean the date that a payment was to have been made under a contract, rather than the time, perhaps long after the trial, when the judgment is finally paid.[61] The convention is now a dead letter and there is little point in speculating further about how it might have been interpreted. It stands mainly as an interesting example of an attempt to bring the *Miliangos* solution into an international instrument. Along with the Canadian statutes it serves as a reminder to drafters to be especially clear in selecting the words used to designate a payment-date conversion. Persons who favour a solution to the currency-of-judgment problem that affords plaintiffs the benefit of currency fluctuation during litigation, regardless of which way it should go, are capable of construing statutes and treaties to achieve that end, even when that is not the goal those instruments were attempting to promote.

Another area where one might expect to find instances of international cooperation on the currency of judgment question is in rules and instruments

different conversion dates: H Smit, 'The Proposed United States—United Kingdom Convention on Recognition and Enforcement of Judgments: A Prototype for the Future?' (1977) 17 *Virginia Journal of International Law* 443, 467.

[59] *Miliangos*, above n 4, 469.

[60] See the discussion in ch 1 at n 51.

[61] See ch 3 n 84. The *European Convention on Foreign Money Liabilities*, discussed below, offers language that might prevent such an interpretation. It speaks of 'the rate of exchange at the date of *actual* payment': below, n 94 (emphasis added).

dealing with international commercial arbitration. It is worth recalling that London arbitral practice was influential in paving the way for the doctrinal shift brought about by *Miliangos*. A year before that case the question of enforcement of a London arbitral award rendered in US dollars had come before the Court of Appeal in *Jugoslavenska*.[62] As noted there by Lord Denning, in recent years some London arbitrators had adopted the novel practice of delivering awards in foreign currencies. Although there were existing judicial statements to the effect that such a practice was improper—statements which had deterred many London arbitral tribunals from giving awards in anything other than sterling—some other panels had begun to ignore the courts on this point.[63] The unanimous judgment in *Jugoslavenska* confirmed that they were correct to do so, and a year later *Miliangos* acknowledged arbitrators' pioneering role in demonstrating that the breach-date rule could, without disaster, be discarded.

However, while arbitral practice may have had the catalytic effect of undermining the forum-currency/breach-date rule, it has not cleared the way for the establishment of any standardised approach to foreign currency obligations. Perhaps by its nature it could not. A glance at some instruments affecting international commercial arbitration will show why. Without a doubt the most successful international agreement in the arbitration sphere is the *New York Convention*.[64] Concluded in 1958 and now in force in 144 countries, it seeks to promote the effectiveness of arbitration agreements by providing a framework for the recognition and enforcement of international arbitral awards. A multilateral agreement on recognition of such awards might helpfully have addressed the foreign currency question and imposed some consistent response. Arbitral awards will often be expressed in a currency different from that of the country where, if they are not voluntarily paid, they will need to be enforced. To the extent that an enforcing court is permitted to convert the arbitral award to the money of the forum and moreover to do so at any one of a number of dates—the date of the award, that of the judgment enforcing it, or that of payment—there may be less than faithful enforcement of the original award. To the extent that enforcing courts in different countries supply different solutions to this problem there will, in practical terms, be disparate answers to what it means to 'enforce' a foreign arbitral award. The existence of such a variety of conversion dates means that the real value of the enforcing judgment may vary according to the conversion date selected. The importance of not varying is precisely what prompted the Court of Appeal in *Jugoslavenska* to anticipate *Miliangos* and hold that when enforcing an arbitral

[62] *Jugoslavenska Oceanska Plovidba v Castle Investment Co* [1974] QB 292, [1973] 3 WLR 847 (CA) (*Jugoslavenska*).

[63] The judicial statements against arbitral awards in anything other than the currency of the forum were those of Diplock LJ in *Margulies Brothers Ltd v Dafnis Thomaidies & Co (UK) Ltd* [1958] 1 WLR 398 (QB) 402 and Salmon LJ in *The Teh Hu*, above n 3, 129.

[64] *Convention on the Recognition and Enforcement of Foreign Arbitral Awards*, opened for signature 10 June 1958, 330 UNTS 38 (*New York Convention*).

award granted in foreign currency courts should do so in that currency. Courts in other countries have been motivated to do the same.

However, nothing in the *New York Convention* compels such a result. It leaves almost all such procedural matters up to the enforcing jurisdiction. It does deal with a couple of procedural issues. For instance, it requires a party seeking to enforce an arbitral award written in a language other than that of the requested court to 'supply a duly certified translation thereof'.[65] However, it offers nothing comparable dealing with the currency question. As a result, enforcing courts remain free to convert foreign-money awards into the money of the forum, and to do so from a range of possible dates, and it seems that none of these actions will amount to a violation of the terms of the *New York Convention*. As we have seen, some courts have thought that arbitral awards granted in a currency other than that of the forum should be enforced in the money in which they were granted, even when forum law was not otherwise receptive to granting judgment in foreign currencies. However, just as enforcing courts remain free, under the *New York Convention*, to apply their own limitation periods to enforcement applications, they remain able to apply their own rules regarding the currency of judgment.[66] In short, in this area where uniformity of result would appear to be a strong value, that value is not compelled and has not been realised.

The silence of the *New York Convention* on the currency issue is not surprising. Its provisions on the mechanism of enforcement are spare. They do not purport to dictate much about how a court recognising an arbitral award should go about the mechanics of enforcing that award. Moreover, it was drafted long before *Miliangos* at a time when there was relative quiet on the currency issue, perhaps due to relative currency stability of the major trading currencies in the mid-1950s. Of course much has changed since 1958 and there has been ample time to consider changes. However, the *New York Convention* has been such a success that there has been no attempt either to generate another multilateral arbitration recognition convention to supersede it or to tamper with it by seeking to amend and update its terms. It remains open for jurisdictions implementing that treaty to stipulate that when recognising an award their courts should enter judgment in the currency of that award. Florida is a jurisdiction that has done so.[67] But the *New York Convention* does not require that.

However, if the chief convention dealing with enforcement of international arbitral awards has not promoted uniformity on the currency-of-judgment question, a little more has been done in the drafting and promulgation of various sets of rules setting out the framework for conducting international arbitrations. Some of these relate to how such proceedings should be held at a given institution,

[65] Ibid, art 35(2).

[66] It seems, for instance, that the law of Austria requires foreign arbitral awards to be converted into local currency for the purposes of enforcement: Judgment of 30 May 2006, 3 Ob 98/06t (Austrian Oberster Gerichthof).

[67] See ch 4, n 64.

others are model laws which contracting parties are free to adopt (in whole or in part) or reject. Such rules do not seek to impose substantive legal standards on parties; they are the arbitration equivalent of civil procedure rules. Since the currency question is one which has sometimes been regarded as procedural it is open to instruments which set out a standardised framework for the conduct of international arbitrations to say something about that question. As the following review will show, there has been a little activity on this front, albeit not a lot.

UNCITRAL's arbitration rules do not seek to direct arbitrators as to the currency in which they should denominate their judgments. Arguably, in individual arbitrations some guidance might be derived from those rules' stipulation that arbitral panels should apply the law chosen by the parties.[68] Even there, however, the rules are not particularly helpful; they provide that tribunals should apply the *substantive* law chosen by the parties and there is room for doubt as to whether a given country's law on the currency-of-judgment question is properly considered substantive (in which case arbitrators would be bound to follow it) or procedural. Of course if the parties went further, as they sometimes do, and specified that any award had to be given in, say, US dollars, that might settle the question.[69] But parties do not always do that. Even if the currency question was uniformly regarded as procedural, so that international commercial arbitrators might be free to impose some uniform approach, the rules give no hint as to what that approach might be; general principles of transnational commercial law offer no resolution to the currency-of-award problem. Any emerging *lex mercatoria* has not developed to that degree of specificity.

The ICSID Rules are similarly silent, as are those of the International Chamber of Commerce.[70] In this there is some similarity between the way international business arbitration has dealt with the currency-of-judgment question and the way it has dealt with—or problematically *not* dealt with—the question of interest on arbitral awards. On the interest question it has repeatedly been pointed out, with respect to international commercial arbitration, that the important matter of awarding compensatory interest 'has been left behind in the march toward

[68] United Nations Commission on International Trade Law Arbitration Rules (Resolution 31/98 adopted by the General Assembly on 15 December 1976), art 33(1). The same is true of the UNCITRAL Model Law: United Nations Commission on International Trade Law Model Law on International Arbitration (UN Doc A/40.17 Annex 1, as adopted by the United Nations Commission on International Trade Law on 21 June 1985), art 28(1). The same is true of the Hong Kong International Arbitration Centre Securities Arbitration Rules: www.hkiac.org/HKIAC/pdf/Rules/Securities%20Arbitration%20Rules.pdf.

[69] Though of course it would not necessarily settle any underlying conversion-date question. That is, if there was an underlying obligation in euros—for instance, because euros were the currency of account under the contract—stipulating that any award had to be in US dollars would not resolve disagreement over the date at which the euros had to be converted to US dollars.

[70] International Centre for the Settlement of Investment Disputes: Rules for the Institution of Conciliation and Arbitration Proceedings; International Chamber of Commerce Rules of Arbitration: www.iccwbo.org/uploadedFiles/Court/Arbitration/other/rules_arb_english.pdf.

uniformity'.[71] Arbitration rules which address many aspects of arbitral procedure but say nothing about pre- or post-judgment interest have left arbitrators in disarray. While some arbitrators have for years been prepared to order pre-award interest, practice on this point is not harmonious and it is often uncertain whether the interest question should be resolved by reference to the governing substantive law (probably the most common result), the *lex arbitri*, some general customary international principles or simply on the basis of what strikes the arbiter as fair and reasonable. As a result, practice with respect to interest is erratic on several issues: whether interest should be awarded at all[72] and, if so, at what rate and for what periods; and whether it should be simple or compounded? A result of this is that contracting parties can have incentives for inefficient breaches, and parties approaching arbitration are deprived of information which would be useful to them if they are contemplating reaching a settlement. Although there has been no shortage of proposals for a uniform solution to this problem, the prospects of any of them being adopted seem slim.[73] The same is true with respect to awards for costs, and, as noted, the currency-of-judgment question.

In addition, this lack of regularity in arbiters' handling of the currency-of-judgment question is not easily amenable to amendment by the courts. This is due to the way in which, in the interest of promoting finality of arbitral decisions, many arbitral frameworks seek to minimise judicial scrutiny of such awards. The 2005 decision of the House of Lords in *Lesotho Highlands Developments Authority v Impreglio* illustrates this nicely.[74] That ruling overturned lower court judgments that had interfered with the way that a tribunal had handled the currency-of-judgment question. Rejecting the views of the judges below, who had regarded the arbitrators' award as being in excess of their powers, the House of Lords concluded that the arbitral panel's mishandling of the currency question was not outside its powers but merely an error of law. As such it was not reviewable by courts: arbitrators might, as a matter of law, err in their administration of the currency-of-judgment problem, but that is not the sort of thing courts should fix. *Lesotho Highlands* is a prime demonstration of judicial fear that vigorous scrutiny of arbitral awards for error of law will erode confidence in the relevant

[71] JY Gotanda, 'Awarding Interest in International Arbitration' (1996) 90 *American Journal of International Law* 40. To similar effect see JDM Lew, 'Interest on Money Awards in International Arbitration', in R Cranston (ed), *Making Commercial Law: Essays in Honour of Roy Goode* (Oxford, Clarendon Press, 1997) 543; N Affolder, 'Awarding Compound Interest in International Arbitration' (2001) 12 *American Review of International Arbitration* 255; JY Gotanda, 'Compound Interest in International Disputes' (2003) 34 *Law and Policy in International Business* 393, 431.

[72] It seems that it is in most cases, but not all, particularly where Islamic law enters into the picture.

[73] In addition to the proposals in n 71 see DJ Branson & RE Wallace, 'Awarding Interest in International Commercial Arbitration: Establishing a Uniform Approach' (1988) 28 *Virginia Journal of International Law* 919.

[74] *Lesotho Highlands Developments Authority v Impreglio* [2005] UKHL 43 (*Lesotho Highlands*). The result of the case may be limited to arbitrations held according to the ICC rules, which go further than most in stipulating that disputants will be deemed to have waived their right to judicial recourse.

jurisdiction's perceived support for the arbitration system. While this hands-off practice may have the beneficial effect of promoting arbitration, it will not have the effect of making arbitrations the site of consistent practice on issues such as costs, interests or the currency of judgment.

The Arbitration Rules of the World Intellectual Property Organization go a little further than those discussed so far. The WIPO rules state that awards made under them 'may be expressed in any currency'.[75] The rules of the London Court of International Arbitration have a similar section.[76] Such provisions give an answer to the question that the UNCITRAL, ICSID and ICC arbitration rules do not explicitly resolve. They make it clear that, regardless of the national substantive law that governs in a given arbitration—a law which might contain rules on the currency-of-judgment question that might require judgment to be conveyed only in that country's money—tribunals are entitled to denominate their awards in any currency. However, provisions of this sort are entirely permissive. They tell arbiters governed by those rules that they are free to express their awards in any currency, regardless of the substantive law governing the contract they are dealing with. Such provisions may have a liberating effect, freeing arbitral panels from out-of-date restrictions bearing on the currency question. However, they do not purport further to standardise arbitral tribunals' resolution of the currency question.

The American Arbitration Association's International Arbitration Rules go a step further. They stipulate that monetary awards 'shall be in the currency or currencies of the contract unless the tribunal considers another currency more appropriate …'.[77] This provision makes it clear that, as under the London and WIPO rules, the currency-of-judgment question is not to be resolved by the governing substantive law. Rather, arbiters acting under the AAA Rules can give awards in a foreign currency even if the substantive law governing the contract they are construing does not does not permit that. The rules go a step beyond that and supply a measure of guidance—albeit not a lot—on the currency-of-judgment question: the currency of the arbitral award is to be ascertained, initially, by looking to the currency of the contract. This is like the rule laid down by the English Court of Appeal in its post-*Miliangos* judgment *The Maratha Envoy*, a rule which was then altered by the feeling-the-loss approach in *The Despina R* and *The Folias*.[78] It is a rule which provides a high degree of advance certainty in ascertaining the metric in which damages will be awarded. However, with the AAA Rules any certainly that might emerge from that default rule is promptly undercut by the words that allow arbitral panels to render awards in other currencies and to

[75] WIPO Arbitration Rules, art 60(a).

[76] Art 26(6). The UK's Arbitration Act 1996, c 23, which is used in many international arbitrations in London, contains a similar provision in s 48(4).

[77] American Arbitration Association, International Dispute Resolution Procedures, art 28(4), www.adr.org/sp.asp?id=33994 (AAA rules), effective 1 September 2000.

[78] See ch 1 at pp 39–42.

do so simply because they think that such a result is 'more appropriate'. Moreover, no assistance is offered as to what sorts of factors should be taken into account in selecting some other currency. Accordingly, if certainty and standardisation are the goals here, then the AAA Rules fail to attain that. However, in at least gesturing towards a standardised rule, the AAA Rules confirm that procedures relating to the conduct of international arbitrations might be an arena in which some universalisation of the currency-of-judgment question could be pursued. Moreover, its default rule—currency of the contract—gives contracting parties some measure of direction in advance of the arbitration.

Another area of potential cross-border regularisation of the currency-of-judgment question is in international agreements dealing with choice of law. These do not seek to impose uniform substantive rules, but rather to promote uniformity of result—that is, to make the outcome of litigation independent of the forum in which that litigation takes place—by imposing uniform choice-of-law rules. With jurisdictions that regard the currency-of-judgment question as substantive, as many US courts do, such conventions might indeed advance predictability of result in a given case. Not all disputes would be subject to the same approach to the currency-of-judgment question, since different disputes would be governed by different laws on the currency question. However, if such a convention was broadly in force then at least any given dispute would be treated the same when it came to selecting the currency of judgment, regardless of where that dispute was entertained.

The problem here, however, as we have seen with conventions like the *CISG* that seek to bring about uniform substantive law in a given area, is that many jurisdictions regard damages as procedural and thus not affected by the substantive law that governs a dispute. The Rome Regulations, which now dictate uniform choice of law rules for most of Europe, illustrate this. The Rome I Regulation which deals with choice of law in contract makes no express reference to the currency-of-judgment question.[79] The same is true of the Rome II Regulation, which since January 2009 has done the same for tort and other non-contractual obligations.[80] Nevertheless, they do have provisions that touch on the assessment of damages, provisions which might be interpreted as addressing the currency of judgment. Article 12(1) of the Rome I Regulation states, in the relevant part:

> The law applicable to a contract by virtue of this Regulation shall govern in particular …
>
> (c) within the limits of the powers conferred on the court by its procedural law, the consequences of a total or partial breach of obligations, including the assessment of damages in so far as it is governed by rules of law ….

In conjunction with the other parts of the regulation that set out the method for determining the law applicable to a contractual dispute, this might conceivably promote uniformity on the currency-of-judgment question: the applicable

[79] Regulation 593/2008 [2008] OJ L177/6.
[80] Regulation 864/2007 [2007] OJ L199/40.

substantive law would dictate the approach to the currency question, regardless of where a cause was heard. However, the provision requires this only 'within the limits of the powers conferred on the court by its procedural law'. So a court of a state whose law did not permit assessment of damages in a foreign currency would not be required to do so under the Rome I Regulation, even if the applicable substantive law dictated that damages should be assessed in that currency. At least that would be so if such a court considered the question of whether it was entitled to award damages in a foreign currency to be a procedural matter, as for instance the courts of England do.[81]

No doubt this provision was the product of a compromise between those who believed that damages were a question for the forum and those who regarded damages as something that should be governed by the applicable law.[82] The provision does appear to promote a greater degree of regularity on the damages question than might have existed in its absence. So, to the extent that uniformity of treatment (in the sense of the currency of judgment being the same regardless of where the suit is brought) is a virtue, that virtue is forwarded by the Rome I Regulation. However, it can readily be seen that such uniformity is far from complete. That is so for a couple of reasons. First, if the national law chosen by the Rome I Regulation as the law applicable to a given contract does not itself provide a certain answer to the currency-of-judgment question—for instance, because it permits a measure of judicial discretion in the selection of such a currency—then the Rome I Regulation does nothing to reduce the uncertainty resulting from such discretion. That is, it does not provide its own rule on the matter. Moreover, as noted, courts are not in all circumstances obliged to defer to the Rome I Regulation's choice of law rule insofar as it might bear on the currency-of-judgment question. That is, if, under the Rome I Regulation's choice of law rules, a given contract is governed by the law of country X, and those laws require that damages be assessed in the currency of country Y, then states party to the Regulation will, in an action before their courts assess damages in the currency of country Y, but only if that is permitted by their own procedural law.

Of course it is not remarkable that any regulation or agreement seeking to impose international uniformity of choice of law, in contract or otherwise, should at some point defer to the procedural law of the forum. Certain routine and technical aspects of litigation inevitably fall to be handled by the local methods regardless of the applicable substantive law, and they thus fall outside the scope of what is affected by standardised choice-of-law rules. It may further be the case that *some*

[81] That is, if the court of a country subject to the Rome I Regulation did not have the power, under its domestic law, to award damages in a foreign currency, but considered the currency-of-damages question to be a matter of substantive law, then it would be required by the Rome I Regulation to apply the applicable law chosen by the Regulation, and thus award damages in a foreign currency in appropriate cases.

[82] P Kaye, *The New Private International Law of the European Community* (Aldershot, UK, Dartmouth Press, 1993) 306.

matters relating to assessment of damages should fall into that category. It is not necessary that the currency-of-judgment question should be one of those matters, but under the Rome Regulations it will be, at least if local courts so decide.

We come now to two initiatives which focus directly and exclusively on the question of foreign currency obligations—though neither of them ever came into force. At its 1952 annual meeting the International Law Association, mindful of problems which had arisen in cases involving the collapse of the reichsmark or the instability of some other currencies following World War II,[83] resolved that its Committee on International Monetary Law study the matter of foreign currency obligations.[84] That committee eventually produced a draft multilateral convention on the matter, a convention that was adopted by the ILA at its 1956 annual meeting in Dubrovnik.[85] The *ILA Convention* touched on a number of matters, including interpretation of contracts, but I focus here just on the provisions dealing with the currency of judgment. Those were three. Article 6 dealt with the handling foreign currency claims in litigation, specifically with the question of pleading:

> In a case of proceedings instituted to recover a sum of money expressed in a currency which is different from that of the forum, the creditor shall claim the sum of money so expressed ....

Article 7 picked up the thread and dealt with how courts should express their judgments. It stated that if the court held for the plaintiff it was then required to give judgment in the currency in which the claim was expressed. The combined effect of Articles 6 and 7 was the abrogation of the rule that was then in effect in common law courts that claims must be expressed and judgments rendered only in the currency of the forum. They allowed for no exception, aside from Article 7 going on to grant courts the power of giving the debtor the option of paying the judgment debt in the equivalent of forum currency at the date of actual payment.

With these two provisions the *ILA Convention* anticipated *Miliangos* by twenty years. Indeed the commentary to these articles made it clear that they were aimed squarely at the old forum-currency/breach date rule which at that time still ruled common law courts around the world:

> Art. 6 is the first of a series of provisions dealing with the peculiar difficulties arising in those cases in which proceedings become necessary. These difficulties exist mainly in the Anglo-American countries by reason of the fact that, in these countries, the plaintiff cannot claim and the Court cannot award any sum of money other than a sum of *moneta fori*.[86]

[83] See, eg: ch 4 at p 155.

[84] International Law Association, *Report of the Forty-Fifth Conference Held at Lucerne August 31 to September 6, 1952* (London, Cambrian News, 1953) viii.

[85] *Payment of Foreign Money Liabilities, Revised Draft Convention*, in International Law Association, *Report of the Forty-Seventh Conference* (London, Cambrian News, 1957) 294 (*ILA Convention*).

[86] Ibid, 291.

The difficulty with these provisions, however, was the very one that arose in the wake of *Miliangos*: it was uncertain how far they were intended to extend beyond claims based in debt—for instance, to actions for damages for tort or breach of contract. And if they did apply to such claims, how would one go about establishing the currency in which the claim had to be expressed and judgment then had to be rendered? Article 6 refers to actions instituted to recover money *expressed* in a currency different from that of the forum. Those words seem to imply that it is concerned only with situations where the obligation has been previously *expressed*—presumably by one or both of the parties, although that is never made clear—in money. That would include a proceeding in debt (like *Miliangos*), presumably also one for the recovery of liquidated damages, and probably some claims in restitution. To the extent that Articles 6 and 7 apply to such claims, they adopted a position that (again like *Miliangos*) advanced a uniform and certain result: the expressed money of a debt was the money in which the plaintiff had to advance any claim for recovery of that debt, and was also the money a court had to use to measure any award it might grant.

However the question of whether Articles 6 and 7 would extend to claims for liquidated damages is far from clear. By way of illustration, if an innocent party to a breach of contract mitigated its loss by expending a certain currency to cure the breach, would that expenditure qualify as an 'expression' of currency such that the claim had to be advanced and, if successful, awarded in that currency? To offer another example, if the victim of a tortious destruction of property expressed its loss on its balance sheet in a certain money, would that qualify as an 'expression', with the same consequences? At first blush one might be inclined to respond in the negative; the currency in question was not 'expressed' in the context of any communication between the parties. However, two other aspects of the *ILA Convention* go on to suggest that it was intended to apply to such situations. Article 9 stated:

> The application of the preceding rules shall extend to all monetary liabilities irrespective of whether they were originally expressed in money or not.

The commentary accompanying all these provisions made it clear that in addition to debt cases they were intended to encompass damages claims.[87]

The problem is that it is simply not clear how the *ILA Convention* would operate in damages cases. Possibly courts would work it out not by seeking to identify the currency in which the plaintiff felt its loss, as the English courts did in extending *Miliangos* to damages claims, but rather identifying the currency which had been 'expressed'. However the above examples suggest this will not always be an uncontroversial concept to apply. It is easy to forgive *Miliangos* for confining itself to debt claims and leaving the damages question for subsequent courts to work out. It would not have been a wise exercise of the judicial function for the House

[87] International Law Association, *Report of the Forty-Seventh Conference*, above n 85, 292.

of Lords in that case to range beyond the debt claim before it and expound on how foreign currency obligations should be dealt with in damages cases. It is less easy to pardon the *ILA Convention* for framing its key provision as applying to claims to recover a sum of money *expressed* in a foreign currency, and then going on to say that it applies to all claims whether *originally* expressed in money or not. Neither the text nor the commentary makes it clear how it would operate in damages cases and it seems obvious that it did not do an adequate job of indicating how the sorts of question posed in *The Despina R* and *The Folias* should be resolved.

There is a further twist to the *ILA Convention*, one that would operate even in a debt claim like *Miliangos*. While Article 6 seems to anticipate *Miliangos* in requiring a debtor to claim in the currency of the debt and the court to make its award in that currency, Articles 8 and 4 depart from the 'for good or ill' aspect of *Miliangos*, at least during the post-judgment period:

> 8 In the event of the depreciation, between the date of judgment and satisfaction of the judgment, of the currency in which the sum of money is due in relation to the currency of the forum, the provisions of Article 4 shall apply and the judgment shall not preclude the creditor from pursuing the claim so arising.
>
> 4 If the debtor does not pay at the date of maturity and if after such date the currency in which the sum of money is due depreciates in relation to the currency of the place of payment, the debtor … shall pay an additional amount equivalent to the different between the rate of exchange at the date of maturity and the date of payment, unless the debtor shall prove that his failure to pay results from 'force majeure' or default of the creditor or that the creditor has not suffered any damage resulting from the delay.[88]

With these provisions the *ILA Convention* goes beyond the currency-of-judgment question and enters the field of substantive law, granting claimants a claim for foreign-exchange losses. It never came into force so there is no case law to assist in interpreting it. It seems clear, however, that the combined effect of Articles 4 and 8 goes beyond that of the comparable provision in the *CIBN* discussed above.[89] That provision had merely provided that a plaintiff-favouring exchange-loss type claim to compensate the plaintiff for adverse fluctuation was not precluded by the *CIBN*. Whether such a claim could succeed was left up to local contract law. The effect of Articles 4 and 8 of the *ILA Convention*, on the other hand, was to grant such a claim (subject to limited defences).[90]

[88] The convention was criticised for an overemphasis on the place of payment. That is, it would appear not to apply to a situation where the parties contemplated that the creditor would immediately convert the money of payment into some other currency: C Evan, 'The ILA Draft Convention on Payment of Foreign Money Obligations: A Critical Analysis' (1958) 85 *Clunet* 406, 450.

[89] At pp 189–90.

[90] Art 8 does use the word 'preclude' but it does so in the context of seeking to alter the rules of res judicata: it provides that a judgment for the creditor on the original claim does not preclude a later judgment for foreign exchange losses arising from the same claim. Accordingly the foreign-exchange loss claim created by art 4 continues to survive a judgment for the initial loss. According to art 4 such a claim is subject only to the requirement that there actually be such a loss and a force majeure defence.

The *ILA Convention* was inspirational a decade later in the drafting of the *European Convention on Foreign Money Liabilities*, doubtless due to the fact that FA Mann played a key role in both.[91] Starting in 1965 and concluding late in 1967, members of the Council of Europe negotiated the *European Convention*, whose preamble provided the epigraph for this chapter. Although signed by several countries,[92] this multilateral convention never came into force, perhaps because most countries did not need it and the UK, to which it was in some degree directed, declined to come on board.[93]

The *European Convention* did not set out a model law. Rather it offered a series of principles and standards which any contracting state would be obliged to incorporate or at least reflect in its national law. It has a number of provisions on the interpretation of contractual terms dealing with the currency and place of payment. It also touches on our concern here, the currency of suit. These closely tracked the equivalent provisions in the *ILA Convention*, with only minor differences in approach. For instance, the *ILA Convention* had required plaintiff debtors to claim in the currency of the debt, and then granted courts the option of rendering judgment in that money or in the forum currency equivalent at the time of payment. The *European Convention* put that choice between those two functional equivalents in the hands of the plaintiff:

> In the event of any proceedings for the recovery of a sum of money expressed in a currency other than that of the forum, the creditor may, at his choice, demand payment in the currency to which he is entitled or the equivalent in the currency of the forum at the rate of exchange at the date of actual payment.[94]

The commentary to the *European Convention* made it even clearer than the *ILA Convention*'s commentary did that it was intended to apply to contractual damages claims as well as debt claims, and even to non-contractual liabilities.[95] At the same time it did nothing to clarify how such an application would operate in practice.

In pre-*Miliangos* days the *European Convention* was championed in the UK by FA Mann, who berated the UK for not even participating in the debates that led to its drafting.[96] Mann was in one respect very forward looking, especially among

It is not obvious that even a foreseeability defence would be open to the defendant in the case of a claim under arts 4 and 8 and in that respect it certainly created a cause of action that went beyond anything available in English law at that time.

[91] *European Convention on Foreign Money Liabilities*, Paris, 11 December 1967, 2 ECA 309, ETS 60 (*European Convention*). Mann was rapporteur for the ILA's monetary law committee that produced the *ILA Convention* and Special Consultant to the group that produced the *European Convention*.

[92] Austria, France, the Federal Republic of Germany and Luxembourg.

[93] At least this was the view expressed by FA Mann, who had acted as a Special Consultant on the project: FA Mann, *The Legal Aspect of Money*, 4th edn (Oxford, Clarendon Press, 1982) 351.

[94] *European Convention*, above n 91, art 5.

[95] Council of Europe, *Explanatory Report on the European Convention on Foreign Money Liabilities* (Strasbourg, Council of Europe, 1968) 8.

[96] FA Mann, *The Legal Aspect of Money*, 3rd edn (Oxford, Clarendon Press, 1971) 372.

those based in England, in anticipating by more than a generation the *Miliangos* solution of making judicial awards in non-forum currency. His unrivalled understanding of the legal nature of money, especially in a comparative context, convinced him that there was nothing to fear in a court's awarding judgment in a non-forum currency and for decades he was a strong academic advocate for that and effective in contributing to the adoption of that position in the *ILA Convention* in the 1950s and the *European Convention* in the 1960s. However, Mann never favoured the 'for good or ill' solution that *Miliangos* would eventually adopt. He thought that as a general rule plaintiffs should get the benefit of currency swings during litigation, regardless of which way they went—which is effectively what the *ILA* and *European Conventions* do, not by giving plaintiffs a choice of conversion dates but by setting a fixed conversion date and then providing that if due to currency fluctuations that date is not beneficial to the plaintiff the plaintiff then has a cause of action to make up the difference. In this respect Mann was out of touch with a strong theme in the English law of judicial remedies, one which is disinclined to grant plaintiffs an unfettered right, during litigation, effectively to speculate at the expense of defendants.

Following *Miliangos*, there was extensive re-examination of the currency-of-judgment question in the UK, and this included a reference to the law commissions of England and Scotland to consider the question whether the *European Convention* should be adopted. They reported in 1981. The party-neutral solution of *Miliangos* was different from the plaintiff-favouring stance of the *European Convention* and the two bodies studying the matter favoured the *Miliangos* approach and recommended against its adoption:

> [T]he fundamental philosophy of the Convention is in sharp contrast to the present law. The main purpose of the Convention appears to be to protect the creditor automatically against a fall in the value of the relevant foreign currency as against the currency of the place where payment is due—eg sterling, where the place of the payment is the United Kingdom—in the case both of judgments debts and other debts. The philosophy of the Convention is therefore quite different from that on which the rules of the present law are based ....[97]

The law commissions were particularly concerned with those provisions of the *European Convention* that gave the plaintiff the benefit of the currency fluctuation regardless of which way it went. In their view, this represented the opposite of the UK approach, where 'once the foreign currency of the creditors debt or loss has been identified, it is regarded as a constant yardstick against which to measure his entitlement'.[98]

[97] The Law Commission and The Scottish Law Commission, *Private International Law: Council of Europe Conventions on Foreign Money Liabilities (1967) and on the Place of Payment of Money Liabilities (1972)*, Law Com No 109, Scot law Com 66, Cmnd 8318 (London, HMSO, 1981) 7–8.

[98] Ibid, 13. The recommendation against adoption was subsequently accepted by the UK government: *Hansard* (HC), 23 December 1981, vol 15, Written Answers, col 420.

As the preceding pages have shown, despite the widespread instance of initiatives to address international transactions and the cross-border effects of private law, no effective solution to the currency-of-judgment question is broadly in force in the international sphere. Many instruments in place to apply in such situations do not deem it to be a matter worth addressing, or perhaps have decided not to address it because they see no hope of resolving it. Others contain provisions which might apply to the issue but which are drafted in such general terms as not to have the effect of requiring courts in the countries to which they apply to reach any particular result. If that is the case then they might as well not address it. Some go a little further and clearly strike down old rules which would stand in the way of a national court granting judgment in anything other than its own money, but they do not go further and provide useful guidance on the question of what money they should grant judgment in. Those that go further and provide some definite answer to that question have not come into force, sometimes for reasons unconnected with the currency question, and sometimes because their resolution of that question has not been right.

6

Closing Observations

... if the breach date rule is abrogated, what is to be put into its place?

Lord Simon[1]

No other aspect of common law damages assessment is as afflicted by uncertainty as the currency-of-damages question. A confusing variety of approaches is in force in the common law world. These vary along a number of axes: whether judgment must be given only in local currency or can be expressed in a foreign one, what conversion date should be selected for any conversion from non-forum money to that of the forum, what sort of factors should guide judicial selection of the conversion date (in particular whether judges are barred, permitted, or even required to take account of fluctuations during the course of litigation), how much unrestricted choice plaintiffs should have to select the currency of their claim, what pre-judgment interest rates should be applied to foreign currency claims, and which of the foregoing questions are to be determined by the substantive law of the claim and which fall to be governed solely by the forum's own procedural rules. In some federal systems—notably the United States and Canada—variation on these questions even exists among the federal components, and between federal courts and those of the states or provinces.

Of course other aspects of damages assessment vary throughout the common law world. Punitive damages, for instance, are more readily awarded in the United States than elsewhere, and awards to compensate for pain and suffering arising from physical injury or for wrongful death can be far higher there too. With foreign currency obligations, however, the variety is more problematic because it arises in the very sort of case that is likely to stretch across international borders. This gives rise to differential treatment of a given dispute depending on which of the concerned forums entertains it. Moreover, the uncertainty that characterises the currency-of-judgment question arises not just between jurisdictions but within them. This is most obvious in those jurisdictions that allow a generous measure of plaintiff choice in selecting the money of their claim or encourage judges to select an exchange date in light of currency changes occurring up to the date of judgment. This permits an element of risk-free speculation by one

[1] In his dissenting speech in *Miliangos v George Frank (Textiles) Ltd* [1976] AC 443 (HL) 483 (*Miliangos*).

party to litigation that is rare elsewhere in the law pertaining to assessment of damages. Even in systems that formally rule out such plaintiff choice or judicial discretion by embracing a mandatory rule on the question, those rules are commonly ones that can make the ultimate award difficult for the parties to predict in advance—as the feeling-the-loss rule did in the illustration that began this book, *The Texaco Melbourne*.

Nor, as the last chapter revealed, has this disarray been rectified by international agreements. Those either ignore the problem by treating it as merely procedural and thus untouchable, subject it to principles that are so general (for instance, that damages must achieve compensation) as not to eliminate existing disparities, or propose solutions that would operate to produce more uncertainty than they eliminate. Nor does there seem much prospect of international agreement eliminating this any time soon. At least there is nothing on the horizon that seems likely to do so.

To the extent that this variety seems troubling it may be tempting to long for the palmy days before 1975 and to blame present woes on the decision of the House of Lords in *Miliangos*.[2] At least within the Commonwealth,[3] it is true that most of the uncertainties outlined above did not exist immediately before that decision. The extension of *Miliangos* from debt actions to damages claims is a bigger step than is sometimes realised—giving rise to some fiendishly tricky questions. *Miliangos* let a genie out of the bottle that cannot be coaxed back in and which has been powerful enough to influence courts throughout the Commonwealth, and even in the United States. However, it was good—not to mention probably inevitable—that it did. By 1975 some civilian courts were already awarding damages in currencies that were not those of the place where they were sitting, and commercial arbitrators were starting to do the same, even when sitting in London. At a time of growing cross-border integration of markets, sinking sterling and increasing resort to arbitration it would have been no easy matter for the common law to remain segregated and retrograde on this question. It might have done so only at the cost of undermining London's attractiveness as a site for international commercial dispute resolution.

The problem—admittedly more acute in Canada, Australia, New Zealand and India than in the UK—has not been that *Miliangos* let a genie out of the bottle, but rather judicial (and sometimes legislative) failure to recognise that it did so and to attend to the consequences. Perhaps the oracular status accorded to that case has masked the fact that key aspects of its reasoning were more rhetorical than vertebrate.

One might think that at least in currency-of-judgment problems arising in contract—which are the majority of them—all of these uncertainties could be tamed or sidestepped by appropriately drafted clauses. Parties negotiating agreements could agree on terms instructing courts or arbitrators to employ a certain approach

[2] Ibid.

[3] The United States is another matter.

to the currency question. Those decision makers in turn could be counted on to be guided by such provisions, thus providing the parties with the required predictability. Certainly courts have become increasingly deferential to party autonomy across a wide spectrum of issues. These include not only arbitration clauses, forum-selection agreements and choice-of-law provisions, but also terms bearing directly on judicial remedies—notably liquidated damages clauses and, especially since 1980,[4] clauses which limit or exclude liability for certain losses.

There is a variety of reasons why there is less scope for contractual provisions to eliminate judicial uncertainty on the currency question than there is for most other areas of damages calculation. A Canadian, American or Indian court that is statutorily required to render judgment only in forum currency will not be bound by a contractual term stipulating that damages must be measured in euros. Even a judge constrained not by statute but only by judicial precedent to measure damages by converting a foreign currency obligation to forum currency as of the date of breach will not usually feel at liberty to follow a contractual term that instructs her to do so at the date of payment; the matter will be regarded as part of the procedural law of the forum, not—as with other remedial matters—the substantive law of the agreement. In short, the peculiar status of national currency as a supporter of national sovereignty effectively means that courts which would be inclined to pay attention to other contractual terms bearing on the calculation of damages cannot be counted on to accord comparable deference to a currency-of-judgment clause.

Even in countries where courts would abide by contracting parties' expressed wishes on the currency-of-judgment question—as English judges would after *The Folias*,[5] or American judges would in those states that have adopted the *Uniform Foreign-Money Claims Act*[6]—the uncertainty problem is by no means eliminated by such terms. If the judgment emanating from such a court has to be enforced by means of recognition in a country whose courts feel compelled to grant judgment only in forum money, then the metric that effectively measures the plaintiff's recovery will alter at the enforcement stage. Clauses attempting to specify the money of judgment are thus inherently less effectual than damages limitations clauses: the latter will be heeded by the initial court and that will effectively penetrate international borders at the enforcement stage. Contractual terms specifying the money of damages cannot be relied on to have that same effect.

Of course certainty is not the be all and end all of damages assessment. There is no point in adopting procedures that pursue that end only at great cost, so that the amounts expended in calculating the amount of the remedy are greater than the remedy itself; there are times when we must settle for rough justice. In addition,

[4] *Photo Productions Ltd v Securicor Transport Ltd* [1980] AC 827 (HL) was a turning point on this issue.

[5] *Services Europe Atlantique Sud (SEAS) v Stockholms Rederiaktiebolag Svea of Stockholm* [1979] AC 685 (HL) (*The Folias*). See the discussion at pp 39–42.

[6] National Conference of Commissioners on Uniform State Laws, *Uniform Foreign-Money Claims Act* (4 August 1989). See the discussion at pp 172–78.

legal principles that can only be stated at a high level of generality—such as the foreseeability requirement—necessarily result in some uncertainty when it comes to application. So it may be unwarranted to declare the currency-of-judgment question a shambles just because it is a field where predictability of the final award is not all that it might be.

However, especially against the background of incomplete capacity for private parties to reduce existing uncertainty through contractual provisions, the room for some jurisdictions to modify their current approach to the currency-of-judgment problem is obvious. Australia, Canada, New Zealand, India, many of the United States of America and all of common law Africa have fallen into a system that allows the metric through which compensation is awarded to be unknowable until a startlingly late stage in the compensation process. The UK, Hong Kong, Singapore and those American states that have enacted legislation based on the *Uniform Foreign-Money Claims Act* have adopted systems that conduce to greater certainty. The *Uniform Foreign-Money Claims Act* goes furthest in this regard in that it provides clear standards for determining the mandatory proper money of a claim and reserves the inherently uncertain feeling-the-loss test for that limited class of cases where its primary rules cannot apply. It is only unfortunate that it did not go further still and adopt the English rule that the pre-judgment interest rate should be determined by the commercial rate applicable to the currency of judgment.[7] The greater problem is that no amount of certainty achieved within any jurisdiction will eliminate the difficulties that exist in the cross-border arena, including international commercial arbitration. Until international action addresses that, traders, litigants and their legal advisors will have to do their best to cope with the confusing situation described and discussed in the preceding chapters.

[7] *Miliangos v George Frank (Textiles) Ltd (No 2)* [1976] 3 All ER 599 (QB). See the discussion at pp 176–77. Jurisdictions that enact the *Uniform Foreign-Money Claims Act* might still adopt the English rule on this point, but the statute would not require them to; it leaves the interest question to the vagaries of state court decision making.

INDEX

www.ingramcontent.com/pod-product-compliance
Ingram Content Group UK Ltd.
Pitfield, Milton Keynes, MK11 3LW, UK
UKHW021908150926
475560UK00003B/253

9 781841 138923